DATE DUE

APR 04 2013			

Demco, Inc. 38-293

HANDBOOK OF DENOMINATIONS

HANDBOOK OF DENOMINATIONS

IN THE UNITED STATES

11TH EDITION

Frank S. Mead

Samuel S. Hill

11th Edition Revised by Craig D. Atwood

Abingdon Press
NASHVILLE

HANDBOOK OF DENOMINATIONS IN THE UNITED STATES
Eleventh Edition

This book is printed on recycled, acid-free paper.

Library of Congress Cataloging-in-Publication Data

Mead, Frank Spencer, 1898–
    Handbook of denominations in the United States / Frank S. Mead, Samuel S. Hill.—11th ed. / revised by Craig D. Atwood
        p. cm.
    Includes bibliographical references and index.
    ISBN 0-687-06983-1 (cloth: alk. paper)
        1. Sects—United States—Dictionaries.   2. United States—Religion—1960—Dictionaries.   I. Hill, Samuel S.   II. Atwood, Craig D.   III. Title.

BL2525 .M425 2001
200'.973—dc21   2001018872

02 03 04 05 06 07 08 09 10 — 10 9 8 7 6 5 4 3 2

MANUFACTURED IN THE UNITED STATES OF AMERICA

In Memory
of
Frank S. Mead (1898–1982)

CONTENTS

PREFACE

Frank Mead's *Handbook of Denominations in the United States* has had a long and esteemed history. Dr. Mead regularly updated the work during his long career; after his death, the task of revision fell to Samuel Hill, the leading scholar in the area of religion in the southern United States. Dr. Hill was able to increase the presence of African American churches and evangelical bodies in the *Handbook*. He also made an effort to reflect the growing presence of world religions in the United States. I had the pleasure of studying under Professor Hill at the University of North Carolina, and it has been an honor to build upon his work in this eleventh edition of the *Handbook*.

With the dawning of a new millennium, it seemed appropriate to make a substantial revision of this classic reference work. To that end, the book has been thoroughly reorganized with the addition of some new categories of churches, such as fundamentalist churches, and there are longer descriptions of each category. The categories are provided to help tell the story of American religion both historically and typologically; they are not intended to be prescriptive or normative. In many cases, one church could be placed in two or more categories, and I apologize to any who feel that they have been "misplaced." Further, many denominations that have been in the work since the 1950s have been omitted from this edition, since they have dwindled or gone out of existence. With few exceptions, the religious organizations included here have at least 5,000 active members. New entries appear in the place of those removed, reflecting the vitality of American religion in the late twentieth century. In addition, the sections on Catholicism and Eastern Orthodoxy have been noticeably enlarged.

Another change is a new directory of churches that includes their Web sites. The Internet proved to be a valuable resource in preparing this edition, and the reader will find that most denominations now make effective use of the new technology.

One editorial decision was particularly difficult. Recent editions of the *Handbook* had entries on Eastern religions in the United States. The presence of non-Western religions is increasing daily through immigration and conversion, and every year American religion becomes more diverse. The old Protestant hegemony has disappeared in this country, and textbooks on American religion can no longer assume that the nation is exclusively or even primarily Christian and Jewish. However, this volume is not a guide to religion in the United States; it is a guide to denominations. Rather than treat the various world religions superficially or drastically limit the space given to various denominations, I decided, therefore, to include only those religions stemming from the Abrahamic-monotheistic tradition.

As all of the religious bodies presented here in some way claim allegiance to the faith of Abraham, they share many similarities in their approaches to ethics, worship, and sacred texts. Most new religions, such as Scientology, new age belief systems, and groups often termed "cults" are thus excluded from this presentation either because of their size or because they are not in the Abrahamic tradition. Again, this focus on Christianity, Judaism, and Islam is not meant to suggest that they alone are real or important religions; rather, it is intended to give the work conceptual coherence and to set definite limits.

A final word is needed regarding membership statistics. Most of the statistics used in the *Handbook* are self-reported from the various religious organizations and appear in the *Yearbook of American and Canadian Churches*. Reports of religious adherence are not always reliable, especially for comparative purposes. Some denominations report all baptized persons whether they ever attend services or not; others report only those who have made an adult profession of faith; and some do not keep membership records at all. It should also be noted that many individuals regard themselves as members of a certain denomination or tradition even though they do not appear in official records. Thus all statistics are merely the best estimate currently available. (The membership statistics are for the U.S., unless otherwise noted.)

I would like to express my thanks to Fran Swajkoski, Kennette Lawrence, and Melissa Hall for their assistance with the database and directory of churches. I am also grateful to Paul Kemeny for his support in this project. Most especially I wish to thank my wife, Julie.

Craig Atwood

RELIGION IN AMERICA

Craig D. Atwood

Frank Mead's *Handbook of Denominations in the United States* has been a standard reference work for half a century, appearing now in its eleventh revision. The *Handbook's* enduring usefulness points to its value for scholars and laypersons alike. Nonetheless, we may well ask why there is a need for such a reference work. What is it that makes American religion so diverse and confusing? Why was it in the United States that the idea of "denominations" emerged so that we can speak of different religious groups without using the often pejorative word *sects*? In order to answer those questions, we need to take a step back in history and review some factors that are central to American religious experience.

First of all, we must be aware that until modern times—indeed, until the rise of the United States—it was assumed that civic harmony depended on religious conformity. There should be "one king, one faith, one law," in the famous phrase of Louis XIV. Religion was seen as the warp of the social fabric, the glue that held different estates together and balanced conflicting interests. Religious diversity was equated with civic unrest and upheaval. The idea that a nation could tolerate not only different Christian churches but also radically different religions was considered lunacy up until the Enlightenment. Modern Americans who have always lived under the Bill of Rights and its guarantee of freedom of worship have difficulty realizing what a truly radical experiment the First Amendment was when proposed by Madison and Jefferson.

Once the Constitution was ratified, the government was forbidden to intervene in matters of personal faith. There have been notable cases in which local and national authorities have indeed impinged this civil right, but for the most part the spirit of freedom of religion has prevailed in the United States for over two centuries. This meant that no force other than popular opinion could prevent the formation of new religious organizations, new churches, and even new religions. Anyone who could gather followers could be the founder of a new denomination. Sometimes these new religions have been dismissed by the public and have become what might be termed cults, but some of them, such as the Mormons, have developed into very popular and dynamic faith traditions.

Rather than leading to the demise of religion as many detractors (and a few supporters) of the First Amendment expected, this freedom of religious expression led to a marked increase in religious belief and practice in the United States during the last two centuries. In contrast to other industrialized nations, the United States continues to have high levels of personal belief, membership in religious organizations, and participation in religious activities. It may appear ironic that the world's first completely secular government has fostered one of the most religious societies, but the reason why is rather simple. In the free-enterprise system of American religion, denominations have always had to compete for the hearts and minds of the masses. Denominations in the United States have had to present their message in a way that appeals to current and potential members. Even those churches that stress hierarchical and traditional values have had to adopt the methods of conversion-oriented churches in order to retain members.

Free competition has made American religion unusually responsive to changes in society as churches adapt popular culture, especially music, for the purpose of attracting members. Each generation has seen the creation of new religious bodies and the transformation of older bodies as churches have tried to address the anxieties of their age and offer hope for the perceivable future. This process of adaptation and change has often led to splits within denominations with one party embracing new techniques, such as large revival meetings, and the other party promoting traditional approaches, such as belief in the classical creeds and use of ancient liturgical forms. New denominations may be innovative or traditionalist, but even the traditionalists have to "sell" members and potential members on the virtues of tradition. The pages that follow will trace the way new churches develop out of older churches. For instance, the majority of Pentecostal churches developed out of the older Holiness churches, which in turn had come out of the Methodist churches, which had themselves originated in the Anglican Church.

The free-enterprise approach to religion has also encouraged experimentation with worship forms, doctrines, and even scriptures. Nineteenth-century America was the birthplace of some of the most dynamic religious movements of modern times. Many of these denominations emerged during the heady days of the Second Great Awakening in the days of the early Republic (1800–30), when it seemed that the common person could achieve any dream.[1] If backwoodsmen could serve in the Congress and farmers create a new government, why shouldn't an angel appear to an ordinary man and reveal a new scripture? Why couldn't a former housewife be the new incarnation of Christ?

Since most of these new religious movements, like the Shakers and the Mormons, have roots in traditional Christianity, they are not generally considered new religions; however, some of them are indeed radical variations on ancient Christian themes. Even among those that stayed closer to traditional Protestantism, there was a widespread sentiment that religious authorities could be ignored and that common people could recreate the church based on their own understanding of the Bible. Out of this conviction arose the denominations associated with Alexander Campbell and Barton Stone (see CHRISTIAN CHURCHES). Later Pentecostals, Adventists, and even the Jehovah's Witnesses would also draw upon this idea of remaking the church according to one's own understanding of Scripture. The old Reformation slogan of "Scripture alone" produced a cornucopia of denominations in the United States as ordinary individuals took up the challenge of interpreting the Bible and judging religious authorities.

A second major factor in the diversity of American religion is immigration. Each wave of immigration brought different national churches. In fact, by the time the Constitution was written there were so many denominations that it would have been difficult, if not impossible, to have created a state church. Among the English colonists there were Congregationalists in New England, Quakers in

---

1. See Nathan O. Hatch, *The Democratization of American Christianity* (New Haven: Yale University Press, 1989), for more information on this formative period of American history. Particularly insightful is the connection between Jacksonian democracy and popular religion.

21

Pennsylvania, Anglicans in New York, Presbyterians in Virginia, and Roman Catholics in Maryland. In addition, there were Dutch, Swiss, and German Reformed; Swedish and German Lutherans; French Huguenots; and Sephardic Jews, just to name the most prominent faiths. Even within the same church, most noticeably the Roman Catholic and Lutheran churches, the United States has been home to an impressive array of ethnic communities that have often posed a challenge to church hierarchies trying to maintain institutional unity. This process continued in the twentieth century as traditional denominations, such as Presbyterians and Methodists, have had to make room for Korean- and Swahili-speaking congregations. Moreover, as many as twelve million American Catholics speak Spanish as their first language.

Religion has provided each immigrant group with an identity in a foreign land, a way of being grounded in the old culture while adjusting to a new and confusing society. Ethnic culture in the United States is inseparable from ethnic religious tradition. Over the decades, though, these ethnic denominations gradually have adapted to the American setting as they have struggled to win the allegiance of third and fourth generations. The transition to English in services is one benchmark of the Americanization process. Gradually they grow to resemble their neighboring churches more than the national churches that gave them birth. Some denominations, most notably Orthodox Judaism, aggressively resist this process of assimilation, but in doing so they adopt American techniques of marketing and group formation. In general, ethnic distinctiveness in religion is eventually confined to ethnic festivals associated with denominational activities.

In the second half of the twentieth century, immigration from Asia and the Caribbean basin has brought the religions of the world, including folk religions such as Santeria, to American shores. This dramatic increase in religious diversity will be one of the major factors of religious life in the United States during the twenty-first century. No longer will the symphony of American religion be composed of variations on the Christian theme.

A third distinctive feature of American religion has been interchurch cooperation in the midst of competition. Again, one might choose an economic analogy and point to the American penchant for large corporations and mergers. Interdenominational, parachurch, and cooperative ministries have brought together believers from different backgrounds throughout American history. In times of disaster it is not at all surprising to see Catholics, Protestants, Jews, and Muslims working hand in hand. The individuals helping are motivated by their religious values, which have been nurtured in a particular faith tradition. But in working together, they learn to respect other faiths.

Sometimes these cooperative efforts have led to the creation of new denominations, such as the United Church of Christ, and sometimes to interchurch agencies, such as the National Association of Evangelicals. More generally such efforts have increased religious toleration on the local level. Here is the essence of denominationalism: diverse religious traditions and organizations that openly compete for adherents while respecting other religious organizations as valid. It is rare, for instance, to hear a Presbyterian in the United States declare that Methodists are not really Christian. Further, as the presence of world religions increases in the United States, one sees this sense of toleration being extended beyond Christian boundaries. Of course, as with every movement, the ecumenical trend has also led to the creation of new denominations that reject this perspective and insist on doctrinal or ecclesiastical conformity and exclusiveness.

Sociologists have noticed the strength of this ecumenism in American religion and have concluded that we are now in a "post-denominational" period when religious identity has lost its place in individuals' lives. It is relatively easy for an Episcopalian to join a Lutheran church. Even the conversion from Catholic to Protestant or vice versa no longer carries the weight it did fifty years ago. There has been a tendency toward homogenization of religion as churches learn from each other and adopt successful practices. Most Americans have an eclectic faith, one stitched together from many different threads of tradition and contemporary ideas and attitudes.

However, this *Handbook* attests to the continuing power and influence of denominations. The drive toward establishing national organizations remains strong, and immigrant religions tend to follow the American model of denominational organization. Denominations help to provide some type of religious identity amid the pluralism of belief. They also provide needed resources for local communities of faith, such as facilities for training ministers, for publishing curriculum resources, and for overseeing certification procedures. Although the character of denominations continues to evolve, there is little indication that they will disappear. It is noteworthy that as denominations move closer to merger, splinter groups always form, thus acknowledging the usefulness of denominational structures even while rejecting the authority of the parent organization.

A fourth major factor in American religion at the beginning of the twenty-first century is the Internet. The potential of the Internet to reach individuals and to spread the word about a particular faith was quickly realized. Religion is one of the major topics discussed in chat rooms and on Web sites. The Internet has even allowed for the creation of new denominations that gather primarily in "cyberspace."

The factors discussed above all figure in the Internet's influence on American religion. Denominations use it to compete for followers, individuals use it as a resource in building their personal belief system, and immigrant churches use it as a resource to keep scattered members of the flock connected with the ethnic tradition. We can expect that as the Internet continues to expand and change, its influence on religious life in the United States will likewise grow and alter.

The *Handbook of Denominations* was written to help individuals navigate the confusing and shifting waters of American religion. It is hoped that this volume will help readers better understand not only American religion in all its diversity but also their neighbors who are of a different faith community.

DENOMINATIONS

ADVENTIST CHURCHES

Throughout the history of Christianity there have been communities and individuals who have awaited the return of Jesus Christ with eager anticipation. From the evidence of the New Testament, it appears that the expectation of the imminent return of the resurrected Christ was widespread among the first generation of Christians. As the apostolic age passed without the Second Coming, hope in the immediate return of Christ waned and the church adjusted to the delay of the Parousia (return of Christ). In place of the earlier fervent hope in the end of history and the consummation of the messianic mission, the church placed its faith in the ongoing presence of the risen Christ through Scripture, sacrament, and faith.

However, when the New Testament canon was sealed, it included many writings about the end time, the most famous of which is the book of Revelation, also known as the Apocalypse. The symbolic language of the Apocalypse, combined with the speculations of Paul in the letters to the Thessalonians, apocalyptic statements by Jesus in the Gospels, and the Old Testament book of Daniel, gave ample scope for the imagination of the faithful during the past two thousand years. The hope that Christ would soon return to rule the world in justice and peace was particularly strong in the United States following the American Revolution. Even the phrase "the New World" conjured up images of the millennial kingdom long awaited.

Ordinary farmers and merchants had defeated the world's greatest military power, had thrown off the rule of the king, and were creating a new nation. It seemed to many, even men like John Adams, that the millennial age was dawning and that Christ would soon appear to take up his rightful throne. The Second Great Awakening, a series of revivals that swept across the western frontier in the early decades of the nineteenth century, added fuel to this fire as reports about the phenomenal activity of the Holy Spirit in converting lost souls circulated around the nation.

The Adventist family of churches in the United States was born in this era of new possibilities and great hopes. Today regarded as conservative Protestants, the Adventists were originally seen as dangerous radicals because of their intense focus on the theme of the return, or Second Advent (coming to our world), of Jesus Christ. By 1844, Adventist groups could be recognized as a distinct religious body separated from the traditional Protestant churches. But modern Adventism began as an interchurch movement whose most vocal proponent was William Miller (1782–1849) of New York, a veteran of the War of 1812. Miller had experienced conversion from skeptical deism to evangelical Christianity during the Second Great Awakening. After his conversion in 1816, Miller became an ardent student of Scripture. Using a Bible that contained the famous chronology of Archbishop Ussher, Miller concentrated his attention on the prophecies of the end time in Daniel and Revelation. Accepting the usual interpretation that the symbolic day of Bible prophecy represents one year, Miller concluded that the 2,300 days of Daniel 8:14 started concurrently with the seventy weeks of years of Daniel 9—that is, from 457 B.C.E., the year of the command to rebuild and restore Jerusalem. He believed that the longer of the two periods would end in or about the year 1843, as calculated by Jewish reckoning. Miller thought that the sanctuary mentioned in Daniel 8:14 was the earth (or the church), which would be cleansed by fire at the Second Advent and that this cleansing would occur sometime between March 21, 1843, and March 21, 1844.

Miller was not the only person fascinated with such apocalyptic reckoning, and his writings struck a chord in the popular culture of the 1830s. Under the direct influence of Miller, a New England pastor published an entire hymnal, *The Millennial Harp,* devoted to the theme of the imminent return of Christ and the restoration of paradise on earth. Miller himself made speaking tours in which he used elaborate charts and chronologies to support his reading of end-time prophecies. All of his research supported his central claim that the Advent would occur in the spring of 1844. Between 50,000 and 100,000 people in the United States believed in Miller's calculations and looked forward to the great day when the world would be cleansed and the righteous would meet Christ.

When March and April passed, and this expectation failed to materialize, some devotees left the movement and returned to their former churches. However, Miller's associates, on the basis of the study of Old Testament typology, arrived at a second date, October 22, 1844. This was to be the great Day of Atonement, prefigured in the Mosaic law. When October 22 also passed with no second coming, vast numbers faced what has been termed "the Great Disappointment." Many gave up on Adventism, some gave up on the Christian faith itself, others simply gave up the desire to fix a date for the Advent. Out of the ashes of the disappointment, new Adventist bodies arose as well.

In the wake of the disappointment, those persons who continued as Adventists formed several smaller bodies. By April 1845, Adventists who had unified during the Millerite movement were becoming divided over the relevance of that movement's interpretations. The majority group abandoned its earlier belief and concluded that the 2,300 years in the prophecy of Daniel 8 would end sometime in the future. A loosely knit organization came into being at a conference in Albany, New York, in 1845. This Albany group held generally to Miller's original theology. They emphasized the personal and premillennial character of the Second Advent, which means that Christ will return in person, not in spirit, before the millennial kingdom comes into being. They also taught that the resurrection of the dead happens in two stages. The faithful are to be raised at Christ's coming, but the rest of humanity will rise a thousand years later. Furthermore, the earth will be redeemed and restored as an eternal abode of the faithful. Known at first as the American Millennial Association, a portion later came to be called the Evangelical Adventist Church. That church has now dwindled to the point of obscurity.

Adventism is based on the conviction that the Second Advent of Christ is the sole hope of the world. The present age is evil and irredeemable, except through the direct action of God. Adventism holds that humanity's nature is fallen because of sin and that those who rebel against the government of God will be ultimately destroyed, while believers, by God's grace, will be saved. After that cataclysmic event, Jesus Christ will reign in triumph through the thousand-year period, or millennium, of Revelation 20:1-6. Thus Adventists are pessimistic about the present but are filled with confidence and hope for God's future. In the meantime, they teach that God's people must be righteous, devout, and disciplined. Those who would be saved should practice a wholesome personal and family life, as well as a life of obedience to God. They should also work diligently toward the evangelization of the whole world in preparation for the return of Christ.

In other areas there have been differing viewpoints among Adventists. Are the dead conscious or unconscious as they await the resurrection? Who are to arise: Both the righteous and the wicked or only the righteous? Is there to be eternal punishment or ultimate annihilation for the wicked? What is the nature of immortality? Does the cleansing of the sanctuary in Daniel 8 refer to a sanctuary in heaven or to one on earth? Should the sabbath be recognized as the first day or the seventh day of the week? Answers to these questions have served to divide various Adventist groups.

ADVENT CHRISTIAN CHURCH

Founded: 1860
Membership: 25,702 in 302 churches (1999)

The Advent Christian Church grew out of the main body of Adventists who reorganized in 1845 following the Great Disappointment (see ADVENTIST CHURCHES). While William Miller was not directly involved in the founding of this church, his preaching and teachings concerning the Second Coming of Christ formed the basis for Advent Christian theological, biblical, and organizational thought.

The doctrine of conditional immortality, or of life only in Jesus Christ, preached by George Storrs (1796–1879) and Charles F. Hudson (1795–1881), also influenced the Advent Christians. Dissatisfied with the widespread teaching of a doctrine of the immortality of the human soul that originated with the Greek philosophers Socrates and Plato, they maintained that only the redeemed receive everlasting life. Similar to the Seventh-day Adventists, the Advent Christian Church teaches that the dead await the resurrection in an unconscious state. When Christ returns, all will rise and face the final judgment. The righteous will be given immortality, but the wicked will suffer eternal extinction as opposed to eternal torment. After the final judgment and destruction of the wicked, Christ will restore the earth and make it the eternal home for the just.

Regarding these doctrines, the position of the Advent Christian Church is very similar to the Seventh-day Adventists; but they reject the prophecies of Ellen Harmon White (see SEVENTH-DAY ADVENTIST). Instead they hold to the Bible as the only source of authoritative teaching, placing great stress on the literal fulfillment of apocalyptic prophecy. The denomination maintains no formal creedal statement, but does have a declaration of principles, adopted by the General Conference in 1900 and revised in 1934, 1964, and 1972. Two sacraments are observed: baptism (of adults by immersion) and the Lord's Supper. Worship is held on the first day of the week rather than on the sabbath.

The first Advent Christian General Conference in 1860 was followed closely by the founding of publications, missions societies, and Aurora University. In 1964, Advent Christian Church merged with Life and Advent Union, an Adventist group with three churches and 300 members, organized by John T. Walsh in 1848. Congregational in polity, the church is grouped in five regional districts in the U.S. and Canada, associated under the Advent Christian General Conference of America. The General Conference meets every three years and maintains denominational offices in Charlotte, North Carolina, which oversee work in missions, urban ministries, church growth, Christian education, publications, administration, women's ministries, and public relations. The denomination also maintains missions in Japan, Mexico, India, Nigeria, Ghana, South Africa, Honduras, the Philippines, and Malaysia.

BRANCH DAVIDIANS

Founded: 20th century
Membership: statistics not available

Largely unknown before 1993, the Branch Davidians became world famous through their fifty-one-day standoff against federal authorities. Relatively unimportant in the current scope of American Christianity, the Davidians remain of historical and social interest.

The events of April 19, 1993, which ended in the fiery deaths of over eighty members, including children, is one of the most tragic and spectacular episodes in American religious history. The members who lived at Mt. Carmel Center, a compound near Waco, Texas, followed their self-proclaimed messiah, David Koresh (1959–1993). Koresh commanded resistance against government officials whom he saw as the armies of the antichrist inaugurating the final apocalyptic battle. It is generally accepted that it was Koresh himself who ignited the fire that took the lives of almost all Davidians still living there.

This group of radical sectarians is a subset of one offshoot of the Adventist movement. They trace a lineage to 1930, when Victor T. Houteff, a Seventh-day Adventist church member in Los Angeles, expounded his new and, he claimed, divinely inspired message in a book, *The Shepherd's Rod.* Houteff found that his prophecies were not acceptable to the Seventh-day Adventist leadership, and in 1935 he took his followers to central Texas. The group believed that the redeemed 144,000 mentioned in the biblical book of Revelation would gather temporarily while directing the establishment of the Davidic kingdom. Living in Texas under theocratic rule, they would await the Second Coming of Christ, who would assume the leadership of the Davidic kingdom on earth.

Houteff and his group broke completely with the Seventh-day Adventists in 1942, and Houteff named his group the Davidian Seventh-day Adventists. In the decades following, various power struggles and disappointments over failed prophecies led to further divisions among the Davidians. Houteff died in 1955; and eventually the group in Waco became known as the Branch Davidians, apparently from one leader's statement that members should "Get off the dead [Shepherd's] Rod and move onto a living Branch."

David Koresh assumed the mantle of leadership over the Waco group in 1986, and the community became ever more isolated and defensive. His sermons and radio broadcasts were filled with imagery of the apocalypse taken from the book of Revelation. He associated the events of the twentieth century with the prophecies of Revelation and urged his followers to prepare for the coming cataclysm, which would destroy and purify the earth as part of the final judgment. Influenced by the "survivalist" literature that proliferated during the cold war era and that fueled militia movements, Koresh and his followers began stockpiling food and arms as they prepared to fight for the "Lamb of

God" (Koresh). Reports of the acquisition of a large cache of weapons and of the sexual abuse of children sparked the interest of the U.S. Attorney General. Four agents of the Bureau of Alcohol, Tobacco, and Firearms were killed and over twenty were wounded when they attempted an ill-advised raid on the Branch Davidian compound. After a lengthy siege, during which Koresh proclaimed his messianic rule, the compound was consumed by fire. The details of the disaster continue to be investigated and debated. The anniversary of the conflagration on April 19 has become an important date to a wide variety of anti-government extremist groups unrelated to the Davidians. It figured in the terrorist attack on a government building in Oklahoma City that killed over two hundred persons, including dozens of children in a day-care center.

Two other Davidian Adventist groups remain, one near Exeter, Missouri, the other near Salem, South Carolina. They, too, stand in the heritage of Houteff and his vision of the restoration of the King David-like theocracy in anticipation of Christ's return. No reliable membership information on these groups or on the remnant that still believe in the messianic status of Koresh is available.

CHURCH OF GOD GENERAL CONFERENCE

Founded: 1921, with roots to the 1840s
Membership: 5,308 in 92 churches (1999)

This church is the outgrowth of several independent local groups of similar faith, some in existence as early as 1800; others date their beginnings from the arrival of British immigrants to this country around 1847. These diverse groups shared in general Adventist theology, such as was popularized by William Miller and others in England and the U.S. in the early nineteenth century (see ADVENTIST CHURCHES). Some of these bodies were at one time organized under the name Church of Christ in Christ Jesus. Others also carried the name Church of God of the Abrahamic Faith for many years. A national organization was instituted at Philadelphia in 1888. It met again in 1889; however, because of strong convictions relating to congregational rights and authority, the national body ceased to function until 1921, when the present general conference was formed at Waterloo, Iowa. The corporate name today is Church of God General Conference, Morrow, Georgia.

31

Members of the Church of God General Conference accept the Bible as the supreme and literal standard of faith. Adventist in viewpoint, the church strongly emphasizes the premillennial second coming of Christ. It holds that when Christ returns, he will establish a literal kingdom of God on earth that will originate in the holy city of Jerusalem, where Christ will rule as the messianic king. From there the kingdom will extend to all the nations of earth. Unlike most Christian churches, the Church of God is Arian in orientation, teaching the absolute oneness of God. Arianism teaches that Christ is the Son of God who did not exist prior to the birth of Jesus in Bethlehem; rather than being a person of the Trinity, the Holy Ghost is the power and influence of God on earth until the return of Christ. The church also promotes the belief in the restoration of Israel as a kingdom at the time of restitution. As with many other Adventist groups, the Church of God General Conference denies the immortality of the soul. The dead remain asleep until the resurrection, when all persons will be judged. The righteous will then receive their reward on earth, but the wicked will be completely destroyed in a second death. Membership depends on acceptance of doctrinal faith, repentance from sins, and baptism (for the remission of sins) by immersion.

Due to the congregational nature of the church's government, the general conference exists primarily as a means of mutual cooperation and development of yearly projects and enterprises. Delegates from each church meet annually to determine denominational plans and policies and elect officers, who serve on a board of directors. The work of the general conference is carried on under the direction of the board of directors, which meets as necessary throughout the year. The general conference supports Atlanta Bible College for the training of pastors, a Publishing Department to produce church literature and curricula; and an Outreach and Church Development Department, which promotes youth work, Sunday school activity, mission, and evangelism in preparation for the return of Christ on earth. The church periodical, *The Restitution Herald,* is published bimonthly. Mission stations are located in India, Mexico, the Philippines, Great Britain, and Peru.

CHURCH OF GOD (Seventh Day)

Founded: 1863
Membership: est. 11,000 in 185 churches (1999)

The Church of God (Seventh Day) grew out of the Adventist movement that developed in the first half of the nineteenth century (see ADVENTIST CHURCHES). Like the larger Seventh-day Adventist Church, the founders of the Church of God believed that Christians should observe the sabbath as defined in the Ten Commandments; however, this body rejected the idea that Ellen Harmon White's visions were divinely inspired (see SEVENTH-DAY ADVENTIST). Under the leadership of Gilbert Cranmer in Michigan, it separated in 1858 from other sabbath-keeping Adventists who endorsed White's visions. A similar group of anti-White sabbatarians who organized themselves in Iowa in 1860 joined the Michigan branch in 1863; the movement subsequently spread to Missouri and Nebraska. Several denominational designations were used in its early history, including Church of Christ and Church of Jesus Christ. The present name was chosen in 1884, and the words "Seventh Day" were added in 1923. In 1888, the united body of the Church of God established a central office in Stanberry, Missouri.

In 1933, owing in part to disparate views on polity and administration, the church divided into two groups. One continued to be headquartered in Stanberry; the other established headquarters in Salem, West Virginia. An attempt at merger in 1949 led to some realignment of membership and the relocation of the Stanberry headquarters to Denver, Colorado, the following year. The Salem organization retained its administrative offices and uses "7th Day" rather than "Seventh Day" in its name. The Salem body claims a membership in excess of 1,000 in seven churches and regards as inappropriate the action of the Stanberry-Denver group in forming a new body.

As with Adventist groups in general, the Church of God promotes the imminent, personal, and visible return of Jesus Christ, who will establish the kingdom of God on earth. The dead await the general resurrection in an unconscious state (asleep in death). When Christ returns, the dead will rise to judgment; the righteous will receive life and dwell on a restored earthly paradise, while the wicked will be

33

extinguished in fire. Two ordinances (or sacraments) are observed, adult baptism by immersion and the Lord's Supper accompanied by foot washing. Membership requires a profession of faith in Christ, belief in the doctrines of the church, consent to fellowship, and baptism.

The beliefs of the Salem and Stanberry-Denver groups vary slightly. The Salem body embraces an idea of apostolic succession and places emphasis on "Biblical organization," which means that the numbers 7, 12, and 70 have particular relevance in church organization. They also teach that the physical Church of God (7th Day) is the "true church." The Denver body does not subscribe to similar positions.

Doctrine in the Denver body is discussed and established by ministerial councils; policy is determined by the general membership in session. In 1987, an attempted merger with the General Council of Churches of God (Seventh Day) in Meridian, Idaho, failed. The Denver body claims a membership in a wide area between Michigan and Texas and on the Pacific Coast. Worldwide membership is reported at more than 60,000. The national organization headquartered in Denver supports Spring Vale Academy, a residential high school in Michigan, and the Summit School of Theology in Denver.

SEVENTH-DAY ADVENTIST

Founded: 1845; 1863
Membership: 861,860 in 4,421 churches (1999)

Today the largest Adventist church is the Seventh-day Adventist Church. It arose in the aftermath of the Great Disappointment, the failure of the Millerites' prediction that Christ would return on October 22, 1844 (see ADVENTIST CHURCHES). The Seventh-day group came from one of the smaller Adventist groups who advocated a radical reinterpretation of William Miller's predictions. They concluded that a significant event had, indeed, occurred in October 1844, but not quite in the way Miller had foreseen. It was not an earthly event that took place on that prophesied day, but an event in heaven itself. Christ's ministry in heaven moved from the Holy to the Most Holy Place. As these Adventists explored the meaning of this transferral to the Most Holy Place, which they understood as the Third Angel's Message (Revelation 14), the group focused on the commandments of God and the faith of Jesus, seeking to show the interrelationship of the Old Testament law and the New Testament gospel. The faithful, they taught, must observe the Ten Commandments literally and faithfully, including the fourth commandment to honor the seventh day as a sabbath.

As early as 1844, a small group of Adventists near Washington, New Hampshire, had begun to observe the sabbath on the seventh day. A pamphlet written by Joseph Bates in 1846 gave the question wide publicity and created great interest. Shortly thereafter, Bates, together with James White, Ellen Harmon (later Mrs. James White), Hiram Edson, Frederick Wheeler, and S. W. Rhodes, with the aid of regular publications, set out to champion the seventh-day sabbath, along with the imminence of the Advent. The observation of the sabbath was to be a way to await the Advent of the Lord; hence the name, Seventh-day Adventist. The growth of the group around these leaders was slow at first, owing to the general derision in which Adventists were held after the Great Disappointment. By 1855, however, that group was prosperous and numerically strong enough to set up headquarters at Battle Creek, Michigan, with a publishing house, the Seventh-day Adventist Publishing Association. In 1860 the name Seventh-day Adventist was officially adopted, and in 1903 the headquarters was moved to its present location in Washington, D.C.

Ellen Harmon White (1827–1915) was the key figure in this rejuvenation of Adventism. When she was only in her teens, she began having visions and receiving messages from heaven. It was her visions that gave shape to the new Seventh-day Adventist Church, doctrinally and structurally. White's followers believed that she was granted insight into the workings of heaven, where the apocalyptic struggle was being played out before it would occur on earth, and that she understood the secret teachings of typology whereby heavenly events are reflected in earthly affairs. She and her husband were also instrumental in connecting the teaching of the Second Advent with new theories about health being promulgated by figures such as the vegetarian John Harvey Kellogg (1852–1943). They consider the human body to be the temple of the Holy Spirit; in consequence, they rigidly abstain from the use of alcoholic beverages, tobacco, and drugs. They advocate sound principles of healthful living through diet, exercise, and philanthropic outlook. Medically, they generally embrace homeopathic and osteopathic principles, eschewing the use of drugs in therapy.

Doctrinally, Seventh-day Adventists today are considered evangelical conservatives, holding to the authoritative nature of the revelation of God through the inspired writings of the entire Bible. The church holds that the great principles of God's law are embodied in the Ten Commandments and exemplified in the life of Jesus Christ. They proclaim a belief in the transcendent, personal, communicating God as revealed in the Father, the Son, and the Holy Spirit, each equally and uniquely divine, personal, and eternal. The gift of prophecy, as exemplified by Ellen White, continues in the church.

Seventh-day Adventists also believe in creation by divine fiat and recognize the fall of the human race through the sin of Adam. Unlike most Christian churches, however, they teach that humans are by nature mortal, but may receive immortality through divine grace and the redemption effected through the atoning work of Jesus Christ. According to Adventist teaching, the dead await the resurrection in an unconscious state until the whole person (body, mind, and soul) is resurrected on the last day when Christ will return in person. The righteous will then receive immortality, while the wicked are destroyed by fire. The visible return of Christ will occur at a time unknown, but it is close at hand. When Christ returns a new earth will be created out of the ruins of the old, and this will be the final abode of the redeemed. Among the distinctive practices, in addition to observing the sabbath as a day of rest and worship, are baptism of adults by immersion and the practice of foot washing in preparation for Holy Communion.

The Seventh-day Adventists are particularly noteworthy for their long tradition of promoting religious liberty and the complete separation of church and state, which at times has led to conflict over issues of conscience, such as being required to say the Pledge of Allegiance, serve in the military, or salute the American flag. Their evangelistic, publishing, educational, and health activities have been highly successful. They consider themselves as a movement established in the fulfillment of Bible prophecy, to prepare humankind for the Second Advent and to revive and restore neglected teachings of the Reformation and the apostolic church.

Seventh-day Adventists operate over fifty publishing houses around the world, four in the U.S. and Canada. The church's message is carried around the world in over 680 languages and dialects, with publications in nearly 200 languages. Included in this message of redemption and preparation for the return of Christ is a message of bodily health and personal responsibility that has had an impact far beyond the boundaries of the church. The Adventist Development and Relief Agency (ADRA) is famous for its work with victims of both natural and human-made disasters. In the U.S. and abroad, the church supports approximately 600 medical units, 900 colleges and secondary schools, and 4,500 elementary schools. There are about 1,500 weekly radio and television broadcasts reaching nearly every country, and approximately 900,000 students are enrolled in Bible correspondence schools.

The entire support of the ministry of the church consists of the tithe. Beyond their tithes, Seventh-day Adventists give generously to missions, local church expenses, and other church enterprises. One of the few Protestant churches that is a worldwide community, the overall administrative body of the church is the executive committee of the general conference, chosen by delegates from the various church groups in the quinquennial sessions. Working under this general conference are lesser governmental units. The North American Division is one of eleven divisions that administer church affairs on different continents. It is composed of nine union conferences that make up the divisional organizations, which in turn comprise fifty-eight local conferences, or missions, the smallest administrative unit. Each unit has a large degree of autonomy in a highly representative form of government. Local congregations elect lay elders, deacons, and other officers; the local conference office supervises all local pastoral and evangelistic work and pays all pastors and other workers in its territory from a central fund. Since the Seventh-day Adventists practice adult (age of accountability) baptism, no infants or children are reported in their world membership, which now exceeds nine million persons in over 42,000 congregations.

BAHA'I

Founded: 1863 (came to the U.S. in 1912)
Membership: 142,245 registered in 1,150 assemblies (2000)

Bahá'i is one of the few religions to emerge in modern times. However, like many other religious bodies, it has roots in the ancient traditions of Western monotheism that can be traced back to the biblical patriarch Abraham. Commonly identified as a sect of Islam, the Bahá'i insist that theirs is a distinct religion that encompasses the truths of all of the great religions of the world, Eastern as well as Western. According to Bahá'i teaching, the reason for much of the violence of the world is that each revelation by the divine has been taken to be the only revelation of the divine. People grasp the universal revelation of the Creator as a special message for them and then force others to give up their religious beliefs. For the Bahá'i, the great religions are all manifestations of the divine pointing to a greater revelation to come.

According to Bahá'i teaching there have been nine great prophets (9 is a sacred number for the Bahá'i): Abraham, Krishna, Moses, Zoroaster, Buddha, Jesus, Muhammad, the Bab, and Baha'u'llah. These were all prophets of the one God, and their insights have helped to move humankind closer to God. They were messengers of God who have educated humankind in a progressive revelation. Each was divine in that he perfectly represented God's will, but each was also human and mortal. As can be seen from the list, though, Bahá'i has a Middle Eastern, in fact, an Iranian/Persian, perspective. With the exception of Krishna and the Buddha, all of the prophets listed or their followers were active in Iran, the last two in the nineteenth century.

The Bahá'i faith originated with the teachings of Mirza Ali Muhammad (1819–50), called "the Bab" (Arabic, for "gate" or "door"), who suffered persecution and was martyred in 1850. The Bab emphasized a messianic theme in Islamic thought; that the Madhi (or "Messiah") would soon appear, reform Islam, and restore the former glory of the Islamic Empire that it had enjoyed in the days of the caliphs. It was a message of hope for thousands of the disenfranchised in Iran, but the Bab's preaching threatened the Persian authorities, who feared that the prophecies about the Madhi might inspire revolution. Thus the Bab was arrested, tortured, and executed. As many as 20,000 of his followers, known as Babi, were also slain during that persecution.

As so often happens in the history of religious persecution, the death of the prophet did not stop his message. One of the Bab's followers was a nobleman, Mirza Husayn-'Ali (1817–1892), long admired for his philanthropy and selflessness. While he was in prison in Tehran in 1852, he began to receive revelations. When he was released, he preached and wrote about his visions. He was exiled from Persia and traveled to Istanbul, the capital of the Ottoman Empire. Exiled from there, he made his way to Palestine. His followers called him Bahá'u'lláh, which means "the Glory of God."

In 1863 Bahá'u'lláh announced publicly that he was the one about whom the Bab had prophesied, the messenger sent by God with a new revelation for the coming age. His words were to prepare a new world order. Beginning in September 1867, Bahá'u'lláh began writing to the leaders of the world, such as Queen Victoria, Napoleon III, Pope Pius IX, and Alexander II of Russia, to inform them of the coming new world order and urge them to assist in the next stage of human development. He maintained that the nations of the world should disarm. Instead of pursuing war, they should pursue justice for all of the world's people. Largely ignored during his lifetime, Bahá'u'lláh's writings were preserved by his followers. They note that his style of writing Arabic differed dramatically when he was receiving divine revelations from when he was writing normally. The revealed writings are venerated by his followers, the Bahá'i, in much the same way as Muhammad's Qur'an is venerated by Muslims. When Bahá'u'lláh died in 1892 his remains were buried in a garden room connected to the mansion in Haifa where he lived for two and a half decades under house arrest. This site, known as the Bahji, is a pilgrimage site for the Bahá'i today.

The message of the Bahá'u'lláh was carried to the wider world by his eldest son, Abbas Effendi (1844–1921), later known as Abdul-Baha, who spent some forty years in captivity before being released in 1908 at the time of the revolution of the Young Turks. He toured Egypt, Europe, and the United States. At Wilmette, Illinois, in 1912, he laid the cornerstone of the first Bahá'i house of worship in the West. The headquarters of the National Spiritual Assembly, the administrative body in the United States, is in that vicinity. The Wilmette temple is a unique structure, in which the number 9, the Bahá'i symbol of unity, is repeatedly emphasized: nine concrete piers, nine pillars, and nine arches; it is set in a park with nine sides, nine avenues, nine gateways, and nine fountains. In 1953 the building was dedicated to the unity of God, the unity of the prophets, and the unity of humankind. Worship services are conducted frequently and are not restricted to weekly programs. A Bahá'i home for the aged was built in Wilmette in 1958.

The chief purpose of the Bahá'i faith is to unite the world in one religion and one social order; hence, its chief principle is the oneness and the wholeness of the human race. Among other dominant principles are independent investigation of the truth, the essential harmony of science and religion, recognition of the divine foundation of all religions, universal compulsory education, equality of all men and women, a spiritual solution for economic problems, the need for a universal auxiliary language, universal peace based on a world federation of nations, elimination of all prejudice, and recognition of the essential unity of humanity.

Unlike many new religious movements, the Bahá'i stress the importance of secular education and the equality of women with men. The oppression of women around the world, Bahá'u'lláh declared, is the cause of much of the world's suffering, and he made education of women a cardinal teaching. In fact, Bahá'is hold that if a family has money to send only one child to school, that child should be a daughter, since the daughter will have fewer opportunities without education. When it comes to family life, though, the Bahá'i are rather traditional and conservative. Women are to be the primary caregivers, but men should assist in raising their family. Sex is to be only within the confines of marriage, and divorce is discouraged. The Bahá'i are also instructed to obey government, to avoid alcohol and narcotics except for medicinal purposes, and to use prayer and fasting as a means of elevating the soul. Bahá'i condemns idleness, exalts any work performed in the spirit of service, and prohibits slavery and other forms of oppression. Interestingly, Bahá'i also condemns religious practices common to other religious groups, such as asceticism and monasticism. Each man and woman is expected to live in a happy and productive family, working for the cause of peace and harmony.

The Bahá'i have no prescribed ritual or clergy, in the belief that each seeker may act upon truth and the spirit without ecclesiastical aid. Unpaid teachers and pioneers give assistance to students. Marriage and funeral services are simple and flexible. Meetings vary from devotional and prayer services to public lectures, study classes, and discussion groups for inquirers to meetings for the Bahá'i community, conventions, and summer and winter schools and institutes. Permanent schools are located in Maine, California, and Michigan, and permanent institutes are in found in Arizona and South Carolina. Events within the communities are scheduled by a special calendar of nineteen months of nineteen days each, with the New Year at the vernal equinox. The Bahá'i day starts and ends at sunset. The high point of Bahá'i community life is the Nineteen-Day Feast, which is open to adults and children and serves to unify the local community. The feast is held every nineteen days; it functions like a sabbath, and it contains three central elements: spiritual devotion, administrative consultation, and fellowship. Other than these, the details of the feast embody local cultural norms for food and celebration. Food, however, is not the central aspect of the feast; rather, the writings of Bahá'u'lláh are. Other scriptures may also be read and studied by the community.

Coordination and direction of international activities are now vested in the Bahá'i Universal House of Justice, a body of nine members elected for terms of five years, located at the World Center in Haifa, Israel. In addition to administrative and judicial functions, this body legislates matters not expressly revealed in Bahá'i scriptures. Another institution, the International Teaching Center, functions through boards of counselors assigned to each continent. Local groups are organized as Spiritual Assemblies, supervised by a National Spiritual Assembly consisting of nine members. Not surprisingly, the Bahá'i viewed the creation of the United Nations as a significant step toward the establishment of universal peace and justice.

Although forbidden from aggressively seeking converts, Bahá'is do enthusiastically teach their religion to others as part of the effort to create a universal society. Since 1963 there has been marked growth in the number of adherents to the religion around the world. Although still a small movement in the United States, Bahá'i claim five million believers across the world who reside in some 230 countries, making it one of the most geographically diverse religions in history. There are approximately 20,000 local assemblies and 165 national assemblies. Within this world fellowship are people of all races, nationalities, and creeds, including former Muslims, Hindus, Christians, and Jews. In addition to the one in Illinois, there are central Bahá'i temples in Frankfurt; Sydney; Kampala, Uganda; Panama City; Delhi; and Apia, Western Samoa. The writings of the Bahá'i faith have been translated into more than 800 languages.

BAPTIST CHURCHES

The Baptists comprise one of the largest and most diverse groupings of Christians in the United States. Technically, there are no such things as Baptist denominations, because Baptists are strongly congregational in polity: Each local congregation is independent of the others. However, Baptist churches are commonly grouped into larger associations for purposes of fellowship. National conventions have been established to carry on educational and missionary work and to administer pension plans. For the purposes of this *Handbook,* these national conventions will be considered denominations.

Most state and regional conventions meet annually with delegates from all Baptist churches in a given area. These conventions receive reports, make recommendations, and help to raise national mission budgets; but they have no authority to enforce their decisions. Baptists have insisted on freedom of thought and expression in pulpit and pew. They have insisted, too, on the absolute autonomy of the local congregation; each church arranges its own worship and examines and baptizes its own members. There is no age requirement for membership, but the candidate is usually of an age to understand and accept the teachings of Christ. Candidates for the ministry are licensed by local churches and are ordained upon recommendation of a group of sister churches.

Doctrine and Polity. Despite their emphasis on independence and individualism, Baptists are bound together by an amazingly strong "rope of sand" in allegiance to certain principles and doctrines based generally on the competency of each individual in matters of faith. While they differ in certain minor details, Baptists generally agree on the following principles of faith: the inspiration and trustworthiness of the Bible as the sole rule of life; the lordship of Jesus Christ; the inherent freedom of persons to approach God for themselves; the granting of salvation through faith by way of grace and contact with the Holy Spirit; two ordinances (rather than sacraments), the Lord's Supper and the baptism of believers by immersion; the independence of the local church; the church as a group of regenerated believers who are baptized upon confession of faith; infant baptism as unscrip-

42

tural and not to be practiced; complete separation of church and state; life after death; the unity of humankind; the royal law of God; the need of redemption from sin; and the ultimate triumph of God's kingdom.

These overall doctrines never have been written into any official Baptist creed for all the churches, but they have been incorporated into two important confessions of faith. The Baptist churches of London wrote a Philadelphia Confession in the year 1689 that was enlarged by the Philadelphia Association in 1742. The New Hampshire State Baptist Convention drew up another confession in 1832. The Philadelphia Confession is strongly Calvinist, the New Hampshire Confession only moderately so.

Baptists in the United States. The Baptist movement in the United States grew out of English Puritanism in the early seventeenth century. Convinced that Puritanism needed further reform, Separatists began to teach that only self-professed believers were eligible for membership in the church. That is, the church is properly made up of only regenerated people. Fleeing persecution under James I, some of the English Separatists settled in Holland, where they encountered the Mennonites (see MENNONITE CHURCHES). Many of the Mennonites principles agreed with their own convictions, including the beliefs that the scriptures are the sole authority for faith and practice, that church and state should be completely and forever separated, and that church discipline should be rigidly enforced in business, family, and personal affairs. Before long the congregation of John Smyth (ca. 1570–1612) accepted another bedrock Mennonite principle and adopted the practice of "believer's baptism"—that is, baptism only of adults who make a profession of faith. Smyth rebaptized himself and his followers in 1609. When he tried to make Mennonites of his people, however, he was rejected by his own congregation. Baptist they would be, but not Mennonite, because that meant a threat to their British heritage. Smyth's people eventually moved back across the channel and established a Baptist church in London.

The first churches were General Baptist churches, which means that they believed in a general atonement for all persons. In the course of time there arose a Particular Baptist Church, which held to the doctrine of predestination associated with the teachings of John Calvin (1509–64). The first British Particular Baptist Church dates back to 1638.

43

In 1631, Roger Williams (ca. 1603–83) came to America and was soon the first great champion of freedom for faith and conscience in North America. Williams was not a Baptist but a Separatist minister when he arrived. Preaching new and dangerous opinions against the authority of the Puritan magistrates, Williams organized a Baptist church at Providence, Rhode Island. John Clarke (1609–76) established another Baptist church at Newport at about the same time. Many scholars date the Providence church to 1639, and the Newport church to 1641. The Baptist movement grew rapidly during the First Great Awakening (a revival of religious interest) of the 1740s, but a dispute soon arose among Baptists over the question of emotionalism. The Old Lights, or Regulars, distrusted revivals, while the New Lights insisted on an experience of rebirth as a condition for membership in their churches. Despite internal disagreements Baptists continued to agitate for religious freedom in the new land and played a significant role in the adoption of the First Amendment.

Many Baptists hold to the belief that the Baptist Church has existed since the days of John the Baptist. Of particular interest in this regard are the Landmark Baptists. The name originated with the writings of James Madison Pendleton (1811–91) and James Robinson Graves (1820–93) in Kentucky and Tennessee in the latter part of the nineteenth century. The four distinguishing tenets of Landmarkism are the following: (1) The church is always local and visible. While members of Protestant churches may be saved, they are not members of true churches. (2) The commission was given to the church; consequently, all matters covered by it must be administered under church authority. Clergy of other denominations are not accepted in Landmark Baptist pulpits. (3) Baptism, to be valid, must be administered by the authority of a New Testament (Baptist) church. Baptisms administered by any other authority are not accepted. (4) There is a direct historic succession of Baptist churches from New Testament times. Baptist churches have existed in practice, though not in name, in every century. These principles are held primarily by the churches of the American Baptist Association, though an estimated one and a half million members of different Baptist churches hold to the Landmark position and doctrine, the largest concentration being in the South and the Southwest. More than fifteen Bible institutes and seminaries are supported by these churches.

Baptist preachers had been particularly effective in converting African Americans to Christianity before emancipation. The great majority of blacks in pre-Civil War days were either Baptist or Methodist. In 1793 there were 73,471 Baptists in the U.S., one-fourth of them black. When the Battle of Bull Run was fought in 1861, there were 200,000 black members of the Methodist Episcopal Church, South, and 150,000 black Baptists. Usually, slaves sat in the galleries of white churches, identifying with the faith of their owners. White preachers, sometimes assisted by black helpers, moved from one plantation to another, holding services more or less regularly. Occasionally a black preacher was liberated to give full time to religious work among blacks, and these ministers had great influence. The first black Baptist church was organized at Silver Bluff, across the Savannah River, near Augusta, Georgia, in 1773. Other churches followed in Petersburg, Virginia, 1776; Richmond, Virginia, 1780; Williamsburg, Virginia, 1785; Savannah, Georgia, 1785; and Lexington, Kentucky, 1790. The slave rebellion led by Nat Turner (ca. 1800–31) in 1831 appears to have been fueled by Christian rhetoric of freedom and divine justice. Whites were so frightened that laws were passed in some sections of the South prohibiting blacks from becoming Christian or building meetinghouses. Almost everywhere slave meetings were monitored by owners, lest unrest be fomented. However, slaves continued to conduct their own meetings hidden from sight and sound of the masters in "the invisible institution." After the Civil War, numerous black Baptist congregations emerged and organized their own conventions. Aided by the Freedman's Aid Society and various Baptist organizations, nearly one million black Baptists were worshiping in their own churches by 1880.

Strongly evangelical in theology, the Baptists were early participants in foreign missions. The English Baptist William Carey (1761–1834) went to India in 1793 and became the pioneer of modern missions. In 1814, Baptists in the U.S. organized their own General Missionary Convention of the Baptist Denomination in the United States of America for Foreign Missions. This convention, representing a national Baptist fellowship, marked the first real denominational consciousness. It was followed eventually by other organizations that welded them firmly together: a general Baptist convention; a general tract society, later called the American Baptist Publication Society; various missionary societies for work at home and abroad; an education society; and the Baptist Young People's Union. These organizations were on a national scale. Their unity was disrupted first by a feeling that home-missions agencies within the body had failed to evangelize Southern territory and later by arguments over slavery. The great division occurred in 1845, when Southerners formed their own Southern Baptist Convention. From that point forward there were both Northern and Southern conventions.

The Baptist Joint Committee on Public Affairs, supported by the American Baptist Churches in the U.S.A., sectors of the Southern Baptist Convention, and some other bodies, is housed in Washington, D.C. This committee serves mainly to spread Baptist convictions on public morals and to safeguard the principle of separation of church and state. The Baptist World Alliance, organized in 1905, now includes more than 40 million Baptists in 170 member bodies. The Alliance meets every five years to discuss common themes and problems and is purely an advisory body. Its headquarters are located in McLean, Virginia.

ALLIANCE OF BAPTIST CHURCHES

Founded: 1987
Membership: est. 64,000 in 130 churches (1999)

The Alliance of Baptists is a confederation of Baptist congregations, primarily in the South, that separated from the Southern Baptist Convention during the conservative/moderate conflict of the 1980s. The Alliance churches stress the historic Baptist principles of individual and congregational autonomy, particularly in regard to biblical interpretation and missions. The Alliance churches encourage the use of modern methods of biblical study, theological education, and free inquiry into the history of Christianity. Most important, the Alliance has dedicated itself to social and economic justice and equity. Women are encouraged to seek ordination and assume leadership roles in the Alliance and in congregations. Leadership of the Alliance is composed of three elected officers who serve no more than two years and a forty-member Board of Directors. The annual meeting of the Alliance is held each spring and reviews all decisions of the Board. There are nine standing committees that supervise such areas as women in ministry and interfaith dialogue.

AMERICAN BAPTIST ASSOCIATION

Founded: 1905
Membership: est. 275,000 in 1,760 churches (1998)

Organized in 1905 as the Baptist General Association, the group adopted its present name in 1924. Teaching that the Great Commission of Christ (Matt. 28:18-20) was given only to a local congregation, members believe that the local church is the only unit authorized to administer the ordinances (baptism and communion) and that the congregation is an independent and autonomous body responsible only to Christ. Because of their belief that no universal church or ecclesiastical authority is higher than a local congregation, members of the American Baptist Association claim that those Baptists organized in conventions are not faithful to Bible missions methods. Maintaining that their own way is the true New Testament form, they hold themselves separate from all other religious groups. They strongly protest the trend of many Baptist groups to identify themselves with Protestantism, since they believe that their faith preceded the Protestant Reformation, and indeed has a continued succession from Christ and the apostles (see BAPTIST CHURCHES).

The Association's doctrine is strictly fundamentalist and includes the verbal inspiration of the Bible, the Triune God, the virgin birth and deity of Christ, the suffering and death of Christ as substitutionary, and the bodily resurrection of Christ and all his saints. The Second Coming of Jesus, physical and personal, is to be the crowning event of the gospel age and will be premillennial. There is eternal punishment for the wicked; salvation is solely by grace through faith, not by law or works. There must be absolute separation of church and state and absolute religious freedom. Members denounce abortion on demand, homosexuality, and premarital sex as being contrary to biblical teachings.

Government of both the local congregation and the annual meeting of the association is congregational in nature. Missionary work is conducted on county, state, interstate, and international levels, the program originating in the local church; and missionaries are supported by the cooperating churches. Educational work is pursued through the Sunday schools, five seminaries, three colleges, and twenty-seven Bible institutes. The greater strength of this group is found in the South, Southeast, Southwest, and West, but much new work has begun in recent years in the East and the North.

47

A comprehensive publishing program includes fourteen monthly and semimonthly periodicals, Sunday school literature designed to cover the entire Bible in a ten-year period, and literature for young people and vacation Bible schools. National and state youth camps are held annually, as are pastors' and missionaries' conferences on regional and national levels.

AMERICAN BAPTIST CHURCHES IN THE U.S.A.

Founded: 1814 or 1845
Membership: 1,454,388 in 5,775 churches (1999)

This body has had several changes in name over the decades. It traces its origins to May 1814, when representatives from various Baptist associations and churches met in Philadelphia to organize the General Missionary Convention of the Baptist Denomination in the United States of America for Foreign Missions. This body quickly became known as the Triennial Convention and was the first national Baptist organization in the United States. The American Baptist Publication Society and the American Baptist Home Mission Society were established in 1824 and 1832 respectively. By 1841, sectional and theological differences centered around the issue of slavery began to erode the unity of the foreign mission board. In 1845, one year after the final meeting of the Triennial Convention, the Northern and Southern groups met and reorganized separately as two foreign mission societies. The women of the Northern churches formed their own home and foreign missionary societies in the 1870s.

Separate appeals for funds to support these competing societies created confusion and dissatisfaction, leading eventually to the formation of the Northern Baptist Convention in 1907. This convention was actually a corporation with restricted powers in conducting religious work, receiving and expending money, and affiliating itself with other bodies. The Convention reorganized in 1950, changing its name to the American Baptist Convention. In 1955, the two women's missionary societies joined administratively with their counterparts, the older foreign- and home-mission societies. In 1950 the first general secretary was elected.

In 1972 the convention adopted its third and present name and restructured to strengthen the representational principle and to integrate more fully the national program bodies into the larger organi-

48

zation. A larger (200-member) general board composed of election-district representatives and at-large representatives makes up the policy-making body. A general council of chief executives and staff of national program boards, chief executives of regions, and other American Baptist bodies serves to coordinate the corporate affairs of the denomination under the leadership of the general secretary.

The denomination is at work in twenty children's homes and special services, seventy-seven retirement homes and communities, twenty-seven hospitals and nursing homes, nine theological seminaries, and sixteen senior colleges and universities. Judson Press is its publishing arm. The Board of National Ministries has workers in thirty-six states. This board supports Bacone College for Native Americans in Oklahoma and carries on widespread work among African Americans, Native Americans, and Asians in the U.S. The Board of International Ministries currently supports missionaries in six countries in Asia (Hong Kong, India, Japan, the Philippines, Singapore, and Thailand), two countries in Africa (South Africa and Zaire), and seven countries in Latin America and the Caribbean (Bolivia, Costa Rica, the Dominican Republic, El Salvador, Haiti, Mexico, and Nicaragua).

In matters of faith, American Baptist Churches hold to typical Baptist doctrines described above. They have historically taken a stand on such controversial issues as abolition, temperance, racial and social justice, and the ordination of women. They have traditionally been a denomination with diversity of race, ethnicity, culture, class, and theology. The ordinances of baptism and the Lord's Supper are considered aids more than necessities for salvation. Generally it may be said that Baptists represented in the American Baptist Churches in the U.S.A. are less conservative in thought and theology than those in the Southern Baptist Convention. American Baptists are represented in the National Council of the Churches of Christ in the U.S.A. and the World Council of Churches; Southern Baptists are represented in neither. American Baptists have made gestures toward union with General Baptists, Southern Baptists, the National Baptist Convention, Seventh-Day Baptists, Disciples of Christ, Church of the Brethren, and the Alliance of Baptists and have welcomed Free Baptists into full fellowship.

BAPTIST GENERAL CONFERENCE

Founded: 1852
Membership: 142,871 in 880 churches (1999)

The history of what is now known as the Baptist General Conference began at Rock Island, Illinois, in 1852. Gustaf Palmquist, a middle-aged schoolteacher and lay preacher, had arrived from Sweden the previous year to become the spiritual leader of a group of Swedish immigrants who had been influenced by the Pietist movement within the (Lutheran) state church of Sweden. At Galesburg, Illinois, he came in contact with Baptists, and early in 1852 he was baptized and ordained a Baptist minister. Visiting the Swedish people at Rock Island, Palmquist won his first converts to the Baptist faith and baptized three in the Mississippi River on August 18, 1852. There were sixty-five churches when the national conference of the Swedish Baptist General Conference of America was organized in 1879.

For several decades the American Baptist Home Mission Society and the American Baptist Publication Society of the American (then Northern) Baptist Convention aided the new work among the Swedish immigrants, but gradually the church became self-supporting. A theological seminary was founded in Chicago in 1871, and the first denominational paper was launched the same year. From 1888 until 1944, foreign missionary activities were channeled through the American Baptist Foreign Mission Society. The Swedish Conference set up its own foreign-mission board in 1944 and today has more than 135 regular and 55 short-term missionaries in India, Japan, the Philippines, Ethiopia, Mexico, Argentina, Brazil, the Ivory Coast, Cameroon, and France.

Following World War I, with its intensified nationalistic conflicts, the transition from Swedish- to English-language church services was greatly accelerated and was practically completed in three decades. In 1945, Swedish was dropped from the name of the conference. With the language barrier removed, the growth of the conference has been rapid and far-reaching. Although its greatest strength lies in the North Central and Pacific Northwest sections of the U.S., home missionaries are at work in all the northern states and some of the southern states. Less than half of the pastors are of Swedish descent, and a large number of churches contain few members of that descent.

The conference owns and controls Bethel College and Seminary in St. Paul, Minnesota, a four-year college and a three-year theological school, with 2,300 students; the seminary also has a campus in San Diego, California. Also affiliated with the conference are three children's homes, seven homes for the aged, and *The Standard,* the official denominational organ issued by the Board of Overseers. Harvest Publications offers Bibles, books, and Sunday school materials.

Basically, the church's doctrine is theologically conservative, with unqualified acceptance of the Word of God, and holds the usual Baptist tenets. It is a strong fellowship of churches, insistent upon the major beliefs of conservative Christianity but with respect for individual differences on minor points.

COOPERATIVE BAPTIST FELLOWSHIP

Founded: 1991
Membership: statistics not available; 1,800 churches (2000)

As with many Baptist groups, the Cooperative Baptist Fellowship (CBF) cannot quite be termed a denomination. It is a recently created and vital fellowship of Baptist churches, primarily in the South. The CBF was formed during the years of struggle within the Southern Baptist Convention (SBC) between conservatives and moderates (see SOUTHERN BAPTIST CONVENTION). Some of the moderates disapproved of the tactics of the conservatives and believed that the Convention itself was in danger of violating the historic Baptist affirmation of individual freedom. In 1991, the new CBF was formed as an alternative body to the SBC, although congregations are free to hold joint membership.

The mission of the Cooperative Baptist Fellowship focuses on ministry rather than theology, as indicated by their mission statement adopted in July, 2000: "We are a fellowship of Baptist Christians and churches who share a passion for the Great Commission of Jesus Christ and a commitment to Baptist principles of faith and practice. Our mission is to serve Baptist Christians and churches as they discover and fulfill their God-given mission." With an annual budget of almost seventeen million dollars, the CBF focuses its work on global missions to the world's ethno-linguistic groups who have little or no exposure to the Christian message and on ministries among the urban

51

poor and other marginalized peoples in the inner cities of the U.S. It also fosters advocacy of historic Baptist values, such as local church autonomy, the priesthood of all believers, and religious liberty. The CBF has partnerships with a dozen seminaries and theological schools and has helped found new schools of theology in historical Baptist colleges in the South.

GENERAL ASSOCIATION OF GENERAL BAPTIST CHURCHES

Founded: 1870
Membership: 67,314 in 719 churches (1998)

The General Association of General Baptist Churches claims its name and origin in John Smyth (ca. 1570–1612) and Thomas Helwys (ca. 1550–ca. 1616) and the group of Baptists organized in England and Holland in 1611 (see BAPTIST CHURCHES). Roger Williams (ca. 1603–83) is held to be the first minister in the American Colonies. General Baptists in the Colonies along the Atlantic coast were at first overwhelmed by the influence of Calvinism (General Baptists have always been Arminian), but their work was reopened by Benoni Stinson (ca. 1798–ca. 1870) in 1823 with the establishment of the Liberty Baptist Church in what is now Evansville, Indiana. They spread into Illinois and Kentucky, and a general association was organized in 1870. Since that time the group has grown steadily; today it is strong throughout the Midwest.

The General Baptist confession of faith is similar to that of Free Will Baptists: Christ died for all; failure to achieve salvation lies completely with the individual; humankind is depraved and fallen and unable to save itself; regeneration is necessary for salvation; salvation comes by repentance and faith in Christ; Christians who persevere to the end are saved; the wicked are punished eternally; and the dead, both the just and the unjust, will be raised at the judgment. The Lord's Supper and believer's baptism by immersion are the only authorized ordinances and should be open to all believers. Some General Baptist churches practice foot washing.

Church polity is similar to that found in most Baptist groups. Churches of a common area are organized into local associations, which in turn are organized into a general association. Both local and general associations are representative bodies and advisory in power.

A peculiar feature of the General Baptist church lies in the use of a presbytery, into which the ordained members of local associations are grouped; they examine candidates for the ministry and for the diaconate. Ministers and deacons are responsible to this presbytery, which exists only on the local level.

The church maintains a liberal arts college with a theological department at Oakland City, Indiana. A publishing house, Stinson Press, is operated at Poplar Bluff, Missouri, where the monthly paper *General Baptist Messenger* is issued, together with Sunday school literature. Foreign missionary work is supported in Guam, Saipan, Jamaica, Honduras, and the Philippines, and home missionary work is actively carried out in various states.

GENERAL ASSOCIATION OF REGULAR BAPTIST CHURCHES

Founded: 1932
Membership: 92,129 in 1,398 churches

Twenty-two Baptist churches of the American Baptist Convention left that organization in May 1932 to found the General Association of Regular Baptist Churches. Their protest was against what they considered the Convention's modernist tendencies and teachings, the denial of the historic Baptist principle of independence and autonomy of the local congregation, the inequality of representation in the assemblies of the convention, and the control of missionary work by convention assessment and budget.

Any Baptist church coming into the General Association is required to withdraw all fellowship and cooperation from any convention or group that permits modernists or modernism within its ranks. Dual fellowship or membership is not permitted. Participation in union evangelical campaigns or Thanksgiving services or membership in local ministerial associations where modernists are involved or present is considered unscriptural. Missionary work is conducted through six approved Baptist agencies that are completely independent of any convention and that are deemed orthodox. Only nine schools are approved; these, too, are guarded against any defection from approved practice or doctrine.

Basically fundamentalist in outlook, the association subscribes to the New Hampshire Confession of Faith (1832) with a premillennial

53

interpretation of the final article of that confession. It holds to the infallibility of the Bible, the Trinity, the personality of Satan as the author of all evil, humankind as the creation of God, and humankind born in sin. Doctrines deal with the virgin birth, the deity of Jesus, and faith in Christ as the way of salvation through grace. The saved are in everlasting felicity; the lost are consigned to endless punishment. Civil government is by divine appointment. There are only two approved ordinances: baptism by immersion and the Lord's Supper.

Church government is strictly congregational. Associated churches have the privilege of sending six voting messengers to an annual convention. A Council of Eighteen is elected—nine each year—to serve for two years. The Council makes recommendations to the association for the furtherance of its work and puts into operation all actions and policies of the association. The Council's authority depends completely on the will and direction of the association. The Regular Baptist Press publishes *The Baptist Bulletin,* a monthly magazine.

NATIONAL ASSOCIATION OF FREE WILL BAPTISTS

Founded: 1935, with roots to Colonial days
Membership: 216,711 in 2,476 churches (1999)

The rise of Free Will Baptists can be traced to the influence of Arminian-minded Baptists who migrated to the American Colonies from England. The southern line, or Palmer movement, began in 1727 when Paul Palmer established a church at Chowan, North Carolina. The northern line, or Randall movement, began with a congregation organized by Benjamin Randall in 1780 in New Durham, New Hampshire. Both groups taught the doctrines of free grace, free salvation, and free will. There were gestures toward uniting the northern and southern groups until the outbreak of the Civil War. The northern body extended more rapidly into the West and the Southwest, and in 1910 this line of Free Will Baptists merged with the Northern Baptist denomination, taking along 857 of its 1,100 churches, all of its denominational property, and several colleges. In 1916 representatives of remnant churches from the Randall movement organized the Cooperative General Association of Free Will Baptists.

By 1921 the southern churches had organized into new associations and conferences, and finally into a General Conference. The division continued until November 5, 1935, when the two groups merged into the National Association of Free Will Baptists at Nashville, Tennessee.

Doctrinally, the church holds that Christ gave himself as a ransom for all, not just for the elect; that God calls all persons to repentance; and that whosoever will may be saved. Baptism is by immersion. One of the few Baptist groups that practice open communion, the Free Will Baptists also practice foot washing. Government is strictly congregational. There are two Bible colleges and two liberal arts colleges. The church's greatest strength is in the South.

NATIONAL BAPTIST CONVENTION OF AMERICA, INC.

Founded: 1895
Membership: est. 3,500,000 in 2,500 churches (1987)

"National Baptist" has been the name of some aspect of organized black Baptist life since at least 1886. By 1876 all of the southern states except Florida had a state missionary convention, but smaller bodies had existed since the 1830s in the Midwest; organized missionary efforts date back to that same period in the North.

The first black Baptist group, the Providence Baptist Association of Ohio, was formed in 1836, and the first attempt at national organization occurred in 1880 with the creation of the Foreign Mission Baptist Convention at Montgomery, Alabama. In 1886, the American National Baptist Convention was organized at St. Louis, and in 1893 the Baptist National Educational Convention was begun in the District of Columbia. All three conventions merged into the National Baptist Convention of America in 1895 at Atlanta. For the next twenty years a single National Baptist body functioned through a variety of activities, the publication of Sunday school material being a major one. It sponsored foreign mission enterprises, especially to African and Caribbean countries; and it founded some colleges and provided support for others, several of them the result of dedication to providing education for the emancipated people on the part of Northern Baptist (see BAPTIST CHURCHES) and other churches.

In 1915 a division arose over the adoption of a charter and the ownership of a publishing house. The group that rejected the charter continued to function as the National Baptist Convention of America. The group that accepted the charter became known as the National Baptist Convention, U.S.A., Inc. The former is frequently referred to as "the unincorporated" (although it did eventually incorporate in 1988) and the latter as "the incorporated," but both trace their beginnings to the Foreign Mission Baptist Convention.

The National Baptist Convention of America, Inc., has its greatest strength in Mississippi, Texas, and Louisiana, with large numbers of members also in Florida and California. It holds an annual convention, and officers are elected each year. There is no central national headquarters, but Nashville, Tennessee, is the home of the publishing house. Publication remains a high priority for the church.

NATIONAL BAPTIST CONVENTION, U.S.A., INC.

> Founded: 1895
> Membership: statistics not available

The largest body of black Baptists in the U.S. shared a common history with the "of America" denomination (see NATIONAL BAPTIST CONVENTION OF AMERICA, INC.) throughout the formative years of the two groups. Its formal origins date from 1895, with many roots and predecessors stretching back to the period around 1840. Until the disagreement that arose over control of the publishing house of the denomination in 1915, there was a single National Baptist body. Once the "of America" convention was created, the Foreign Mission Board became the "U.S.A." body's center of operations.

The "U.S.A." body has widespread distribution. In 1990 it opened its World Headquarters in Nashville, Tennessee, where a section of the publishing industry has been located since the 1890s and where its Sunday School Board is still located. Nashville is also the home of a seminary that has been operated (jointly with the Southern Baptists) since 1924. This convention meets annually, and its officers are elected annually. Those officers and a Board of Directors with fifteen members conduct the Convention's business.

If publishing control has been the most conspicuous fact in the "of America" body, presidential influence has been the "U.S.A." body's most visible feature. That was particularly true during the tenure (1953–82) of Joseph H. Jackson. A powerful and effective leader, Jackson promoted the theory and practice of racial uplift in the tradition of Booker T. Washington (1856–1915). "From protest to production" was Jackson's motto. He led the body to steer clear of political and social involvements on any large scale. That policy placed this group mostly outside the civil rights movement of the period 1954–72, in which many black Baptist pastors and lay leaders worked for racial justice. As a result, another National Baptist schism occurred, out of which the Progressive National Baptist Convention was formed in 1961 (see PROGRESSIVE NATIONAL BAPTIST CONVENTION, INC.). Since that period, however, this once less publicly involved body has shifted its practice and has been active in civil rights causes and voter registration drives.

This denomination, too, has been active in missionary, educational, and publication ministries. Recently it has established a ministerial pension plan. It has shown a particularly high degree of commitment to the support of colleges and seminaries, among them Morehouse School of Religion in Atlanta, Georgia, and Virginia Seminary in Lynchburg. The educational institutions are typically supported by Baptist churches and individuals rather than being affiliated officially with the Convention. The body supports missionary stations in the Bahamas, Jamaica, Panama, and Africa.

NATIONAL MISSIONARY BAPTIST CONVENTION OF AMERICA

Founded: 1988
Membership: est. 2,500,000 (1992)

The recent origin of this body of black Baptists (which came into being in 1988) accurately suggests the degree of historical heritage it shares with the two older National Baptist bodies. Once again the issue of control over denominational publication ventures led to a rupture. This new fellowship opposed the private ownership and leadership of the Convention's Sunday school congress and publishing house. It sought an organizational plan by which the Convention itself would control the congress and publishing activities.

The convention meets in September annually, and the governing boards hold two additional meetings. The National Missionary Baptist Convention is headquartered in Los Angeles, California, and its greatest strength lies in the population of the Pacific Coast states.

NATIONAL PRIMITIVE BAPTIST CONVENTION, U.S.A.

Founded: 1907
Membership: est. 1,000,000 in 1,530 churches (1995)

The black population of the South, throughout the years of slavery and civil war, generally worshiped with the white population in their various churches. That was true of the forerunners of this group, formerly the Colored Primitive Baptist Church. The members attended white Primitive Baptist churches until the time of emancipation, when their white co-worshipers helped them establish their own churches, granting letters of fellowship and character, ordaining deacons and ministers, and assisting in other ways.

The doctrine and polity are similar to that of the Primitive Baptists (see PRIMITIVE BAPTIST), though earlier the members were opposed to all forms of church organization. There are local associations and a national convention, organized in 1907. Each congregation is independent, receiving and controlling its membership. Unlike the Primitive Baptists, since 1900 this group has been establishing aid societies, conventions, and Sunday schools, over the opposition of some older and more traditional members.

NORTH AMERICAN BAPTIST CONFERENCE

Founded: 1865
Membership: 45,738 in 271 churches (1999)

This Baptist conference began among German Baptist churches in North America in the nineteenth century. German Baptists first settled in New Jersey and Pennsylvania, where Quakers offered the religious freedom they sought. The scattered churches later became the North American Baptist Conference, organizing the first local churches in the 1840s. The local conference idea was enlarged as the number of churches increased and as German immigration spread westward. In 1865 delegates from the eastern and western conferences met in a General Conference in Wilmot, Ontario. A Triennial Conference is now the chief administrative unit.

Twenty associations meet annually to elect their own officers and committees and to guide their own work. The Triennial Conference is made up of clergy and lay representatives from all the churches and superintends the work of publication, education, international missions, and church planting. A general council acts for the conference between sessions. Few congregations continue to use the German language in worship.

German Baptists were a part of what is now Colgate-Rochester Divinity School in Rochester, New York. In 1935, they established a seminary of their own, the North American Baptist Seminary, which relocated from Rochester to Sioux Falls, South Dakota, in 1949. The conference supports ten homes for the aged and efforts at church planting in Japan, Brazil, Nigeria, Cameroon, West Africa, Russia, the Philippines, and Mexico.

Theologically, there is little variance from the basic Baptist position. In general, North American Baptists follow the New Hampshire Confession (1832), stressing the authority of Scripture, the revelation of God in Christ, regeneration, immersion, separation of church and state, and the congregational form of government.

PRIMITIVE BAPTIST

Founded: 1827
Membership: est. 72,000 in 1,000 churches (1995)

Primitive Baptists have the reputation of being the strictest and most exclusive of all Baptist churches. Certainly they have held to the Baptist belief in local autonomy to an unusual degree. In fact, they have never been organized as a denomination and have no administrative body of any kind beyond the local church. The movement originated in a nineteenth-century protest against money-based mission and benevolent societies introduced in the early nineteenth century. Of particular concern was the assessing of churches to support missions, missionaries, and Sunday schools. The Primitive Baptists maintained that there were no missionary societies in the days of the apostles and none directed by the Scripture; therefore, there should be none now.

Spearheading this protest against new measures, in 1827 the Kehukee Association in North Carolina condemned all money-based and centralized societies as being contrary to Christ's teachings. Within a decade, several other Baptist associations across the country made similar statements and withdrew from other Baptist churches.

59

The various associations adopted the custom of printing in their annual minutes their articles of faith, constitutions, and rules of order. These statements were examined by the other associations, and, if they were approved, there was fellowship and an exchange of messengers and correspondence. Any association not so approved was dropped from the fellowship.

Calvinism runs strongly through the Primitive Baptist doctrine. In general, the members believe that through Adam's fall, all humankind became sinners; human nature is completely corrupt, and humans cannot by their own efforts regain favor with God; God elected God's own people in Christ before the world began, and none of these saints will be finally lost; Christ will come a second time to raise the dead, judge all people, punish the wicked forever, and reward the righteous forever; and the Old and New Testaments are verbally and infallibly inspired. The two biblically authorized ordinances are the Lord's Supper and baptism of believers by immersion. All church societies are human inventions and are denied fellowship.

Pastors are to be called by God, come under the laying on of hands, and be in fellowship with the local church of which they are members in order to administer the two ordinances. No theological training is demanded of ministers. While there is no opposition to such education, the position is that the Lord might call an educated person, but lack of education should not bar a person from the ministry. Some, but not all, Primitive Baptists still practice foot washing. In spite of their opposition to money-based missionary societies, they are intensely evangelistic, and their preachers travel widely and serve without charge, except when hearers wish to contribute to their support. The movement is concentrated in the South.

PROGRESSIVE NATIONAL BAPTIST
CONVENTION, INC.

Founded: 1961
Membership: est. 2,500,000 in 2,000 churches (1995)

This group of Baptists came into being in 1961, after several years of tension and discussion, breaking away from the National Baptist Convention, U.S.A., Inc. In that year, Martin Luther King, Jr. (1929–68) nominated Gardner C. Taylor as president of the convention against longtime president Joseph Jackson, who was opposed to the protest movement of King. The National Baptist Convention, U.S.A., followed a policy of disengagement from the civil rights movement and other social justice struggles during the revolutionary years following the 1954 Supreme Court decision concerning desegregation of public facilities. Following the defeat of Taylor, who called for unity within the National Baptist Convention, U.S.A., the Rev. L. Venchael Booth, chairman of the Volunteer Committee for the Formation of a New National Baptist Convention, issued a call for a meeting at his church in Cincinnati, Ohio. One of the central objectives of the new convention was support for the "freedom fighters" in the civil rights movement. The first president was Dr. T. M. Chambers, who served until 1967, at which point Gardner Taylor was elected to that office.

Once the convention was established, it became a focal point of the civil rights movement, and many leaders of that movement assumed significant positions in the new convention. In addition to King and Gardner, this included the famous preachers Ralph David Abernathy (1926–90) and Benjamin Mays (1895–1984). From its inception, the Progressive body has taken a highly active role in civil rights, social justice, and political causes. It also took a strong stand against apartheid in South Africa.

Headquartered in Washington, D.C., the Progressive National Baptists are organized into four national regions. Eight departments include women, laymen, young adult women, young adult men, ushers, youth, moderator's council, and Christian education. From its beginning, the convention has has been ecumenical in spirit, seeking to work harmoniously with other Christian denominations.

REFORMED or SOVEREIGN GRACE BAPTISTS

Founded: 1954
Membership: statistics not available

This collection of Baptists represents a theological movement more than a denominational structure; thus it is impossible to give accurate membership statistics. However, it is estimated that there are 300 to 400 congregations in the U.S. and Canada who have embraced a strict adherence to "five-point Calvinism" as represented in the London Confession of 1689 and the Philadelphia Confession of 1742. They profess belief in the tenets of total human depravity, unconditional election, limited and definite atonement, irresistible (or invincible) calling, and the perseverance of all true saints. "Reformed" in their name refers to the doctrines of the Reformation, especially Calvinism. They agree for the most part with the doctrines of the Synod of Dort (1618–19), along with the Anabaptist doctrine of a called-out church. They have been heavily influenced by the nineteenth-century theologian and popular preacher Charles Spurgeon (1834–92). A series of special meetings conducted by Rolfe P. Barnard (1904–69) led to the first "Sovereign Grace Bible Conference," which was held in Ashland, Kentucky, in 1954. The conference gave rise to this fellowship of churches.

These Baptists differ from most other Baptists in their stress on theology rather than revivalism, but they also differ from other Calvinist Baptists who may deny the necessity of preaching to all or hold to a Landmark concept of the church (see BAPTIST CHURCHES). The churches involved are completely autonomous, independently supporting an unlisted number of missionaries and the publishing of church literature. Membership is concentrated mainly in the northeastern and southern states.

SEPARATE BAPTISTS IN CHRIST
(General Association)

Founded: ca. 1700
Membership: est. 10,000 in 101 churches (2001)

The first Separate Baptists arrived in the U.S. in 1695 from England. They were especially active during the days of the preaching of George Whitefield (1714–70) in the early eighteenth century and in the conflict between the Old Light and the New Light sects. In 1787, Separate and Regular Baptist churches in Virginia merged into the United Baptist Churches of Christ in Virginia. Additional mergers and gestures toward union arose in New England and other states, but a few Separate Baptist churches maintained their independence. Separate Baptists do not claim to be Protestants: "We have never protested against what we hold to be the faith once delivered to the saints."

All creeds and confessions of faith are rejected by Separate Baptists; however, there is an annual statement of articles of belief by the several associations and the general association. These include statements of faith in the infallibility of the scriptures and in the Trinity; regeneration, justification, and sanctification through faith in Christ; and the appearance of Christ on judgment day to deal with the just and the unjust. The election, reprobation, and fatality of Calvinism are rejected. Unlike most other Baptists, these churches observe three ordinances (sacraments): baptism of believers by immersion only, the Lord's Supper, and foot washing.

The General Association of Separate Baptists has incorporated a mission program called Separate Baptist Missions, Inc. Through this program, support is given to various mission fields and efforts, both in the U.S. and abroad.

SEVENTH DAY BAPTIST GENERAL CONFERENCE

Founded: 1802, with roots to 1671
Membership: est. 4,800 in 80 churches (1995)

Differing from other groups of Baptists in its adherence to the seventh day (Saturday) as the sabbath, the Seventh Day Baptists first appeared as a separate religious body in North America in the Colonial period. Stephen and Ann Mumford came from England in 1664 and entered into a covenant relationship with those who withdrew from John Clarke's (1609–76) Baptist Church in order to observe the sabbath. In 1671, they officially organized a congregation. Other churches were organized in Philadelphia and New Jersey. From these three centers, Seventh Day Baptists followed the westward migration.

Similar to other Baptists, Seventh Day Baptists maintain a belief in salvation through faith in Christ; believer's baptism by immersion; insistence on intellectual and civil liberty; and the right of every person to interpret the Bible under God. They hold only baptism and the Lord's Supper as ordinances and practice open communion.

Local churches enjoy complete independence, although all support the united benevolence of the denominational budget. For fellowship and service, the churches are organized into eight regional associations, and these often assist local church councils in the ordination of deacons and ministerial candidates. The highest administrative body is the General Conference, which meets annually and delegates interim responsibilities to its president, executive secretary, and general council. The conference promotes denominational giving, channeled through mission, publishing, and educational agencies. It also accredits ministers certified to it by ordaining councils and local churches.

The denomination participates in the ecumenical movement at local, regional, national, and world levels. The Seventh Day Baptist conferences include those in Australia, Brazil, England, Germany, Guyana, India, Jamaica, Malawi, Mexico, Myanmar, the Netherlands, New Zealand, Nigeria, the Philippines, Poland, and South Africa as well as in the U.S. and Canada.

SOUTHERN BAPTIST CONVENTION

Founded: 1845
Membership: 15,851,756 in 41,099 churches (1999)

The largest non-Catholic denomination in the United States is the Southern Baptist Convention (SBC), whose membership, as its name suggests, is most numerous in the South. In recent years, however, the SBC has been expanding in all regions of the country. The annual convention increasingly is being held in cities outside the southern homeland, partly because so many members live in those areas and are entitled to have geographical access to national convention meetings. The name "Southern" has, therefore, become something of a misnomer.

The SBC came into being during the years leading up to the Civil War, and in many ways, the division of the Baptists North and South merely foreshadowed that American tragedy. Although there were significant disagreements between Baptists in the two regions over the question of centralized organization (the South favored one organization to control the various cooperative ministries), it was the issue of slavery that led directly to the formation of a separate Southern Baptist Convention. Specifically, the issue was whether slaveholders could be accepted as foreign missionaries. The mission board, located in Boston, refused to send slaveholders into the fields, and in May 1845, the Southern Baptist Convention (SBC) was organized in order to establish boards for foreign and home missions.

Three hundred churches in eight southern and border states entered the new organization; a hard struggle for existence lay ahead. Along with the rest of the South, the Southern Baptist churches suffered great losses during the war. Homes, schools, churches, the livelihood of citizens, indeed, the very pattern of southern society were destroyed, with devastating effect on religious bodies. An anti-missionary movement further decimated Baptist ranks. Membership continued to decline when former slaves withdrew to form their own societies and conventions. The recovery of the Southern Baptist Convention was impressive, however. In 1845 there were 351,951 members, of whom 130,000 were black; by 1890, there were 1,235,908 members, predominantly white. In the late twentieth century, African Americans began returning to the Southern Baptist fold.

Southern Baptists have generally held to a more conservative theology than their northern relatives, but the basic tenets of belief are the same. The Southern Baptist heritage is more definitely Calvinist; one of the ironies of Baptist history is that the Southern Baptist Convention adheres more firmly to the New Hampshire Confession of Faith than do American Baptist churches (see AMERICAN BAPTIST CHURCHES). Church polity and government are comparable in the two conventions. Membership and ministry have usually been exchanged in harmony and understanding.

In 1997 the Convention was reorganized. Twelve denominational agencies work with thirty-nine state conventions and two fellowships in home and foreign missions, Sunday schools, educational institutions, and ministerial retirement. The North American Mission Board operates throughout the U.S. and its territories, with nearly five thousand missionaries active in the field. It cooperates with black Baptist churches; works among migrants in the South, Native Americans in the West and Southwest, ninety-eight language groups, and deaf persons; and provides loans for church construction. In 1998, SBC churches reported 407,264 baptisms in the U.S. and another 333,034 around the world. Nearly 1,500 churches were started in 1998 alone.

The International Mission Board sponsors more than 4,500 missionaries in 127 nations, and in 1998 it operated 43 hospitals and 295 clinics, with a staff of 38 physicians, 72 nurses, 9 dentists, and 45 other personnel. Half of the Convention's Cooperative Program allocation of funds goes to overseas missions. The Board was also active in disaster relief in the Balkans and Central America. Over $10,000,000 was spent on 423 hunger and relief projects in 57 countries.

LifeWay Christian Resources (formerly the Sunday School Board) is the world's largest publisher of religious materials. It provides the literature for some 37,000 SBC churches. The SBC maintains six theological seminaries with more than 12,600 students.

Rapid growth and expansion beyond the southern region is only one of the major stories about the Southern Baptist Convention in recent years. Another is the factionalism within the body. Since 1978, the elected president, who has key appointive powers, has been elected from the more conservative sector of the Convention. Conservatives are now solidly in the majority and have exerted control over the seminaries, agencies, and boards that belong to the entire Convention. Conservatives distinguish their position as a commitment to biblical inerrancy. Others in the convention take their stand on what may be termed the infallibility of biblical authority and a commitment to the principle of independence. In the larger arena of contemporary American Christianity, both groups are on the conservative side of most issues.

In the late 1990s, controversy arose over the issue of women's ordination. At the SBC annual convention in June 2000, delegates voted to limit pastoral/leadership roles to men. Amending the "Baptist Faith and Message" confession of faith first formulated in the 1920s, the convention stipulated that "while both men and women are gifted and called for ministry, the office of pastor is limited to men as qualified by Scripture." The 2000 gathering also reaffirmed the convention's position on the inerrancy of Scripture, put the convention on record as supporting the death penalty in cases of murder and treason, and refused to be deterred from evangelistic efforts by outside criticism.

Earlier in 2000, a group of Southern Baptists opposed to "fundamentalist domination" of churches and state Baptist conventions met in Atlanta, Georgia, and formed the Network of Mainstream Baptists. Over 100 representatives from 15 states adopted the label "mainstream" to express their adherence to what they called traditional Baptist beliefs and practices. While eschewing any attempt to develop an alternative organization, those in attendance pledged to work to thwart further conservative advance, both theological and political, within the SBC.

Another significant development within the Southern Baptist Convention in the 1990s was the adoption on June 20, 1995, of a resolution to renounce its racist origins and to apologize for its founders' defense of slavery. In its apology to African Americans, the resolution declared that members of the church must "unwaveringly denounce racism, in all its forms, as deplorable sin" and repent of "racism of which we have been guilty whether consciously or unconsciously." As of 2000, more than 1,900 SBC congregations were predominantly African American.

BRETHREN AND PIETIST CHURCHES

An international religious revival began in Germany in the late 1600s with the writings of Jakob Philip Spener (1635–1705). Spener decried the barren intellectualism, theological factionalism, and general ineffectiveness of the Protestant churches of his day. He called for a new type of Reformation that would complete the promise of Luther's Reformation. Luther had reformed the church doctrinally and liturgically; Spener wanted to reform it morally and spiritually. He called for pastors to find ways to make the doctrine of the priesthood of all believers effective in the hearts and souls of the people. To do this, he proposed that pastors form small groups of believers to meet for study, prayer, and mutual encouragement. The staples of modern church life, such as Sunday school, youth fellowship, and women's circle meetings, grew out of this idea. Also, Spener urged pastors to leave polemics aside and concentrate on edifying preaching that could transform individuals from sinners to laborers for God. This "religion of the heart" spread throughout Protestant Germany and profoundly influenced John Wesley's (1703–91) early Methodist movement. When Pietism, as it was called in Germany, came to the U.S. in the 1740s, it helped to fuel the First Great Awakening.

In the 1750s Philip Otterbein (1726–1813), a German Reformed pastor of Pietist leanings, began his career as an evangelist in Pennsylvania and Maryland. His activities led to the formation of the United Brethren Church, later called the Evangelical United Brethren (EUB). This body was one of the groups that eventually formed The United Methodist Church in 1968. Although there are only a few, relatively small denominations in the U.S. that emerged out of German Pietism, Christianity in all its varieties has been influenced by this spiritual movement.

Many Pietist bodies use the name "Brethren" in various forms. For them, the church is primarily a company of brothers and sisters in Christ joined together by the Holy Spirit for mutual edification. The inner spiritual life, piety, is cultivated in prayer and study of Scripture and through association with fellow believers. For most Brethren, the local church is central, but they are often bound in close-knit national communities. The church claims their primary loyalty and is understood more as a community of people who love God and one another than as part of an organization or a body that formulates doctrine. Brethren do not emphasize rigid doctrinal standards; rather, the Spirit of God within each person, binding them together in love, takes precedence for them. They usually live a simple, unadorned life. In their early decades in Europe and the United States, most Brethren were separatists from the state and conventional churches. While not manifesting a judgmental attitude, they devoted themselves to a moral purity that set them apart from other Christians as well as from general society.

Many Pietist groups took the New Testament literally and endeavored to put its teachings into practice, even in the minute details of their daily living. At the heart of their religious ritual was the love feast, or agape, the serving of the Lord's Supper, preceded by a ceremony of foot washing. They saluted one another with a kiss of peace, dressed in the plainest of clothing, covered women's heads at services, anointed their sick with oil for healing and consecration, refrained from worldly amusements, and refused to take oaths, go to war, or engage in lawsuits. Those Pietist groups that were not Brethren tended to be more embracing of the secular world.

Many of the Brethren churches stem from the work of Alexander Mack, Sr. (1679–1735), in Schwarzenau in Wittgenstein, Germany. After his experience of conversion, Mack was convinced of the need for those who had experienced regeneration to form separate communities modeled on the early church's practice of sharing goods in common. Exiled from the Palatinate for preaching separatism, Mack gathered a company of fellow refugees and in 1708 took the bold, and at that time illegal, step of rebaptizing adult believers. Eventually persecution in Germany led these German Baptists to emigrate to the U.S.

They were known for years simply as German Baptist Brethren, but that title has largely disappeared, except in the case of the Old German Baptist Brethren, who were also known as "Dunkers." The terms "Brethren" and "Dunker" have been the cause of much confusion. Dunker is a direct derivation of the German *tunken*, "to dip or immerse," and is identified with the peculiar method of immersion employed by this group of churches in which the new believer is immersed three times, face forward, in the name of the Father, the Son, and the Holy Ghost.

BRETHREN CHURCH
(Ashland)

Founded: 1882
Membership: 13,227 in 118 congregations (1999)

In 1882 the Church of the Brethren (see CHURCH OF THE BRETHREN) voted to expel a member for advocating Sunday schools, missions, a paid clergy, congregational polity, and more freedom in dress and worship. The supporters of such changes withdrew and formed the Progressive Convention of the Tunker Church in Ashland, Ohio. The following year it was officially organized as the Brethren Church. Most Brethren churches are still found in Ohio, Pennsylvania, and Indiana. The church's college and a seminary in Ashland, Ohio, have historically been at the center of its ministry.

Theologically, the Brethren Church tries to seek a balance between the Calvinist and Arminian perspectives on salvation; however, for the Brethren, style of life is more important than doctrine. The believing community of faith leads believers into the path proposed in the Sermon on the Mount. Nonetheless, the church suffered a schism during the fundamentalist/modernist controversy that gripped American Christianity in the 1920s and 1930s. The more conservative ministers formed the Fellowship of Grace Brethren Church (see FELLOWSHIP OF GRACE BRETHREN CHURCHES).

The church has three retirement homes, a publishing company, and a missionary board. It cooperates with the Church of the Brethren in relief activities around the world. It also works with the Mennonites (see MENNONITE CHURCHES) in the area of evangelism.

BRETHREN IN CHRIST CHURCH

Founded: 1778
Membership: 20,010 in 252 congregations (1999)

The church began as a result of a spiritual awakening that took place in Lancaster, Pennsylvania, in the 1760s, inspired by the preaching of Philip Otterbein (1726–1813; see BRETHREN and PIETIST CHURCHES) and Martin Boehm (1725–1812). The group that gathered along the Susquehanna River was called simply the River Brethren until the Civil War. Primarily of Mennonite (see MENNONITE CHURCHES) descent, the River Brethren separated from the Mennonites over the issue of triple immersion in baptism.

The River Brethren were pacifists, and with the outbreak of the Civil War and the institution of a national military draft, it became necessary for the Brethren to obtain legal recognition as an established religious organization in order to protect the objectors. A council meeting in Lancaster County, Pennsylvania, in 1863 adopted the name Brethren in Christ Church, but the group was not legally incorporated until 1904.

The Brethren in Christ Church pledges loyalty to the following doctrines: the inspiration of the Holy Scriptures; the self-existent, Triune God; the deity and virgin birth of Christ; Christ's death as atonement for our sins and his resurrection from the dead; the Holy Spirit, who convicts the sinner, regenerates the penitent, and empowers the believer; justification as forgiveness for committed sins and sanctification as heart cleansing and empowerment by the Holy Spirit; observance of the ordinances of God's house; temperance and modesty of apparel as taught in the scriptures; the personal, visible, and imminent return of Christ; the resurrection of the dead, with punishment for the unbeliever and reward for the believer; and worldwide evangelism as the supreme duty of the church.

While the government of this church is largely in the hands of the local congregations, there are eight regional conferences and a general conference, which is the ultimate authoritative body. A board of administration has oversight of the general conference and of general church property and financial transactions. The church maintains offices in Grantham, Pennsylvania; its publishing arm, Evangel Publishing House, is in Nappanee, Indiana.

The church has two institutions of learning: Messiah College at

Grantham, Pennsylvania, and Niagara Christian College at Fort Erie, Ontario, Canada. Missionaries are at work in Africa, India, Japan, London, Colombia, Nicaragua, Venezuela, and Cuba and are engaged in Mennonite Central Committee work around the world.

CHURCH OF GOD (Anderson, Indiana)

Founded: 1881
Membership: 234,311 in 2,353 churches (1998)

Although not directly related to the Pietist movement and the Brethren churches, the Church of God headquartered in Anderson, Indiana, is deeply influenced by Wesleyan theology and Pietist practice. There are several other organizations called the Church of God, most of which are Pentecostal bodies, but the Church of God in Anderson, Indiana, has a different history and perspective from those groups. Daniel S. Warner (1842–1925) and several associates rejected denominational hierarchies and formal creeds. They preferred to rely on the Holy Spirit and the Bible alone as a way to restore both unity and holiness of life in the church. Their goal was not to establish another denomination but to transcend denominational loyalties through allegiance to Christ.

The Church of God's generally accepted doctrines include the divine inspiration of the scriptures; forgiveness of sin through the atonement of Christ and repentance of the believer; the experience of holiness; the personal (amillenial) return of Christ; the kingdom of God as established on earth; resurrection of the dead; and a final judgment in which the righteous are rewarded and the wicked punished. Baptism by immersion is viewed as a witness to the new believer's regeneration in Christ and inclusion in the family of God. The Lord's Supper reminds participants of the grace experienced in the life of the believer. As with many Pietist groups, foot washing is practiced in acknowledgment and acceptance of the servant ministry of Christians to each other and to the world. None of these practices, termed ordinances, are considered mandatory conditions of Christian experience or fellowship.

The church is congregational in government with each local church being autonomous. Ministers meet in voluntary state and regional conventions, which are chiefly advisory. The General Assembly meets in connection with the annual international convention held at Anderson. In 1996 and 1997 the assembly initiated a restructuring of the church's work in the U.S. The result was the formation of Church of God Ministries, Inc. The church's ministries emphasize outreach, congregational ministry, and service to pastors and others. Warner Press serves as the church's publisher of curriculum and other materials.

There is no formal membership in the Church of God (Anderson), but persons are assumed to be members on the basis of conversion and holiness of life. Its largest membership concentrations are in the midwestern states, the Pacific Coast states, and western Pennsylvania. It supports Anderson University and School of Theology, two other liberal arts colleges, and one Bible college. It carries on work in eighty-four countries, involving approximately 446,000 worshipers.

CHURCH OF THE BRETHREN

Founded: 1708
Membership: 138,304 in 1,095 churches (1999)

The Church of the Brethren was formed in 1708 in Schwarzenau, Germany (see BRETHREN and PIETIST CHURCHES). Its founders were five men and three women, most under thirty years of age, who gathered in homes for Bible study and prayer. The early Brethren were influenced by the Anabaptists as well as by Pietism, and they covenanted to be a people shaped by personal faith in Christ, prayer, and study of Scripture. They stressed daily discipleship and service to neighbor. Severe persecution and economic conditions prompted virtually the entire movement to migrate to North America between 1719 and 1729. Included was their leader and first minister, Alexander Mack, Sr. (1679–1735).

Commonly known as German Baptist Brethren, or even Dunkers or Dunkards, in its bicentennial year, 1908, the group adopted "Church of the Brethren" as its official name. "Brethren" was seen as a New Testament term that conveyed the kinship and warmth of Jesus' early followers.

Although non-creedal from its inception, the Church of the Brethren has held firmly to basic tenets of the Free Church, or Believers Church, tradition. Among the most distinctive Brethren practices are the baptism of confessing believers by threefold immersion and the anointing of the ill for spiritual and bodily health. The Last Supper is observed by a service of foot washing that symbolizes servanthood, a fellowship meal that symbolizes family, and the commemorative Eucharist that symbolizes Saviorhood.

As one of the three historic peace churches, together with Friends (see FRIENDS) and Mennonites (see MENNONITE CHURCHES), Brethren have long held an official peace witness, expressed often in conscientious objection to military service. During World War II, Civilian Public Health camps were maintained for religious objectors who performed work in the national interest. During and after the war, many of the programs were continued under the alternative service provisions of Selective Service, and voluntary service abroad, a forerunner of the Peace Corps, was introduced.

Also growing out of the peace concern was a worldwide program of relief, reconstruction, and welfare, conducted by the Brethren Service Commission and later by the World Ministries Commission, as a service of love to those suffering from war, natural disasters, or social disadvantage. Since 1948, Brethren Volunteer Service has enlisted nearly 5,000 men and women for one or two years of social service at home and abroad. Work with migrant laborers, inner-city dwellers, prison inmates, refugees, and victims of abuse exemplify the types of activity undertaken. Increasingly, older volunteers have enrolled in the program, quite often after they have reached retirement age.

Numerous projects initiated by the group have become full-scale ecumenical enterprises. Among them are the Heifer Project International, Christian Youth Exchange, Christian Rural Overseas Program (CROP), Sales Exchange for Refugee Rehabilitation Vocation (SERRV; handcraft sales for Third World producers), and International Voluntary Service. Other pioneering ventures were agricultural exchanges begun with Poland in the 1950s and with China in the 1980s and ecumenical exchanges with the Russian Orthodox Church in the 1960s.

In polity, the Brethren combine both congregational and presbyterian practices, with final authority vested in an Annual Conference of elected delegates. The General Board of elected and ex officio members is the administrative arm of the church. Congregations are organized into twenty-three districts in thirty-six states, usually with one or more full-time executives in each district. The heaviest concentration of churches is in Pennsylvania, Virginia, Maryland, Ohio, Indiana, and Illinois.

The Brethren are related to six accredited liberal arts colleges: Bridgewater College in Virginia; Elizabethtown and Juniata colleges in Pennsylvania; University of LaVerne in California; Manchester College in Indiana; and McPherson College in Kansas. The church sponsors one graduate school, Bethany Theological Seminary, in Richmond, Indiana. General offices are in Elgin, Illinois, also the home of Brethren Press, which produces the monthly publication *Messenger* and various books and curriculum resources.

CHURCH OF THE UNITED BRETHREN IN CHRIST

Founded: 1800, with roots to 1767
Membership: 24,603 in 253 congregations (2000)

This group had its origins in the Pennsylvania awakening led by Philip Otterbein (1726–1813) and Martin Boehm (1725–1812) in the 1760s. In 1800 the ministers of the Brethren officially adopted the name United Brethren in Christ and elected Otterbein and Boehm as the first bishops. In 1815 they adopted a confession of faith based on one that Otterbein had written in 1789. The United Brethren took a strong stand against slave holding in the 1820s; thus they did not spread in the South, but did make the western U.S. a mission area. In 1841 a constitution was adopted. When the constitution was changed in 1889, some members viewed the changes as unconstitutional and separated from the main body. The main body of United Brethren eventually merged with the United Methodists (see METHODIST CHURCHES), leaving the name "United Brethren" to the smaller group.

United Brethren believe in the Trinity and in the deity, humanity, and atonement of Christ. Observance of "scriptural living" is required of all members, who are forbidden use of alcoholic beverages and membership in secret societies. Baptism and the Lord's Supper are observed as ordinances.

Local, annual, and general conferences are held. The highest governing body, the General Conference, meets quadrennially. It is composed of about seventy delegates from around the world, including ministers, district superintendents (presiding elders), general church officials, bishops, and lay delegates. General church offices are located in Huntington, Indiana; the majority of local churches are found in Pennsylvania, Ohio, northern Indiana, and Michigan. Both

74

men and women are eligible for the ministry and are ordained only once as elders. Missionary societies administer evangelism and church aid in the U.S. and in Costa Rica, El Salvador, Honduras, Hong Kong, India, Jamaica, Macau, Mexico, Myanmar, Nicaragua, Sierra Leone, and Thailand. Worldwide membership numbers over 36,000. The church works in harmony with evangelical groups in other denominations.

The United Brethren Church maintains a college and a graduate school of Christian ministries at Huntington, Indiana, with secondary schools in Sierra Leone.

EVANGELICAL COVENANT CHURCH

Founded: 1885
Membership: 96,526 in 636 congregations (1999)

The Evangelical Covenant Church is not a Brethren church but grew out of Pietism in Sweden. It traces its roots from the Protestant Reformation through the biblical instruction of the Lutheran state church of Sweden to the great spiritual awakenings of the nineteenth century. The Covenant Church was founded by Swedish immigrants in the Midwest and adheres to the affirmations of the Reformation regarding the Holy Scriptures as the Word of God and the only perfect rule for faith, doctrine, and conduct. It has traditionally valued the historic confessions of the Christian church, particularly the Apostles' Creed, but emphasizes the sovereignty of the Word over all creedal interpretations.

The Covenant Church's evangelical emphasis includes the necessity of the new birth, the ministry of the Holy Spirit, and the reality of freedom in Christ. It values the New Testament emphasis on personal faith in Jesus Christ as Savior and Lord and the church as a fellowship of believers that recognizes but transcends theological differences. Baptism and the Lord's Supper are seen as divinely ordained sacraments. While the denomination has traditionally practiced the baptism of infants, it has also recognized the practice of believer baptism.

The local church is administered by a board elected by the membership; its ministers, ordained by the denomination, are called, generally with the aid and guidance of the denominational Department of the Ministry and the conference superintendent. Each of the nine regional conferences elects its own superintendent. The highest authority is vested in an annual meeting composed of ministers and laypeople elected by the constituent churches. An administrative board, elected by the annual meeting, implements its decisions.

The Covenant Church sponsors churches in the Czech Republic, Columbia, Congo, Ecuador, France, Germany, Japan, Laos, Mexico, Russia, Spain, Taiwan, and Thailand. Educational institutions include North Park University and North Park Theological Seminary in Chicago, Illinois. The church maintains fourteen retirement communities and nursing homes serving over 4,000 residents in seven states, two hospitals, and fifteen camps and conference centers across North America.

EVANGELICAL FREE CHURCH OF AMERICA

Founded: 1950
Membership: est. 260,000 in 1,250 congregations (2000)

The origins of the Evangelical Free Church lay in a meeting between a group of independent congregations and several churches of the old Swedish Ansgarii Synod and Mission Synod at Boone, Iowa, in 1884. They formed a fellowship of "free" congregations to be known as the Swedish Evangelical Free Mission (later changed to Swedish Evangelical Free Church). In that same year, two Norwegian-Danish groups began fellowshipping, one on the East coast and one on the West. In 1912, these merged to form the Norwegian-Danish Evangelical Free Church Association. In 1950 the Swedish denomination merged with the other Scandinavian bodies to form the present Evangelical Free Church.

By common agreement, the 1884 fellowship was to be a body of self-governing congregations. Churches were to elect delegates to an annual conference, which was advisory to the churches but which would legislate national and international ministries of the denomination itself. A society of ministers and missionaries was organized in 1894. Initially, the only qualification for membership in the local church was evidence of conversion and commitment to the Christian life.

The Evangelical Free Church holds to a view of scriptural inerrancy, the necessity of evangelization, and congregational polity. Local churches are autonomous. In 1950 the merged denominations adopted a twelve-point doctrinal statement, which is now incorporated into the constitution of most local congregations. The constitu-

76

tion stresses faithfulness to evangelical beliefs while avoiding disputes over minor matters. Affirming both the rational and the relational dimensions of Christian faith, the church maintains that sound Christian doctrine must be coupled with dynamic Christian experience, facilitating a ministry of love and reconciliation.

The Evangelical Free Church maintains administrative offices in Minneapolis, Minnesota. The president works with various boards and leadership teams to guide the several ministries of the denomination. Some five hundred missionaries serve stations in over forty countries around the world. The church sponsors Trinity International University, which includes Trinity Evangelical Divinity School, with the main campus located in Deerfield, Illinois; other campuses of the university are maintained in Chicago, Illinois; Miami, Florida; and Santa Ana, California. Trinity Western University in Langley, British Columbia, is also affiliated with the church.

FELLOWSHIP OF GRACE BRETHREN CHURCHES

Founded: 1939
Membership: 30,371 in 260 congregations (1997)

This body was part of the Brethren Church (Ashland) that separated from the main Church of the Brethren in the early 1880s (see BRETHREN CHURCH [ASHLAND]). In part as a result of the fundamentalist/modernist controversy of the 1920s and 1930s, that church further divided. In 1939 the Ashland group and the Grace group went their separate ways. The Grace group represents more nearly a Calvinist viewpoint in theology; the Ashland group, more nearly an Arminian position.

In 1969, the Grace group adopted its own statement of faith that expressed the church's fundamental beliefs: the primacy of the Bible; the trinitarian God; the incarnation of the divine Son of God, the Lord Jesus Christ; the work of the Holy Spirit; the sinfulness of humans; salvation through Christ; the church as made up of believers; the Christian life as a way of righteousness; the ordinances of baptism and the threefold Communion service (which includes foot washing and the love feast); the reality of Satan; the Second Coming; and the future life. The group was separately incorporated in 1987 as the Fellowship of Grace Brethren Churches. The constitution adopted in

1997 reaffirms the Fellowship's commitment to Scripture as the sole guide and authority in all matters of faith, doctrine, and practice.

Grace Brethren churches are grouped geographically into districts, which hold annual conferences. The entire church holds an annual conference, often held at Winona Lake, Indiana, where the group's headquarters are located. This conference, made up of delegates from Fellowship churches, elects a board of directors, known as the Fellowship Council, and general church officers. The church supports both international and North American missionary and relief efforts, and it maintains Grace College and Seminary in Winona Lake.

MORAVIAN CHURCH (*Unitas Fratrum*)

Founded: 1457 (came to the U.S. in 1735)
Membership: 47,134 in 153 congregations (1999)

The Moravian Church is one of the few pre-Reformation Protestant churches (the Waldensians are another). Its roots go back to John Hus (ca. 1372–1415), a Czech reformer who was burned at the stake at the Council of Constance in 1415. The followers of Hus founded two churches, the more conservative Utraquists and the apocalyptic Taborites; the latter were destroyed in battle in 1453. In 1457, dissatisfied with the lifestyle and worship of the Utraquists, a leader known as Brother Gregory organized a small band of like-minded people into a community dedicated to living according to the Sermon on the Mount and the example of the early church. They called their pacifist, communitarian body *Jednota Bratrska,* "the Unity of the Brethren"; at times they used the Latin form, *Unitas Fratrum,* which remains the official name of the church. In 1467 the group established an independent episcopacy and clergy.

Persecution under the Hapsburgs following the Thirty Years War (1618–48) almost exterminated the church. In 1722 groups of Protestants, led by a carpenter, Christian David, began fleeing from Moravia. At the invitation of Count Nicholas Ludwig von Zinzendorf (1700–60), one of the leaders of German Pietism, the refugees settled on his estate in Saxony. There they built the town of Herrnhut, a highly structured religious community that would be the model for similar communities in the U.S. The count allowed the Moravians to revive the discipline of their ancestors' church.

Under the direction of Zinzendorf, the Moravians carried out an extensive mission enterprise, beginning with work among the slaves on St. Thomas, an island in the Virgin Islands. The Moravian evangelist David Zeisberger (1721–1808) had great success among the native tribes of the northern United States, but that effort was virtually destroyed by the massacre of Moravian Indians at Gnaddenhutten, Ohio, in 1777 by an American militia during the Revolutionary War.

The Moravians attempted to establish a settlement in Georgia in the 1730s, but the only lasting result of that work was the conversion of John Wesley (1703–91) to "heart religion." Permanent work was established in Pennsylvania, especially in the Lehigh Valley (Bethlehem and Nazareth), and in the Piedmont area of North Carolina (Salem). In the nineteenth century, the church supported work among German and Scandanavian immigrants in the upper Midwest. Recent growth in the United States comes mainly from immigration from Central America and the Caribbean, where the Moravians have long had a strong presence.

It is sometimes said that the Moravians never developed a unified system of doctrine. That may be an overstatement, but it certainly is true that no doctrine is peculiar to them; the church is broadly evangelical, insisting on the principle "in essentials unity, in nonessentials liberty, and in all things charity." The scriptures are held to be the inspired Word of God and an adequate rule for faith and practice. The main doctrinal emphases may be said to be the love of God manifested in the redemptive life and death of Jesus, the inner testimony of the Spirit, and Christian conduct in everyday affairs. In addition to infant baptism and Holy Communion, the Moravians observe the practice of the love feast, a simple meal taken communally.

There is only one Moravian Church worldwide, but it is divided into twenty governing units, called provinces. There are three provinces in North America: Northern (including Canada), Southern, and Alaska. The highest administrative body in each is the provincial synod. Composed of ministers and laypeople, it meets every three or four years to direct missionary, educational, and publishing work and to elect a Provincial Elders' Conference, which functions between synod meetings. Bishops, elected by provincial and general synods, are the spiritual, not the administrative, leaders of the church.

Missionary work has always been a primary concern. There are nearly 800,000 Moravians worldwide, more than half in Tanzania and South Africa. In addition to nursing homes, church camps, a publishing house, and mission enterprises, the church also sponsors a mission to Tibetan refugees in northern India and a rehabilitation center for persons with handicaps at Ramallah, on the West Bank of the Jordan River.

Always committed to education, the church founded Moravian College and Theological Seminary in Bethlehem, Pennsylvania, and Salem College in Winston-Salem, North Carolina.

OLD GERMAN BAPTIST BRETHREN
(Old Order Dunkers)

Founded: 1881
Membership: 6,050 in 55 churches (1999)

While the Brethren Church left the Church of the Brethren because the latter body seemed too conservative in the early 1880s, the Old German Baptist Brethren (Old Order Dunkers) left because they considered the Church of the Brethren not conservative enough. The dissenters stood for the old order and traditions. The salient point in their opposition lay in their suspicion of Sunday schools, salaried ministers, missions, higher education, and church societies.

The basic objections still hold but with certain modifications. Children are not enrolled in Sunday schools, but are encouraged to attend the regular services of the church and to join the church by baptism during their teens; however, the decision is left entirely to the individual. Many congregations list a majority of members between fifteen and forty years of age. The church today is not completely opposed even to higher education; a few of the youth enter high school and take training in college or professional schools.

The church stands for a literal interpretation of the scriptures in regard to the Lord's Supper and practices closed Communion, which excludes all but its own members. While it advocates compliance with the ordinary demands of government, it opposes cooperation in war. Any member who enters into military service will fall under the judgment of the church. Non-cooperation in political and secret societies is required; dress is plain, and all amusements deemed worldly are frowned upon. The group has no salaried ministers and enforces complete abstinence from alcoholic beverages; the members refuse to take oaths or engage in lawsuits, the sick are anointed with oil, the heads of the women are veiled at worship, and wedding ceremonies are not performed for previously divorced persons.

There are no missions or educational work. An annual conference that rules on matters on which the scriptures are silent is held each year at Pentecost. Most of the congregations are in Ohio, Indiana, and Pennsylvania.

UNITY OF THE BRETHREN

Founded: 1903, with roots to the 1850s
Membership: 3,218 in 27 congregations (1998)

Czech immigrants to Texas began forming Protestant congregations in the 1850s. In 1903 these scattered churches were joined into the Evangelical Unity of the Czech-Moravian Brethren in North America. Drawing on the ancestry of Protestantism in Bohemia and Moravia, in 1959 the Brethren adopted the name "Unity of the Brethren" (Latin, *Unitas Fratrum;* Czech, *Jednota Bratrska*), which dates from 1457. Conservative in theology and lifestyle, the church shares some features with other Brethren bodies, but has a distinct history. A synod meets every two years.

CATHOLIC CHURCHES

Christians in many different churches profess their faith in "the one, holy, catholic church" using the words of the Apostles' Creed. "Catholic" in this sense does not necessarily refer to a particular religious institution but to the idea of the universality of the church. The Catholic Church is the church that exists around the world and through the ages. Obviously, though, religious institutions will have differing understandings about the institutional expression of that catholicity. In this section are included those bodies that hold most dearly to a view of the church that is universal in time and space. These are churches that see themselves in unbroken continuity with the institutional expression of Christian faith since the days of the apostles. They differ markedly from Restorationist bodies (see CHRISTIAN CHURCHES), for example, which view most of Western history as a decline and fall of the church and thus sought to restore the New Testament church without the use of rituals, creeds, and structures that had developed over time. Most of the bodies discussed in this volume represent variations on Protestantism, but it is important to remember that most of the world's Christians remain in the Catholic Church.

For most Catholic churches, the Holy Spirit continued to work through historical development in order to bring the faith to its richest and fullest expression. In particular, the writings of the Church Fathers (e.g., Jerome [c. 345–c. 420] and Augustine [354–430]) instruct the faithful in how to understand the Scripture and live a Christian life. It was during the Patristic Age (the age of the Church Fathers, from the close of the first century to the close of the eighth century) that much Catholic doctrine, polity, and devotion were established.

The history of the Catholic Church for a thousand years is the history of Christianity. There is not space in this volume to give a full account of that history, but it should be noted that during the first five centuries of Christianity there were numerous struggles over the nature of Christian doctrine and ecclesiastical authority. Gradually the lines of orthodoxy were established through the authority of creeds, especially the Nicene Creed, and the episcopacy (bishops, archbishops, and patriarchs). During this process of development there was no real division between Eastern and Western Christianity.

The East and the West did develop some distinctive liturgical and administrative practices, however, due in part to the greater sophistication of Byzantine (Eastern) culture. Most important, the Eastern bishops and theologians tended to define the church in terms of orthodox belief and practice, while in the West institutional allegiance became paramount, particularly during the rising social chaos of the early Middle Ages. The church in the West gained secular authority and power when it emerged as the only body strong enough to rule after the barbarian onslaught beginning with the sack of Rome in 410 C.E. Ravaged first by Goths, Vandals, and Franks then by Saxons, Danes, Alemanni, Lombards, and Burgundians, Western Europe found its only steadying hand in the institutional church, which kept the flame of faith burning in its various congregations and the candle of wisdom alive in its monastic schools.

Therefore, in the West the word *catholic* was increasingly applied to those who were loyal to the bishop of Rome as the head of the universal church. The first mention of the term *catholic* ("universal") was made by Ignatius of Antioch about 110–15 C.E., but it was Augustine who provided the theological and philosophical structure that gave the papacy its justification and defense. Although there were disputes about the authority of the papacy throughout the Middle Ages, the consensus in Western Christianity was that there should be a single ecclesiastical institution with a single head who served as Christ's representative in the church.

Until at least 1054 the bishop of Rome and the bishop of Constantinople served as the heads of the Western and Eastern churches, respectively, without one asserting absolute authority over the other. By the time the Fourth Crusade conquered Constantinople instead of Jerusalem in 1204, the break between East and West was complete. However, the Roman Catholic Church was the most significant force in Western society for most of the Middle Ages. It preserved and spread Christianity during the days of barbarian invasion; preserved and spread classical education through monasteries, convents, cathedral schools, and universities; stabilized feudal society; promoted architectural and artistic achievements; and established the basis for the Western legal system.

Schisms, heresies, and divisions began appearing in the late Middle Ages, but it was the Protestant Reformation, ignited by Martin Luther (1483–1546), that splintered Western Christianity. Roman Catholic scholars acknowledge that there were corrupt individuals within the church and that reform was necessary. Indeed, reform was underway even before the Reformation; Luther was a reformer within the church before he broke away. Erasmus (1469–1536) and Savonarola (1452–98) wrote and preached against the corruption and worldliness of certain Roman Catholic leaders and laypeople, but they stayed within the church. Roman Catholic historians and theologians recognize that these reformers had a point, but the church asserts that while priests and bishops may err or be corrupt, the one true church cannot err. Thus Luther was wrong in rebelling; but rebel he did, and the Roman Catholic Church suffered its most fateful division.

In some ways, the Reformation encouraged the Roman Catholic Church to reform and reorganize itself. Indeed, some historians, Catholic and Protestant alike, would date the founding of the Roman Catholic Church as a self-conscious and distinctive religious body to the great Council of Trent (1545–63) when many Catholic doctrines were officially defined for the first time and where the current ecclesiastical structure was codified. The Tridentine (or post Council of Trent) church was in many ways a stronger and more effective institution than the Renaissance church. The newly established Society of Jesus (Jesuits) led the way in winning back areas lost to Protestantism and, along with the Franciscans, in courageously bringing Christianity to the recently discovered lands east and west of Europe.

Having reformed the papacy of many of the abuses that had fueled the Reformation, the Tridentine church increasingly looked to the papacy as the guarantor of Catholic unity and continuity. As the Enlightenment took hold in Europe in the eighteenth century and revolutions convulsed the European kingdoms in the nineteenth, Catholic bishops and theologians held up the Roman pontiff as the symbol of stability, authority, and order in church and society. This led to the declaration of papal infallibility by the First Vatican Council in 1870, a move that inspired a number of Catholics, calling themselves Old Catholics, to separate from the Roman Catholic Church. Also during the second half of the nineteenth century, Anglicans in the Oxford Movement, a group centered at Oxford in the 1830s and 1840s that sought to restore the High Church ideals of the 17th century to the Church of England, began stressing Anglican continuity with the Catholic tradition, leading to a variety of Anglo-Catholic bodies (see EPISCOPAL/ANGLICAN CHURCHES).

The most significant event in the twentieth century was the Second Vatican Council (1962–65). Pope John XXIII summoned all the bishops of the church to the twenty-first ecumenical council, and, following John's death, Pope Paul VI reconvened the council. The council approved the use of the vernacular in the Mass, allowed for modern methods of biblical study and interpretation, encouraged active involvement of the laity in the life of the parish, and allowed Roman Catholics to engage in ecumenical and interfaith dialogue. Before Vatican II, Catholics were forbidden to attend meetings of the World Council of Churches; now Catholic observers attend council sessions, and bishops of the church have entered into theological dialogue with several larger Protestant denominations. Since then, the church has been rebuilding bridges to the Orthodox churches (see ORTHODOX and ORIENTAL ORTHODOX CHURCHES) and has even exonerated Martin Luther of heresy.

In 1968, Pope Paul VI reaffirmed the official church position against any form of artificial birth control. Many theologians, priests, and laypeople protested this, voicing opposition to the encyclical *Humanae Vitae;* the hierarchies of such countries as France, Canada, Belgium, Holland, Switzerland, Austria, and West Germany interpreted the papal position in the light of freedom of the individual conscience.

The present pope, John Paul II, from Poland, is the first non-Italian pope since the 1520s. A true internationalist in itinerary and in linguistic skills, he is a firm traditionalist in matters of doctrine and practice, notably on family and gender issues. With respect to social and political concerns, he qualifies as a progressive. The mixture of "liberal" and "conservative" in him seems to mirror many tensions in this global Christian community.

AMERICAN CATHOLIC CHURCH

Founded: 1989
Membership: est. 25,000 in 100 parishes (2000)

Reacting to the conservative response after the Second Vatican Council and to papal rulings regarding birth control, ordination, and theological debate, the American Catholic Church was founded as "a progressive alternative" in 1989. It is a federation of independent churches served by duly ordained priests. Members of the church are committed to basic Catholic beliefs and sacramental theology, and the church stresses the importance of prayer, spirituality, community, and love for one's neighbor and self. The church affirms that authority rests in the "sensus fidelium" (the sense of the faithful) and that communion is open to all. The rite is modern but in the tradition of the Roman Catholic and Orthodox churches.

EASTERN RITE CATHOLIC/UNIATE CHURCHES

Founded: various dates
Membership: est. 500,000 (2000)

The Eastern Rite churches hold a special position within the Roman Catholic Church. Historically and liturgically they are closely related to the Eastern Orthodox (see ORTHODOX and ORI-

85

ENTAL ORTHODOX CHURCHES) churches, but each has chosen to come under the jurisdiction of the Roman Catholic Church while preserving its own distinctive language, rites, and canon law. Most of these churches, for instance, are permitted to have married clergy and have always served both the bread and the wine of the Eucharist to the laity.

There are five major families of Uniate churches: Alexandrian (Copts and Ethiopians), Antiochene (Maronites, Syrians, Malankarese), Armenian, Chaldean (Chaldean and Malabarese), and Byzantine (Hungarian, Yugoslav, Melkites, Ukranian). The largest Eastern Rite church is the Ukrainian Catholic Church, which was formed when Ukrainian subjects of the king of Poland were united with Rome in 1596. This church was outlawed by the Soviet Union following World War II, but has resumed open activity since the collapse of the USSR. The Maronites of Lebanon established ties with Rome during the Crusades.

Each of the Eastern Rite churches is headed by its own Patriarch who has jurisdiction over the bishops, the clergy, and the people of that rite. All of the patriarchs are members of the Congregation for the Oriental Churches, which governs the relations of the Vatican with the Eastern Rite Churches.

LIBERAL CATHOLIC CHURCH

Founded: 1916
Membership: est. 6,500 in 27 churches (2000)

This church originated in 1916 in Great Britain as a branch of the Old Catholic Church (see OLD CATHOLIC CHURCHES) movement that began in Holland in the eighteenth century. Its founding bishops included members of the Theosophical Society (see SPIRITUALIST and THEOSOPHICAL BODIES). The group took the name "Liberal Catholic Church" in 1918. Tracing its orders to an apostolic succession that runs back to the Roman Catholic Church under the reign of Pope Urban VIII (1568–1644), the Liberal Catholic Church aims at a combination of traditional Catholic forms of worship with the utmost freedom of individual conscience and thought. It claims to be neither Roman nor Protestant, but still catholic in the broadest sense of the word. During the 1940s and

86

1950s, a dispute between church authorities in London and some American bishops led to a division between the Liberal Catholic Church International (LCCI) and the Liberal Catholic Church, Province of the U.S. (LCC).

The Nicene Creed is generally used in Liberal Catholic services, but there is no requirement of submission to any creed, Scripture, or tradition. Members seek, not a common profession of belief, but service to humanity through corporate worship in a common ritual. While the LCC places more emphasis on the precepts of the Theosophical Society, *theosophia* ("divine wisdom") is stressed in both bodies, and worship incorporates many basic tenets of Eastern mysticism. Paramount in the thinking is a central inspiration from faith in the living Christ, based on the promises of Matt. 18:20 and 28:20. These promises are regarded as "validating all Christian worship," but special channels of Christ's power are found in the seven sacraments of the church: baptism, confirmation, the Holy Eucharist, absolution, holy unction, holy matrimony, and holy orders. As with the Old Catholic churches, Liberal Catholic priests and bishops may marry, and they exact no fee for the administration of the sacraments; LCC priests are employed in secular occupations, but LCCI churches may offer a salary to their priests if financially able. Liberal Catholics permit the remarriage of divorced persons and are open to gay and lesbian persons. However, neither church ordains women. The presiding bishop of the LCC churches is headquartered in New York City. The LCCI churches maintain St. Alban Theological Seminary in San Diego, California; the publishing arm, St. Alban Press, is also located in San Diego.

MARIAVITE OLD CATHOLIC CHURCH, PROVINCE OF NORTH AMERICA

Founded: 1906 (came to the U.S. in 1972)
Membership: statistics not available

Mariavites are a unique type of Old Catholic Church (see OLD CATHOLIC CHURCHES). They derive their name from the Latin *Mariae vitae imitantur,* meaning "to imitate the life of Mary," the mother of Christ. This ideal originated in late nineteenth-century Poland, a heavily Roman Catholic country. The Mariavite Order of priests and sisters was founded August 2, 1893, by Maria Felicia

Kozlowska (1862–1921), a Third Order Franciscan, and Jan Kowalski (1871–1942), a diocesan priest. Kozlowska had earlier formed a community of sisters in response to visionary experiences; and Kowalski took up the movement about five years later, adding a community of secular priests. The motto of the order was, "Everything for the greater glory of God and the honor of the Most Blessed Virgin Mary." From the beginning, its members endeavored to practice an ascetic/mystical religious life, in accordance with the primitive Rule of St. Francis of Assisi. Their goal was to maintain a deep inner spiritual life among themselves and their faithful by being pastors and servants, not through cloistered or contemplative communities. Candidacy requirements were firm and sacrificial, with a tendency toward the ascetic.

Ecclesiastic and civil opposition marked the early decades of the Mariavites in Poland. The Roman Catholic Church (see ROMAN CATHOLIC CHURCH) was skeptical of their mystical claims and denied their application for recognition as a religious order. In 1906 the group formed a church independent of Rome, and in 1909 it became part of the Old Catholic Church at Utrecht, Holland. That church had been independent of Rome since 1871. At the time of Kozlowska's death in 1921, the Mariavite movement had some 50,000 adherents. However, the group went into decline; and the Old Catholics severed communion with the Mariavites in 1924. The latter were perceived as growing more fanatical, evidenced by Kowalski's ordination of women to the priesthood. Kowalski was eventually imprisoned by the Nazis and died in a concentration camp.

Mariavites first came to the U.S. around 1930. During World War II it was impossible for the churches to maintain close contact with Europe, and by 1972 the U.S. church had become autonomous and self-reliant. Archbishop Robert Zaborowski has led the church since 1974; its headquarters are in Wyandotte, Michigan. According to its own reports, this church has grown rapidly since 1972; some reports claim as many 300,000 members. However, information is difficult to obtain from church officials and actual membership is uncertain.

The church's faith is based on the Old Catholic tenets of faith and morals contained in the canonical books of Holy Scripture in the Old and New Testaments, as well as on the early traditions of the universal church that were dogmatically defined at the first seven ecumenical councils. The traditional seven sacraments and three creeds

88

(Apostles', Nicene, and Athanasian) are acknowledged. Worship is celebrated according to the Tridentine Rite of 1570 in Latin, English, and Polish in the U.S. The principal purpose of the Mariavite Church, which came to be known as the Work of Great Mercy, is "the propagation of devotion to the Most Blessed Sacrament and the invocation of the Perpetual Help of Mary as a means of final salvation for a world perishing in its sins."

OLD CATHOLIC CHURCHES

Founded: 1871 (came to the U.S. in 1914)
Membership: statistics not available

Old Catholic churches in the U.S. are an outgrowth of the Old Catholic movement, centered in the See of Utrecht in the Netherlands. Conflicts between Dutch Catholics and the papacy date to the Jansenist controversy over grace and determinism in the eighteenth century, which resulted in a schism in the Roman Catholic Church in Holland. The schismatic Dutch body continued its existence into the next century, attracting new followers when Pope Pius IX (1846–78) affirmed the First Vatican Council's statement on papal infallibility in 1870 (see CATHOLIC CHURCHES).

A significant number of Swiss, German, and Austrian Roman Catholic priests also refused to accept the doctrine of papal infallibility and were excommunicated in 1871. Ignatz von Döllinger (1799–1890) presided over a number of conferences attended by Old Catholics—that is, Catholics who could not accept the new dogma on papal authority—and representatives of the Anglican and Lutheran churches in the mid-1870s. Old Catholic bishops were ordained by the bishops of Utrecht and were eventually welcomed into communion with the Anglican Church and several Orthodox bodies.

In 1889 the Declaration of Utrecht was issued as the doctrinal statement of Old Catholics. The declaration affirms the main lines of the Catholic tradition up to about the year 1000. Especially important for the Old Catholics are the first seven ecumenical councils (before the division between East and West) and most of the medieval liturgy. However, the declaration rejected more recent doctrines of the Roman Catholic Church, especially papal infallibility, the immaculate conception of Mary, and compulsory celibacy of the priesthood. The church maintains that the five patriarchal Sees of the ancient church remain the equal heads of the church. The Slavic branch of the Old Catholic Church has a separate history (see POLISH NATIONAL CATHOLIC CHURCH OF AMERICA).

The Old Catholic movement in the U.S. first emerged with the work of Père Joseph René Vilatte (1854–1929) in Wisconsin near Green Bay, where several parishes were organized. A group of English-speaking Old Catholics were also gathered together by a former Roman Catholic monk, Augustine de Angelis (William Harding), who had organized a community of men devoted to the Religious Rule of St. Benedict at Waukegan, Illinois around the turn of the century. The Old Catholic episcopacy in the United States was established in 1914 when the English Archbishop Arnold Harris Matthew (1852–1919) consecrated Bishop de Landas Berghes et de Rache (1873–1920), a prince of the house of Lorraine-Brapan. He was succeeded by Father Carmel Henry Carfora (1878–1958), an Italian Franciscan friar, who led the church until his death in 1958.

At that time, the North American Old Catholics split into several ecclesial bodies, not all recognized by Old Catholics in Europe. Perhaps as many as seventeen bodies have claimed to be Old Catholic in the U.S., but the major bodies originating in the Utrecht movement are the Old Catholic Church of America, the Old Roman Catholic Church of North America, the North American Old Catholic Church, the North American Old Roman Catholic Church (Archdiocese of New York), and the Old Roman Catholic Church (English Rite). Most of the Old Catholic churches have fewer than ten parishes in the United States.

In the U.S., the Old Catholics often represent a more conservative form of Catholicism despite their early identification as "liberal." The sweeping liturgical and devotional changes of the Second Vatican Council led some conservative priests to join the Old Catholics in order to preserve the old traditions, such as prayers for the dead. Several conservative churches in the Anglican (see EPISCOPAL/ANGLICAN CHURCHES) tradition may be classified with the Old Catholic churches as well. Most of these bodies use the 1928 edition of *The Book of Common Prayer,* reject the ordination of women, and emphasize catholic ritual in worship. Most of these bodies would agree with the statement of purpose for the Holy Catholic Church (Anglican Rite): "to perpetuate the Faith, Order, Worship and Witness of Western Catholicism as it existed in the Church of

England from around 200 A.D., to the time of the Great Schism, and set forth by the 'ancient catholic bishops and doctors,' and especially as defined by the Seven Ecumenical Councils of the undivided Church."

POLISH NATIONAL CATHOLIC
CHURCH OF AMERICA

Founded: 1897
Membership: est. 150,000 in 125 parishes (2000)

The Polish National Catholic Church, along with a few smaller Slavic national churches in the U.S., represents a different type of the Old Catholic (see OLD CATHOLIC CHURCHES) movement as Eastern European immigrants sought to have parishes in their native tongue. The Polish body was formally organized at Scranton, Pennsylvania, on March 14, 1897, in protest over the lack of a Polish bishop and a desire to have more control over parish affairs. Some Poles, priests and parishioners alike, felt that the policies of Cardinal James Gibbons (1834–1921) gave too much power to the Roman Catholic hierarchy over the parishioners and permitted "an unlawful encroachment upon their right to private ownership and paved the way for the political and social exploitation of the Polish people." After building a new church, the congregation of Sacred Heart parish in Scranton wanted to retain ownership of the property, but their bishop directed that the deed be turned over to the diocese. Some 250 families then began work on a new church, St. Stanislaus, and called a native Pole, Francis Hodur (1866–1953), to be their priest. A constitution for the new church was adopted by the Scranton parish in 1897, claiming the right to control all churches built and maintained by Poles and to administer such property through a committee chosen by each parish. This action was not accepted by authorities in Rome, and Hodur was subsequently excommunicated.

Other Polish parishes followed the Scranton example and began referring to themselves as "National Churches." Joining together, they held their first synod at Scranton in 1904, with 146 clerical and lay delegates representing parishes in Pennsylvania, Maryland, Massachusetts, and New Jersey. Hodur was chosen bishop-elect; he was consecrated in 1907 at Utrecht, Holland, by three bishops of the Old Catholic Church. Following the first synod, the vernacular, first

91

Polish and then English, gradually replaced Latin as the liturgical language—although, to be sure, Hodur had begun to use a Polish mass as early as 1901. A second synod at Scranton in 1909 officially adopted the church's present name.

The Polish National Catholic Church adopted the "Confession of Faith," written by Bishop Hodur, at a general synod in Chicago in 1914. The confession includes belief in the Trinity; the Holy Spirit as the ruler of the world and the source of grace; the necessity of spiritual unity of all Christians; Christ's one body, the church, apostolic and universal, as teacher, steward of grace, and a light unto salvation; the equal right of all to life, happiness, and growth in perfection; equal responsibility to God of all people and nations; immortality; and the future justice and judgment of God. The church recognizes the same sacraments as the Old Catholic, Orthodox (see ORTHODOX and ORIENTAL ORTHODOX CHURCHES), and Roman Catholic churches (see ROMAN CATHOLIC CHURCH). Two forms of confession are in general use: a private confession for children and youths, and a general confession for adults only.

A general synod is the highest legislative authority. It meets every four years, except for such special sessions as may be necessary, and is composed of active bishops, clergy, and lay delegates from every parish. The administration and destiny of this church, according to its constitution, rest with the Prime Bishop. A Supreme Council meets annually or on call and is composed of all active bishops, plus six clergy and fourteen lay delegates approved by the general synod. In like manner, the authority of the diocese is vested in a diocesan bishop and a synod, which meets every four years. There are five dioceses: Buffalo-Pittsburgh, Canadian, Central, Eastern, and Western. Each parish is governed by an elected board of trustees. Polish and English are used in worship and in the educational programs of parish schools taught largely by pastors. Clergy have been allowed to marry since 1921, but only with the knowledge and permission of the bishops.

The Polish National Union, a fraternal and insurance organization established by Bishop Hodur in 1908, is set up as an adjunct to parish life. There is a theological seminary in Scranton, Pennsylvania, and a home for the aged, Spojnia Manor, in Waymart, Pennsylvania. Missionary work was begun in Poland in 1919, ending in the 1950s with the formation of a separate denomination in Poland, the Polish Catholic Church. The Polish National Church maintains ties with the

Old Catholics in Europe, and it has entered into dialogue with the Roman Catholic Church. Sacramental intercommunion with the Episcopal Church was formalized in 1946 but was ended in 1978 over the issue of ordination of women in the Protestant body.

ROMAN CATHOLIC CHURCH

Founded: ca. 60 C.E. (came to the U.S. in 16th century)
Membership: 62,391,484 in 19,627 parishes (2000)

History in the United States. The Roman Catholic Church is the largest single religious body in the United States and has the oldest continuous institutional existence. It is difficult to give a precise date for the origin of this church, since there is disagreement over the distinctive nature of the church. There are indications that Christianity came to the city of Rome as early as 50 C.E., but the structure of papal supremacy that has characterized the Roman Catholic Church took centuries to develop. Officially, the Roman Catholic Church traces its beginning from the moment of Christ's selection of the apostle Peter as guardian of the keys of heaven and earth and chief of the apostles (Matt. 16:18-19). According to Catholic teaching, Peter, martyred in Rome under Nero, was the first bishop of Rome and thus the first pope. During the second, third, and fourth centuries its claim to the theological primacy of Rome was reinforced by practical developments in the church and Western society.

Although for most of its cultural and political history the U.S. has been dominated by Protestants, it is important to remember that Roman Catholicism came to the New World with Christopher Columbus. Missionaries came with Coronado and other early Spanish explorers to the southern and western regions of what would become the United States. The first permanent parish was established at St. Augustine, Florida, in 1565, half a century before the first Protestant baptism in the Americas.

The intrepid French explorers, voyageurs, and colonizers, such as Cartier, Jolliet, and Marquette, who live in North American lore were Roman Catholics. They were generally accompanied by missionaries or were missionaries themselves. New France became a vicariate apostolic in 1658, with Bishop Laval at its head. The See of Quebec (1675) had spiritual jurisdiction over the vast French provinces in North America, reaching down the valley of the Mississippi to Louisiana.

In 1634, Roman Catholics from England founded Maryland in part as a refuge for Catholics during the turmoil of the English Civil War and Puritan Commonwealth. Catholic activity in the English colonies was restricted by law, however, even in Maryland, until after the American Revolution. In 1763, there were fewer than 25,000 Roman Catholics in a colonial population of 2.2 million, and they were under the jurisdiction of the vicar apostolic of London. Even so, among the signatures on the Articles of Confederation, the Declaration of Independence, and the Constitution are found those of three Catholics: Thomas Fitzsimmons (1741–1811), Charles Carroll (1737–1832), and Daniel Carroll (1730–96). Religious equality became law with the adoption of the Constitution in 1787.

The status of the Roman Catholic Church in the new nation was unclear until the Reverend John Carroll (1735–1815) of Baltimore, elder brother of Daniel Carroll, was named Superior, or perfect apostolic, of the church in the new United States. In 1800, he was the head of some 150,000 Roman Catholics. By 1890 that number had grown to 6,231,417, primarily due to the flood of emigration from the Catholic countries of Europe.

Catholics faced a number of unique problems in the U.S. There is only one Roman Catholic Church worldwide, with a single head, unlike most Protestant churches, which have separate national organizations. For example, while there is an Anglican communion worldwide, it is made up of largely independent Anglican churches in the various former British colonies. Episcopalians in the U.S. (see EPISCOPAL/ANGLICAN CHURCHES) are not under the direct authority of the Archbishop of Canterbury the way Roman Catholic bishops are under the authority of the pope. Thus there has been tension in the Roman Catholic Church over the issue of Americanization: How much independence could the American bishops exert while still remaining obedient to Rome? This was a particularly touchy problem following the First Vatican Council (1869–70), when the European leaders rejected a number of ideas, such as democratic government, that were at the core of American values. James Gibbons (1834–1921), the archbishop of Baltimore and primate of the Catholic Church in America, guided the church through these difficult issues and gained permission for Catholics in the U.S. to participate fully in American political and social life while remaining loyal to the Roman church. Ultimately, the Second Vatican Council (1962–65) approved of many proposals long advocated by American bishops.

Another issue in the U.S. has been the effect of Protestant movements on Catholicism. For instance, the Pentecostal movement began making inroads in Catholic parishes in the 1970s, and now the number of "Spirit-filled" Catholics—that is, those who believe in and claim charismatic gifts, such as speaking in tongues, healing, interpretation, and prophecy—is over 300,000. Many more have had some measure of contact with what is broadly called charismatic Catholicism.

Dissension is a common feature in contemporary church life. Some of the most troublesome issues have to do with clerical celibacy, birth control, abortion, the role of women in the church, and the official positions of the church on political and economic matters.

Beliefs and Practices. The faith and doctrine of the Roman Catholic Church are founded upon what the First Vatican Council referred to as "that deposit of faith given to it by Christ and through his apostles, sustained by the Bible and by tradition." Thus, like other Catholic and Orthodox bodies, the church accepts the decisions of the first seven ecumenical councils; however, for Roman Catholics, the later councils of the Western church, such as the Fourth Lateran Council (1215), are also authoritative. These councils, down to the Second Vatican Council, clarify and enrich without changing the "deposit of faith," and they become part of the apostolic tradition. The church also accepts the Apostles' Creed, the Nicene-Constantinople Creed, the Athanasian Creed, and the Creed of Pius IV, also called the Creedal Statement of the Council of Trent. These creeds set forth many doctrines common to most Christian bodies, such as the Trinity (Father, Son, and Spirit are fully and completely divine without losing their distinctiveness) and the full humanity and divinity of Christ.

The creeds also define a number of beliefs and practices that are more distinctively Catholic. Like the Orthodox, Roman Catholics stress the sacraments more than do most Protestants; the sacraments are a visible means of receiving God's grace and are thus holy. For Catholics there are seven sacraments: (1) Baptism, necessary for membership in the church, is administered to infants and to adults by pouring or immersion; anointing with the holy chrism in the form of a cross follows baptism. (2) Confirmation is by the laying on of hands, ordinarily by a bishop; but today priests also may confirm if necessary. (3) The Eucharist, or Holy Communion, is the central act

95

of Catholic devotion. The laity may receive the Eucharist in the forms of bread and wine. This is not a mere sign or ritual for believers. The body and blood of Christ are considered actually present in the eucharistic elements so that the worshiper communes spiritually and physically with the Savior. (4) Through the sacrament of reconciliation (formerly called penance), post-baptismal sins are forgiven. (5) Anointing of the sick is for the seriously ill, the injured, or the aged. (6) The sacraments of holy orders is for the ordination of deacons, priests, and bishops. (7) Marriage is a sacrament that "cannot be dissolved by any human power"; this rules out remarriage after divorce. However, improper marriages may be annulled.

Members are required to attend Mass on Sundays and on obligatory holy days, to fast and abstain on certain appointed days, to confess at least once a year, to receive the Holy Eucharist during the Easter season, to contribute to the support of the church, and to strictly observe the marriage regulations of the church. The Roman Catholic liturgical calendar is more elaborate than that of Protestant churches, with days to remember and venerate hundreds of heroes of the faith, known as saints. Of particular importance in Roman Catholic devotion in the United States and around the world is Mary, the mother of Christ, who serves as an intercessor for the faithful.

The central act of worship is the Mass; its two principal parts are the liturgy of the Word and the liturgy of the Eucharist. Until 1963 Latin was the only appropriate liturgical language. Now the entire Mass is recited in the vernacular by both priest and people. Many Catholics also participate in devotions such as benediction, the rosary (a cyle of prayers usually counted on a string of beads), stations of the cross (prayers occasioned by depictions of Christ's journey from Pilate's house to the tomb), and novenas (a period of nine days of public or private devotion).

Polity. The government of the Roman Catholic Church is hierarchical, but lay members of the parishes assume much responsibility. The trend since Vatican II has been toward more and more lay participation. At the head of the structure stands the pope, who is also Bishop of Rome and "Vicar of Christ on earth and the Visible Head of the Church." His authority is supreme in all matters of faith and discipline.

Next is the College of Cardinals. Although laypeople once were appointed as cardinals, the office has been limited to priests since 1918. Many cardinals live in Rome, acting as advisers to the pope or as heads or members of the various congregations or councils that supervise the administration of the church. When a pope dies, cardinals elect the successor and hold authority in the interim. The Roman Curia is the official body of administrative offices through which the pope governs the church. It is composed of Roman congregations, tribunals, and pontifical councils and acts with the delegated authority of the pope.

In the U.S. there are 11 active cardinals, 45 archbishops (7 of whom are cardinals), 336 bishops, and more than 46,000 priests; there are 34 archdioceses and 151 dioceses. An archbishop is in charge of an archdiocese and has precedence in that province. Bishops, appointed by Rome usually upon suggestions from the U.S. hierarchy, are the ruling authorities in the dioceses, but appeals from their decisions may be taken to the apostolic delegate at Washington, D.C., and even to Rome. The parish priest, responsible to the bishop, is assigned by the bishop or archbishop and holds authority to celebrate Mass and administer the sacraments with the help of such other priests as the parish may need. Priests are educated in theological seminaries, typically connected to Roman Catholic colleges and universities. The usual course of study covers a period of eight years— four years of philosophy and four years of theology. Those in religious orders (see below) also spend one or two years in a novitiate.

The clergy of the church also include deacons. Since the restoration of the Permanent Diaconate in 1967, more than 11,000 men have completed the training course and been ordained deacons. Most of these men are married and over the age of thirty-five. They are empowered to preach, baptize, distribute Holy Communion, and officiate at weddings. Most deacons support themselves in secular jobs and exercise their ministry during weekends and evenings.

Three ecclesiastical councils form an important part of the Roman Catholic system: (1) The general, or ecumenical, council is called by the pope or with his consent; it is composed of all the bishops, and its actions on matters of doctrine and discipline must be approved by the pope. (2) The plenary, or national, council is made up of the bishops of a given country; its acts, too, must be submitted to the Holy See. (3) Provincial and diocesan councils make further promulgation and application of the decrees passed by the other councils and approved by the pope.

With the most centralized government in christendom, the Holy

97

See at Rome has representatives in many countries of the world. Roman Catholic churches have been established in over 230 countries, with a total membership of more than one billion. The majority of Italians, Spanish, Irish, Austrians, Poles, Latin Americans, Belgians, Hungarians, southern Germans, Portuguese, French, and Filipinos are baptized Roman Catholics. The Society for the Propagation of the Faith is the overall representative missionary body. The U.S. sent about 5,800 missionaries to over 130 countries in 1998–99.

Almost every diocese publishes a weekly newspaper; more than 400 Catholic newspapers and magazines are published in the U.S. and Canada. Some of the largest and most influential periodicals are *The National Catholic Reporter, Commonweal, America, Columbia, U.S. Catholic, St. Anthony Messenger, Catholic Digest, Catholic World, Ligourian, Catholic Twin Circle,* and *The National Catholic Register.*

Religious Orders. At least since the fourth century, religious orders have been an integral part of Catholicism. *The Official Catholic Directory 2000* lists a total of 137 religious orders for men and 441 for women. These orders differ widely in their work. Some are "contemplative," the members remaining in monasteries or cloistered convents. Those in active or mixed religious orders engage in teaching, caring for the sick, missionary work, writing, or social work. Brothers and sisters are required to take vows of poverty, chastity, and obedience but are not ordained; they engage primarily in educational and philanthropic work.

Originally monks or nuns were individuals who embraced an ascetic lifestyle of poverty and celibacy as a way to share in the witness of the martyrs who died for the faith. Voluntary asceticism was viewed as a way to "take up the cross" and follow Christ. Over time more organization and discipline were provided for those who chose to serve Christ fully instead of serving a family or personal ambition. In the sixth century, Benedict of Nursia established a monastery on his estate of Monte Cassino. His rule for the men there became the basis for all Western monasticism, male and female. Among the key features of his rule were the vow of obedience to the abbot (head of the monastery) in addition to poverty and chastity, moderation of ascetic excess, and participation in physical labor in addition to prayer.

Through the centuries other religious orders were established, some in an attempt to reform perceived abuses in an older order, some in order to respond to some unmet need in the church and society. Among the most important of these orders were the Cistercians and the Carthusians, established in the twelfth century in protest against the luxury and laxity of many Benedictine houses. With the rapid urbanization of Europe in the late Middle Ages, the mendicant orders were established to reach out to secular society. The Franciscans embraced a radical devotion to poverty and initially lived by begging. The Dominicans also stressed poverty, but they focused their efforts on preaching, especially in areas where heresy was strong. Known as friars, rather than monks, members of these orders quickly established a strong presence in the burgeoning universities of the Middle Ages. There are now 235 Roman Catholic colleges and universities in the U.S., including Notre Dame, Fordham, Georgetown, Boston College, St. Louis University, Marquette, Loyola, and Villanova, most of them closely connected with various religious orders.

Numerous orders were established during the Reformation in order to reform the Roman Catholic Church internally and to respond to the Protestant challenge externally. Chief among them was the Society of Jesus (Jesuits). Today, many priests are also members of a religious order. Parishes in the U.S. are often under the charge of a particular order, such as the Franciscans.

Religious orders have provided an important focus of ministry for women in the Roman Catholic Church for more than 1,800 years. Some of the male orders have branches for women, but in general women have established their own institutions within catholicism. There are the Carmelites who produced the great mystic Teresa of Avila (1515–82); the Ursulines, who embraced a mission of educating young women; and the Sisters of Mercy, founded by Mother Teresa of Calcutta (1910–97). In the U.S., women religious have been the backbone of the extensive Roman Catholic parochial school system. In the 1990s there were some 7,000 parochial and private schools in this country with about two million students, including over 1,300 Roman Catholic high schools.

Women religious have also been vital in staffing Catholic hospitals and establishing countless charitable institutions. It is indicative of the work of Roman Catholic women that the first American officially to be declared a saint of the church was Elizabeth Seton (1774–1821), noted for her sacrificial role in alleviating social misery. The National Conference on Catholic Charities helps to coordinate charity and welfare work on state and national levels; work is also conducted by several religious orders whose members devote full time to the relief of the poor in homes or institutions, and many dioceses have bureaus of charity.

The Society of St. Vincent de Paul is perhaps the largest and most effective charitable organization, but many others—particularly women's orders, such as Little Sisters of the Poor, Sisters of Charity, Daughters of Charity of the Society of St. Vincent de Paul, and Sisters of Mercy—are active among the poor in Catholic hospitals, orphanages, and homes for the aged. The church operates 1,414 homes for the aged and 149 orphanages. More than 77 million patients are treated annually in 593 general and special hospitals and 557 health-care centers. One of every three beds in the nation's private hospitals is provided by the Catholic hospital system.

Besides religious orders and congregations, Roman Catholics may join secular institutions whose members also observe poverty, chastity, and obedience but do not wear distinctive garb or live together in a community. Before receiving approval as secular institutes engaged in apostolic work, these groups may operate as approved "pious unions."

Ethnic Parishes. One of the major issues that has faced the Roman Catholic Church in the U.S. has involved immigration. Catholics in Europe were united in their obedience to Rome, but they were organized on national lines. Spaniards had Spanish priests, Spanish bishops, and venerated Spanish saints. Likewise, the Catholic churches of Ireland, Germany, France, Poland, and elsewhere had their own national character. There was a strong impulse for these ethnic identities to determine the structure of the Catholic Church in America. In other words, there were those who wanted to recreate the old national churches on American soil with separate hierarchies for each major ethnic group. There would have been many Catholic churches; all were loyal to Rome, but separated from each other in the U.S. Cardinal Gibbons again charted the course that led to a parochial system in which local parishes could be organized on ethnic lines, but the national church would be a single American church. Thus diversity and unity were preserved.

There is much that Catholics share in common; however, it is important to note the rich diversity of traditions within Catholicism in the U.S., even in a single metropolitan area. When immigrants arrive in this country, they tend to group in neighborhoods in major cities and there re-create some familiar features of the Old World. Thus, although the basic elements of the Mass are the same in every Roman Catholic parish and the same high holy days are observed, at the local level there are many variations liturgically and in popular devotion. A sampling of a few of the major Catholic ethnic groups within the U.S. includes:

Irish. It is estimated that more than four million people fled Ireland for the U.S. during the nineteenth century, joining at least one hundred thousand more who arrived before the American Revolution. Irish emigration was connected with the subjugation of Ireland to the British crown. Once Protestantism was firmly established in England, Catholicism became a mark of national resistance for the native Irish who clung tenaciously to their faith. In the New World, Catholicism continued to be a bond among the immigrants and to the homeland. Countless Irish benevolent and mutual aid societies were established in the U.S., often with a close connection to the church. St. Patrick's Day became a major holiday in many northern cities and an expression of Irish pride. Within the Roman Catholic Church in the U.S., the Irish played a major role. From the time of the first American bishop, John Carroll, until today most dioceses and archdioceses have had more prelates of Irish birth or descent than of any other nationality. In many ways, the Irish have largely defined American Catholicism, and it was a bishop of Irish descent, James Gibbons, who established the pattern for Catholicism in America.

Italians. By 1908 more than two and half million persons had emigrated from Italy to the U.S., settling mainly in the major cities of the Northeast, particularly New York City, and the upper Midwest. The Franciscans provided most of the pastoral leadership for Italian immigrants, and notable among them were Father Pamfilo da Magliano, founder of St. Bonaventure's College at Allegany, New York (1858), and Father Leo Paccillio, pastor of the first Italian parish in New York, St. Anthony's. The Franciscans were followed by the Jesuits, the Scalabrini Fathers, the Salesians, the Passionists, and the Augustinians. In some cases priests of other nationalities learned Italian in order to minister to the needs of the Italians in areas where no Italian priest was available. Italian Catholics continued to honor the patron saints of their native Italian towns, naming benevolent societies after them and holding parish festivals on the saints' days. Particularly important in this regard have been St. Anthony and St. Joseph.

101

Hispanic. Catholicism came to the New World primarily by way of Spain, whose monarchs were strong supporters of the Counter Reformation. The first universities in the Americas were founded in the Spanish colonies, and indigenous cultures blended with the religious practices of the conquering Spaniards to create a great variety of vibrant subcultures of the faith. Missionaries to the American Southwest made some progress in converting native peoples, and by 1800 beautiful adobe missions dotted the West. For most of U.S. history, Mexicans have been the dominant Hispanic group, and in some cities it is common to see devotion to the Virgin of Guadalupe and the spectacular Day of the Dead festival, which is celebrated around the time of Halloween. Since World War II immigration has increased from other Latin American countries, making the Hispanic population the fastest growing portion of the Roman Catholic Church in the U.S. In large part due to a shortage of priests and economic distress, there has not been as great a tendency toward the creation of parishes along national lines as there was in nineteenth century. Some parishes do primarily use Spanish, and many parochial schools teach in Spanish; but in general there has been a blending of immigrants from different Latin American countries and cultures.

Poles. Poland gradually disappeared as a political entity during the eighteenth century as Russia, Prussia, and Austria divided the territory among them. Partition, however, did not destroy Polish identity or patriotism. Particularly in western Poland, German efforts to assimilate the Poles into German Protestant culture served to heighten devotion to the Roman Catholic Church. There were Poles in the U.S. during colonial days, and some served prominently in the American Revolution; but the immigration of the Polish masses began in the 1850s. In 1851, Father Leopold Moczygemba (1824–91), a Franciscan, came to the U.S. and soon after induced nearly one hundred families from Upper Silesia to come to Panna Maria, Texas, where they built the first Polish church in the U.S. in 1855. Immigration, particularly from Polish Prussia, increased rapidly, primarily to Illinois, Michigan, and Pennsylvania. By 1890 there were some 130 Polish churches served by 126 priests. Most of the more than 120 schools were conducted by the Felician Sisters and the School Sisters of Notre Dame. The election of the first Polish pope, John Paul II, in 1978 was a great boon to Polish Catholics in the U.S.

102

CHRISTIAN CHURCHES
(The Stone-Campbell Movement)

Protestantism, with its emphasis on the Bible alone as the basis of faith, has always sought to remain true to the church of the apostles in the New Testament. Most Protestants have been willing to accept some historical development of the church and its doctrine in the post-biblical period, accepting the Apostles' Creed, for example. There have been others, though, who have seen most of the history of Christianity as the story of a decline from New Testament purity. These Christians have attempted to "restore" original or "primitive" Christianity by purging the church of all nonbiblical elements, including creeds and confessions of faith. During the Second Great Awakening (beginning at the end of the 18th century and continuing through the first two decades of the 19th century), this restorationist impulse grew particularly strong. In politics, the U.S. had "restored" Greek democracy; many thought Americans could also restore the structure and doctrine of the original church in the new land. By returning to the New Testament alone, without recourse to creeds or rituals, the restorationists also hoped to end fraternal strife among churches.

Thomas Campbell (1763–1854) was a Scottish Presbyterian who left his church in Ireland to come to western Pennsylvania in 1807. Campbell was convinced that the historical creeds and confessions of the church were a source of Christian division rather than union, and he preached that all Christians should share in the Lord's Supper together. When his views led to a censure from the Presbyterians (see PRESBYTERIAN CHURCHES) in 1809, he formed the Christian Association of Washington County, Pennsylvania, and published the *Declaration and Address*, which was to become the Magna Carta of the restorationist movement. In that document he argued that "schism, or uncharitable divisions" in the church were "anti-Christian, anti-Scriptural, and anti-natural" and "productive of confusion and every evil work." The church and church membership should be based solely upon the belief and practices of New Testament Christianity, he maintained; the articles of faith and holiness "expressly revealed in the Word of God" were quite enough, without adding human opinions or creedal inventions. The Bible,

103

Campbell asserted, was a reasonable book that any reasonable person could read and understand; therefore, there is no need for creeds or other human interpretations. God has spoken clearly, and the Bible lays down the rules for church practices. "We will speak when the scriptures speak, and remain silent when they are silent." With that phrase, Campbell abolished many traditional church practices, such as days of fasting and the use of musical instruments in worship.

Campbell's son, Alexander (1788–1866), was less scholarly than his father, but more dynamic and consistent in his application of his father's principles. He convinced Thomas that infant baptism was not Christian, and in 1812 all of the Campbells were immersed by a local Baptist minister. However, even the Baptists were not biblical enough for the Campbells. Father and son continued their independent evangelical work, and Alexander fought many public battles against atheism, Mormonism, Unitarianism, creedalism, sectarianism, emotionalism, and even slavery; but he was singularly unsuccessful in bringing about church unity. His noncreedal church became one of the first independent denominations to be born in the United States.

The other major branch of the nineteenth-century restorationist movement had its origins in the convictions of James O'Kelly (1757–1826), a Methodist minister; Abner Jones (1772–1841), a Baptist; and Barton Stone (1772–1844), a Presbyterian. In 1792, O'Kelly withdrew from the Methodist Church (see METHODIST CHURCHES) in protest over the recently established episcopacy. He especially objected to the power of bishops to appoint ministers to their charges. O'Kelly and his followers organized under the name Republican Methodist; the new church insisted that the Bible be taken as the only rule and discipline and that Christian character be made the only requirement for church membership.

Abner Jones, convinced that "sectarian names and human creeds should be abandoned," left the Vermont Baptists (see BAPTIST CHURCHES) in 1801 to organize First Christian Church at Lyndon, Vermont. This was done from a desire to secure a wider freedom of religious thought and fellowship. Like O'Kelly, Jones insisted that piety and character be the sole test of Christian fellowship.

When the Second Great Awakening swept through Tennessee and Kentucky in the early 1800s, preaching focused on the need for conversion rather than denominational or doctrinal distinctions. Barton Stone was instrumental in the famous Cane Ridge, Kentucky, revival, which began on August 7, 1801. Somewhere between 10,000 and 25,000 people appeared during the weeklong revival in which preachers from a variety of churches took part. Participants described the event as a new Pentecost where thousands were converted, often with dramatic emotional displays. The experience of the revival convinced Stone that salvation has little to do with church affiliation and that "deeds are more important than creeds." The egalitarian promise of the American Revolution was being felt in Cane Ridge and other Western "camp meeting" revivals, but the controversy over them led to a schism in the Presbyterian Church.

The groups led by O'Kelly, Jones, and Stone engaged in a long series of conferences that resulted in agreement on six basic Christian principles: (1) Christ, the only head of the church; (2) the Bible, sufficient rule of faith and practice; (3) Christian character, the measure of membership; (4) a right, individual interpretation of the Scripture, as a way of life; (5) "Christian," the name taken as worthy of the followers of Christ; (6) unity, Christians working together to save the world.

By 1832 the "Stoneites" and the "Campbellites" had come together for a meeting in Lexington, Kentucky. Stone used the word *Christian* to designate his group, feeling that all of God's children should be known as such. Alexander Campbell used the phrase "Disciples of Christ." After 1832, some of the Christians and the Disciples of Christ merged; both names are still used, but commonly and officially the body is known today as the Christian Church (Disciples of Christ).

Early in the movement, Walter Scott (1796–1861) popularized the term *Restoration,* meaning the restoration of the New Testament pattern and practice. Like Stone, Scott was suspicious of the values of the current revivalistic frenzies; he related faith more to the mind than to emotions. He stressed the importance of faith together with repentance of sin and baptism by immersion. Very soon thereafter, however, differences arose among the restorationists, and, over time, distinct fellowships emerged. Devoted in varying ways to the restoration ideal, several of these groups continue to be influential.

CHRISTADELPHIANS

Founded: 1844
Membership: est. 15,000 in 170 ecclesias (2000)

Less clearly connected to the original restorationist movement than the other bodies discussed under this heading, the Christadelphians did grow out of the Disciples of Christ. When John Thomas (1805–71) came to the United States from England in 1832, he soon joined the Disciples. Things did not go well for him in that body; he believed that the Disciples neglected many important biblical doctrines. Therefore, he left the Disciples in 1844 to found a number of societies that preached the need for a return to primitive Christianity. Loosely organized, those various societies bore no name until the outbreak of the Civil War, when their members' doctrine of nonresistance forced them to adopt a name in order to avoid the draft. They chose the term *Christadelphians,* or Brothers of Christ.

Christadelphians are both Unitarian and Adventist in theology. They reject belief in the devil, maintaining that the scriptures teach that Christ is not God the Son, but the Son of God. They believe that Christ was not preexistent, but was born of Mary by the Holy Spirit, that is, by the power of God. Humankind is mortal by nature, and Christ is the only means of salvation. Eternal life comes only to the righteous. Strong millenarians, they believe that Christ will come shortly to reward with immortality those who are worthy. In the U.S., some Christadelphians, called Unamended, believe Christ will raise only those who died in the faith; all other persons will simply remain dead, without consciousness. Other Christadelphians, known as Amended, believe that Christ will raise all responsible persons, rewarding the righteous and annihilating the wicked. Both groups believe the faithful will be gathered together, and the world will be ruled from Jerusalem for a thousand years. They hold the Bible to be the inspired Word of God, inerrant in its original text.

The church is congregational in policy; local organizations are known, not as churches, but as ecclesias. Membership is by profession of faith, and baptism is by immersion. There are no paid or ordained ministers in the usual sense; each ecclesia elects serving brethren, among whom are managing brethren, presiding brethren, and lecturing brethren. Women take no part in public speech or prayer, though all vote equally in the affairs of the ecclesia.

106

Christadelphians do not vote in civil elections or participate in war, and they refuse to accept public office. There are no associations or conventions, but there are fraternal gatherings for spiritual inspiration. Many meetings are held in rented halls, schools, or private homes, though a number of ecclesias have their own buildings.

Home-missions work is local, usually in the form of lectures and instruction in Christadelphian doctrine and righteous living. Foreign missions and ecclesias are found in 60 countries. Summer Bible schools are held in several states. Found in over 40 states from coast to coast, this loosely organized movement has greater numbers in Great Britain, New Zealand, Australia, Canada, and Germany. Most of the approximately 700 ecclesias outside the U.S. hold the Amended position regarding resurrection.

CHRISTIAN CHURCH (Disciples of Christ)

Founded: 1832 or 1812
Membership: 834,037 in 3,792 congregations (2000)

Among the dozen largest religious groups in the United States, the Christian Church (Disciples of Christ) might be called the most American. It was born on the nineteenth-century American frontier out of a deep concern for Christian unity.

Alexander Campbell (see CHRISTIAN CHURCHES) enlarged upon the concept that every congregation should be autonomous and completely independent—that creeds, clerical titles, authority, and privilege had no justification in Scripture; that the Lord's Supper should be served at every Sunday service; and that baptism should be by immersion for adult believers (persons old enough to understand the meaning of the ordinance). He argued eloquently for Christian union and freedom of individual faith, and he welcomed to his independent church at Brush Run, Pennsylvania, all who came with faith in Christ as the Son of God and the Messiah. He met the same kind of opposition his father, Thomas, had met and, with his congregation, joined an association of Baptists (see BAPTIST CHURCHES), only to separate from that body in 1830. In 1832 he and many of his followers joined with the Christian movement of Barton Stone (see CHRISTIAN CHURCHES).

The first national convention of the Disciples of Christ and the first missionary society (American Christian Missionary Society) were

107

organized in 1849; state conventions and societies had begun to meet in 1839. The group grew rapidly during and following the Civil War period, especially in Ohio, Indiana, Illinois, Tennessee, and Missouri, in spite of internal conflicts over ecclesiastical organization. The differences between conservatives and progressives became acute in such matters as the organization of missionary societies and instrumental music in the churches; the Churches of Christ (see CHURCHES OF CHRIST) separated from the Disciples during that debate.

In matters of belief, conservative and progressive attitudes were and still are important, and the church allows for variance of opinion and freedom in interpretation, stemming from the conviction that there is no creed but Christ and no saving doctrines save those of the New Testament. It could be said that the Disciples are God-centered, Christ-centered, and Bible-centered; beyond that, faith is a matter of personal conviction, but there are areas of general agreement and acceptance. The Disciples are firm in their belief in immortality but do not accept the doctrine of original sin; they hold that all people are of a sinful nature until redeemed by the sacrifice of Christ; they are not concerned with speculation about the Trinity and the nature of a triune God. They have no catechism and no set orders of worship. Faith in Christ as Lord is the only requirement.

For more than a century Disciples of Christ were strictly congregational in polity, but increasingly it was felt that such an arrangement, with overlapping boards and agencies and no representative voice, needed restructuring in the interests of efficiency and economy. Following a seven-year study and discussion led by a 130-member commission, a whole new design of organization was adopted at Kansas City in 1968. Under the new plan, entitled *Provisional Design for the Christian Church (Disciples of Christ)*, the whole church works under a representative government referred to as "three manifestations"—local, regional, and general.

The local church is still the basic unit, and each congregation manages its own affairs, has its own charter and bylaws, owns and controls its property, calls its ministers, establishes its own budgets and financial policies, and has voting representatives in regional and national assemblies.

The congregations are grouped in 35 regions, organized to provide help, counsel, and pastoral care to members, ministers, and congregations. Each region organizes its own boards, departments, and committees. The regions certify the standing of ministers and provide counsel in such matters as ordination, licensing, location and installation of ministers, and the establishment or dissolution of pastoral relationships. The General Asembly of the church meets every two years; this assembly includes 8,000 to 10,000 people, lay and clergy, from across the church. The General Board, a body of 160 voting members, meets annually for the purposes of long-range planning and setting general policies for the whole church. Finally, the Administrative Committee, with 44 voting members, meets twice annually. The Office of Communication is located in Indianapolis, Indiana; the church's publishing arm, the Christian Board of Publication, is in St. Louis, Missouri.

Membership continues to be largest along a crescent from Pittsburgh to San Antonio. Highly valuing education, the Disciples of Christ were instrumental in founding schools on the frontier. There are now 21 colleges and seminaries in covenant relation with the Disciples, the largest of which is Texas Christian University, in Fort Worth, Texas. The church's National Benevolent Association operates 83 facilities and programs in 22 states, serving over 30,000 a year in residential facilities and community-based programs. Still committed to the cause of Christian union, the Disciples have long participated in the ecumenical movement, including the Consultation on Church Union.

CHRISTIAN CHURCHES AND CHURCHES OF CHRIST

Founded: 1830s; 1920s
Membership: 1,071,616 in 5,579 churches (1988)

Even more so than most Baptist (see BAPTIST CHURCHES) groups, these independent churches reject the designation as a denomination. Indeed, they have no formal organization other than the local congregation. There are several parachurch agencies formed to meet specific needs, such as homes for the aged and for needy children or particular missions. It was in part the issue of increasing centralized organization that led the Christian Churches to separate from the Disciples of Christ; however, there is evidence that throughout the nineteenth century the union between the Campbellites (Disciples of Christ) and the Stoneites (Christian Churches and Churches of Christ) was strained (see CHRISTIAN CHURCH [DISCIPLES OF CHRIST]).

In the 1920s, during the heyday of the fundamentalist/modernist controversy in the U.S., many Christian Churches and Churches of Christ separated from the Disciples over what they felt was the Disciples' liberalism. Christian Churches and Churches of Christ stress the divinity of Christ, the authority of the Bible, the indwelling of the Holy Spirit for the believer, future reward or punishment, and God as a loving, prayer-answering deity. They baptize by immersion and observe the Lord's Supper in open Communion every Sunday. Many Christian Churches and Churches of Christ still maintain the nineteenth-century practice of the extended revival, known as the "camp meeting."

In recent years, some of the Christian Church congregations have experienced enormous growth, reaching audiences of up to 20,000 worshipers. The group supports over twenty colleges, most of which are preacher-training schools insulated from liberal influences. Standard Publishing, in Cincinnati, Ohio, is identified with this group as well.

The North American Christian Convention, an annual preaching and teaching assembly, draws as many as 20,000 attendees to an annual nondelegate gathering each July. Active in foreign missions, with a missionary presence in about a dozen foreign countries and a domestic missionary presence as well, these churches sponsor a National Missionary Convention that meets each fall, with an attendance of between 3,000 and 5,000.

CHRISTIAN CONGREGATION, INC.

Founded: 1887
Membership: 118,209 in 1,438 churches (1999)

The philosophy and work of the Christian Congregation, formed in Indiana in 1887, revolve around the "new commandment" of John 13:34-35. The origins of the group go back to Barton Stone, but in 1887 a number of ministers desired greater coordination of activities and formally organized a church. The charter was revised in 1898 and again in 1970.

The group is a fellowship of clergy and laypeople who seek a non-creedal, nonsectarian basis for union. Unlike many other descendents of the restorationist movement, the Christian Congregation is pacifistic and opposes all war and sectarian strife. Inspired by the preaching of John Chapman and John L. Puckett, the church insists that "the household of faith is not founded upon doctrinal agreement, creeds, church claims, names, or rites," but solely on the relationship of the individual to God. The basis of Christian fellowship is love; the actual relation of Christians to one another transcends all individual belief or personal opinion. Because of its teachings concerning the sanctity of life, the church condemns abortion, capital punishment, and all warfare. Independent Bible study is encouraged. They believe that the ethical demands of the Scripture transcend all national and racial barriers and should unite all persons in activism for peace.

Although churches and pastorates are located in almost every state in the union, the church remains strongest in the areas where Barton Stone preached and the original Christian Congregation groups were located: Kentucky, the Carolinas, Virginia, Pennsylvania, Ohio, Indiana, Tennessee, and Texas. The greater part of the group's work is carried on in rural and mountain areas. Polity is congregational. A general superintendent presides over a board of trustees; relations among the superintendent, the board, and the people are purely advisory.

CHURCHES OF CHRIST

Founded: 1906, with roots to the 1820s
Membership: est. 1,500,000 in over 10,000 churches (2000)

The largest of the bodies in the American restoration movement, Churches of Christ are located throughout the nation but are concentrated in the South and the Southwest. As with the Christian Church (see CHRISTIAN CHURCHES AND CHURCHES OF CHRIST), the Churches of Christ reject the idea of denominationalism and have no central headquarters; therefore, accurate statistics are impossible to attain. This group has no governing bodies, but they do cooperate voluntarily in international radio programs sponsored by any congregation.

The Churches of Christ are anti-creedal and look for a Christian union based on the Bible alone. They assert that the Bible is "the beginning place," in and through which God-fearing people can achieve spiritual oneness. All Christians are to "speak where the Bible speaks and to be silent where the Bible is silent" in all matters

111

pertaining to faith and morals. Consequently, members recognize no other written creed or confession of faith. In all religious matters, there must be a "thus said the Lord."

The leaders among the Churches of Christ in the nineteenth century were more conservative than their counterparts among the Disciples of Christ. Stressing a strict adherence to the New Testament pattern of worship and church organization, they refused to join any inter-congregational organization, such as a missionary society. Worship was simple, and they opposed the addition of instrumental music on the grounds that the New Testament did not authorize it and that the early church did not use it. Around the beginning of the twentieth century, the differences between the conservative and the more liberal wings of the restoration movements became evident, and in the 1906 census of religious bodies, Churches of Christ were listed separately for the first time.

Today one of the outstanding features of Churches of Christ is their acceptance of the Bible as a true and completely adequate revelation. This basic concept has resulted in such practices as weekly observance of the Lord's Supper, baptism by immersion, a cappella singing, a vigorous prayer life, support of church needs through voluntary giving, and a program of preaching and teaching the Bible. This concept also explains the autonomy of local churches, governed by elders and deacons appointed under New Testament qualifications; dignified worship services; enthusiastic mission campaigns; and far-flung benevolence, all financed by local churches.

Key doctrines of Churches of Christ include belief in the Father, the Son, and the Holy Ghost as members of one Godhead; in the incarnation, virgin birth, and bodily resurrection of Christ; and in the universality of sin after the age of accountability, its only remedy the vicarious atonement of the Lord Jesus Christ. Strong emphasis is also laid on the church as the body and bride of Christ. A figurative, rather than literal, view is prevalent with reference to the book of Revelation. Church membership is contingent upon an individual's faith in Jesus Christ as the only begotten Son of God, repentance, confession of faith, and baptism by immersion for the remission of sins. Church attendance is stressed. Churches of Christ maintain that the final judgment of all religious groups is reserved to the Lord. This view, however, still allows for a vigorous evangelism that finds unacceptable the "doctrines, practices, names, titles, and creeds that have been grafted onto the original practice of Christianity."

Clergy are ordained rather than licensed, and they hold tenure in their pulpits under mutual agreement with the elders of the churches in which they preach. Ministerial authority is essentially moral; the actual governance of the church is vested in its elders.

A vigorous missionary program is carried on in 92 nations outside the U.S., and in recent years a strong movement to extend the influence of the church in the northeastern states of the U.S. has developed. Counting native workers on the foreign field and mission activities within the U.S., more than 1,000 missionaries or evangelists are supported by groups other than those to which they preach. Generally patriotic, the Churches of Christ maintain a quota of chaplains in the U.S. military.

Churches of Christ support 24 Bible colleges, liberal arts colleges, and universities and 27 high schools and/or elementary schools in the U.S. They also sponsor numerous facilities for care of the aged. The church publishes over one hundred periodicals, newspapers, and magazines. The oldest publication, *The Gospel Advocate,* has been published continually since the 1850s, except when it ceased during the Civil War due to lack of mail delivery. The churches also carry on an active ministry through the Internet. Since the status of these institutions is unofficial, and none is authorized to speak for the entire church, their conformity in ideas and teachings is all the more remarkable.

CHURCH OF CHRIST, SCIENTIST
(Christian Science)

Founded: 1879
Membership: approx. 2,200 churches (1998)

The Church of Christ, Scientist (Christian Science), is a form of Christianity that was born on American soil and has no direct connection to any other Christian group. Generally described as "a religious teaching and practice based on the words and works of Christ Jesus," Christian Science was regarded by the founder, Mary Baker Eddy (1821–1910), as "the scientific system of divine healing," the "law of God, the law of good, interpreting and demonstrating the divine Principle and rule of universal harmony." She believed that

God is "the Principle of all harmonious Mind-action." Eddy included most of these definitions and descriptions in *Science and Health with Key to the Scriptures* (1875, 1883). This volume and the Bible are the twofold textbooks of Christian Science.

Christian Science originated from Eddy's personal experience. Having suffered from a form of paralysis much of her life, in 1866, in Lynn, Massachusetts, after reading the account of Christ's healing of a man with a form of palsy (Matt. 9:1-8), Eddy recovered almost instantly. Already fascinated with the idea of spiritual causation found in Swedenborgianism (see SWEDENBORGIAN CHURCH) and deeply immersed in the Bible, Eddy was convinced that God was the source of her healing. She began to regard God as the divine mind, which is infinite love. From these roots came Christian Science.

Under her direction, the Church of Christ, Scientist, was established at Lynn in 1879; shortly thereafter she moved the church and its headquarters to Boston. In 1892 she formed the present worldwide organization; the church in Boston became the mother church of Christian Science.

Applied not only to the healing of sickness but also to the problems of life generally, the tenets and doctrines of Christian Science are often confusing to outsiders and call for careful explanation. They begin with the conviction that God is the only might, or "Mind"; God is "All-in-all," the "divine Principle of all that really is," "the all-knowing, all-seeing, all-acting, all-wise, all-loving, and eternal; Principle; Mind; Soul; Spirit; Life; Truth; Love; all substance; intelligence." The inspired Word of the Bible is accepted as "sufficient guide to eternal Life."

Another tenet of Christian Science doctrine states: "We acknowledge and adore one supreme and infinite God. We acknowledge His Son, one Christ; the Holy Ghost or divine Comforter; and man in God's image and likeness." Jesus is known to Christian Scientists as Master or Way-shower. They accept his virgin birth and his atoning mission "as the evidence of divine, efficacious Love, unfolding man's unity with God through Christ Jesus the Way-shower," and believe that he was "endowed with . . . the divine Spirit, without measure." Humankind "is saved through Christ, through Truth, Life, and Love as demonstrated by the Galilean Prophet in healing the sick and overcoming sin and death." The crucifixion and resurrection of Jesus are held as serving "to uplift faith to understand eternal Life, even the allness of Soul, Spirit, and the nothingness of matter."

The "allness" of spirit and "nothingness of matter" involve the basic teaching of Christian Science concerning reality. As *Science and Health* explains, "All reality is in God and His creation, harmonious and eternal. That which He creates is good, and He makes all that is made. Therefore the only reality of sin, sickness, or death is the awful fact that unrealities seem real to human, erring belief, until God strips off their disguise. They are not true, because they are not of God."

In Christian Science belief, God forgives sin through destroying it with "the spiritual understanding that casts out evil as unreal." The punishment for sin, however, lasts as long as one's belief in sin endures.

Adherents of Christian Science do not ignore what they consider "unreal"; rather, they seek to forsake and overcome error and evil through Christian discipleship, prayer, and progressive spiritual understanding of God's "allness" and goodness; they strive to see the spiritual "body," created in God's likeness, as the only real body. Error is "a supposition that pleasure and pain, that intelligence, substance, life, are existent in matter."

Christian Scientists commonly rely wholly on the power of God for healing rather than on medical treatment. Healing is not held to be miraculous, but divinely natural; disease is understood to be basically a mental concept that can be dispelled by active Christian discipleship, spiritual regeneration, and application of the truths to which Jesus bore witness.

For Christian Scientists, heaven is not a locality but "harmony; the reign of Spirit; government by divine Principle; spirituality; bliss, the atmosphere of Soul." Hell is "mortal belief; error; lust; remorse; hatred; revenge; sin; sickness; death; suffering and self-destruction; self-imposed agony; effects of sin; that which 'worketh abomination or maketh a lie.'" Mortal mind is "the flesh opposed to Spirit, the human mind and evil in contradistinction to the divine Mind." Prayer is "an absolute faith that all things are possible to God—a spiritual understanding of Him, an unselfed love." Baptism is not observed as a traditional ceremony, but is held to be a continuing individual spiritual experience, "a purification from all error."

The local Churches of Christ, Scientist, enjoy their own forms of democratic government within the general framework of bylaws laid down by Eddy in the *Manual of the Mother Church*, which also provides for Christian Science college organizations. Reading rooms,

115

open to the general public, are maintained by all churches. The affairs of the mother church are administered by the Christian Science Board of Directors, which elects a president, First and Second Readers, a clerk, and a treasurer. The board of directors is a self-perpetuating body that elects all other officers of the church annually, with the exception of Readers, who are elected by the board for a term of three years.

Important in the Christian Science movement are the Readers, teachers, and practitioners. There are two Readers in each branch church, usually a man and a woman elected by the church members. In all services on Sundays and Thanksgiving Day, they read alternately from the Bible and from *Science and Health*. The lesson-sermons of Sunday services are prepared by a committee and are issued quarterly by the Christian Science Publishing Society. This system is followed by all Christian Science churches throughout the world. A midweek meeting, conducted by the First Reader alone, features testimonies of healing from sin and sickness.

Practitioners devote their full time to healing and are listed in a directory in the monthly *Christian Science Journal.* A board of education consists of three members: a president, a vice president, and a teacher of Christian Science. Under the supervision of this board, a Normal class is held once every three years. Teachers are duly authorized by certificates granted by the board to form classes. One class of not more than thirty pupils is instructed by each teacher annually.

A board of lectureship consists of about sixty members, appointed annually by the board of directors. At the invitation of branch churches, free public lectures are given by these members all over the world. A Committee on Publication serves as an ecumenical and informational office, representing the denomination to the press and the public. The Christian Science Publishing Society carries on broadcasting activities and produces several publications, including: *Christian Science Sentinel, The Christian Science Journal, Christian Science Quarterly—Bible Lessons, Herald of Christian Science*, and *The Christian Science Monitor.* A number of nursing homes for members who rely wholly on spiritual means for healing are independently maintained throughout the world.

At a time when its members were frequently citing the rapid growth of the denomination, Eddy ruled that membership statistics should not be made available for publication, believing that the number of members is no indication of true spiritual growth.

CHURCH OF GOD AND SAINTS OF CHRIST

Founded: 1896
Membership: est. 40,000 in approx. 200 congregations (1999)

The Church of God and Saints of Christ is a Christian body that tries to live according to a literal understanding of Old Testament law. As such, they are sometimes called "Christian Israelites"; however, they have no direct relationship to historical Judaism. The church was begun by William Saunders Crowdy (1847–1908), who was born to slave parents in Maryland. After serving in the Union Army, Crowdy bought a farm near Guthrie, Oklahoma. Active in the Baptist church, in 1893 Crowdy began having disturbing visions and hearing voices. He dreamed of tables covered in filth, each of which had the name of a denomination. Then he saw a clean table that came down from heaven; on it was the name "Church of God and Saints of Christ." Later he received guidelines for his new church, which were known as the "Seven Keys."

Crowdy began preaching on the streets in towns and villages in the Midwest and drew crowds most places he spoke. He baptized many into the faith and in November of 1896 he formally organized the Church of God and Saints of Christ in Lawrence, Kansas. Subsequently Crowdy took his message to Chicago and found success there. Arrested numerous times because of his ministry, he made converts in prison as well. The Seven Keys formed the core set of doctrines: repentance of sin; baptism by burial into water upon confession of faith; unleavened bread and water for Christ's body and blood; foot washing by elders; obedience to the commandments; the holy kiss; and the Lord's Prayer. Crowdy eventually traveled to New York, founding a church there in 1899; and later that year he moved on to Philadelphia, holding meetings and preaching on street corners along the way. In Philadelphia he founded a church and also several businesses; the Church of God and Saints of Christ continues to stress the importance of individual enterprise and business acumen as marks of religious life.

Crowdy taught that his followers should celebrate a number of Jewish holy and feast days. Of particular importance are the observance of the sabbath on the seventh day, Passover, the Day of Atonement, and the Jewish new year. Members believe their church is built on the patriarchs and prophets of the Jewish tradition, and "Jesus the Anointed" is their chief cornerstone. They differentiate between prophetic Judaism, "which seeks to follow the living insight into the spiritual idea to its fullest implication," from "legalistic" Judaism. They accept the Decalogue as the standard of conduct for all humankind. Men and women are instructed to wear particular clothing on the sabbath according to the season of the year, and men are expected to wear the yarmulke and a tallith.

An executive bishop stands at the head of the church and of the bishops' council; the church maintains headquarters in Cleveland, Ohio. The *Newsletter* (Church of God and Saints of Christ), published every two weeks, serves to inform members through sermons, lectures, and announcements. An a cappella choir formed of members of the church has released recordings of gospel music to critical acclaim.

COMMUNITY CHURCHES, INTERNATIONAL COUNCIL OF

Founded: 1950
Membership: est. 200,000 in approx. 500 churches (1999)

Not a denomination in the traditional sense, the International Council of Community Churches provides services to several hundred independently organized and operated community churches in the U.S. and around the world. Community Churches date from the mid-1800s, but were first organized nationally in 1933. Community Churches are a result of the desire to eliminate over churching in some communities and to solve attendant economic and staffing problems; to replace the restrictiveness and divisiveness of denominationalism with self-determination and Christian unity; to refocus primary loyalty from organizations outside a community to the community itself; and, by addressing specific needs within a community, to effect a more relevant religion.

Since each church is adjusted to the needs of a different community, there is much variety among Community Churches in worship, work and witness styles, and methods. Several general categories exist. Federated and United Churches have resulted from mergers of congregations previously affiliated with certain denominations. Some have continued alignments with two or more denominations; others have become entirely independent. Some individual congregations also have severed denominational ties; others have affiliated with the Community Church movement while continuing relationships with one or more denominations. However, the majority of Community Churches never have had denominational affiliation.

The stated purposes of the council are (1) to be an answer to Christ's prayer: "That they may all be one" (John 17:21 NRSV); (2) to affirm the worth and dignity of every person; (3) to attend to human need and suffering throughout the world; (4) to seek and share the truth; (5) to build toward a new world of peace.

The current organization resulted from a 1950 merger of two other councils: one composed of predominantly black congregations, the other of churches with predominantly white memberships. The council holds an annual conference to which every member church can send two voting members, at least one of which must be a lay person. This conference elects a president, an executive director, a board of trustees, and other officers who carry on the business of the Council between conferences. The executive director and a small staff oversee the projects of the Council on a daily basis; headquarters are in Frankfort, Illinois. The Council's services include ecclesiastical endorsement, personnel placement, continuing education, direct and brokered consultation for help in various areas, and supportive networks for clergy and their spouses and children. Publications include *The Christian Community,* a monthly newspaper; *The Pastor's Journal,* a quarterly for professionals; and materials from the Community Church Press.

It should be noted that many of the Council's member churches do not use the word *Community* in their names. Moreover, many churches that do include this term in their names are affiliated with a denomination, are members of a national organization outside the historic movement, or are independent congregations.

CONGREGATIONAL CHURCHES

The proper form of church polity or structure of authority has been an issue in Christianity since New Testament times. The dominant Catholic/Orthodox tradition resolved that issue in favor of episcopacy or rule by bishops. As the Protestant Reformation developed in the sixteenth century, polity became one of the key issues. The Reformed tradition, associated with John Calvin (1509–64) and John Knox (ca. 1513–72), rejected episcopacy in favor of a presbyterial system in which a council of clergy had authority. In England, dissent took corporate form in the Puritan movement, of which Congregationalism represented the most radical wing. In Congregationalism, the assembled body of believers on the local level has authority. Many Christian bodies, such as the Baptists (see BAPTIST CHURCHES) and the various Christian Church groups (see CHRISTIAN CHURCHES), hold to congregational polity.

In 1609, John Robinson (1575–1625) fled persecution in England and settled at Leiden in the Netherlands, with the exiled congregation from Scrooby in Nottinghamshire, England. There he met William Ames (1576–1633), Congregationalism's first great theologian, who was also a fugitive from the ecclesiastical courts of England. In conversation with Ames and others, Robinson was converted from rigid Separatism to Congregationalism.

For twelve years, Robinson and his congregation enjoyed peace and freedom under the Dutch. However, they were haunted by the conviction that their children would not grow up as English people, and a large part of the company sailed for the American colonies in 1620 aboard the historic *Mayflower*. In a hostile new world, with the wilderness before them and the sea at their backs, they helped to lay the foundations of the American commonwealth. They established their own covenant together as believers and citizens, thus establishing early forms of democratic government.

Between 1630 and 1640, 20,000 more Puritans arrived at Massachusetts Bay. Even less inclined toward Separatism than was the Plymouth colony, the settlers of the bay established an effective "theocratic" government. Church and commonwealth were that society's two instruments. Contrary to popular belief, it was not a stern and rigid regime of the saints, but it was strict and could be as intolerant of religious dissent as the Church of England was. The story of the banishment of radicals like Anne Hutchinson (1591–1643) and Roger Williams (1603–83) are well known. When four Quakers (see FRIENDS), including a woman, were hanged on Boston Common in the 1660s (after the end of the Puritan Commonwealth in England), there was a public outcry in England. Following the Golden Revolution, New England was forced to accept the Act of Toleration in 1689.

Congregationalists like Jonathan Edwards (1703–58) of Northampton played leading roles in the First Great Awakening in the 1730s and 1740s. That revival was marked not only by the eloquence of George Whitefield (1715–70) but also by the vigorous writings and preaching of Edwards, whose books are now regarded as American classics.

Congregationalists in New England were leaders in the American Revolution, and during the next century Congregationalism played a major role in developing American institutional and religious life. In the field of education, this church had already made tremendous contributions. Members of this church founded Harvard in 1636. Yale (founded 1707) was a project for the education of Congregationalist clergy in Connecticut. Dartmouth (founded 1769) developed from Eleazer Wheelock's (1711–79) school for Native Americans. These schools were among the first colleges in North America.

Interest in missions among Congregationalists began the day the Pilgrims landed at Plymouth. John Eliot (1604–90), Thomas Mayhew (c. 1620–57), Jonathan Mayhew (1720–1766), and David Brainerd (1718-47) worked among Native Americans during the Colonial era. Eliot spent seven years mastering Algonquian and translated the Bible (NT 1661, OT 1663) and published a catechism in 1653, the first book to be printed in a Native American language. By 1674 there were four thousand "praying Indians" in New England and twenty-four native preachers.

The American Board of Commissioners for Foreign Missions, organized in 1810, was concerned at first with both home and foreign missionary work. On it served not only Congregationalists but also representatives of Presbyterian (see PRESBYTERIAN CHURCHES), Dutch Reformed, and Associate Reformed churches (see REFORMED CHURCHES). Missionaries were sent to more than thirty foreign countries and American territories. In Hawaii, Congregational missionaries taught a whole nation of people to read and write and laid the foundations of a constitutionally democratic government. The rise of denominationalism worked against the complexion of the American Board, and by the 1950s all non-Congregationalists had withdrawn to go their separate ways.

In 1826, the American Home Missionary Society was founded, and in 1846 the American Missionary Association, which was active in the South before the Civil War, was founded. It was especially effective toward the end of that conflict with its "contraband" schools for black persons, one of which became Hampton Institute.

Meanwhile, differences of opinion between theological liberals and conservatives were developing within the church. Strict Calvinists and Trinitarians were opposed by Unitarians (see UNITARIAN UNIVERSALIST ASSOCIATION). A famous sermon by William Ellery Channing (1780–1842) at Baltimore in 1819 made a division inevitable. The American Unitarian Association was established in 1825, and almost all of the older Congregational churches in eastern Massachusetts went Unitarian; only one Congregational church was left in Boston. Debate and legal action over property and funds were not concluded until about 1840.

In spite of Unitarian defection, Congregationalism continued to grow until a national supervisory body became necessary. A council held at Boston in 1865 proved so effective that a regular system of councils was established. Following conferences between the associations into which the churches had grouped themselves, the first of these national councils was called at Oberlin, Ohio, in 1871. Known as the National Council of the Congregational Christian Churches, it met biennially and acted as an overall advisory body for the entire fellowship.

The "wider fellowship" was taken seriously; unity and cooperation across denominational lines have been outstanding characteristics of Congregationalism. Christian Endeavor, at one time the largest young people's organization in Protestantism, was founded in 1881 by a Congregationalist, Francis E. Clark (1851–1921). By 1885 it had become interdenominational, known the world over as the United Society of Christian Endeavor.

In 1925, the Evangelical Protestant Church of North America joined the National Council of Congregational Churches in the Evangelical Protestant Conference of Congregational Churches. This group in turn merged with the Christian Church in 1931 to become the Congregational Christian Churches; and in 1957, this body joined with the Evangelical and Reformed Churches to form the United Church of Christ. These affiliations witness to the widening fellowship and vision of Congregationalists.

CONGREGATIONAL CHRISTIAN CHURCHES
(National Association)

Founded: 1955
Membership: 66,262 in 416 churches (2000)

This association was organized in order to "preserve historical Congregational forms of freedom and fellowship (the Congregational Way)." It is the largest of several Congregational bodies that did not participate when the General Council of Congregational Churches and the Evangelical and Reformed Church merged with the United Church of Christ in 1957 (see UNITED CHURCH OF CHRIST). The National Association brings local churches together for counsel, inspiration, and fellowship, but still preserves the independence and autonomy of the local churches. It describes its mission as encouraging and assisting local churches "in their development of vibrant and effective witnesses to Christ in congregational ways."

There is no binding ecclesiastical authority and no required creed or program. Members "are bound together not by uniformity of belief but by the acceptance of a covenant purpose to be 'the people of God.' " The association leaves to each church any decision to participate in social and political questions and action.

A moderator presides over an annual meeting of representatives of all the member churches; an executive committee of twelve, elected for four-year terms, acts for the association between meetings. An executive secretary and a staff of twelve are employed by the National Association to oversee day-to-day operations; headquarters are in Oak Creek, Wisconsin. Six commissions (Christian education, Communication Commission, women's work, youth, world Christian relations, and spiritual resources) work under the direction of the executive committee. Five divisions of the National Association provide a Missionary Society, a Building and Loan Fund, the Congregational Foundation for Theological Studies, the

Division for Ministry, and Congregational Church Development. A unique feature of the organization is its Referendum Council, which, upon call of 10 percent of the churches and by a two-thirds vote, may modify any action or proposal of any of the national bodies or officers of the association.

There is widespread missionary work in the U.S. and in the Philippines, Mexico, Hong Kong, Formosa, Greece, Italy, Germany, Brazil, Central America, and southern India. The *Congregationalist,* a denominational periodical founded in 1849, was revived in 1958 as the journal of the association.

CONSERVATIVE CONGREGATIONAL CHRISTIAN CONFERENCE

Founded: 1948
Membership: 40,414 in 242 churches (1999)

The origins of this group go back to 1935 and the work of H. B. Sandine, a pastor in Hancock, Minnesota, who was convinced that the Congregational Christian churches had departed from the beliefs, policy, and practices of historic Congregationalism. He carried on an educational effort through mimeographed documents until 1939, when his efforts were consummated in a monthly publication, *The Congregational Beacon.* This later became *The Congregational Christian* and, finally, the bimonthly *Foresee.* A Conservative Congregational Christian Fellowship was organized at Chicago in 1945. The ongoing process of merger among Congregational bodies (see CONGREGATIONAL CHURCHES) precipitated the Fellowship's reorganization into the Conservative Congregational Christian Conference in 1948.

The Conference's statement of faith is conservative and evangelical. It includes belief in: the infallibility and authority of the scriptures; the Trinity; the deity, virgin birth, sinlessness, atoning death, resurrection, ascension, and promised return of Jesus Christ; regeneration by the Holy Spirit; the resurrection of both the saved and the lost; and the spiritual unity of all believers in Christ.

Local churches are completely autonomous. An annual meeting of clergy and lay representatives from member churches elects a board of directors and a set of officers for the Conference. The national officers include a president, a vice president, a recording secretary,

124

an executive director (conference minister), a treasurer, and a controller, all of whom are elected for three-year terms. The board of directors manages the property and directs the general business of the conference; an executive committee is composed of the officers, with the president as chair. Fifteen subordinate committees guide the various efforts of the conference. General offices are located in St. Paul, Minnesota.

Work is largely in the areas of missions, church planting, and Christian education, carried on through recognized evangelical home and foreign mission agencies, Bible institutions, colleges, seminaries, and Sunday school publishing houses. The conference is especially active in the fields of church extension, pastoral placement, and regional activities.

UNITED CHURCH OF CHRIST

Founded: 1957, with roots to Colonial days
Membership: 1,401,682 in 5,961 congregations (1999)

Four churches of significant importance in American history constitute the United Church of Christ: the Congregational churches, the Christian Church (see CHRISTIAN CHURCHES), the Evangelical Synod, and the Reformed Church in the U.S. (see REFORMED CHURCHES). The first two bodies merged in 1931 to become Congregational Christian Churches. They were joined in 1957 by the merger of Evangelical and Reformed churches. The union was complete when the constitution was adopted at Philadelphia in July 1961.

On July 8, 1959, at Oberlin, Ohio, representatives of the Congregational Christian Churches and the Evangelical and Reformed Church, upon merging into the United Church of Christ, adopted the following statement, understood as a "testimony rather than a test of faith."

We believe in God, the Eternal Spirit, Father of our Lord Jesus Christ and our Father, and to his deeds we testify: He calls the worlds into being, creates man in his own image and sets before him the ways of life and death. He seeks in holy love to save all people from aimlessness and sin. He judges men and nations by his righteous will declared through prophets and apostles. In Jesus Christ, the man of Nazareth, our crucified and risen Lord, he has come to us and shared our common lot, conquering sin and death and reconciling the world

125

to himself. He bestows upon us his Holy Spirit, creating and renewing the Church of Jesus Christ, binding in covenant faithful people of all ages, tongues, and races. He calls us into his Church to accept the cost and joy of discipleship, to be his servants in the service of men, to proclaim the gospel to all the world and resist the powers of evil, to share in Christ's baptism and eat at his table, to join him in his passion and victory. He promises to all who trust him forgiveness of sins and fullness of grace, courage in the struggle for justice and peace, his presence in trial and rejoicing, and eternal life in his kingdom which has no end. Blessing and honor, glory and power be unto him. Amen.

Although this statement was not intended to set forth doctrinal positions (the doctrines and theological positions of the four churches now within the United Church of Christ remain as they were), or to stand as a substitute for the historic creeds, confessions, and covenants of the churches involved, it served as a witness to the faith, charity, and understanding of the merging groups.

The United Church of Christ represents a union of congregationalism and presbyterianism. The church establishes congregationalism as the rule for the local congregation and presbyterianism as the basis of organization of the member churches' connectional life. The constitution is explicit: "The autonomy of the local church is inherent and modifiable only by its own action. Nothing . . . shall destroy or limit the right of each local church to continue to operate in the way customary to it."

Alongside the local church stand associations, conferences, and the general synod. Local churches in a geographical area are grouped into an association, which is concerned with the welfare of the churches within its area. It assists needy churches; receives new churches into the United Church of Christ; licenses, ordains, and installs clergy; adopts its own constitution, bylaws, and rules of procedure; and is made up of the ordained ministers and elected lay delegates of the area. Associations meet regularly and are related to the general synod through their conferences.

Associations are grouped into conferences, again by geographical area, with the exception of the Calvin Synod, a nongeographic conference made up of churches from the Hungarian Reformed tradition. The voting members of a conference are ordained ministers of associations in the conference and lay delegates elected from local churches. A conference acts on requests and references from the local churches, associations, general synod, and other bodies. It

126

meets annually, and its main function is to coordinate the work and witness of its local churches and associations, to render counsel and advisory service, and to establish conference offices, centers, institutions, and other agencies.

The General Synod is the highest representative body; it meets biennially and is composed of conference delegates and voting members of boards of directors of the Covenanted Ministries of the church. The General Synod nominates and elects a General Minister and President, an Associate General Minister, and members of the Boards of Directors of the Covenanted Ministries: Office of General Ministries, Local Church Ministries, Wider Church Ministries, and Justice and Witness Ministries. An Executive Council is elected by the General Synod to act for the synod between its meetings. It recommends salaries for officers of the church as part of a national budget, has responsibility for the church's publications, prepares the agenda for all meetings of the General Synod, and appoints committees not otherwise provided. It also submits to the General Synod "any recommendation it may deem useful" for the work of the church. General church offices are located in Cleveland, Ohio, as is the church's publishing arm, Pilgrim Press.

Since 1985, the United Church of Christ has enjoyed an ecumenical partnership with the Christian Church (Disciples of Christ). Both denominations are active in the Consultation on Church Union; and they join in common witness through Global Ministries, which operates teaching and service ministries throughout the world. The United Church of Christ remains a leader in cooperative Christianity, especially through its ministries in education, social action, and service.

Twenty-nine colleges and universities are related to the United Church of Christ, six of which are historically African American.

DIVINE SCIENCE

Founded: 1898
Membership: 16 churches (2000)

The principles and practice of Divine Science were developed in the late nineteenth century through the work of Aletha Brooks Small, Fannie Brooks James, Nona Lovell Brooks (all sisters), and Malinda E. Cramer. When the sisters, who lived in Denver, Colorado, met Cramer, of San Francisco, California, they all realized they had developed similar ideas independently. They joined forces in 1898 and organized the Divine Science College and the First Divine Science Church of Denver.

The core of Divine Science teaching is the principle of the all-inclusive God-mind: "The principle of the omnipresence of God means He is the One Presence containing all Wisdom, Power, and Substance." Human beings are understood to be the children of God, to be of God, and to be like God; knowledge of this truth frees persons to attain a larger concept of God and the understanding of one's higher nature. Acording to Nona Brooks, the essence of Divine Science is "the practice of the presence of God." Adherents carry out this practice through study of the Bible and other writings (including writings by the founders), through prayer, through contemplation, and through meditation.

All of the founders had the experience of divine healing, and the emphasis on healing naturally persists. Healing comes through an understanding of the nature of God and the Universal Law and is "the cleansing of the inner man from all that is unlike God." Divine Science does not deny the existence of visible matter but interprets form and substance as manifestations of God. Practitioners believe that the human mind is linked with the divine mind. Thoughts, feelings, words, and actions have an impact on one's life, health, and circumstances. Prayer is therefore seen as a way to transform one's own mind, not as a way to change the mind of God. Jesus is recognized as a man who realized his full divine potential and shows the way for others to do likewise.

For many years local churches and colleges of Divine Science were independent of one another. In 1957 some of the ministers and key workers met and organized the Divine Science Federation International. This organization serves its member churches and centers and cooperates with Brooks Divinity School, in Denver, which trains clergy, teachers, and practitioners, and with Divine Science School, in Washington, D.C. Churches, centers, and study groups are found in several major U.S. cities and abroad; Federation headquarters are in St. Louis, Missouri. Divine Science is also affiliated with the International New Thought Alliance.

EPISCOPAL / ANGLICAN CHURCHES

The Anglican Church is the Church of England, which severed allegiance to the papacy during the Protestant Reformation. In doing so, however, the Church of England sought to maintain an unbroken historical continuity to the Christian church in England from the early fourth century. The historical succession of bishops, or the episcopacy, is the visible sign of this long tradition of English Christianity, and as Great Britain established colonies around the world, the Anglican Church, in various national forms, was established throughout the then British Empire. It has often been viewed as a "middle way" between Roman Catholicism and Protestantism, and during the past five hundred years, there has been tension in Anglican churches between those who favor a more Catholic/traditional stance and those who adopt more Protestant principles.

It was King Henry VIII who first rejected papal supremacy (in favor of royal supremacy) in the 1530s. During the reign of his successor, Edward VI, the Anglican Church became more clearly Protestant and adopted *The Book of Common Prayer,* which has exerted considerable influence on the worship and piety of all English-speaking churches, and the Forty-two Articles of Religion (reduced to Thirty-nine Articles under Queen Elizabeth I). Tensions arose over issues of episcopacy, royal supremacy, and the prayer book during the reign of Elizabeth I. The so-called Puritans advocated for a more Reformed/Calvinist style of Christianity (see CONGREGATIONAL CHURCHES), but episcopacy was firmly established in the Anglican Church following the English Civil War and Interregnum in the seventeenth century.

The Anglican Church took its current form during the era of Richard Hooker (ca. 1554–1600), late in the sixteenth century. Aesthetic in orientation, it incorporates theology into liturgy and makes use of the senses of sight and taste as well as those of hearing and speaking. This church relies on the traditional liturgy in its worship; but it is distinctive in leaving undefined the exact nature of the Communion bread and wine, regarded as a spiritual mystery. The church acknowledges no central authority, although bishops are important symbols of unity. Its sources of belief and practice are the Bible, the tradition of the church, and reason. Anglican clergy are called priests and have the authority of the apostolate.

The Anglican Church came to the United States along with English colonization. When Sir Francis Drake (ca. 1540–96) came ashore in 1578 in what is now California, his chaplain, Francis Fletcher, planted a cross and read a prayer as Drake claimed the new land for the Elizabeth I. Later colonists came to Virginia with Sir Walter Raleigh (ca. 1552–1618), whose chaplain baptized a native named Manteo and the first English immigrant baby, named Virginia Dare. With Captain John Smith (ca. 1580–1631) came chaplain Robert Hunt (ca. 1568–1608), who stretched a sail between two trees for a shelter and read the service from *The Book of Common Prayer.*

In the southern colonies, the Church of England became the established church, but many colonists who had emigrated to escape royal authority in religious matters were suspicious of the established church. The church was staffed by British clergy and supported by public taxes and assessment. The Society for the Propagation of the Gospel was established in England in 1701 to help support the poorly paid American clergy and spread the work of the church westward. The American branch of the church was technically under the jurisdiction of the bishop of London, since there was no American bishop during the Colonial period. This meant that it was necessary for colonial ministers to make the long journey to England for ordination, and few could afford it. This, coupled with the rising tide of revolutionary fervor, placed the colonial Church of England in an unenviable position.

Yet the church did well, and membership grew rapidly. William and Mary College was established in 1693; King's Chapel in Boston was opened in 1689; in 1698 a church was established at Newport, Rhode Island, and another, Trinity Church, in New York City.

Nonetheless, the American Revolution almost destroyed the colonial Church of England. Under a special oath of allegiance to the king, the clergy either fled to England or Canada or remained as Loyalists in the Colonies in the face of persecution. The church did provide many leaders of the American cause, however, including George Washington, Thomas Jefferson, Patrick Henry, John Jay, Robert Morris, John Marshall, John Randolph, Charles Lee, and "Light-Horse" Harry Lee. Still, in the popular mind, episcopacy was associated with the British crown rather than with independence. At war's end the church had no bishop, no association of the churches, and not even the semblance of an establishment. Few thought there was a future for Anglicanism in the U.S.

However, the clergy who remained in the new nation reorganized the church, and in 1783 a conference of the churches met at Annapolis, Maryland. They formally adopted the name "Protestant Episcopal Church." It was Protestant to distinguish it from Roman Catholicism, episcopal to distinguish it from the Presbyterian and Congregational churches. Also in 1783, the clergy in Connecticut elected Samuel Seabury (1729–96) as their prospective bishop. He went to England and waited a year for consecration by English bishops but was denied. He then went to Scotland and obtained consecration there in 1784.

Ultimately, the British Parliament and the Church of England accepted the existence of a separate American church. Two other bishops-elect (from New York and Pennsylvania) were consecrated by the Archbishop of Canterbury in 1787. In 1789, during the first meeting of the House of Bishops, the church constitution was adopted in Philadelphia, *The Book of Common Prayer* was revised for American use, and the Protestant Episcopal Church became an independent, self-governing body. Over time it would be subject to several schisms and reunions.

ANGLICAN CATHOLIC CHURCH

Founded: 1977
Membership: est. 12,000 in 200 parishes (1988)

In 1977 an international congress of nearly 2,000 Anglican bishops, clergy, and laypeople met in St. Louis to voice their opposition to changes in the Episcopal Church (see EPISCOPAL CHURCH), particularly the ordination of women and revisions to the prayer book. From this meeting of conservative bishops came the Anglican

Church of North America, which changed its name to the Anglican Catholic Church in 1978 when a constitution was adopted. This body reaffirmed faith in the seven ecumenical councils of the church and a commitment to catholic principles. Bishop Albert Chambers was the head of the new body.

The American dioceses of this international body use only the 1928 American version of *The Book of Common Prayer.* The Eucharist is celebrated each Sunday and on holy days, but daily celebration is encouraged. Clergy are expected to say the daily offices, including the monthly recitation of the psalter. Seven sacraments are observed: baptism, confirmation, holy Eucharist, holy matrimony, holy orders, penance, and unction of the sick.

Following the 1977 convention of conservative bishops, the Anglican Catholic Church continued to experience division and subdivision. The Province of Christ the King has maintained a separate existence since 1979 and has about fifty parishes nationwide. The United Episcopal Church was formed in 1980. The Anglican Rite Jurisdiction of the Americas was established in 1991 through a merger of the American Episcopal Church and a sizable portion of the Anglican Catholic Church.

EPISCOPAL CHURCH

Founded: 1789
Membership: 2,317,794 in 7,390 parishes (1998)

The largest body to come out of the Church of England in the United States has simply been known as the Episcopal Church since 1967. It has been one of the most influential churches in American history and has provided many national leaders, including presidents, supreme court justices, and generals. In the nineteenth century, it was also actively involved in establishing Sunday schools, Bible societies, theological seminaries, colleges, hospitals, boarding schools, guilds for men and women, and a domestic and foreign missionary society. By 1830 the Protestant Episcopal Church had 12 bishops, 20 dioceses, 6,000 clergy, and 1,250,000 communicants.

The Protestant Episcopal Church was the only major denomination that did not divide over the issue of slavery and the secession of the Confederate States. There were New England clergy who were abolitionists, and a Louisiana bishop, Leonidas Polk (1806–64), was a Confederate general under Lee; but Polk prayed for Bishop Charles McIlvaine (1799–1873) of Ohio in public, and the Ohioan prayed for Polk. They were still in one church. A temporary Protestant Episcopal Church in the Confederate States was organized to carry on the work in the South, but the names of Southern bishops were still called in the general convention in New York in 1862. Once the war was over, the Episcopal house was quickly reunited.

The prayer book and the episcopacy remained the glue that held this diverse and active church together. W. A. Muhlenberg (1796–1877) called for a wider catholicity in the Protestant Episcopal Church, which resulted in the famous Chicago Lambeth Quadrilateral on Church Unity in 1888. From this activity came a further revision of the *American Book of Common Prayer* in 1892.

Members of the Episcopal Church profess two of the ancient Christian creeds: the Apostles' Creed and the Nicene Creed. The articles of the Church of England, with the exception of the 21st and modification of the 8th, 35th, and 36th, are accepted as a general statement of doctrine, but adherence to them as a creed is not required. The clergy also make the following declaration: "I do believe the Holy Scriptures of the Old and New Testaments to be the Word of God, and to contain all things necessary to salvation; and I do solemnly engage to conform to the doctrine, discipline, and worship of the Episcopal Church."

The church expects its members to be loyal to the "doctrine, discipline and worship of the one Holy Catholic and Apostolic Church" in all the essentials, but permits great liberty in nonessentials. It allows for variation, individuality, independent thinking, and religious liberty. Liberals and conservatives, modernists and fundamentalists find common ground for worship in the prayer book.

Two sacraments, baptism and the Eucharist, are recognized as "certain sure witnesses and effectual agencies of God's love and grace." Baptism by pouring, sprinkling, or immersion is necessary for both children and adults. Baptism by any church in the name of the Trinity is recognized as valid. Baptized persons are confirmed as members of the church by the bishop. Adults who receive laying on of hands by a bishop at baptism are considered confirmed. Without stating or defining the holy mystery, the Episcopal Church believes in the real presence of Christ in the elements of the Eucharist. The church also recognizes a sacramental character in confirmation, penance, orders, matrimony, and unction.

The episcopal form of government is a federal union, each diocese autonomous in its own sphere, originally associated with others for the maintenance of a common doctrine, discipline, and worship. To those objectives have been added the unification, development, and prosecution of missionary, educational, and social programs. Each diocese functions through a bishop (elected locally, with the approval of the episcopate and representatives of clergy and laity from the whole church), who is the spiritual and administrative head. There is a diocesan legislative body made up of the clergy of the diocese and representatives of the local congregations, which meets annually; a standing committee of clergy and laity, advisers and assessors to the bishop; and, usually, a program board.

The typical pattern for the local congregation is the parish, which elects its own minister (rector or priest), who is vested with pastoral oversight of the congregation and, with the wardens and vestry representatives, administers the temporal affairs and the property of the parish. Each parish and parochial district (mission or chapel) is represented in the annual diocesan convention by its clergy and elected lay delegates (usually in proportion to the congregation's constituency); each diocese is represented in the triennial General Convention of the church by its bishop (or bishops) and clergy and lay deputies elected in equal numbers (at present, four of each). Between sessions of the General Convention, the work of the church is carried on by the presiding bishop and an executive council. The church maintains headquarters in New York City.

Some Episcopal churches are "high," with elaborate ritual and ceremony; others are described as "low," with less involved ceremony and more of an evangelistic emphasis. But all value the prayer book, which contains the heart of both New Testament and Old Testament devotions. Members have built stately cathedrals in the U.S., such as the Cathedral of St. John the Divine in New York City, the third largest in the world, and the Cathedral of Saints Peter and Paul, the national cathedral in Washington, D.C. Stained-glass windows, gleaming altars, vested choirs, and a glorious ritual not only are beautiful, but also give the worshiper a deep sense of the continuity of the Christian spirit and tradition.

Financial support is given to fund U.S. dioceses, the Navajoland Episcopal Church (an area mission in the Southwest), and several small, primarily rural, western dioceses. Special emphasis is placed on urban ministries, ministry in college communities, and ministry to

African American, Hispanic, Native American, and Asian American congregations. Overseas missions are located in all U.S. territories and in the Dominican Republic, Haiti, India, Japan, the Middle East, Liberia, Mexico, Okinawa, Taiwan, and Central America.

The church sponsors twelve accredited seminaries in the U.S., plus three overseas; nine colleges; one university; over eighty homes for the aged; over ninety institutions and agencies for child and youth care; and over forty hospitals, homes, and convalescent clinics. It has religious orders of monks and nuns, sisters and friars; nine communities for men, eleven for women, and two for both men and women.

Two major developments in the past few years have been subjects of debate and division in the Episcopal Church: prayer book revision and the ordination of women to the priesthood. The General Convention of 1976 gave first approval to *The Proposed Book of Common Prayer,* the first revision of the American prayer book since 1928 and the first to use contemporary language. Much of the Elizabethan idiom, however, has been retained. The Holy Eucharist, morning and evening prayer, the service for burial of the dead, and all the collects for the church year appear in both contemporary and traditional language; Archbishop Cranmer's (1489–1556) "Great Litany" was somewhat revised, but appears in its traditional form. All other services, including those for baptism, matrimony, confirmation, and ordination, were revised or rewritten in contemporary idiom. The new prayer book was passed by an overwhelming majority at the 1979 convention. A new hymnal, the first since 1940, was approved in 1982.

The issue of women's ordination is extremely complex. Actually, it has to do with the historical doctrine of the uninterrupted line of succession in the historical episcopate, the apostolic succession, in which only men had been ordained in the threefold ministries of deacon, priest, and bishop. The opposition to ordination of women came from two groups: those who believed it impossible for women to be priests and those who believed that the General Convention, albeit the supreme legislative authority of the Episcopal Church, had no right to decide this question without some kind of ecumenical council.

The general convention of 1970 authorized the ordination of women to the diaconate. Ordination of women to the priesthood finally passed in 1976. In 1988, the Reverend Barbara C. Harris was elected Suffragan Bishop of Massachusetts, and in February 1989, she was ordained the first woman bishop in the historic succession.

EPISCOPAL ORTHODOX CHRISTIAN ARCHDIOCESE OF AMERICA

Founded: 1963
Membership: est. 6,000 in 200 churches (2000)

Until 1999, this body was known as the Anglican Orthodox Church, and it was established when the Rev. James Parker Dees resigned from the priesthood of the Protestant Episcopal Church in 1963 to protest what he believed to be "its failure to proclaim firmly the biblical doctrine, and . . . its emphasis on the social gospel and pro-communist program." His group sought to preserve the traditional Anglicanism, especially the belief in the fundamental (King James) Bible truths and morality, the 1928 *Book of Common Prayer,* the Thirty-nine Articles of Religion without revision, the homilies, the doctrines of the Anglican Reformers, and other basic Anglican traditions and church government. Dees was consecrated bishop by Bishop Wasyl Sawyna of the Holy Ukrainian Autocephalic Orthodox Church and Bishop Orlando J. Woodward of the Old Catholic succession.

The doctrines of the virgin birth, the atoning sacrifice of the cross, the Trinity, the resurrection, the Second Coming, salvation by faith alone, and the divinity of Christ are emphasized. The clergy of the church are trained at Cranmer Seminary in Statesville, North Carolina.

Although remaining small in number in the U.S., the Episcopal Orthodox Christian Archdiocese of America has sponsored movements in Africa and Asia that have grown exponentially. In 1999, the American body came under the jurisdiction of the Anglican Rite Synod in the Americas, which is itself under the jurisdiction of the Philippine Independent Catholic Church.

INTERNATIONAL COMMUNION OF THE CHARISMATIC EPISCOPAL CHURCH

Founded: 1992
Membership: 600 parishes (2000)

Founded by Bishop Austin Randolph Adler, this communion seeks to combine Pentecostal/charismatic experience with liturgical worship. It is a new and growing fellowship of charismatic churches that maintain their identification with traditional Episcopalianism.

136

Tracing its origins to an expressed desire among various evangelicals in the 1970s for connection with "historical Christianity," the church endeavors to bring the rich sacramental and liturgical life of the early church to searching evangelicals and charismatics.

The Charismatic Episcopal Church holds to traditional Christian doctrine as expressed in the Apostles' and Nicene creeds; doctrine was given explicit formulation in the "San Clemente Declaration 1999." Church teaching gives priority to worship and liturgical practice in community life. Stressing that it is not a splinter group but an intentional religious community drawing on a rich theological and liturgical heritage, the Communion intends to "provide a home for all Christians who seek a liturgical-sacramental, evangelical, charismatic church and a foundation for their lives and gifts of ministry."

The Communion maintains relations with groups in over twenty countries, reporting a worldwide communicant membership of over 200,000 in approximately 1,000 parishes. As an Episcopal communion, the governance of the church is in the hands of bishops who are understood to be pastors of the church and who must be rectors in thir own parishes. The office of the Patriarch and that of the General Secretary are in San Clemente, California.

NATIONAL ORGANIZATION OF THE NEW APOSTOLIC CHURCH OF NORTH AMERICA

Founded: 1862
Membership: 36,254 in 385 congregations (1999)

The New Apostolic Church of North America is a variant or schism of the Catholic Apostolic Church movement in England, a movement that originated with Edward Irving (1792–1834), a Presbyterian pastor in London. It is difficult to place this body into a category because it emerged from the evangelical movement in the Anglican Church, adopted some Pentecostal practices, and over the years moved closer to Roman Catholic practice and piety. The founders of the church believed in the imminent return of Christ, and in preparation for the eschaton they attempted to recreate the apostolic offices of the church. Thus there were apostles, prophets, evangelists, pastors, and so on. The twelve apostles held their first conference in 1835. Soon the movement spread to the U.S. and

Germany, where several Roman Catholic priests became members in secret. Debate arose in 1860 over the appointment of new apostles to fill vacancies left by attrition. Because of his insistence on twelve apostles at the head of the true church and his proposal of the election of new ones, Bishop Schwarz of Hamburg was excommunicated from the Catholic Apostolic Church in 1862. To lead the dissenting body, a priest named Preuss was elected to the office of apostle "through the spirit of prophecy," and Bishop Schwarz served under him until his own elevation to the apostolic office.

Under Preuss and Schwarz, the New Apostolic Church spread from Europe to North America, where today it is organized into districts under apostles, bishops, and elders. This church teaches that only the apostles have received from Christ the commission and power to forgive sin. Each church has a rector and one or more assistants (priests, deacons, etc.) who usually serve without remuneration. All clergy and other "office-bearers" are selected by the apostleship. The American church is a constituent of the international organization supervised by Chief Apostle Richard Fehr in Zurich, Switzerland.

The New Apostolic Church of North America accepts the Apostles' Creed, but adds a number of articles that stress the authority and inspiration of the living apostles as well as the Bible, the apostolic ordinances of the laying on of hands, the necessity of gifts of the Holy Spirit, freewill offerings, and the speedy, personal, pre-millennial return of Christ. Three means of grace are found in three sacraments: baptism (including children), Holy Communion, and Holy Sealing (the dispensing and reception of the Holy Spirit). Work "along broader interior and missionary lines" is conducted in the U.S., Canada, Mexico, and Puerto Rico. The international organization has more than nine million members in over 52,000 branches around the world.

REFORMED EPISCOPAL CHURCH

Founded: 1873
Membership: est. 6,400 in 125 parishes (1998)

The Reformed Episcopal Church was organized in New York City by Bishop George D. Cummins (1822–76), eight clergy, and twenty laypersons who had been members of the Protestant Episcopal Church. This body emerged during the long Tractarian controversy in England and the United States, in which the issues of church ritual and ecclesiastical authority became prominent. Cummins was a leader of the evangelical party, which objected to the increased use of vestments, ornaments, and sacerdotal rituals in the Episcopal Church. He also protested what he perceived to be intolerance of other Protestant churches among those influenced by the Oxford Movement, the movement in the Church of England that sought to restore the high church ideas and practices of the seventeenth century. In October 1873, Cummins participated in an ecumenical, evangelical communion service held in Fifth Avenue Presbyterian Church in New York. In the face of public criticism from other bishops, and in the conviction that the catholic nature and mission of the Protestant Episcopal Church were being lost, Cummins withdrew to found the new denomination. Later in 1873 he drew up The Declaration of Principles, the basis of the Reformed Episcopal Church, which are understood to be "an expression of evangelical understanding of the traditional Thirty-nine Articles of Anglicanism."

Doctrine and organization are similar to those of the parent church, with several important exceptions. The Reformed Episcopal Church rejects the doctrines that the Lord's table is an altar on which the body and blood of Christ are offered anew to the Father, that the presence of Christ in the Lord's Supper resides in the elements of bread and wine, and that regeneration is inseparably connected with baptism. It also denies that Christian ministers are priests, in any sense other than that in which all believers are a "royal priesthood." Clergy ordained in other churches are not reordained upon entering the ministry of the Reformed Episcopal Church, and members are admitted on letters of dismissal from other Protestant denominations.

Worship is liturgical; at Sunday morning services, the use of *The Book of Common Prayer,* revised to remove certain sacerdotal elements, is required. Parishes may use the 1928 prayer book. At other services its use is optional, and the minister may pray extemporaneously at any service.

Parish and synodical units prevail in the administration of the church. The triennial General Council is like the General Convention of the Episcopal Church; however, its bishops do not constitute a separate house. The church has seven dioceses in North America (four in the U.S.) and carries out oversees work in India, France, Brazil, Uganda, and Germany. There are seminaries in Philadelphia, Pennsylvania; Summerville, South Carolina; and Shreveport, Louisiana.

SOUTHERN EPISCOPAL CHURCH

Founded: 1962
Membership: statistics not available

With the motto "clinging to an unchanging faith in a changing world," this body represents another form of conservative Anglicanism in the U.S. It was founded in Nashville, Tennessee, by clergy who felt that the Episcopal Church was being threatened by liberalism and who called for a return to the traditional faith and practices of Anglicanism (see EPISCOPAL/ANGLICAN CHURCHES). Among the main tenets of the church are an emphasis on the truth of the Scripture, the usefulness of the apocryphal books, and the unchanging nature of the ancient creeds.

Bishop B. H. Webster became the first Presiding Bishop, succeeded in 1990 by Bishop Huron C. Manning, Jr. By 1992, the Southern Episcopal Church had grown to include five dioceses and missionary districts, with congregations spread throughout the U.S., Puerto Rico, Canada, Ireland, and India. The church maintains a seminary in Port Richey, Florida.

FRIENDS (QUAKER)

Dating from the 1650s in England, the Society of Friends, or Quakers, is an unconventional but esteemed Protestant body. Because they affirm the "Inner Light," the spiritual nerve center that God has placed in every person, classical Friends deny the validity of clergy, liturgy, and sacraments. The fact that every person has this inward spiritual endowment has prompted Friends to stand for the equality of all people and thus to oppose slavery and to be exceptionally service minded. Despite their small numbers, Friends have had a deep and lasting influence on Western society. Contributions in both religious and humanitarian spheres have won them universal respect and admiration, and their loyalty to their quiet faith offers a challenge and inspiration to all churches.

History. The Society of Friends began with the vision of George Fox (1624–91), a British seeker after spiritual truth and peace during the turmoil of the English Civil War and its aftermath. After failing

140

to find satisfactory truth or peace in the churches of his time, Fox discovered what he sought in a direct personal relationship with Christ: "When all my hopes in [churches] were gone . . . I heard a voice which said, 'That is the Inner Voice, or Inner Light, based upon the description of John 1:9: "the true Light, which lighteth every man that cometh into the world. (KJV)"'" This voice, Fox maintained, is available to all and has nothing to do with the ceremonies, rituals, or creeds over which Christians have fought. Every heart is God's altar and shrine.

This idea of the Inner Light was revolutionary. It implied that theology and dogma mean nothing, that people need not attend "steeple houses" to find God, and that it is wrong to pay taxes to support the state church clergy. This was seen as rebellion, but Fox and his early followers went even further. They not only refused to go to church, they also insisted on freedom of speech, assembly, and worship. They would not take oaths in court and would not go to war. They doffed their hats to no one, king or commoner, and they made no distinction in gender or social class. They condemned slavery and England's treatment of prisoners and the mentally ill. The names they adopted—Children of Truth, Children of Light, and Friends of Truth—aroused ridicule and fierce opposition. When Fox, hauled into court, advised one judge to "tremble at the Word of the Lord," the judge call him "a quaker," thus coining a term that became a name for the movement.

Quakers were whipped, jailed, tortured, mutilated, and murdered. Fox spent six years in jail; others spent decades, some dying there. From 1650 until 1689, more than 3,000 suffered for conscience's sake, and 300 to 400 died in prison; but in spite of that persecution, the group grew, and the Religious Society of Friends was founded in 1652. When Fox died in 1691, Quakers numbered 50,000.

Friends soon brought their message to the American colonies. Ann Austin (d. 1665) and Mary Fisher (ca. 1623–98) arrived in Massachusetts from Barbados in 1656. They were promptly accused of being witches and were deported. Two days later, eight more Friends arrived from England. Hastily, laws were passed to keep them out. The whipping post was liberally applied, but it failed to stop the Quaker missionaries. Eventually, four were hanged in Boston. Quakers kept coming into New England, New York, New Jersey, Maryland, Virginia, and Pennsylvania. Rhode Island and

Pennsylvania welcomed them from the beginning, and the persecution in the communities that did not welcome them ended with the passage of the Act of Toleration of 1689.

William Penn (1644–1718), the son of a British admiral, was granted the colony of Pennsylvania by the British Crown. He made this colony a refuge for his fellow Quakers. When he arrived in Philadelphia in 1682, he sat under an elm at Shackamaxon and made a treaty with the Indians, the "only treaty never sworn to and never broken." Penn's "Holy Experiment" allowed complete religious toleration in the colony of Pennsylvania, removing the government from the business of religion. This was a milestone on the path to full religious freedom in the American Constitution.

A new phase of Quaker life began as persecution waned, and Quakers settled down to business and farming. Known for their peacefulness and honesty, many grew prosperous. During that period of quiet in the early eighteenth century, meetings and community life became well organized. It was a time of creativity and mystical inwardness, and closely knit family life was emphasized. Quaker philanthropy increased and became widely admired. Their ideas on prison reform began to take effect, and their schools increased in number and attendance.

The Quakers lost control of the Pennsylvania legislature in 1756 over the issue of taxation to pay for a war against the Shawnee and the Delaware peoples. Quaker leaders, now looking within rather than without, began to enforce such strict discipline upon their members that they became, in fact, a "peculiar people." Members were disowned or dismissed for even minor infractions; thousands were cut off for "marrying out of Meeting." Pleasure, music, and art were taboo; sobriety, punctuality, and honesty were demanded in all matters; dress was painfully plain; and speech was biblical. They were "different" and dour; they gained few new converts and lost many old members during this period.

Divisions arose within the ranks during those years. The Hicksites separated in 1827, the Wilburites in 1845, the Primitives (a small group now nonexistent) in 1861. Of these separations, the one led by Elias Hicks (1748–1830) is of primary concern. Hicks was a rural Long Island Quaker, and his liberal and rational theological views brought him into conflict with those who were more orthodox and evangelical. Two-thirds of the Philadelphia Yearly

Meeting withdrew with the Hicksites (a name never officially adopted), and similar divisions followed in New York, Ohio, Indiana, and Baltimore. Other separations were led by Joseph John Gurney (1788–1847), whose followers gradually moved into mainstream evangelical piety, polity, and practice, and John Wilbur (1774–1856), a quietist who sought a return to traditional Quaker faith and practice.

Service and Peace Work. Even during the rather quietistic phase of Quaker life, Friends continued to work for peace, public education, temperance, democracy, and the abolition of slavery. In 1688 the Friends of Germantown, Pennsylvania, announced that slavery violated the Golden Rule. It took nearly a century for Quakers to rid their own society of slavery, but they did so years in advance of any other religious body in the U.S. Sellers or purchasers of slaves were forbidden membership in the society by the end of the eighteenth century. The writings of Friends John Woolman (1720–72) and John Greenleaf Whittier (1807–92) helped to further the abolition movement in American society, and once the Civil War was over, Friends threw their strength into such organizations as the Freedman's Aid Society. Ever since, they have been active in education and legislative protection for African Americans.

During World War I, Friends from all branches of society were at work in the American Friends Service Committee (A.F.S.C.) in relief and reconstruction efforts abroad. The A.F.S.C. remains today one of the most effective of such agencies in the world. Its volunteers have erected demountable houses, staffed hospitals, plowed fields, raised domestic animals, and driven ambulances. Famine relief and child-feeding programs have been instituted in Serbia, Poland, Austria, Russia, and Germany. The A.F.S.C. and its British counterpart were jointly awarded the Nobel Peace Prize in 1947.

Friends served in the medical corps of both world wars, and some went into combat. They also worked to relieve displaced Japanese Americans during World War II, and they cooperated with Brethren (see BRETHREN and PIETIST CHURCHES) and Mennonites (see MENNONITE CHURCHES) in locating conscientious objectors in work of real importance on farms and in reformatories, hospitals, and mental institutions.

No Quaker body has ever departed from the declaration to Charles II in 1661: "The spirit of Christ, which leads us into all Truth, will never move us to fight and war against any man with outward weapons, neither for the Kingdom of Christ, nor for the kingdoms of this world." However, there is great tolerance for individual variations in this position. During World War II, the formal Quaker position favored applying for conscientious-objector status, either as a noncombatant within the military or in alternate service. In the case of the Vietnam war, corporate positions shifted to encourage men to practice draft refusal and go to jail if necessary. In both cases, a wide variety of positions was accepted; the emphasis was on following individual conscience. Friends who enter military service are no longer disowned from membership, but many leave the society and join a church that does not profess pacifism. Conversely, pacifists brought up in other traditions often join the Friends in young adulthood.

Friends have not been satisfied to work merely in relief efforts. Peace conferences have had a prominent place, ranging from local to international and covering all age groups. Scores of youth conferences and camps in the U.S. and in foreign fields testify to Friends' devotion to the way of Christ as they understand it. Young Quaker volunteers in summer camps have inspired goodwill among nations and among minority groups within nations.

Quakers have always valued education, stressing its importance among members of the various Friends groups and working to make it available to as many persons in the larger society as possible. Among Quaker affiliated colleges and universities are Bryn Mawr, Haverford, and Swarthmore colleges in Pennsylvania; Guilford College in North Carolina; Earlham College and Earlham School of Religion in Indiana; Wilmington College in Ohio; Friends University in Kansas; Whittier College in California; and George Fox University in Oregon.

Worship and Polity. The Inner Light is the heart of Quaker theology and practice. Friends believe that grace, the power from God to help humankind pursue good and resist evil, is universal among all people. They seek not holiness but perfection—a higher, more spiritual standard of life for both society and the individual—and they believe that truth is unfolding and continuing. They value the Bible but prefer to rely on fresh individual guidance from the Spirit of God, which produced the Bible, rather than follow only what has been revealed to others.

Worship and business in the society are conducted in monthly, quarterly, and yearly meetings. The monthly meeting is the basic unit, made up of one or more meetings (groups) in a neighborhood. It convenes each week for worship and once a month for business. It keeps records of membership, births, deaths, and marriages; appoints committees; considers queries on spiritual welfare; and transacts all business. Monthly meetings join four times a year in a quarterly meeting to stimulate spiritual life and decide on any business that should be brought to the attention of the yearly meeting. The yearly meeting corresponds to a diocese in an episcopal system. There are standing committees on such subjects as publications, education, the social order, missions, peace, charities, and national legislation; trust fund incomes are allocated, and the work of the society is generally supervised. In Friends' business meetings at every level, there often is frank inquiry into members' conduct of business and treatment of others.

Group decisions await the "sense of the meeting." Lacking unity of opinion, the meeting may have a "quiet time" until unity is found, or it may postpone consideration of the matter or refer it to a committee for study. Minority opinion is not outvoted, but convinced. Every man, woman, and child is free to speak in any meeting; delegates are appointed at quarterly and yearly meetings to ensure adequate representation, but enjoy no unusual position or prerogatives.

Church officers, elders, and ministers, are chosen for recognized ability in spiritual leadership, but they too stand on equal footing with the rest of the membership. To the Friends, all members are ministers. A few full-time workers are paid a modest salary, and "recorded" ministers who serve as pastors in meetings that have programmed worship also receive salaries.

Worship may be either programmed or unprogrammed, but the two are not always distinct. The former more nearly resembles an ordinary Protestant service, although there are no rites or outward sacraments. While Friends believe in spiritual communion, partaking of the elements is thought unnecessary. In unprogrammed meetings there is no choir, collection, singing, or pulpit; the service is devoted to quiet meditation, prayer, and communion with God. Any vocal contributions are prompted by the Spirit.

In the traditional Quaker marriage observance, the bride and groom simply stand before a meeting and make mutual vows of love and faithfulness. Among many pastoral meetings, however, the minister of the meeting officiates.

If Friends were ever exclusive, they no longer are. A world outreach has been evident and growing in the late years of the twentieth century. Friends' United Meeting and Friends General Conference are members of the World Council of Churches, and the Philadelphia Yearly Meeting belongs to the National Council of the Churches of Christ in the U.S.A. Friends World Committee for Consultation (F.W.C.C.), organized at Swarthmore, Pennsylvania, following the Second World Conference of Friends in 1937, functions as an agent, or clearinghouse, for interchange of Quaker aspirations and experiences through regional, national, and international inter-visitation, person-to-person consultations, conferences, correspondence, and a variety of publications. The F.W.C.C. maintains a world office in London, England, and is a nongovernmental organization (NGO) related to the United Nations, through cooperation with the A.F.S.C.; it helps to operate a program at U.N. headquarters to forward world peace and human unity. Something of a world community has been set up in the Wider Quaker Fellowship, in which non-Friends in sympathy with the spirit and program of Quakerism may participate in the work without coming into full membership.

EVANGELICAL FRIENDS INTERNATIONAL

Founded: 1990
Membership: 36,760 in 288 meetings (1995)

This is one of the newest, and largest, organizations of Friends meetings in the U.S. It grew out of the Evangelical Friends Alliance, which was formed in 1965 to encourage evangelical emphases and denominational unity. The Evangelical Friends represent one part of the general evangelical renewal that profoundly shaped American Christianity in the latter part of the twentieth century. However, this Quaker evangelical movement also grew out of new research into the early years of Quakerism that pointed to its strongly Christ-centered, evangelical character.

The Evangelical Friends are organized into six regions of the U.S., with commissions devoted to missions, education, youth ministry, and communication. Worship is programmed and includes Scripture readings, congregational singing, and a sermon by the pastor. The theology is generally conservative, and Evangelical Friends cooperate with other evangelical bodies. Of primary concern is the Great Commission (Matt. 28:19) to make disciples of all nations.

FRIENDS GENERAL CONFERENCE

Founded: 1900
Membership: est. 32,000 in 620 meetings (1999)

Friends General Conference is an association of fourteen yearly meetings and regional associations and seven monthly meetings of Friends (Quakers) in the United States and Canada. It is less a denomination than a service organization that provides resources for yearly and monthly meetings. Most of these meetings are unprogrammed, meaning that worshipers meet in silence, expecting that one or more Friends may be moved by the Spirit to speak. No pastors are employed; the responsibilities handled by pastors in other denominations are shared among the members of the meeting. This groups of Friends emphasizes the Quaker belief that faith is based on direct experience of God and that God is found in every individual.

Friends General Conference serves the members of affiliated meetings by preparing and distributing educational and spiritual materials, providing opportunities for Friends to share experiences and strengthen the Quaker community, and helping monthly and yearly meetings to nurture and support the spiritual and community life of Friends in North America. It is best known for the annual "Gathering of Friends," which attracts between 1,500 and 2,000 Quakers from all over North America. Friends General Conference offices are in Philadelphia, Pennsylvania. The Conference publishes various books and religious education materials and supports *Friends Journal*, a magazine for Friends and other seekers.

FRIENDS UNITED MEETING

Founded: 1902
Membership: 33,908 in 379 meetings (1999)

Friends United Meeting brought together in one cooperative relationship eighteen yearly meetings in the U.S. and six abroad (in East Africa, Cuba, and Jamaica) with a somewhat different status. Now there are twenty-seven meetings that work together in many departments, such as missionary service and the production of Sunday school materials. While each yearly meeting is autonomous, they

147

come together for spiritual stimulation, business, and conference every three years.

The ministries are carried forward between triennial sessions by two planning commissions and the general board, which convenes semiannually. Offices are located in Richmond, Indiana, as is the Friends United Meeting's publishing arm, Friends United Press. The press produces a variety of materials, from books of poetry and religious reflection to religious education materials to the monthly magazine *Quaker Life*.

Affirming the importance of personal religious experience, this group embodies a creative balance of central Quaker accents, evangelism and social concern, mission and service, worship, and ministry. Friends of various persuasions work together within the Friends United Meeting spectrum. It seeks to implement its commitment as a classic "peace church," supporting ministries throughout North America and the world. Its support of higher education, with seven colleges spread from North Carolina to the Midwest to California, is remarkable in view of the size of its membership. A seminary, Earlham School of Religion, is located in Richmond, Indiana.

RELIGIOUS SOCIETY OF FRIENDS
(Conservative)

Founded: 1845; 1904
Membership: est. 1,500 (1999)

Known also as Wilburites, this group resulted from a division over the nature of Scripture and the gift of ministry (see FRIENDS). Joseph John Gurney, a British evangelical Quaker who came to the U.S. in 1837, taught essentially evangelical doctrine and his followers adopted mainstream Protestant polity and practice. John Wilbur, a conservative Friend from Rhode Island, while not denying the authority of the Bible and its teachings, felt that Gurney's preaching substituted a creed for the immediate revelation of the divine Spirit. The term *conservative,* therefore, refers more to adherence to traditional Quaker faith and practice than to theological doctrines as such. Both Gurney and Wilbur had large followings, and from 1845 through 1904, there were Quaker separations in various regions. Many of the divided Friends came together as the twentieth century

148

progressed, but some conservative Friends remained outside the larger organizations.

The major conservative Friends group is the North Carolina Yearly Meeting (Conservative) of the Religious Society of Friends. Tracing their origins to the first yearly meeting established in the state in 1698, this Friends group established itself as a separate body in 1904 over the issues of "the immediate and perceptible guidance of the Holy Spirit," the leadership of Christ in the church, and the traditional Quaker worship practice. These Friends cooperate with other Quaker groups in various areas of service and in inter-visitation.

FUNDAMENTALIST/BIBLE CHURCHES

Representing the most conservative form of Protestantism, socially and theologically, fundamentalism was one of the most potent forces within American Christianity in the twentieth century. It is also one of the most difficult to categorize and study because of the variety within fundamentalism and the fact that fundamentalism exerts an influence beyond the many different fundamentalist churches. Fundamentalist churches tend to be Congregationalist (see CONGREGATIONAL CHURCHES) and Baptist (see BAPTIST CHURCHES) in orientation; therefore, structure exists primarily on the local level. Pastors tend to found their own congregations and work to build them into major bodies that are loosely joined to like-minded congregations. Rather than having traditional denominational structures, fundamentalist churches tend to establish a variety of cooperative ministry programs, such as radio and television ministries, sponsorship of foreign missions, and educational programs. Bible colleges, often associated with local congregations, are one of the backbones of fundamentalism. Graduates of these Bible colleges often serve in denominations that are not in themselves fundamentalist.

Fundamentalism grew out of nineteenth-century American evangelicalism and revivalism. Dwight L. Moody (1837–99), founder of Moody Bible Institute, was one of the key figures in the formation of fundamentalist organizations, but the roots of the movement go back to the Plymouth Brethren (see CHRISTIAN BRETHREN) in

England. The early Brethren dismissed with clergy and encouraged any members with spiritual gifts to preach, evangelize, and offer the sacraments. One of the key preachers was John Nelson Darby (1800–82), who stressed the importance of biblical prophecy, especially that found in the apocalyptic books, for understanding human history. Darby taught that history was divided into seven dispensations, the first six of which ended in a cataclysm, such as the great flood. The seventh dispensation will be the millennial age that Christ will inaugurate. Cyrus Scofield (1843–1921) made Darby's theory the centerpiece of his popular reference Bible early in the twentieth century.

Fundamentalism thus ran directly counter to modern trends in biblical scholarship and scientific theories about the origin, age, and evolution of the universe. *The Fundamentals: A Testimony to the Truth* was a popular pamphlet series designed to defend the Bible from critics. It appeared between 1910 and 1915 and included nearly one hundred articles that sought to defend the deity of Christ, the virgin birth, the historical resurrection, the inerrancy of Scripture as the Word of God, and the reality of sin and Satan.

World War I put the fundamentalist controversy on hold as Christians of all kinds joined in the war effort, but by 1920, the fundamentalist controversy heated up as Baptist and Presbyterian (see PRESBYTERIAN CHURCHES) fundamentalists fought to preserve their churches from modernism. This early period culminated in the famous Scopes "Monkey Trial" of 1925 over the teaching of evolution in the public schools. Following that celebrated trial, fundamentalists began organizing separate congregations, schools, and inter-church organizations. The formation of the State of Israel in 1948, which had been a key prediction of fundamentalist preaching, and the threat of nuclear destruction during the cold war era gave renewed vigor to fundamentalist preaching and writing. Prone to fractures and doctrinal disputes (like other Christian movements), fundamentalists since the Second World War have increasingly established cooperative ministries with other evangelicals.

Many fundamentalist bodies are closely connected to the Holiness movement (see HOLINESS CHURCHES). Some of the major fundamentalist denominations are discussed below, but it should be noted that there are thousands of fundamentalist (or nearly fundamentalist) bodies in the U.S.

AMERICAN EVANGELICAL CHRISTIAN CHURCHES

Founded: 1944
Membership: statistics not available

The American Evangelical Christian Churches (AECC) are less a denomination than an inter-church organization that offers credentials for ministers. Congregations associated with the AECC are autonomous but agree to a fundamentalist statement of belief. Clergy credentialed by the AECC serve in a variety of capacities, including prison ministry, military and hospital chaplaincy, as well as outreach to truckers, bikers, and others without a permanent Christian community.

Ministerial applicants must subscribe to "Seven Articles of Faith": (1) the Bible as the written Word of God; (2) the virgin birth; (3) the deity of Jesus Christ; (4) salvation through the atonement of Christ; (5) the guidance of life through prayer; (6) the return of Christ; and (7) the establishment of the millennial kingdom. Upon completion of training, ministerial students are granted licenses enabling them to perform all the functions and offices of the ministry, with the exception of officiating at marriages. Full ordination is withheld until the licentiate has become pastor of a regular congregation or is engaged in full-time evangelistic or missionary work. Twelve regional offices in the U.S. and one in Canada supervise the work of the organization.

BAPTIST BIBLE FELLOWSHIP INTERNATIONAL

Founded: 1950
Membership: est. 1,200,000 in 4,500 churches (1997)

Baptist Bible Fellowship was founded by some one hundred Baptist (see BAPTIST CHURCHES) ministers and missionaries to promote fellowship among independent Baptists in three main areas of church life: evangelism, education of church workers, and the founding of churches. Many of the founders had been part of the World Fundamental Baptist Missionary Fellowship, which had grown out of the Baptist Bible Union, founded in 1921. The Baptist Bible Fellowship's statement of faith was based on that of the Baptist Bible Union. It is strongly fundamentalist in character, emphasizing

151

the inerrancy of Scripture, the virgin birth, the deity of Christ, the substitutionary atonement, the resurrection of the body of Christ, biblical miracles, and the literal millennial kingdom on earth. Ministers and members of the fellowship use only the King James Version of the Bible in English-speaking churches.

The Baptist Bible Fellowship also teaches that Jesus was a Baptist in his thinking and work. They recognize baptism by immersion only, participate in Communion only with members of their own church, and are adamantly opposed to dancing, drinking, smoking, movies, gambling, and sex outside of marriage. No formal membership statistics are kept, but there are approximately 850 missionaries at work in over a hundred mission fields around the world. In the U.S. their greatest strength is in the Great Lakes region and the Southwest.

Baptist Bible College in Springfield, Missouri, and Baptist Bible College East in Boston, Massachusetts, are owned and supported by these independent Baptists. Recently the Baptist Bible Graduate School of Theology was founded in Springfield, Missouri. Other schools supported by the fellowship are Pacific Coast Baptist Bible College and Spanish Baptist Bible Institute in Miami, Florida.

BAPTIST MISSIONARY ASSOCIATION OF AMERICA

Founded: 1950
Membership: 234,732 in 1,334 churches (1999)

Organized at Little Rock, Arkansas, as the North American Baptist Association, this group changed its name to Baptist Missionary Association of America in 1968. It concentrates on fostering and encouraging missionary cooperation. There are workers in home missions and missionary work abroad in Mexico, Japan, Brazil, Taiwan, Portugal, Cape Verde Islands, Uruguay, Guatemala, Costa Rica, Nicaragua, Australia, Italy, France, Africa, India, Bolivia, Honduras, Korea, and the Philippines. A strong publications department issues literature for Sunday school and training classes, pamphlets, books, tracts, and magazines in both English and Spanish. The association also owns and operates a printing business in Brazil, where literature is printed in Portuguese for use in Africa and Europe. A worldwide radio ministry is also maintained.

The members are thoroughly fundamentalist in conviction, placing strong emphasis on the verbal inspiration and accuracy of Scripture, direct creation, the virgin birth and deity of Jesus, his blood atonement, justification by faith, salvation by grace alone, and the imminent personal return of Christ to earth. The Lord's Supper and baptism are accepted as ordinances, and baptism is considered "alien" unless administered to believers by the divine authority as given to the Missionary Baptist churches. With its roots in the American Baptist Association, this body carries on the Landmark Baptist movement (see BAPTIST CHURCHES), holding to the historic succession of independent Baptist churches from the time of Christ.

Churches are completely autonomous in the Baptist tradition and, regardless of size, have an equal voice in the cooperative missionary, publication, evangelical, and educational efforts of the association. Member churches must, however, conform to the doctrinal standards of the association. Three junior colleges and several orphans' homes are maintained on a state level, and a theological seminary is located in Jacksonville, Texas.

BEREAN FUNDAMENTAL CHURCH

Founded: 1947
Membership: est. 8,000 in 51 churches (1997)

In the mid-1930s, Dr. Ivan E. Olsen became the first pastor of the Berean Fundamental Church, an independent congregation in North Platte, Nebraska. Following the biblical principle of evangelism found in Acts 1:8, Olsen assisted in planting sixteen other churches in surrounding communities. In 1947 the churches formed the Berean Fundamental Church Council, Inc. Currently, there are churches in eight states—California, Colorado, Kansas, Minnesota, South Dakota, Oregon, Wyoming, and Nebraska—and one in Manitoba, Canada.

The member churches possess a common constitution, stressing the basic doctrines of Christianity and the verbal, plenary inspiration of Scripture (the inerrancy of the Bible in all matters of faith and morals); the virgin birth of Christ; the deity of Christ; the blood atonement; the bodily resurrection of Christ; and the return of Christ to earth, following the rapture and preceding the millennial kingdom. The local assemblies are also Bible centered and evangelistic.

Berean Fundamental churches support a variety of independent

153

faith missions, draw their pastors from various seminaries and Bible institutes, and freely choose their own Sunday school curricula and church literature. The Berean Fundamental Church Council, Inc., supports its own Maranatha Bible Camp and Conference Grounds near North Platte.

BIBLE FELLOWSHIP CHURCH

Founded: 1858
Membership: 7,169 in 56 churches (1998)

This body was formed in the 1850s when Mennonite (see MEN-NONITE CHURCHES) leaders in Pennsylvania resisted the more evangelical style of some of the younger generation. The evangelical Mennonites formed their own group. Originally it was called the Evangelical Conference, but the name was changed in 1959 when a new confession of faith was adopted. The church now has a more fundamentalist outlook, but retains some of its Mennonite heritage.

Bible Fellowship Church doctrinal emphases include salvation through the death and resurrection of Christ, transformed life through new birth by the Holy Spirit, the authority and trustworthiness of the Bible as the Word of God, the culmination of history in the Second Coming of Jesus (pre-millennialism), and a shared life in the church of believers, with every member's being responsible for the propagation of the gospel through evangelism and missions. Churches are found mainly in Pennsylvania, New Jersey, New York, and Ontario, Canada.

The churches support missions on five continents, the Pinebrook Junior College, the Victory Valley Camp for children and youth, a home for the aging, and Pinebrook-in-the-Pines, a conference and retreat center—all in Pennsylvania.

BIBLE PRESBYTERIAN CHURCH

Founded: 1938
Membership: est. 10,000 in 32 congregations (2000)

On June 11, 1936, during the fundamentalist-modernist controversy, a group of about 300 people, led by J. Gresham Machen (1881–1937) of Princeton Theological Seminary, met in Philadelphia to form a new church that would be faithful to the Bible. The name chosen was Presbyterian Church of America, and Machen was unanimously elected the first moderator. A year later it became apparent that the new church was actually composed of two groups with views so divergent as to make continued unity impossible. Therefore, on September 6, 1938, one group formed the Bible Presbyterian Church; the other retained the name Presbyterian Church of America, but was denied its use by the courts and subsequently took the name Orthodox Presbyterian Church.

The founders of the Bible Presbyterian Church stated their basic convictions clearly: "We are persuaded that the great battle in the world today is the faith of our fathers versus modernism, compromise, indifferentism, and worldliness. With all our hearts we throw our strength into the great task of winning lost souls to Jesus Christ by the Gospel of the Grace of God."

In 1941, the Bible Presbyterians joined with other like-minded churches to found the American Council of Christian Churches, in opposition to the National Council of Churches; in 1948 the International Council of Christian Churches was formed to provide a worldwide association (membership in 1998 included 700 branches in over 100 nations).

The word *Bible* is included in the name of this church to emphasize its Bible-based position. It is thoroughly fundamentalist and subscribes to the Westminster Standards (the Confession of Faith, the Shorter and Larger Catechisms). It opposes all forms of the social gospel and liberation theology and refuses to cooperate with those who compromise such doctrines as the inerrancy and infallibility of the Bible, the virgin birth and deity of Christ, his blood atonement and bodily resurrection, and his literal coming again. It continues to oppose the policies of both the National Council of the Churches of Christ in the U.S.A. and the World Council of Churches because of what it calls their "departure from historic Christianity."

Properties of the local church are guaranteed to the church itself. Local congregations may call their pastors "without interference" from presbyteries or synods. Any church may withdraw at any time "for reasons sufficient to themselves." The work of the church is carried on through independent agencies rather than denominational boards. Among its approved agencies are Western Reformed Seminary, Cohen Theological Seminary, Faith College of the Bible, and two Independent Boards for Presbyterian Missions, one foreign, the other home. Presbyteries and synods are meetings for edification and fellowship rather than administration. Greatest strength is in the Midwest.

CHRISTIAN AND MISSIONARY ALLIANCE

Founded: 1887
Membership: 347,973 in 1,973 churches (1999)

A. B. Simpson (1843–1919), a Presbyterian (see PRESBYTER-IAN CHURCHES) minister in New York City, left that church to carry on independent evangelistic work in 1882. This led to the formation of two societies: the Christian Alliance, for home missions work, and the Evangelical Missionary Alliance, for work abroad. These merged in 1897, forming the Christian and Missionary Alliance. The Alliance remained a confederation for over seventy-five years, but it formalized its status with bylaws and a constitution in 1974.

Strongly evangelical, the Alliance believes in the inspiration and inerrancy of the Bible, the atoning work of Christ, the reality of supernatural religious experience, sanctification, and the pre-millennial return of Jesus Christ. It stresses the centrality of Christ as Savior, sanctifier, healer, and coming king.

The Alliance has ministries in sixty-six countries. In the U.S. and Puerto Rico, work is carried on in twenty-one geographic and ten intercultural districts. Ethnic groups include Cambodian, Dega, Haitian, Hmong, Jewish, Korean, Laotian, Native American, Hispanic, and Vietnamese. Each member church or group is engaged in missionary and evangelical activities. An overall conference of delegates, the General Council, meets annually in various cities in the U.S. The Christian and Missionary Alliance in Canada became autonomous in 1980 but continues to send and support overseas missionaries jointly with the U.S. Alliance.

True to its original purpose, the Alliance sponsors foreign missions work in Latin America, Africa, Asia, the Pacific Islands, the Middle East, Europe, Australia, and New Zealand. There are over one thousand Alliance missionaries and some 15,000 national pastors and workers ministering to nearly two million persons.

When the charismatic Assemblies of God was founded, about one-tenth of that constituency resulted from the departure of people from

156

the Christian and Missionary Alliance. The two groups have a close-knit history, are doctrinally similar, and maintain ties of fellowship.

CHRISTIAN BRETHREN (Plymouth Brethren)

Founded: 1820s
Membership: est. 100,000 in 1,150 churches (1997)

The Plymouth Brethren is a widely used, but unofficial, designation for a loose grouping of churches with early nineteenth-century roots in the British Isles. Within these churches, the common terminology is simply "Brethren" or "Christian Brethren," but they are to be distinguished from Brethren churches associated with the Pietist movement (see BRETHREN and PIETIST CHURCHES). Similar to the Restorationist bodies in the U.S., the early Brethren envisioned a basis for Christian unity by forsaking denominational structures and names in order to meet simply as Christians. The autonomy of the local congregation is another feature of the movement, coupled with the doctrinal understanding that a church is not a building, but the gathering of people who meet there.

The weekly hour-long "remembrance meeting" is probably the surest way to identify a Brethren assembly. The centrality of the Communion service is characteristic: In accordance with the meaning of "priesthood of all believers," the service is unstructured. Brethren have consistently refused to restrict the administration of baptism or the Lord's Supper to ordained ministers, thus effectively eliminating a clergy/laity distinction and the traditional concept of ordination. Anyone, man or woman, in the assembly is free to speak. A preacher may serve full-time with a congregation, but will not be identified as clergy or be given control of the congregation.

The Brethren are committed to all the fundamentals of conservative Christianity, including the verbal inspiration of Scripture. They emphasize gospel preaching and the necessity for personal conversion. Except for the weekly breaking of bread and the absence of collections at other meetings, their services are much like those of evangelical Baptist (see BAPTIST CHURCHES) or free and Bible churches.

Among American evangelicals, Brethren have had an influence out of proportion to their numbers. Their pre-millennial theology helped to shape evangelicalism, especially in the proliferation of independent churches and mission boards. Many have responded to the Brethren emphasis on plurality of leadership and participatory worship in the local church. Brethren are also characteristically found in leadership positions in interdenominational evangelistic campaigns and the founding and operation of nondenominational Bible schools, colleges, seminaries, and parachurch organizations. They have only one multiple-year, college-level institution, Emmaus Bible College in Dubuque, Iowa.

As a result of a division in England in 1848, there are two basic types of assemblies, commonly known as exclusive and open. Led in the beginning by John Nelson Darby (1800–82), the exclusive assemblies produced most of the movement's well-known Bible teachers, such as William Kelly and others. They operated on the premise that disciplinary action taken by one assembly was binding on all. As a result, once started, a division continued, until by the end of the century the exclusive Brethren were divided into seven or eight main groups. Recent mergers have reduced that number somewhat, and an important American group has merged with the open assemblies.

Open assemblies were led by George Muller (1805–95), well known for his orphanages and life of faith. The Brethrens' strength has always been in evangelism and foreign missions. Lacking the exclusive disciplinary premise, local disputes spread only as far as there was interest and involvement; thus open assemblies have never experienced worldwide division.

The Brethren are strongest in Pennsylvania, North Carolina, Florida, Michigan, Illinois, New Jersey, Iowa, and California. Apart from the metropolitan areas of Los Angeles and San Francisco, only scattered assemblies exist in the western half of the U.S.

CONSERVATIVE BAPTIST ASSOCIATION OF AMERICA (CBAmerica)

Founded: 1947
Membership: est. 200,000 in 1,200 churches (1998)

The Conservative Baptist Association is officially described as a "voluntary fellowship of sovereign, autonomous, independent, and Bible-believing Baptist churches." The founders of this association were active in an earlier organization known as the Fundamentalist

Fellowship, founded in 1920 within the American (then the Northern) Baptist Convention (see BAPTIST CHURCHES). This group of conservative church people opposed what they considered the infiltration of liberal and modernist tendencies and teachings into that convention. The basic disagreement was doctrinal, having to do with fundamentally different views and interpretations of the scriptures and of theology. The dispute was aggravated by the inclusive policy of the American Baptist Foreign Mission Society, under which missionaries of both conservative and liberal theology were sent to home and foreign fields.

As an association, this body should be distinguished from the Conservative Baptist movement as a whole. Several Conservative Baptist institutions, such as the Conservative Baptist Foreign Mission Society, the Conservative Baptist Home Mission Society, and a number of schools and colleges, function as part of the movement but are separate from the association.

The work of the association includes providing resources and personnel in areas of Christian education, leadership training, new church planting, financial services to clergy and staff, stewardship ministries, women's ministries, and retirement advisory services; serving in pastoral placement; printing and distributing literature, books, and Sunday school material; endorsing chaplains for the U.S. armed forces; and providing a national magazine, *The Conservative Baptist.*

Doctrinally, the church stands for the infallibility of the scriptures; God as Father, perfect in holiness, infinite in wisdom, measureless in power; Christ as the eternal and only begotten Son of God—his sinlessness, virgin birth, atonement, resurrection, and ascension; the Holy Spirit as coming forth from God to convince the world of sin, of righteousness, and of judgment; the sinfulness of all people and the possibility of their regeneration, sanctification, and comfort through Christ and the Holy Spirit; the church as the living body, with Christ as head; the local church as free from interference from any ecclesiastical or political authority; the responsibility of every human being to God alone; and the ordinances of baptism and the Lord's Supper.

Associational and regional officers are elected at annual meetings; a board of directors is made up of the associational officials and eighteen regional representatives, elected for three-year terms. The Association maintains offices in Littleton, Colorado. It supports five schools, including seminaries in Portland, Oregon, in Denver,

159

Colorado, and in Dresher, Pennsylvania, with extension campuses in other states.

GRACE GOSPEL FELLOWSHIP

Founded: 1944
Membership: est. 60,000 in 128 churches (1992)

Dispensational and pre-millennial, this fellowship had its beginnings as a pastors' fellowship at a conference of pastors and missionaries at the Berean Bible Church in Indianapolis, Indiana, in 1943. A year later, at Evansville, Indiana, its purpose was defined in a constitution: "to promote a fellowship among those who believe the truths contained in [our] doctrinal statement and to proclaim the Gospel of the Grace of God in this land, and throughout the world."

That doctrinal statement includes belief in the Bible as infallibly inspired by God; in the total depravity of the human race; in redemption by God's grace through the blood of Christ by means of faith; in eternal security for the saved; in the gifts of the Spirit (as enumerated in Eph. 4:7-16); and that the human nature of sin is never eradicated during this life. Its members believe in baptism by the Holy Spirit but hold that, while water baptism is biblical, it is not relevant to the present dispensation. Any church may vote to become affiliated with Grace Gospel Fellowship, provided it meets the doctrinal standards.

Outside the U.S., more than 1,000 churches are found in Zaire, Puerto Rico, India, the Philippines, Australia, South Africa, Tanzania, and South America. Grace Bible College and the headquarters of the Fellowship are located in Grand Rapids, Michigan. Closely connected to Grace Gospel Fellowship are Grace Ministries International, Grace Publications, and Grace Youth Camp in Indiana.

INDEPENDENT FUNDAMENTAL CHURCHES OF AMERICA (IFCA International, Inc.)

Founded: 1930
Membership: 61,655 in 659 churches (1999)

This body was organized at Cicero, Illinois, by representatives of various independent churches anxious to safeguard fundamental doctrine. Members must agree with doctrines of the verbal plenary inerrant inspiration of the Bible; the virgin birth, deity, and sinless life of Jesus Christ; the death, burial, and resurrection of Christ to provide salvation for all; the person and work of the Holy Spirit; the reality of Satan and his destructive work today; the personal and bodily return of Jesus Christ; and the bodily resurrection of all people, some to eternal life and some to "everlasting punishment."

This body is less a traditional denomination than a sponsoring agency for autonomous churches and ministries. It has two types of membership: one for churches and organizations, the other for clergy, missionaries, evangelists, and lay workers. It has a strong commitment to various forms of chaplaincy, particularly military and prison ministries. It also publishes *Voice* magazine and other materials devoted to evangelical/fundamentalist ministries. There are five Bible camps, seven Bible institutes, and two children's homes. Conferences are scheduled regularly to promote fellowship among fundamentalist churches and workers.

The president of the body presides over an annual conference in which the members have voting power; an executive committee of twelve serves for three years. The constituent churches are completely independent but are required to subscribe to the statement of faith of the organization. A home office is maintained in Grandville, Michigan.

HOLINESS CHURCHES

The Holiness movement grew out of the Methodist Church beginning in the mid-nineteenth century (see METHODIST CHURCHES). Early Methodist ministry in the U.S. focused primarily on conversion and church extension, at times neglecting John Wesley's (1703–91) emphasis on sanctification and moving on toward perfection. As Methodism became more established, there was renewed interest in the doctrine of perfection. One of the key figures in this revival of holiness teaching was the traveling evangelist and writer Phoebe Palmer (1807–74), who experienced sanctification by the Holy Spirit in 1837. She worked tirelessly to bring others to a similar experience of holiness.

Toward the end of the nineteenth century, the Holiness movement had spread throughout the country, becoming a source of controversy in local Methodist churches. Congregations divided; holiness-minded preachers left the Methodist Church in order to work independently; and a wide-variety of small, often "store-front," churches sprang up in virtually every U.S. community. Over time, many of these independent congregations formed denominations.

Holiness teaching generally rejects various forms of popular entertainment, such as dancing, movies, popular music, make-up, ornate clothing, gambling, drinking, and smoking. In many ways, the Holiness movement represents a countercultural movement in the U.S., but its adherents continue to live and work in the midst of the wider society.

Many Holiness churches use the word *Apostolic* in their names to emphasize their aim of returning to the life of the New Testament church, when the Holy Spirit was perceived to be particularly active. After 1900, many in the Holiness movement embraced further works of the Holy Spirit, such as speaking in tongues and physical healing (see PENTECOSTAL CHURCHES).

Since the Holiness movement is focused more on lifestyle and an experience of conversion followed by sanctification, it is to be distinguished from the more doctrinally oriented fundamentalist movement. However, there has been much cross-fertilization between these two forms of conservative Protestantism.

APOSTOLIC CHRISTIAN CHURCH OF AMERICA

Founded: 1830s (came to the U.S. in 1847)
Membership: 12,800 in 91 churches (1999)

This is the only Holiness group that originated in Europe. It began in Switzerland when S. H. Froehlich had a dramatic conversion experience that he felt marked the New Testament pattern of Christian experience. Froehlich's church first took the name Evangelical Baptist, but adopted the Apostolic title as it embraced the doctrine of holiness. Froehlich himself came to the U.S. in the 1850s and ministered to Swiss and German immigrants in the Midwest. By that time, another Swiss pastor, named Benedict Weyeneth, already had organized the first congregation in the U.S. in upstate New York.

The theology of the church is conservative and reflects some of the concerns of German Pietism (See BRETHREN and PIETIST

CHURCHES). The basic doctrine is salvation by grace through faith in Jesus Christ. Those who are saved experience a change of heart through regeneration and a life of godliness guided and directed by the Holy Spirit.

The church consists of members who have been converted to Christ, are reborn and baptized, and who strive for sanctification and of such friends of the truth who sincerely and earnestly strive to attain adoption by God in Christ. Members are noted for a life of simplicity, separation from worldliness, and obedience to the Bible, which is embraced as the infallible Word of God. Members may serve in the military, but do not bear arms since that violates the commandment to love one's enemies. Though they strive to be good citizens, they do not swear oaths.

The local churches are independent in polity but united in fundamental organization. Each church is served by elders authorized to baptize, lay on hands, serve the Lord's Supper, and conduct meetings for the exercising of church discipline.

There are no educational institutions for clergy, and they are not paid. Moreover, they are not expected to prepare sermons but depend entirely on the inspiration of the Holy Spirit. A very close knit fellowship and strong sense of community exist throughout the denomination, evidenced in the observance of the kiss of peace. Doctrinal authority and national governance of the church rest with a council of approximately fifty elders.

A smaller, related body is called the Apostolic Christian Church (Nazarene).

APOSTOLIC FAITH CHURCH

Founded: 1907
Membership: est. 4,500 in 50 churches (2000)

This body was organized in Portland, Oregon, by the Rev. Florence L. Crawford in order to "reestablish, maintain, and teach all the doctrines as taught by Christ and his apostles in the days of the early church." The church is trinitarian, fundamentalist, and Arminian in theology. It presents the doctrines of fundamentalism, stressing justification by faith, entire sanctification, and the baptism of the Holy Spirit as evidenced at Pentecost. Branches exist in several foreign countries, with more members in Africa than in the U.S.

Although the church keeps baptismal records there are no membership reports. A born-again experience and subscription to the doctrines of the group are required for membership. It is a church without a collection plate, with no offering being taken during services. True to the Holiness tradition, worldly amusements (dancing, theater, card playing, drinking, smoking) are banned. Members are required to dress conservatively, and marriage with unbelievers is not permitted.

Governing bodies consist of a board of five trustees, of which the general overseer of the denomination is chair, and a board of twenty-four elders. A headquarter church, a campground, and a publishing house that circulates evangelical literature in more than sixty languages and dialects are located in Portland.

APOSTOLIC OVERCOMING HOLY CHURCH OF GOD

Founded: 1916
Membership: 10,714 in 129 churches (2000)

Bishop W. T. Phillips (1893–1973), a former member of the Methodist Church (see METHODIST CHURCHES), became deeply concerned with the teaching of the doctrine of holiness and, after four years of study and preaching on the topic, organized the Ethiopian Overcoming Holy Church of God in 1916 in Mobile, Alabama. "Ethiopian" was later changed to "Apostolic."

Active in twenty-two states, the West Indies, Haiti, and Africa, the church's clergy, both men and women, are supported by tithes. Worship includes foot washing and divine healing. Services generally are emotionally expressive, with participants speaking in tongues and engaging in ecstatic dances.

It is claimed that this church existed even from the days of Enos, when Christianity was known to be in existence in Abyssinia. Marriage to the unsaved, the use of tobacco, foolish talking, jesting, and use of slang are forbidden.

In doctrine, sanctification and holiness are stressed, along with the deity of Christ, the final resurrection of the dead, and the punishment of evil at the time of the last judgment at the Second Coming of Christ. A special relief fund provides for the needs of orphans, widows, and aged and disabled members. A publishing facility is located in the headquarters building in Birmingham, Alabama. An executive bishop and six other bishops supervise the work of the church; a general assembly made up primarily of representatives from local churches meets each June.

CHURCH OF CHRIST (Holiness) U.S.A.

Founded: 1894
Membership: 10,383 in 167 churches (1998)

A Baptist preacher in Alabama and Mississippi, C. P. Jones, seeking a new church and faith that would make him "one of wisdom's true sons . . . like Abraham, a friend of God," founded this church. The body retained its Holiness emphasis when other early black churches moved into Pentecostalism (see PENTECOSTAL CHURCHES). The Church of Christ (Holiness) seeks to spread the gospel around the world, to reclaim those who have fallen away from the faith, to encourage believers to experience sanctification, and to support divine healing. The church has a strong eschatological focus as well.

Doctrinally, the church emphasizes original sin, the Holy Spirit as an indispensable gift to every believer, and Christ's atonement and Second Coming. There are two sacraments: baptism and the Lord's Supper. Foot washing and divine healing are employed as aids to the growth of spiritual life. The church has bishops who speak for the church, but its government is representative, with final authority vested in a biennial convention made up of elders, clergy, and local lay leaders. There are seven dioceses, each under a bishop's charge.

Missionary work is conducted in the U.S. and in Liberia and Nigeria. The church supports the Christ Missionary and Industrial College at Jackson, Mississippi, and a national publishing house in Chicago, Illinois.

CHURCH OF GOD (Holiness)

Founded: 1886
Membership: est. 8,000 in approx. 140 churches (2000)

The Church of God (Holiness) is an association of autonomous congregations that was founded by former Methodists (see METHODIST CHURCHES) who were active in the Southwest

Holiness Association. They believed that entire sanctification was a biblical doctrine that described the teaching as a second definite work of God's grace in the heart and life of the believer subsequent to regeneration, at which time the believer is cleansed of the effects of original sin and is completely submitted to the controlling hand of the Holy Spirit.

The church today has about 120 English-speaking congregations concentrated in Missouri and Kansas, and a rapidly expanding work among Hispanics in the U.S. The Home Missions Department also works with Haitian immigrants in New York City and sponsors a Navajo mission in the Southwest. The World Missions Department has works in Bolivia; Grand Cayman, Cayman Islands, British West Indies; Cayman Brac, Cayman Islands, British West Indies; St. Croix and St. Thomas, Virgin Islands; Anguilla, Jamaica, Tortolla, and Virgin Gorda, British West Indies; Nigeria; Mexico; and the Ukraine.

In addition to Kansas City College and Bible School, located in Overland Park, Kansas, the church operates many day schools around the U.S. and maintains the Harmony Hill Youth Ministries near Fulton, Missouri. The printing house is the Herald and Banner Press, which produces Sunday School literature for all ages, devotional books, and the periodical *The Church Herald and Holiness Banner.*

A General Convention is held annually in June, to which each congregation may send delegates to represent its interests, the allotment depending upon the size of the local body. The main function of the General Convention is to elect members to boards and committees of the church.

CHURCH OF THE NAZARENE

Founded: 1908
Membership: 627,054 in 5,101 congregations (1998)

The Church of the Nazarene is one of the largest and most influential of the Holiness bodies, and it is one that has self-consciously held to its Wesleyan roots. The church resulted from the merger of three independent Holiness groups already in existence in the U.S. In 1907, an eastern Holiness body, the Association of Pentecostal Churches of America, located principally in New York and New England, joined with a California body, the Church of the Nazarene.

166

The two churches agreed on the name "Pentecostal Church of the Nazarene." Then in 1908, this body merged with a Southern group known as the Holiness Church of Christ. By 1919, the word *Pentecostal* had acquired a different connotation, and the church removed it from the name. While many were involved in the founding of the church, perhaps the principal figure was Phineas F. Bresee (1838–1916), who became its first general superindendent.

The church's theological background is Wesleyan. Four of the first five general superintendents of the Church of the Nazarene, including Bresee, were former Methodist (see METHODIST CHURCHES) ministers, and the church's *Manual* is similar to the Methodist *Book of Discipline.*

The doctrine of the church is built around the justification and the sanctification of believers by faith. This includes a believer's entire sanctification as a second work of grace, subsequent to regeneration. All clergy, both men and women, and local church officials must profess this experience of entire sanctification. Other doctrines include belief in the plenary inspiration of the scriptures as containing all truths necessary to Christian faith and living; the atonement of Christ for the whole human race (i.e., Arminianism); the justification, regeneration, and adoption of all penitent believers in Christ; the Second Coming of Christ; the resurrection of the dead; and the final judgment.

Members believe in divine healing but never to the exclusion of medical agencies. The use of tobacco and alcoholic beverages is denounced. Two sacraments, baptism by sprinkling, pouring, or (most often) immersion and Communion are accepted as "instituted by Christ." Baptism of young children is allowed, but believer's baptism predominates.

Pastors are called by local churches; each district is supervised by a district superintendent, who may be elected for a four-year term by the members of the District Assembly. The General Assembly, the highest body of the church, elects six general superintendents whose terms last until the next General Assembly, and the General Board, consisting of an equal number of lay and clergy members. The General Board meets annually and oversees the five administrative divisions of the church: World Mission, Church Growth, Sunday School Ministries, Communications, and Finance. The church is organized in 109 world areas and supports some 600 missionaries. There is strong emphasis on evangelism. The church's International Center is located in Kansas City, Missouri.

Worldwide, the church supports ten liberal arts colleges, two graduate theological seminaries, and forty-three Bible colleges. Outside North America, the church operates two hospitals, thirty-eight medical clinics, three nurse training colleges, one teacher training college, one junior college, and 430 primary and secondary schools that serve over 51,000 children. The books, periodicals, and curriculum of the church are produced at the Nazarene Publishing House in Kansas City.

CHURCHES OF CHRIST IN CHRISTIAN UNION

Founded: 1909
Membership: 10,104 in 216 congregations (2000)

This church began when five ministers and several lay persons withdrew from Christian Union churches at the 1909 meeting of that group at Marshall, Ohio. The Christian Union had been founded in 1864 in Ohio "to promote fellowship among God's people, to put forth every effort to proclaim God's saving grace to the lost . . . and to declare the whole counsel of God for the edification of believers." Some of the clergy in the Christian Union felt that key doctrines were being neglected, and so the Churches of Christ in Christian Union was organized "to allow a complete freedom in the preaching of full salvation as stated doctrinally by John Wesley." The first council was held that year at Jeffersonville, Ohio, and district councils have been held since that date. In 1945, legislation was enacted to provide for the organization of additional councils, and the church now reaches into seventeen states and several countries abroad. The Reformed Methodist Church merged with the Churches of Christ in Christian Union in September 1952.

Churches in this body are generally evangelistic in faith and work; camp meetings, revivals, and soul-winning campaigns are held regularly throughout the denomination. Worship follows simple forms, with little prescribed ritual. Emphasis is placed "on the blessing of God rather than on the ingenuity of man." A general council meets every two years at Circleville, Ohio, the body's headquarters. Circleville Bible College trains clergy and lay workers.

WESLEYAN CHURCH

Founded: 1843
Membership: 121,356 in 1,594 congregations (1999)

The first Holiness denomination in the U.S., this church arose as a protest against slavery, led by Orange Scott (1800–47) and other New England Methodists (see METHODIST CHURCHES). When the Methodist bishops urged silence, these abolitionists opposed the episcopacy and organized a separate Wesleyan Methodist Connection. This separation predated by one year the historic division of the Methodist Episcopal Church and the Methodist Episcopal Church, South. Following the Civil War and Emancipation, the Wesleyan Methodist Connection embraced the Holiness movement. The ideas of entire sanctification and full temperance seemed important enough to continue the separation from the Methodists. In 1947 a central supervisory authority was established and the word *Connection* was changed to *Church.*

The teaching of entire sanctification is still central in the church, and candidates for church membership are required to disavow the use, sale, or manufacture of tobacco and alcoholic beverages and to refrain from membership in secret societies.

This body was called Wesleyan Methodist Church of America until it merged with the Pilgrim Holiness Church in 1968. That church was one of the bodies that emerged during the Holiness revival of the late nineteenth century. It was close in doctrine and polity to the Church of the Nazarene (see CHURCH OF THE NAZARENE) and thus close to Methodism and in agreement with Wesleyan doctrines; therefore, there was no change in doctrinal emphasis when the two churches united.

Areas of greatest strength of the Wesleyan Church are Indiana, Michigan, Ohio, and North Carolina. A growing evangelistic and missionary activity is directed from the church headquarters in Indianapolis, Indiana. Missionaries work in many countries of Asia, Africa, the Caribbean, Latin America, and Europe. The church supports four liberal arts colleges and one Bible college and maintains good relations with several conservative seminaries in the Wesleyan tradition.

169

HUTTERIAN BRETHREN

Founded: ca. 1530 (came to the U.S. in 1870s)
Membership: est. 42,800 in 428 communities in the U.S. and Canada (1997)

This is one of the few American bodies to stem directly from the Anabaptist movement during the Protestant Reformation (the Mennonites being another; see MENNONITE CHURCHES). The Anabaptists took the ideas of the Reformers farther than the civil magistrates would allow. They rejected infant baptism and insisted on separation of church and state. The New Testament, particularly the Sermon on the Mount (Matt. 5:1–7:29), was taken as the literal authority for true Christians; therefore, the Anabaptist Brethren embraced nonviolence.

The Hutterian Brethren Church was founded by Jacob Hutter, a sixteenth-century Tyrolean Anabaptist who advocated communal ownership of property. The community thrived in the underpopulated areas of Central Europe, particularly Moravia, but was always under the threat of persecution. Hutter himself was martyred in Austria in 1536. Over time, Hutterites migrated to Russia, where the need for hard-working and peaceful farmers was evident. As persecution there increased in the nineteenth century, many Hutterites left Russia for Canada and the U.S.

Most Hutterites are of German ancestry and use that language in their homes and churches. Aside from the idea of common property, they are quite similar to the Old Order Amish (see OLD ORDER AMISH CHURCHES); they seek to express their Bible-centered faith in brotherly love and aim at the recovery of New Testament spirit and fellowship. They feel this requires nonconformity to the world; accordingly, they practice nonresistance, refuse to participate in local politics, and dress in traditional attire. They maintain their own schools, in which the Bible is paramount.

ISLAM

Islam is second only to Christianity in size and geographical scope among world religions, but it is only in the last quarter of the twentieth century that Muslims have been a significant presence in the United States. As a result, Islam is poorly understood in the U.S., and Muslims have been subject to unfair stereotyping, particularly since the Shi'ite revolution in Iran. Militant Islamic fundamentalists are a small percentage of Muslims.

Islam is a monotheistic religion that has close historical and theological ties to Christianity and Judaism. Like them, it seeks to build a just and peaceful society based on a rational moral code. Islam has had a long and glorious tradition. In fact, when the Christian West was in its so-called Dark Ages, Islamic countries were renowned for their science, art, and philosophy. In the nineteenth and twentieth centuries, many Islamic regions were colonized by the Western nations. Their development was impaired by colonial rule, and for many Muslims anti-Western sentiment grew strong. For Muslims living in the U.S., there is the ever-present question of how much one can live like an American and remain faithful to the commandments of Allah.

History. According to Muslims, Islam actually began with the Patriarch Abraham, with whom God made a covenant. Abraham was obedient to God; therefore, Abraham was a Muslim—one who submits to the will of Allah. His was the true religion that later suffered corruption. The oldest son of Abraham was Ishmael, whom the Arabs claim as their forebear.

Historically, though, Islam as an organized religion developed out of Judaism about 600 years after the birth of Christ. Within a hundred years Muslims would conquer much of the ancient Christian world: Syria, Palestine, Egypt, North Africa, and Spain. In 1453, the great Christian city of Constantinople became the Islamic capital of Istanbul. But it all began with one man.

Muhammad was a member of the Quraysh tribe of Mecca, an important center for trade and religion in Arabia. Mecca housed the Ka'ba, a very important shrine among the people of Arabia. Thousands made pilgrimage each year to visit the Ka'ba and see or touch the holy stone contained therein. They also left gifts before the idols placed in the shrine.

171

When he was twenty-five years old, Muhammad married a wealthy widow and managed her extensive holdings and trade. Every year during the month of Ramadan the family would leave the heat of the city to live in one of the cool caves nearby. During one of these family retreats, Muhammad received a call to be a prophet. He heard a voice that told him to read. When he protested that he could not read, the voice commanded him again. He then left the cave and saw the angel Gabriel, who told him that he was to be God's messenger.

Later it was revealed to Muhammad that he was called to reform the religion of the people of Mecca. They must get rid of their idols and worship only the true God of Abraham, Isaac, and Ishmael. Muhammad's first converts were his first wife, Khadijah, his cousin Ali, and his friend Abu Bakr. Muhammad's attempted reforms offended his own tribe, which profited from the pilgrimages and gifts to the idols in the Ka'ba. After some thirteen years of struggling to convert the people of Mecca, a group of pilgrims from Yathrib, now known as Medina, heard Muhammad preach and accepted him as Allah's prophet. Messianic hopes were high among the Jews in Yathrib, and for a brief period early Muslims and Jews were united.

In 622 C.E., Muhammad fled to Yathrib at night in order to avoid assassination. This is known as the *Hijrah,* and it begins the Muslim calendar. Dates in Islamic lands are counted in years after the *Hijrah,* just as Christian lands date events before and after the birth of Jesus. In Yathrib/Medina, Muhammad laid the foundation for the religion of Islam and became a great chieftain.

After several years Muhammad entered Mecca as a conqueror. The residents converted, and the idols were destroyed. Soon afterward Muhammad became the virtual emperor of Arabia and outlawed all forms of idolatry. Only monotheists—Muslims, Jews, and Christians—were tolerated. Before Muhammad died in 632 C.E., it is said that he was taken by Gabriel to Jerusalem, where he visited the Temple site. There Muhammad ascended into heaven and met Moses and Jesus.

The death of Muhammad was a blow to his followers, but they remembered that he was a mortal and not a god. Muslims follow the teachings of Muhammad; they do not worship him. The first five successors of the prophet are known as the Caliphs. They were instrumental in defining the nature of Islam and ensuring its long-term survival. In 662 C.E. the leadership of Islam passed to the

Umayyad dynasty after a period of internal dispute. It was at this point that Shi'ite Islam was born.

In 750 C.E. the leadership of the Islamic Empire passed into the hands of the Abbasids in Persia, who built the capital city of Baghdad. They would rule one of the most glorious empires of the world until the Mongols invaded in the mid-thirteenth century. Eventually Islam spread to Africa, India, Indonesia, and Central Asia.

Theology and Practice. The basic idea of Islam is submission to the will of Allah. This will is expressed in the Qur'an and in Islamic law. Over the years Muhammad received many divine messages in a state of trance. These prophecies, called *surahs,* were written down by his hearers and later collected and edited in the book we know as the Qur'an, or simply the Reading. They are organized according to length rather than content or chronology. Other sayings of the prophet, the *sunnahs,* were recorded in the *Hadith.* They are respected, but are not considered scripture.

Like Judaism, Islam is a religion of law and observance. This law (*Sharia*) includes not only what Westerners would consider criminal matters, such as theft, but also instructions on how family life and society should be organized. It also includes laws regarding religious observance, devotion, and worship. Muslims have always needed teachers to educate people about the law and to interpret the law so that it may be applied to every circumstance of life. These teachers are sometimes called Imams. Often the Imam will be the head of the mosque.

Over time, four major schools of legal interpretation emerged in Islam. Today, 90 percent of all Muslims belong to one of these four schools, but each school accepts the others as orthodox. This scheme of four orthodox schools of interpretation is known as Sunnism. It is contrasted to Shi'ism, which remained closer to the old Arabic traditions.

Some things are basic to all forms of Islam (excluding the Nation of Islam in the U.S.). There are five major beliefs in Islam: (1) There is only one God; (2) there are angels; (3) there have been many prophets, but there is only one message; (4) there will be a final judgment; (5) it is possible to have knowledge of God and God's will. Islam emphasizes the intellect; therefore, every Muslim is a student. There is a saying that God's first creation was the pen and that the first word God revealed to Muhammad was *read.* It is obligatory in Islam to read, study, and seek knowledge; the ink of the scholar is considered to be more valuable than the blood of a martyr.

More important than these tenets are the five pillars of Islam: (1) *Shahada:* "There is no God but Allah and Muhammad is his prophet"; (2) *Salat:* five prayers daily facing Mecca; the prayers are proscribed, as is the bodily posture; (3) *Zakat:* ritual almsgiving; today Muslims are expected to give 2.5 percent of their income to the needy; (4) *Siyam:* a one-month fast during Ramadan in imitation of the practice of Muhammad; and (5) *Hajj:* a pilgrimage every Muslim is expected to make to Mecca at least once in his or her life. Today more than two million do so each year, at great cost to the Saudi Arabian government, which provides hospitality. Every Muslim must follow these five pillars in order to attain heaven, but provisions are made for the weak, the poor, and the infirm.

This is not the sum of Islam, however. Islamic law covers every aspect of life. It is a practical religion that gives guidance for daily life rather than encouraging asceticism. For instance, celibacy is condemned, and large families are encouraged. Moderation in all things, even religion, is stressed. Some things, like images, alcohol, and pork, are forbidden. Other things, like divorce, are permitted but discouraged. Thus there is some variation in Muslim customs because they reflect local traditions. Islam in the U.S. is different from Islam in Pakistan; however, the Islamic ideal is that the whole world will become submissive to the will of God.

Islam in the United States. Since changes were made in American immigration policy in 1965, an average of 30,000 Muslims a year have immigrated to this country. This influx of immigrants, the generally high birth rate of Muslims, and the increasing number of conversions to Islam mean that in this century Islam will certainly surpass Judaism as the second largest religion in the U.S. Muslim immigrants, like their Catholic and Jewish predecessors, have located primarily in the urban centers of the Northeast, the Midwest, and the West Coast. American Muslims come from over sixty different nations; therefore, there has been some difficulty in relating divergent cultural expressions of the religion. The architectural style of mosques, leadership styles, and attitudes toward gender roles differ widely among American Muslims; however, Muslims in general are much more conservative than mainstream American culture. Despite the diversity of American Islam, certain things, such as learning Arabic, reciting the prayers, and reading the Qur'an, unite Muslims of all national origins.

In the twentieth century, Islam began attracting significant numbers of African American converts. For many of them, Islam represented an alternative to Christianity, which they associated with slaveholders. Further, Islam represented a connection with their ancestors, for at least some of the Africans brought in bondage to these shores had been Muslims in their homeland. Finally, Islam offered a practical discipline and control over one's destiny that many felt was denied to them in the dominant culture.

It was Malcolm X (1925–65) who did the most to spotlight Islam in the African American community. He had originally been a leader in the Nation of Islam (see NATION OF ISLAM); however, he rejected that organization when he made his Hajj to Mecca and encountered Sunni Islam in its full international and interracial character. He saw that racism of every kind is condemned in Islam: All Muslims are equal in the eyes of God and will face the same judgment, and all Muslims making the Hajj wear the same white robes of penitence and submission to Allah. Malcolm X was murdered just as he was establishing his own Islamic organization for African Americans, but many followed his example and continued his cause. Among them were notable athletes who took Muslim names, such as Muhammad Ali and Karem Abdul Jabbar. African American Muslims tend to establish their own mosques and publishing houses, but the same is true of Muslims who have recently immigrated. Perhaps 25 percent of American Muslims are of African descent.

NATION OF ISLAM

Founded: 1920s
Membership: est. between 800,000 and 1 million (2000)

The Nation of Islam was an expression of the African pride movement of Marcus Garvey (1887–1940) and others in the first decades of the twentieth century (see AFRICAN ORTHODOX CHURCH). Timothy Drew became convinced that Islam was the true religion of black people and founded Moorish Science Temple in Newark, New Jersey, and took the name Noble Drew Ali (1886–1920). According to Drew, African Americans were Moors whose forebears had lived in Morocco. Only by leaving the distorted white religion of Christianity could African Americans be free. His followers divided into several groups when he died in 1920.

Wallace D. Fard (b. ca. 1877) led a group in Detroit, Michigan. He called himself the reincarnation of Noble Drew Ali and taught "The Religion of the Black Men of Asia and Africa," based at first on the Bible and the Qur'an. Fard's ideas eventually became more radical, attacking the Bible as a book of lies and claiming that African Americans were gods while the white race was the serpent devil that would ultimately be destroyed. Fard announced that he was a tool in the hands of Allah, called to tell the truth about the races and prepare for the final judgment. After his mysterious disappearance in 1933, his followers claimed that he had been Allah personified.

Fard was succeeded by Elijah Poole (1897–1975), known as Elijah Muhammad. Elijah Muhammad continued to preach Fard's gospel of black revolution by which African Americans would end white domination. He called for the creation of an independent Black Nation of Islam within the U.S. Building on the desperate conditions of poverty in the inner-city ghettos, the movement spread across the country and became increasingly militant after World War II.

Elijah Muhammad encouraged his members to spread his teachings among the millions of African American males imprisoned in the U.S. Among his prison converts was Malcolm X (1925–65), one of the towering figures of the Black Power movement of the 1960s. Malcolm used the symbol X to reject the name acquired during slavery. He urged African Americans to take charge of their own destiny rather than relying on the charity of white liberals. He also rejected the pacifist Christian approach of Martin Luther King, Jr., during the civil rights movement. Rather than calling for integration of African Americans into white society, Malcolm X and the Nation of Islam promoted a separate culture. His preaching helped to build membership in the Nation of Islam, but subsequently disagreements developed between Malcolm X and Elijah Muhammad after Malcolm discovered orthodox Islam. Malcolm was murdered in New York City in 1965, but his ideas have remained influential.

After his death in 1975, Elijah Muhammad was succeeded by his son Warith Deen Mohammed, who reoriented and decentralized the movement. He also moved the organization closer to the normative Islamic tradition. Meanwhile, a splinter group led by Louis Farrakhan, based in Chicago, Illinois, continued to emphasize the more radical aspects of the Nation of Islam, especially black nationalism and the racial theories of Fard. Farrakhan's statements and actions have evoked both admiration and condemnation. Warith Deen Mohammed, meanwhile, joined with other Muslim leaders in

1992 to form the Muslim American Society, which claims a membership of 200,000.

Although subject to controversy and occasional violence, the Nation of Islam has achieved some definite accomplishments. It established a chain of industries, such as barbershops, supermarkets, bakeries, restaurants, cleaning establishments, and farms, to relieve poverty among African Americans. Black Muslims do not gamble, smoke, drink, overeat, or buy on credit. They arrange parole for convicts and offer guidance for those released. They claim to give blacks self-respect and a sense of identity, and they have reached many persons whom the mainstream Christian churches have been unable to reach.

SHI'ISM

Founded: 662 C.E.
Membership: 100 million in world, perhaps 100,000 in U.S. (2000)

The Shi'ites broke away from mainstream Islam (see SUNNISM) over the issue of the succession of the Caliphs. Shi'ites believe that leadership should have remained in the family of the prophet rather than passing to the Umayyads. Initially a resistance movement against the Umayyad domination of Islam, the Shi'ites soon became the official religion of Iraq and developed their own distinctive system of jurisprudence. The Shi'ites use the title "Imam," rather than "Caliph," to refer to the true leader of Islam. Most Shi'ites expect a "Twelfth Imam" to appear at the start of the messianic age. The clergy in Shi'ism generally have more authority to interpret Islamic law and observances than in Sunni Islam.

SUFISM

Founded: 8th century
Membership: statistics not available

Sufism is a mystical tradition in Islam (see ISLAM) that originated sometime before the tenth century. It is similar to Hasidic Judaism (see JUDAISM) in its teaching that God is in all things, in its focus on divine joy at all times, and in its use of dancing to help induce religious experience. Unlike the Hasidim, though, the Sufi do

177

not establish separate communities. Rather, Sufi masters teach the Sufi arts in any number of schools or religious orders. Sufism is not for all Muslims, but for those who are specially called; however, the teachings of the Sufi are available to all. In general, Sufism places less emphasis on legalism and more on religious experience and an embrace of all people in divine love. Sufi texts have become popular in the U.S., and there is a Sufi Order of the West, but it is not accepted as orthodox by most Muslims.

SUNNISM

Founded: 622 C.E. (major influx in the U.S. after 1965)
Membership: est. between 3.5 and 6 million in approx. 1,500 mosques

Ninety percent of the world's one billion Muslims are in one of the four orthodox branches of Sunni Islam (see ISLAM). Membership figures are very rough estimates, since there are no central organizations for Muslims and many mosques do not keep or report statistics. The Islamic Society of North America (ISNA), located in Plainfield, Indiana, is the largest organization that provides support for Muslim ministries. In particular, it helps to establish full-time Islamic schools and reviews textbooks for Muslims. It also helps Muslims observe dietary laws while under U.S. government control (e.g., in the military or prison). The ISNA also has programs aimed at keeping youth involved in Islam and in training Islamic workers.

JEHOVAH'S WITNESSES

Founded: ca. 1870
Membership: 990,340 in 11,257 congregations (1999)

The Jehovah's Witnesses are among the most zealous religious bodies in terms of promotion of their beliefs. Meeting in Kingdom halls (not in churches), members witness and publish their faith in testimony and in a remarkably comprehensive missionary effort. They do not believe in separation into clergy and laity, since "Christ Jesus did not make such a separation," and they never use titles like "Reverend." All members are expected to give generously of their time in proclaiming their faith and teaching in private homes. Called "publishers of the Kingdom," they preach only from the Bible. Pioneers, or full-time preachers, are required to give at least 90 hours per month; special pioneers and missionaries donate a minimum of 140 hours per month and are sent to isolated areas and foreign lands where new congregations can be formed. All pioneers provide for their own support, but the society gives a small allowance to some, in view of their special needs. This missionary activity has made Jehovah's Witnesses one of the most widely known (although not widely understood) churches in the U.S.

It was Charles Taze Russell (1852–1916) who established the Witnesses, and until 1931 they were known as Russellites, Millennial Dawn People, or International Bible Students. Russell, the first president, is acknowledged not as founder (there is no human founder), but as general organizer. Witnesses claim to have been on earth as an organization for more than 5,000 years (based on Isa. 43:10-12; Hebrews 11; John 18:37).

Russell was deeply influenced by Adventist thought, which captivated American attention around the middle of the nineteenth century (see ADVENTIST CHURCHES). He developed his own Adventist ideas based on personal study of the Bible, and his lectures attracted huge crowds. To date, some thirteen million copies of his books have been circulated, and they have profoundly influenced the Witnesses. The first formal Russellite group was organized in Pittsburgh, Pennsylvania, in 1870, and soon after a board of directors was elected by vote of all members who subscribed ten dollars or more to support the work (a practice discontinued in 1944). In 1884, Zion's Watch Tower Tract Society was incorporated. In 1939, the name of this corporation was changed to Watchtower Bible and Tract Society, and it remains one of the world's largest publishers.

When Russell died in 1916, Joseph F. Rutherford (1869–1942), known widely as Judge Rutherford, became president. He had been a lawyer and occasionally sat as a circuit court judge in Missouri. His numerous books, pamphlets, and tracts supplanted those of Russell, but his neglect of some aspects of Russell's teaching brought dissension.

The vast literature of the Witnesses (all circulated without bylines or signatures) quotes extensively from the Bible and relates the eschatological teachings of the church. Witness theology is based on the idea of theocracy, or rule of God. It teaches that there is only one

God; Jesus is a creature, not God. In the beginning, the world was under the theocratic rule of the Almighty. At that time all was "happiness, peace, and blessedness." But Satan rebelled and became the ruler of the world, and from that moment, humankind has followed his evil leading. Then came Jesus, "the beginning of the creation of God" (Rev. 3:14, KJV), as the prophets had predicted, to end Satan's rule.

Witnesses maintain that Jesus' heavenly rule, after he paid the ransom sacrifice of his death on earth, began in 1914. Russell had seen World War I as the final apocalyptic struggle that would usher in the return of Christ. When that did not happen, Rutherford reorganized the movement and announced in 1918 that Christ then "came to the temple of Jehovah." With Jesus now enthroned in the temple of Jehovah, the rule of Satan was nearly over, and so Rutherford began to send out his followers to preach the good news in the final days.

God, according to Witness belief, will take vengeance on wicked human beings in our time. God is now showing great love by "gathering out" multitudes of people of goodwill, to whom God will give life in the new world that is to come after the battle of Armageddon. This is to be a universal battle; Christ will lead the army of the righteous, composed of the "host of heaven, the holy angels," and they will completely annihilate the army of Satan. The righteous of the earth will watch the battle and the suffering of God's enemies, but they will not participate.

After the battle, Witnesses teach, the believers in God and God's servants will remain on the earth. Those who have proved their integrity in the old world will multiply and populate the new earth with righteous people. A resurrection of the righteous will also take place, as an additional means of filling the cleansed earth with better inhabitants. After the holocaust, "righteous princes" will rule the earth under Christ, "King of the Great Theocracy." One special group—the 144,000 Christians mentioned in Revelation 7 and 14—will become the "bride of Christ" and rule with him in heaven.

Administration of the group changed during Rutherford's presidency. The governing body today is in the hands of older and more "spiritually qualified" men who base their judgments on the authority of Scripture. This is not considered a governing hierarchy, but an imitation of early apostolic Christian organization. Under direction of the leaders at headquarters, local congregations of Witnesses (always called congregations, never churches) are arranged in circuits, with a traveling minister who spends a week with each congregation. Approximately twenty congregations are included in each circuit, and circuits are grouped into districts, with some forty in the U.S.; circuit organizations are now found in 211 countries and islands around the world.

The headquarters is located at Bethel Home in Brooklyn, New York. Staff engage primarily in editorial and printing work and receive an allowance of $45.00 a month, in addition to room and board. They write, print, and distribute literature in almost astronomical proportions. The official journal, *The Watchtower,* has a circulation of 16,400,000. More than one billion Bibles, books, and leaflets have been distributed since 1920; they are made available in at least 200 languages.

Although predictions of Armageddon have repeatedly been disappointed, Witnesses maintain their belief in its imminence. They have been especially active in opposing what they consider the three allies of Satan: false teachings of the churches, tyranny of human governments, and oppression by big business. This "triple alliance" of ecclesiastical, political, and commercial powers has misled humankind, the Witnesses claim, and must be destroyed at Armageddon before the new world can be born. They refuse to salute the flag, bear arms in war, or participate in the political affairs of government, not because of pacifist convictions, but because they desire to remain apart from what they consider expressions of Satan's power over humankind.

This attitude has brought them into conflict with law enforcement agencies; they have also endured whippings, assaults by mobs, stonings, being tarred and feathered, the burning of their homes, imprisonment, and detention in concentration camps. All of this they have accepted in a submissive spirit. Their position is that they will obey the laws of the earth when those laws are not in conflict with the laws of God.

JUDAISM

Judaism is one of the oldest religions of the world. Today there are about twelve million Jews in the world, half of whom live in the

United States. Judaism can refer to both a religion and an ethnicity, and there are many Jews who do not belong to a synagogue or follow even the basics of the Jewish religion. There is, of course, disagreement among Jews as to what truly makes a person Jewish—whether it is a matter of birth, cultural heritage, or religious observance. Perhaps as many as half of the Jews in the United States are not observant.

Unlike Christianity, which is generally defined in terms of doctrines and beliefs, Judaism as a religion is defined by practices and ethics primarily. Put briefly, Jews understand themselves as the people to whom God gave the commandments to observe as their obligation to God. By following God's instructions, the "chosen people" in turn become a blessing to the entire world as they help to establish God's realm of justice and peace (*shalom*).

History. Jews trace their heritage back to the patriarch Abraham, who answered the call of God and left his home in Mesopotamia to seek a promised land beyond the Jordan River. According to tradition, Abraham's grandson was Jacob, whose name was changed to Israel after he wrestled with an angel one night. The children of Israel were the fathers of the twelve tribes of ancient Israel.

The defining event for the Israelites and their descendents was the exodus. After many years serving as slaves to Pharaoh in Egypt, a prophet named Moses was called by God to lead the people to freedom. Moses parted the waters of the Sea of Reeds (traditionally the Red Sea) and led the people to Mt. Sinai. There he established their laws and gave instructions on how they should live. Israel's obligations to God became known as the Torah ("Law" or "Instruction"). Torah is the centerpiece of all forms of Judaism down to the present day.

Around 1000 B.C.E., King David established a strong and prosperous centralized government with a standing army and efficient bureaucracy. He captured the Canaanite city of Jerusalem and made it the capital of his realm. Despite his personal flaws and failings, David was heralded as the perfect king, God's own son. Prophets and priests alike proclaimed that God had made a special covenant with the house of David so that there would always be a son of David, one of the anointed (in Hebrew, *Messiah*) on the throne in Jerusalem. David's son Solomon expanded the kingdom and built a large central temple in Jerusalem. Jerusalem was proclaimed to be the holy city, the dwelling place of God. Centuries after the destruction of the Temple, Jerusalem is still viewed as a holy city by most Jews.

After Solomon's death, the kingdom divided into two unequal parts. The smaller southern kingdom of Judah consisted primarily of the tribe of Judah. The capital city was Jerusalem, where the descendents of David ruled until the sixth century B.C.E. The words *Judaism* and *Jew* come from "Judah." The northern kingdom was known as Israel, and its capital was Samaria. In the early eighth century B.C.E. this kingdom was destroyed by the Assyrians. The people were dispersed, never to reunite. From that time on, the southern kingdom assumed the heritage of Israel. Around 587 B.C.E., the kingdom of Judah was conquered by the Babylonians, and thousands of citizens were taken into captivity. During the forty years of exile, the prophets, priests, scribes, and scholars began the process of codifying the writings that became the sacred Scripture.

Eventually the Jews were allowed to return to the land of the patriarchs and built a nation under Persian and later Greek control. There was no longer a king; instead the high priest served as the chief administrator of Judea. In the second century B.C.E., their Hellenistic overlord, the Syrian Emperor Antiochus IV, tried to crush the Jews and their religion in order to make them more subservient to his rule. Copies of the Torah (the scrolls of the first five books of the Bible) were burned, Jews were forbidden to circumcise their boy babies (the physical sign that one is in the covenant), and the Temple was desecrated by the sacrifice of an unclean animal to a pagan deity. Rather than crush the spirit of the Jews, these measures led to open revolt. This revolt of the Maccabees on behalf of the right of Jews to observe the commandments of God is commemorated each year at Hanukkah.

Within a hundred years of the revolt against foreign domination, though, Judea fell into Roman hands and at the time of Jesus was administered by a Roman governor. Rebellion again broke out in 66 C.E., but this time, the Jews were defeated. Jerusalem and the Temple were destroyed in 70 C.E. By that time, there were Jewish communities throughout the Roman and Persian worlds, and they grew in importance when the heart of Judaism was destroyed. The Diaspora, or scattering, of the Jews was facilitated by the development of a mobile form of religion that was based in the family and small community. It takes only ten men to form an assembly or synagogue and conduct worship. Even without a synagogue, Judaism can be observed in the home, in secret if need be.

After the rise of Islam (see ISLAM), which has many affinities to Judaism, Jews met with a measure of toleration in the Islamic

Empire and many Islamic countries. Jews often had positions of great power and influence, particularly in the learned professions, such as medicine. Jews in the Islamic world generally spoke Arabic or other local languages and even translated the Torah into Arabic. They assimilated outwardly while maintaining Jewish observance and theology. These Jews of the Mediterranean basin would eventually be called Sephardic, from the Hebrew word for "Spain." Spain had a thriving Jewish community until Isabella and Ferdinand consolidated their rule over the Iberian Peninsula. In 1492, the year Columbus sailed west, the Jews were forced to leave Spain or face the wrath of the Spanish Inquisition. Many Sephardic Jews made their way to the New World, settling in Brazil, New York, and Rhode Island.

Jews in the Christian kingdoms of the West had a more tenuous existence than did those in Islamic lands. During the struggle to define Christianity as separate from Judaism in the patristic period, much anti-Semitism found its way into Christian theology and practice. Throughout the Middle Ages, Jewish communities were subject to harassment by Christian mobs. In the thirteenth and fourteenth centuries Jews were expelled from England and France. Many made their way eastward into the sparsely settled lands of Germany, Poland, Hungary, and Russia. There they established separate communities, often building entire farming villages, where they could observe the Torah in relative peace. These Jews became known as Ashkenazi, from the Hebrew word for "Germany," and they developed a unique German dialect known as Yiddish, which is written in Hebrew letters. The Ashkenazi were generally less sophisticated and secular than were the Sephardim.

Persecution of the Ashkenazi Jews in Russia began in earnest in the nineteenth century, and thousands emigrated to the U.S. Soon anti-Semitism increased in Germany and throughout Central Europe. Hatred of Jews reached a fever pitch in the first half of the twentieth century. When the National Socialist (Nazi) Party came to power in Germany through popular elections, they encouraged violence against Jews. Adolf Hitler (1889–1945) and his aides put in place a series of anti-Jewish laws that stripped Jews of their rights. Soon, he began shipping Jews to concentration camps, where as many as six million, along with millions of Gypsies, Slavs, and other hated groups, were brutally tortured and murdered. This Holocaust marked a watershed in Jewish history that continues to affect Judaism in profound ways. Never before had the threatened destruction of the Jewish people been so close to fulfillment. Perhaps half of the world's Jewish population died during the Nazi era.

The founding of the State of Israel in 1948 was connected with the horrors of the Holocaust. Since the nineteenth century, when many peoples of Europe had agitated for their own nations, there had been calls for a Jewish nation. This Zionist, or Jewish nationalist, movement was led by Theodor Herzel (1860–1904), who laid the groundwork upon which the Jewish homeland would be erected. Initially a rather small movement among secularized Jews, many of whom had socialist convictions, Zionism grew in power as Jews learned the truth about the Holocaust. A Jewish state free from Gentile control seemed to be the best solution to Jewish survival. In the 1960s and 1970s, religious Jews became firm supporters of the Jewish state as well; and many people perceived a link between the future of Israel as a nation and the establishment of the long-hoped for messianic age. In the last quarter of the twentieth century there was a growing fundamentalist movement focused on Zionist goals.

Jews in the United States. There were Jews in the U.S. during the Colonial period, and President Washington was able to assure a delegation of Jewish leaders that the new Constitution of the United States guaranteed freedom of worship and conscience to all people, not just Christians. Despite numerous incidents of anti-Semitism, many Jews saw the U.S. as the new promised land where they could live and worship in relative security. Some Jews embraced American culture so completely that they redefined Judaism in terms familiar to liberal Protestants. Hebrew was dropped, except in special services, the rules of ritual observance were relaxed, and organs were added to synagogues. Some synagogues even began worshiping on Sunday rather than on the sabbath. Other Jews rejected this extreme assimilation to the Protestant American mainstream and retained traditional elements of worship and observance.

The massive influx of Eastern European Jews, the Ashkenazi, profoundly affected the American Jewish community. Millions of immigrants settled in the major Northern cities, creating large Jewish neighborhoods where they could maintain much of their Old World identity in the midst of industrial America. Many of the most famous American entertainers came out of this Yiddish culture, with its distinctive foods and traditions. The Ashkenazi tended to be more conservative than the Sephardic Jews who had lived in the U.S. for

185

decades. Over time, however, much of this Yiddish culture has fallen away. By the end of the twentieth century, Judaism was so well established in American society that an observant Jew, Joseph Liebermann, could be nominated for vice president.

While the local synagogue is very important to Jewish life in the U.S., there are hundreds of Jewish organizations that help to define and defend Judaism. They range from those focused on Jewish rights to youth societies. There are some 200 periodicals and newspapers and two news syndicates dedicated to Judaism. The American Jewish Committee is organized to protect the civil and religious rights of Jews around the world. It seeks equality in economic, social, and educational opportunities and gives aid and counsel in cases of intolerance and persecution.

Jewish institutions of higher learning, affiliated with the various movements, serve the community nationwide, not only training rabbis, but also providing general Jewish learning for all interested people. The most important are (Orthodox) Rabbi Isaac Elchanan Theological Seminary of Yeshiva University in New York City; (Reform) Hebrew Union College—Jewish Institute of Religion in New York, Cincinnati, Los Angeles, and Jerusalem; (Conservative) Jewish Theological Seminary in New York City; and Reconstructionist Rabbinical College in Philadelphia. Yeshiva University in New York City is the only Jewish college that awards a B.A. degree; Brandeis University in Waltham, Massachusetts, is the only nonsectarian Jewish sponsored college or university in the U.S.

Theology and Practice. Rabbinic Judaism was the only form of Judaism to survive ancient times. It actually developed at the same time that Christianity was being formed. In fact, in the first century, Christianity was simply one of many forms of non-rabbinic Judaism. By the sixth century, the two religions had developed the basic structures, theology, and practices that define each to the present.

Judaism as a religion is based on the Hebrew Scriptures (for Christians, the Old Testament), but it is distinct from the form of religion described in those texts. The ancient religion of the Israelites focused on cultic observances, particularly animal sacrifice, and revelation given by prophets. Priests were in charge of seeing that cultic rites were properly performed and that ritual purity was maintained. Prophets served social and religious functions as well. They were men (and occasionally women) through whom God spoke, especially in judgment. Prophets challenged the leaders of society, even the king, to live by the ethical demands of the covenant. Justice for the poor, the outcast, and the oppressed was a major theme of the prophetic judgment.

Over time, scribes codified the pronouncements of the prophets and the laws of the priesthood, producing an enormous body of legal and ethical material that has profoundly shaped Western society. However, many of the laws and instructions contained in the scriptures clearly reflect the world of an ancient agricultural people. Later Jews would try to understand them in radically different historical and social contexts.

Rabbinic Judaism grew out of the Pharasaic movement. The Pharisees were a Jewish party that controlled most of the synagogues in and around Palestine. They differed from the priests and other Jews by their strict interpretation of the demands of the Torah: It should be observed as faithfully as humanly possible. To make observance of the Torah easier, the Pharisees taught, Jews should keep themselves separate from Gentiles, especially at meals, when it would be hard to observe the dietary restrictions of the Torah. Marriage to Gentiles was also generally forbidden. The Pharisees deemphasized Temple observances and the sacrifice of animals and focused on the demands of the Torah in day-to-day living. Justice, not sacrifice, was what God demands, the prophet Micah had said, and the Pharisees agreed. For the Pharisees, prayer and study of Torah served the religious needs that the priests had once met.

One of the key concepts of rabbinic Judaism is that there are two Torahs. The written Torah was given to Moses and is contained in the scrolls of Moses (Genesis, Exodus, Leviticus, Numbers, and Deuteronomy). These writings were revealed by God through the prophetic lawgiver, but the written Torah can be very confusing and difficult to observe unless you live in a small agricultural society. Here is where the second Torah comes in. This is the oral Torah, which was also communicated to Moses by God on Mt. Sinai. The oral Torah is the key to understanding Scripture and to applying the teachings of Scripture to one's daily life. The written Torah says to observe the sabbath and keep it holy. The oral Torah tells you how to do this. According to tradition, this oral Torah was passed down by a succession of prophets and scribes, such as Ezra.

After the destruction of the Temple, though, it became necessary to codify and clarify this oral tradition and preserve it in written

187

form. This culminated in the production of the Talmud around 600
C.E. The Talmud is one of the masterpieces of world literature and
intellectual history. It contains the debates of the rabbis on questions
of biblical interpretation and how to understand and apply the Torah.
There are, in fact, two Talmuds, one produced in Babylon by the
descendents of Jews who had not returned to Israel, and one produced in Palestine centuries after the destruction of the Temple. The
Talmud has two main parts, one of which, the *Haggadah,* deals with
biblical interpretation, customs, legends, and edifying stories. The
other part concerns *Halakah,* the rules of the covenant with God.
Halakah involves the 613 commandments that Jews are to obey and
practice in their daily lives. This can be difficult as the world
changes, so the Talmud also provides guidelines for the rabbis to
continue the tradition of interpreting *Halakah.* This process of interpretation, adaptation, and even disagreement over the meaning of
Torah is the thread that runs through the history of Judaism.

There are some features of Jewish theology and observance that
are common throughout the various branches of Judaism. The core
of Jewish theology is the concept of the oneness of God. There is
only one God, and God's will is known in the covenant. Every day
the practicing Jew repeats the ancient verse that introduces the Ten
Commandments in Deuteronomy: "Hear, O Israel! The LORD is our
God, the LORD alone" (Deut 6:4 NJPS). There is but one Creator,
who ultimately controls the destiny of humankind and the world.

Humankind, created by this one God, is inherently good. There is
no idea of original sin in Judaism. Humans are made in God's image
and are endowed with an intelligence that enables them to choose
between good and evil. Torah assists in this process of choosing good
over evil, but all people, Jews and Gentiles alike, will be judged. The
righteous (or just) will be rewarded and the wicked punished.
However, concern for life after death is an issue of minor signifi-
cance for most Jews. More important is the way one lives in this life.
Judaism looks forward to the establishment of a divine kingdom of
truth and righteousness on the earth. Orthodox Jews believe the time
will come when God sends the Messiah, the descendent of David
who will restore the kingdom. Other Jews speak of a messianic age.
To work toward the divine kingdom, Jews have been established by
God as "a kingdom of priests and a holy nation," the "servant of the
Lord."

Judaism follows a liturgical calendar, dating from ancient times. It

188

is based on the lunar year rather than the solar year, so the dates vary from year to year. The year begins in the autumn with Rosh Hashanah, a new year festival that begins the High Holy Days. For ten days, Jews are encouraged to examine their lives and make reconciliation with those they have wronged, including God, in preparation for Yom Kippur, the Day of Atonement. On this day, God judges the sins of the people and provides for atonement.

Some weeks after Yom Kippur is Succoth, the Feast of Tabernacles or Booths, during which Jews relive the years of wandering in the wilderness. Hanukkah, in December, commemorates the purification of the Temple during the Maccabean revolt. This feast day has grown in importance in the U.S. because of the commercial power of Christmas. Pesach, or Passover, in the spring is a memorial of the liberation of Jews from Egypt. Shabuoth, also known as the Feast of Weeks or Pentecost, follows Passover in late May or early June. It was once a harvest festival but now commemorates Moses' receiving of the Torah.

Other observances follow the life cycle of the individual. These include the circumcision of male children on the eighth day after birth, the *bar/bat mitzvah* (a rite of entry into adult accountability for the covenant), weddings, and funerals. Also important in Judaism is the observance of the sabbath (sundown Friday until sundown Saturday) as a sacred day of rest and study of the Torah. Most synagogues have sabbath services, although sabbath observance is actually a home obligation.

Local congregations have full independence. There are no synods, assemblies, or hierarchies of leaders. Jewish worship varies according to theology and culture. Traditional Orthodox synagogues, for instance, have no instrumental music, the congregation worships with covered heads, and the men and women sit separately. In Reform, Conservative, and Reconstructionist houses of worship, sermons are in English and there is no segregation by sex.

At the head of the congregation stands the rabbi, trained in seminary and fully ordained. He (in some cases, she) officiates at marriages and grants divorce decrees in accordance with Jewish law after civil divorce has been granted by the state. Rabbis conduct funerals and generally supervise burial as Jewish law requires. Orthodox rabbis may supervise the slaughtering of animals and validate other aspects of dietary law. Many congregations engage readers, or cantors, who lead most of the service.

CONSERVATIVE JUDAISM
(United Synagogue of Conservative Judaism)

Founded: 1913
Membership: est. 1,500,000 in 800 synagogues (2000)

Solomon Schechter (1847–1915), head of the Jewish Theological Seminary in New York and founder of the United Synagogue of Conservative Judaism, provided the conservative movement with its intellectual and organizational foundation. The basic conviction of Conservative Judaism is that the whole Jewish community should be united in a type of Judaism that is based on the North American experience and adapted to modern living, but still devoted to the Torah and *Halakah*. In other words, Conservative Judaism is willing to make changes in Jewish custom, such as segregated seating for men and women, but strives to observe the requirements of the Torah as closely as possible in a modern setting.

Education has been a major focus of the Conservative movement. The oldest department of Schechter's United Synagogue is the department of education, which produces and sets standards for textbooks and Jewish school curricula. The United Synagogue congregational religious school system had over 100,000 students in 1996. There is also a Solomon Schechter Day School system, a network of 68 schools throughout the continent with a combined enrollment of over 17,000 children. Youth programs are designed to help Jewish teens and young adults learn to live as Jews in a Gentile world.

Conservative Judaism emphasizes observance of the sabbath, Jewish holy days, and *kashrut* ("rules of purity"). Synagogues are encouraged to have schools for children and follow the *Halakah*. Each congregation is free to accept changes in *Halakah* observance recommended by the Committee on Jewish Law and Standards if and when they so decide.

HASIDIC JUDAISM

Founded: roots to the 1700s
Membership: est. 165,000 (2000)

Hasidic Jews are often confused with the Orthodox; however, they represent one of the most distinctive types of Judaism (see

JUDAISM). Like the Amish (see MENNONITE CHURCHES) among Christians, the Hasidim are so conservative that they generally wear the same style of clothing as their ancestors did in the nineteenth century. By choice they live in segregated communities and clearly define themselves against the dominant culture. They are similar to the Orthodox in their strict observance of *Halakah* and literal approach to the Torah, but theologically and liturgically they are far removed from orthodoxy. Hasidic Judaism developed in Eastern Europe during the early 1700s when groups of pious laypersons began reading the Kabala (medieval Jewish mystical writings) and followed the Torah strictly. In doing so they developed a number of controversial practices, such as rocking back and forth during prayer, that set them off from others in the synagogue. The key figure in early Hasidism was Israel b. Eliezar Ba'al Shem Tov (ca. 1700–60), known as the Besht, who would enter into an ecstatic state and be guided by the Spirit of God. The Besht was a charismatic figure who attracted a large following of disciples, for whom he served as an adviser and guide. His visions and revelations soon took on the force of truth among his followers.

In 1780, Jacob Joseph wrote *Toledot Ya'akov Yosef,* a memoir that included many sayings of the Besht. This was the first attempt at any kind of theoretical formulation of Hasidic beliefs. Among these beliefs are that the separation between the Creator and the creation is merely an illusion. God is hidden in the creation, but is present in this hiddenness. There is only one God, and God is all. God is completely in creation; therefore, we are all one with God. The key to the religious life and to understanding the Torah is to understand and experience the reality of union with God. This mystical idea undergirds all of the life of the Hasidim. Rituals are not meaningless if the mind and heart are properly prepared. The proper attitude for devotion and life is joy rather than melancholy. Melancholy and despair are the great enemies of faith because these emotions deny the reality of God's presence in the world. If God is all, then we must be joyful. Distinctive Hasidic practices, such as dancing in worship, flow from this burning desire for a joyful union with God through celebration of creation.

The key to the spread and development of Hasidism was the Zaddikim, the holy men, who continued to demonstrate the real presence of God in the world through their own experience and activities. These Zaddikim were seen as mediators between God and the community, offering people vicarious fulfillment through their spiritual accomplishments. Now known as Rebbes, these charismatic figures continue to shape Hasidism. The most influential Rebbe in the U.S. was Menachem Schneerson (1902–94), the Lubavitcher Rebbe in New York City.

ORTHODOX JUDAISM
(Orthodox Union)

Founded: 1898
Membership: est. 1,000,000 in 1,000 synagogues (2000)

Orthodox Judaism developed in the nineteenth century in Europe in reaction to the rise of what would be called Reform Judaism. The Orthodox sought to preserve synagogues from what they viewed as corruption and to maintain traditional forms of worship and observance of *Halakah*. This often included preservation of Eastern European customs. For the Orthodox, the Torah is binding on all Jews and is not subject to interpretation or change. The Orthodox Union in America was founded by Dr. Henry Pereira Mendes (1852–1937), a Sephardic leader in New York. He hoped that this union would unify traditionalists, promote the observance of the Torah, and halt Jewish assimilation.

Initially the Union focused on protecting Jewish children and immigrants from Protestant missionaries and promoting the strict observance of the sabbath. Another concern was the difficulty of maintaining the rules of *kashrut* (kosher laws) in the U.S. In 1924, the Orthodox Union created the first non-profit kosher certification program, which now certifies over 200,000 products and supervises over 2,000 corporations with 4,000 certified plants in 56 countries. The Orthodox Union also helps American soldiers to follow *kashrut,* even on the battlefield, and educates the public about Jewish dietary restrictions.

The Orthodox view intermarriage and assimilation as threats to the survival of Judaism. The National Conference of Synagogue Youth (NCSY), an outreach ministry for teenagers, stresses Jewish identity and the need to marry within the faith. The NCSY spurred the birth of the North American Teshuva movement as well. Following the social disruptions of the 1960s, there was a revival of interest in traditional Jewish faith and practice among American youth. Many Conservative synagogues moved more toward

Orthodox observance. Orthodox Jews have been particularly active in working with Russian Jewry and have been strong supporters of the State of Israel.

RECONSTRUCTIONIST JUDAISM
(Jewish Reconstructionist Federation)

Founded: 1954
Membership: est. 100,000 in approx. 100 synagogues (2000)

Originating in 1934 under the leadership of Mordecai M. Kaplan (1881–1983) of the Jewish Theological Seminary in New York City, Reconstructionism is a movement indigenous to the United States. Reconstructionism defines Judaism as an evolving religious civilization, and it attempts to assure the physical and spiritual survival of Judaism by demonstrating that a maximum Jewish life can be lived within the setting of a modern democratic state. Viewing Judaism as a civilization, Reconstructionists have strong commitments both to Jewish tradition and to the search for modern meaning.

Reconstructionists accept that Judaism has evolved over the centuries; rabbinic Judaism is not identical to the Judaism of King David, for instance. However, they do not want to break with the historical process. Instead, "the past has a vote" in determining what the present and the future will be. The whole Jewish heritage, not just the Talmud, is embraced as a resource for building a Jewish civilization in the midst of modern culture. As such, the Zionist cause figures prominently in Reconstruction, but so too does an energetic program of scholarly endeavor to give laypersons resources for understanding the Jewish heritage.

Theologically, Reconstructionists believe it is the duty of all Jews to question and to study in order to find unique paths to the divine. They believe in a God who inhabits this world and especially the human heart. This God is the source of generosity, sensitivity, and concern for the world.

REFORM JUDAISM
(Union of American Hebrew Congregations)

Founded: 1873
Membership: est. 1,500,000 in approx. 890 synagogues

The earliest roots of Reform Judaism can be traced to the Hashalah movement in Europe during the Enlightenment. In the 1740s, Moses Mendelsohn (1729–86) urged his fellow Jews to learn from the secular world and speak the languages around them instead of Hebrew or Yiddish. He translated and published the scriptures in German and encouraged others to translate the Talmud so that both Jews and Gentiles would be able read and understand them. Those in the Hashalah movement advocated that Jews fully assimilate into their local culture, that they speak, dress, act, and even eat like those around them. This would be the path of emancipation from persecution: Jews would overcome cultural alienation and be able to participate fully in life around them. Some of the more religious in the movement sought to reform Judaism from what they considered an archaic past, thus they are known as Reform Jews.

Rabbi Isaac Mayer Wise (1819–1900) brought the Hashalah movement to the U.S. when he emigrated in the 1840s. His American plan (*Minhag America*) included new liturgies for use in the congregations. The prayers dropped all mention of rebuilding the Temple in Jerusalem, for example. Wise attempted to unify Judaism in the U.S. by convoking a Cleveland Conference, where he called for an "American Judaism, free, progressive, enlightened, united, and respected." In 1873, Wise founded Hebrew Union College in Cincinnati, one of the most important Jewish schools in the U.S., and for many years he was a leader in the Union of American Hebrew Congregations.

Since Wise's time, Reform Judaism has continued to understand Judaism in terms of "ethical monotheism," in which the ethical demands of the Torah are vital rather than the ceremonial and dietary aspects. Reform Judaism promotes assimilation into American culture in part as a way to move this nation toward the pursuit of justice and peace.

LATTER-DAY SAINTS
(Mormons)

Best known as Mormons, Latter-day Saints are neither Protestant nor Catholic, and they have one of the most distinctive theologies of all Christian bodies. In addition to the Old and New Testaments, the Latter-day Saints base their beliefs on the *Book of Mormon,* discovered by Joseph Smith, Jr. (1805–44) in the 1820s, and two later works by Smith, *Doctrine and Covenants* and *The Pearl of Great Price.* They believe that the authentic church, having gone underground for many centuries, was restored with the new revelations to Smith. In the mid-nineteenth century, the Latter-day Saints were able to build a civilization based on Mormon teaching in the Utah Territory. Attacked by mobs and once invaded by U.S. Army troops, they founded a religious community in what was once a desert and have established themselves as one of the outstanding religious groups in the nation. Few churches live with such clear identity and manage such a high degree of loyalty and dedication.

Today, the Saints are conservative politically and morally, giving a predominant place to family life. However, they have had one of the most tempestuous histories of any church in the U.S.

History. The early years centered on the prophet and translator of the *Book of Mormon,* Joseph Smith, Jr., who organized the movement with six charter members at Fayette, New York, in 1830. Smith grew up in the famous "Burned-over District" of upstate New York, so called because of the frequency and intensity of the religious revivals there during the Second Great Awakening at the close of the seventeeth century and the early years of the eighteen century. Smith claimed to have experienced a series of heavenly visitations, beginning with the appearance of God and Jesus Christ in 1820. During these visits he was informed that all existing churches were in error and that the true gospel was yet to be restored. It would be revealed to him, and he was to reestablish the true church on earth.

An angel named Moroni led Smith to a hill called Cumorah near Manchester, New York, where he found a book written on gold plates left there by an ancient prophet named Mormon. Later Smith was given a "seer stone" that gave him the knowledge to translate the mysterious hieroglyphic writings. The plates contained the sacred records of the ancient inhabitants of North America, righteous Jews who had fled from Jerusalem in 600 B.C.E. and sailed to North America in a divinely designed ark. According to Smith, he returned the metal plates to the angel. There were eleven other persons besides Smith who claimed they had seen the book before it was returned.

The "priesthood of Aaron" was conferred upon Smith and his scribe, Oliver Cowdery (1806–50), by a heavenly messenger, John the Baptist, who instructed them to baptize each other. In 1829, a year before the founding of the church, three other divine visitors, Peter, James, and John, bestowed upon Smith and Cowdery the "priesthood of Melchizedek" and gave them the keys of apostleship.

Opposition arose as the church gained strength, and in 1831 the Mormons left New York for Ohio, where headquarters were established at Kirkland. Smith moved on to Independence, Missouri, in 1838, where he and his followers planned to build the ideal community, with a temple at its heart. Friction with other settlers there became so acute that they left Missouri during 1838 and 1839 and settled at Nauvoo, Illinois. Violence followed them and reached its peak when Joseph Smith announced his intention to run for the U.S. presidency and acted to shut down a newspaper that had criticized him. He and his brother, Hyrum Smith (1800–44), were murdered by a mob at Carthage, Illinois, in 1844.

With Smith's death, the Quorum of the Twelve Apostles was accepted as the head of the church, and Brigham Young (1801–77) was made president of the Quorum. A defeated minority, objecting that Young was not the legal successor to Smith, withdrew to form other churches. Some followed James J. Strang (1813–56) to Wisconsin to form the sect known as Strangite; others joined various other dissenting groups. The largest body of "anti-Brighamites" believed that the leadership belonged to direct descendants of Joseph Smith, and in 1847 these people, led by Joseph Smith III (1832–1914), formed the Reorganized Church of Jesus Christ of Latter-day Saints.

Young held his office with the vote of the majority, and he had the administrative ability to save the church from disruption and further division. He led the Saints when they were driven out of Nauvoo in February 1846 and began their epic march to what is now Utah. They arrived in Salt Lake Valley in July 1847, and there they built the famous Mormon Tabernacle.

Some sources indicate that Joseph Smith, Jr., informed his associates in the 1840s that polygamous marriages were sanctioned and even commanded by God. Such marriages had been contracted secretly for some time before the practice was announced publicly by Brigham Young in 1852. Following the Civil War, the U.S. federal government mounted an increasingly intense campaign against Mormon polygamy. In 1882, the Edmunds Act provided stringent penalties, and in 1887 the church was unincorporated and its properties confiscated. In 1890 the U.S. Supreme Court ruled it constitutional to deny all privileges of citizenship to members of the church. Also in 1890, the church president issued a manifesto that officially discontinued the contracting of new polygamous marriages. Some followers of Joseph Smith III deny that polygamy was ever sanctioned by the church; but a few in other groups believe that it will never end.

CHURCH OF CHRIST (Temple Lot)

Founded: 1867, with roots to 1830
Membership: est. 2,400 in 32 congregations (2000)

After the death of Joseph Smith, Jr., in 1844, and following the western trek of the Mormons (see LATTER-DAY SAINTS), a number of those who remained in the Midwest became convinced that the church leaders were advocating new teachings quite at variance with the original doctrines. By 1852 there were two protesting groups. One was known as the New Organization; the other, centered in Crow Creek, Illinois, functioned under the name Church of Christ. This latter group returned to Independence, Missouri, in response to a revelation given in 1864 through the presiding elder at the time, Granville Hedrick.

In the "appointed year" of 1867 they returned to the land dedicated in 1831 by Joseph Smith, Jr., for the building of the Lord's Temple. Their belief is that the Lord will designate the time of building. Although the church cannot build until the appointed time, they nevertheless have a sacred obligation to "hold and keep this land free; when the time of building comes, it can be accomplished as the Lord sees fit." This church won court battles with other Mormon bodies to maintain control of these lots.

This Church of Christ puts its faith in the pattern and thought of the church "as it existed at the time of Christ and His apostles." Hence the highest office is that of apostle, of which there are twelve. They are charged with the missionary work and general supervision of the church. Temporal affairs are administered directly by the General Bishopric, under the direction of the General Conference and the Council of Apostles. Local churches administer their own affairs but must keep their teachings and practice in harmony with those of the denomination.

The church accepts the King James Version of the Bible and the *Book of Mormon* as its standards. It holds that all latter-day revelation, including that of Joseph Smith, Jr., must be tested by these scriptures; thus it does not accept all that was given through Smith. Because changes were made in the early revelations, this church prefers *The Book of Commandments* to *Doctrine and Covenants*, which includes changes. For this reason, the doctrines of plural marriage, baptism for the dead, celestial marriage, and plurality of gods are not accepted.

CHURCH OF JESUS CHRIST
(Bickertonites)

Founded: 1862
Membership: 2,707 in 63 congregations (1989)

The founders of this church were at one time members of a Pennsylvania Mormon (see LATTER-DAY SAINTS) body led by Sidney Rigdon (1793–1876), who refused to join the western march under Brigham Young, denouncing Young's teaching of polygamy, the plurality of gods, and baptism for the dead. In 1846 his followers purchased a farm near Greencastle, Pennsylvania. A small group led by William Bickerton, one of Rigdon's elders, did not go to Greencastle, but remained at West Elizabeth. In 1862 they were formally organized as the Church of Jesus Christ. The name "Bickertonites" is employed to distinguish this body from other Mormon groups; members prefer that it be known as the Bickerton Organization.

Foot washing is practiced, and members salute one another with the holy kiss. Monogamy, except in case of death, is required. Members are also called to obedience to all state and civil laws. The church has its own edition of the *Book of Mormon* (in English and Italian) and publishes a monthly periodical, *The Gospel News,* along

198

with other denominational material. A general conference meets annually at the headquarters in Monongahela, Pennsylvania. Missionary work is conducted in Italy, Nigeria, Mexico, and among Native Americans of the United States and Canada.

CHURCH OF JESUS CHRIST OF LATTER-DAY SAINTS

Founded: 1830
Membership: 5,113,409 in 11,315 congregations (1999)

This is the main body of Mormons (see LATTER-DAY SAINTS), headquartered in Salt Lake City, Utah, where the great tabernacle is located.

Beliefs and Practices. Mormonism clearly comes out of the Christian tradition, and in some respects resembles conservative Protestant churches; but certain aspects of the theology of Latter-day Saints depart from traditional Christian theology. For example, in Mormon teaching there are three persons who comprise the Godhead: the Father, the Son, and the Holy Ghost. However, the Father and the Son both have bodies of flesh and bone. It is also maintained that persons will be punished for their own individual sins, not for Adam's transgression. All humankind, even those who have already died, may be saved through the atonement of Christ and by obedience to the laws and ordinances of the gospel. Mormons hold that Christ will return to rule the earth from his capitals in Zion (Salt Lake City) and Jerusalem, following the restoration of the ten tribes of Israel.

For this Mormon group, revelation is not to be regarded as confined to either the Bible or the *Book of Mormon*; it continues today in the living apostles and prophets of the Latter-day Saints church. Latter-day Saints are to adhere to the official pronouncements of the living president (prophet) of the church. Subjection to civil laws and rules is advocated, together with insistence on the right of the individual to worship according to the dictates of conscience.

Ordinances include faith in Christ, repentance, baptism by immersion for the remission of sins, the laying on of hands for the gift of the Holy Ghost, and the observance of the Lord's Supper each Sunday. Baptism is necessary for salvation. Like Pentecostal churches (see PENTE-COSTAL CHURCHES), Mormons believe in the gift of tongues and of interpretation of tongues, visions, prophecy, and healing.

199

Two practices, baptism for the dead and sealing in marriage for eternity, are exclusive to this church. Baptism and salvation for the dead are based on the conviction that persons who died without a chance to hear or accept the gospel cannot possibly be condemned by a just and merciful God. The gospel must be preached to them after death; they find authority for this practice in 1 Pet. 4:6. Baptism is considered as essential for the dead as it is for the living, even though the rites will not finally save them without personal faith and repentance. The ceremony is performed with a living person standing proxy for the dead.

Marriage has two forms: marriage for time and marriage for eternity (celestial marriage). Mormons who are married by only civil authority still remain in good standing in the church, but marriage for time and eternity in the church's temples is regarded as a prerequisite for the highest opportunity for salvation.

Polity. Latter-day Saints recognize two priesthoods: (1) the higher priesthood of Melchizedek, which holds power of presidency and authority over offices of the church and whose officers include apostles, patriarchs, high priests, seventies, and elders, and (2) the lesser priesthood of Aaron, which guides the temporal affairs of the church through its bishops, priests, teachers, and deacons.

The presiding council of the church is the First Presidency, made up of three high priests—the president and two counselors. Its authority is final in both spiritual and temporal affairs. The president of the church is "the mouthpiece of God"; through him come the laws of the church by direct revelation.

Next to the presidency stands the Council of the Twelve Apostles, chosen by revelation to supervise, under the direction of the First Presidency, the whole work of the church. The church is divided into areas, regions, and stakes (geographical divisions) composed of a number of wards (local churches or parishes). Members of two quorums of seventy preside over the areas, under the direction of the Twelve. High priests, assisted by elders, are in charge of the stakes and wards. Members of the Melchizedek priesthood, under the direction of the presidency, officiate in all ordinances of the gospel. The stake presidents, ward bishops, patriarchs, high priests, and elders supervise the work within the stakes and wards of the church. The Aaronic priesthood is governed by three presiding bishops, known collectively as the Presiding Bishopric, who also supervise the work of the members of the priesthood in the stakes and wards. In June

1978, it was ruled that "all worthy male members of the church may be ordained to the priesthood without regard for race or color."

Mission. The church influences all aspects of the life of every member; it supplies relief in illness or poverty and assists with education and employment when necessary. This church maintains, as part of a self-help welfare system, storehouses for community food and clothing. Members operate vegetable, seed, and wheat farms; orchards, dairies, and cannery processing facilities; sewing centers; soap-processing plants; and several grain elevators. Through this system the church donates thousands of tons of surplus clothing annually to needy populations around the world and sponsors water and agricultural projects in underdeveloped countries. The welfare system also includes sheltered workshops for persons with handicapping conditions and a variety of social services, including adoption and foster-care agencies.

Some 37,000 young Mormons currently serve as full-time missionaries throughout the world without compensation; they devote eighteen months to two years to spreading the teaching of their church at home and abroad. Only about 100 persons in full-time leadership positions receive a salary or living allowance.

The Latter-day Saints grew tremendously in the twentieth century and in the last half of the century became very influential in national politics. Many states in the western U.S. now have significant Mormon populations, and the church has spread worldwide.

Education is of great importance to this Mormon group. The church's largest institutions are Brigham Young University in Provo, Utah, and Ricks College in Idaho. Some 425,000 secondary and post-secondary students worldwide are enrolled in seminary and institute classes, which provide religious instruction.

REORGANIZED CHURCH OF JESUS CHRIST OF LATTER-DAY SAINTS

Founded: 1860, with roots to 1830
Membership: 137,065 in 1,236 congregations (1999)

This church claims to be the true continuation of the original church organized by Joseph Smith, Jr., with leadership passing to his son Joseph Smith III in 1860. It bases this claim of succession on the book of *Doctrine and Covenants*. Court actions on two occasions, in

Ohio in 1880 and in Missouri in 1894, are cited in naming it the legal continuation of the original church.

The Reorganized Church rejected the claims of the Mormons (see LATTER-DAY SAINTS) led by Brigham Young because of their abandonment of this rule of succession, along with other doctrinal disagreements. Those holding to the lineal succession eventually reorganized, the first collective expression of this movement coming at a conference in Beloit, Wisconsin, in 1852. Joseph Smith III was chosen president in 1860 at Amboy, Illinois. All of his successors have been descendants of the founder. Since 1920, headquarters have been located in Independence, Missouri, where a temple was built late in the twentieth century.

Although the doctrine of polygamy was endorsed by Young's group in 1852, the Reorganized Church held polygamy to be contrary to the teachings of the *Book of Mormon* and the book of *Doctrine and Covenants* of the original organization. It also differs on the doctrine of the Godhead, celestial marriage, and baptism of the dead.

Basic beliefs include faith in the universality of God the Eternal Father, Jesus Christ as the only begotten Son of the Father, the Holy Spirit, the worth and dignity of persons, repentance of sin, baptism by immersion, the efficacy of various sacramental ordinances, the resurrection of the dead, the open canon of scriptures and the continuity of revelation, the doctrine of stewardship, and the accountability of all people to God.

The work of the church is supported by tithes and free-will offerings. This is regarded as a divine principle, and the tithe is calculated on a tenth of each member's annual increase over needs and just wants.

Church doctrines, policies, and matters of legislation must have the approval and action of a delegate conference held biennially in Independence. General administration of the church is by a First Presidency of three high priests and elders, a Quorum of Twelve Apostles who represent the presidency in the field, and a pastoral arm under the high priests and elders. Bishops are responsible for church properties, the stewardship of members, and church finances.

The Reorganized Church has been active in developing ministries and understanding as it has expanded since 1960 into non-Western cultures. With work in over thirty countries, it has a worldwide membership of nearly 250,000. It sponsors several homes for the elderly, medical clinics, and educational facilities both in the U.S. and abroad. It seeks to dedicate itself to the pursuit of world peace and reconciliation. The ordination of women was approved in 1984, and by 2000 more than 3,500 women had been ordained to ecclesiastical orders.

In 2000, church officials and members agreed to change the name of this Mormon church to Community of Christ, effective in April 2001.

LUTHERAN CHURCHES

In the early sixteenth century, a German theologian named Martin Luther (1483–1546) set out to reform the Roman Catholic Church (see CATHOLIC CHURCHES) of his day. Although he did not intend to create a new church, his followers were nicknamed "Lutherans." These Protestants, as they would later be called, meant to affirm the message of the Bible as the sole authority for church life and Christian belief and practice without rejecting the historical church. To this day, Lutheranism retains much of the tradition of the ancient and medieval church, including a sense of participation in the historic people of God and in the traditional liturgy, revised to accord with Protestant biblicism. Lutherans are devoted to sound doctrine, systematically developed and expressed in thoughtful preaching. Luther's teaching on justification by faith and on the universal priesthood of believers might be called the cornerstone of Protestantism.

History. The story of Luther's rebellion against the Roman Catholic Church is well known. His position, briefly, was that the church and the papacy had no divine right in things spiritual; Scripture, not the priest or the church, has final authority over conscience. "Whatever is not against Scripture is for Scripture, and Scripture is for it," said Luther. People are forgiven and absolved of their sins, he believed, not by good works or by a church rite (especially not through the purchase of indulgences offered for sale at that time by the Roman Catholic Church) but by their Spirit-empowered turning from sin directly to God. Justification is attained through faith, not through ceremony; and faith is not subscription to the dictates of the church, but "the heart's utter trust" in Christ. "The just shall live by faith" was the beginning and the end of Luther's thought. He held that the individual conscience is responsible to God alone. He also held that the Bible is the clear, perfect, inspired, and authoritative Word of God and guide for humankind.

In 1529 Luther wrote both his *Large Catechism* and his *Small Catechism*. A year later, Philip Melanchthon (1497–1560) authored the statement of faith known as the Augsburg Confession. The year 1537 brought the Schmalkald Articles of Faith, written by Luther, Melanchthon, and other German Reformers; in 1577, the Formula of Concord was drawn up. These documents, which offer an explanation of Luther's ideology and theology, form the doctrinal basis of Lutheranism.

The German Reformation resulted not in a united Protestantism, but in one with two major branches: Evangelical Lutheranism, with Luther and Melanchthon as leaders, and the Reformed Church (see REFORMED CHURCHES), led by John Calvin (1509–64), Ulrich Zwingli (1484–1531), and John Knox (ca. 1513–72). Evangelical Lutheranism spread to Poland, Russia, Lithuania, Bohemia, Austria, Hungary, France, and Holland. It became the state church of Denmark, Norway, Sweden, Finland, Iceland, Estonia, and Latvia.

Lutherans in the United States. It was mainly from Germany and Scandinavia that Lutheranism came to the United States. A Lutheran Christmas service was held at Hudson Bay in 1619; the first European Lutherans to remain permanently in this country arrived at Manhattan Island from Holland in 1623. The first independent colony of Lutherans, New Sweden, was established at Fort Christiana along the Delaware River in 1638, at present day Wilmington, Delaware. The great influx of Lutheran immigrants, however, went to Pennsylvania, where by the middle of the eighteenth century Lutherans numbered 30,000, four-fifths of whom were German, the remainder Swedish.

The first churches were small and poor, often without pastors. The situation was relieved with the coming of Henry Melchior Muhlenberg (1711–87) from the University of Halle. He brought about the first real Lutheran organization in 1748 by uniting the pastors and congregations in Pennsylvania, New Jersey, New York, and Maryland into what came to be called the Ministerium of Pennsylvania, the first of many Lutheran synods in the U.S. Others followed slowly: New York in 1786, North Carolina in 1803, Maryland in 1820, Ohio in 1836.

Each synod adjusted itself to its peculiar conditions of language, natural background, previous ecclesiastical relationship with Lutheran authorities abroad, and geographical location. The need for even further organization was evident from the ever-increasing flood of Lutherans from Europe, resulting in the formation of the General Synod in 1820. With the formation of a national synod, the last real bonds with Europe began to break, and American Lutheranism was increasingly on its own.

The General Synod was obliged to extend its efforts farther and farther west, and the Missouri Synod was formed in 1847. From 1850 until 1860, one million Germans arrived in the U.S., the majority of whom were Lutheran. The German Iowa Synod was organized in 1854; in the same year, the Norwegian Lutheran Church was established; the Augustana Synod was created in the new West in 1860. By 1870, Lutherans were the fourth largest Protestant group in the country, with approximately 400,000 members.

The Civil War brought the first serious break in Lutheran ranks, with the organization of the United Synod of the South in 1863; three years later a number of other synods, led by the Ministerium of Pennsylvania, withdrew from the General Synod to form the General Council. To increase the complexity, Lutheran immigrants continued to arrive in larger and larger numbers. These immigrants spoke different languages and came from nations where the church was organized in different ways. From 1870 until 1910, approximately 1.75 million Scandanavians arrived, bringing a slightly different form of Lutheranism than the older, now established German congregations. Numerous small synods were organized.

At one time there were 150 Lutheran bodies in the U.S.; consolidation, unification, and federation have now reduced that number to less than a dozen. In 1917 three larger bodies united in the Norwegian Lutheran Church of America. Some of the Midwest German synods merged in the Joint Synod of Wisconsin in 1918; in that same year, the General Synod, the General Council, and the United Synod of the South merged into the United Lutheran Church. The synods of Iowa, Ohio, and Buffalo, New York, merged into the American Lutheran Church in 1930, and no fewer than eight Lutheran churches were included in mergers from 1960–62. The movement toward unification continued to the end of the century, with the old barriers of speech and nationality disappearing.

In 1988 the American Lutheran Church merged with the Lutheran Church in America and the Association of Evangelical Lutheran Churches to form the Evangelical Lutheran Church in America.

On the international front, united efforts are noticeable also. Groups of lay and ministerial delegates from major Lutheran churches in twenty-two countries formed a Lutheran World Federation in 1947 for the purpose of relief and rehabilitation on a global scale among Lutherans. Perhaps the most cooperative effort in the history of American Lutheranism is found in Lutheran World Relief, through which more than $300 million in cash and food (including U.S. government-donated commodities) has been distributed throughout the world.

Belief and Practices. In spite of their divisions, there has been real unity among Lutherans, based more on faith than on organization. All the churches represent a single type of Protestant Christianity, built on Luther's principle of justification by faith alone. Lutherans maintain that the Bible is the inspired Word of God and the rule and standard of faith and practice. They confess their faith through the three general creeds of Christendom (Apostles', Nicene, and Athanasian), which they believe to be in accordance with the scriptures. They also believe that the Augsburg Confession is a correct exposition of the faith and doctrine of evangelical Lutheranism, although there is disagreement over which version is preferred. The two catechisms of Luther, the Schmalkald Articles, and the Formula of Concord are held to be faithful interpretations of Lutheranism and of the Bible.

The two Lutheran sacraments, baptism and the Lord's Supper, are not merely signs or memorials, but channels through which God bestows forgiving and empowering grace upon humankind. The body and blood of Christ are believed to be present "in, with, and under" the bread and wine of the Lord's Supper and are received sacramentally and supernaturally. Infants are baptized, and baptized persons are believed to receive the gift of regeneration from the Holy Spirit.

Polity. The local congregation is usually administered between its annual meetings by a church council consisting of the pastor and a number of elected lay officers. Pastors are called by the voting members of the congregation.

Congregations are united in synods composed of pastors and lay representatives elected by the congregations and have authority as granted by the synod constitution. In some instances, there are terri-

206

torial districts or conferences instead of synods, operating in the same manner and under the same restrictions; some may legislate, while others are for advisory or consultative purposes only.

Synods (conferences or districts) are united in a general body that may be national or even international and are called variously "church," "synod," or "conference." Some of these general bodies are legislative in nature, some consultative; they supervise the work in worship, education, publication, charity, and mission. Congregations have business meetings at least annually; synods, districts, and conferences hold yearly conventions; the general bodies meet annually or biennially.

APOSTOLIC LUTHERAN CHURCH OF AMERICA

Founded: 1872
Membership: est. 9,000 in 58 churches (2000)

Sometimes called the Church of Laestadius for Lars Levi Laestadius (1800–61), a naturalist, a revivalist, and a minister of the state church of Sweden, this church originated with Finnish immigrants in and around Calumet, Michigan, in the middle years of the nineteenth century. They first worshiped in the Lutheran Church of Calumet under a Norwegian minister. However, differences between the two national groups led to the formation, in 1872, of a separate Finnish congregation, led by Solomon Korteneimi. The church was first incorporated in Michigan in 1879 under the name "Finnish Apostolic Lutheran Church of America," which actually was a merger of independent Apostolic Lutheran congregations. Spreading over Michigan, Minnesota, the Dakotas, Massachusetts, Oregon, Washington, and California, the new church was divided into two districts, eastern and western, with foreign missions in Nigeria, Liberia, and Guatemala.

Conservative in theology, this church stresses the infallibility of Scripture and the importance of a scriptural Christian experience of justification by faith. Such an experience is required for voting membership in spiritual matters; supporting members may vote on temporal matters only. The church accepts the ecumenical creeds and puts strong emphasis on the confession of sins, absolution, and regeneration. Confession may be made to another Christian, but if someone has fallen into sins unknown to others, private confession is not sufficient; the person "should confess them publicly before the congregation and receive absolution."

Local congregations are quite free to govern themselves. At the annual church convention, where every congregation has a vote, three members are elected to a nine-member executive board for three-year terms; the board elects a president, a vice president, a secretary, and a treasurer.

ASSOCIATION OF FREE LUTHERAN CONGREGATIONS

Founded: 1962
Membership: 32,984 in 241 congregations (1999)

This association was formed by congregations of the Lutheran Free Church, which rejected merger with the newly formed American Lutheran Church in 1962 (see LUTHERAN CHURCHES). It has its roots in a revival movement that swept through Scandinavian Lutheran churches in the late nineteenth century. It is conservative theologically and maintains that the local congregation is subject to no authority but the Word of God. Doctrinal emphases include the inerrancy and supreme authority of the Bible as the Word of God, congregational polity, the spiritual unity of all true believers, evangelical outreach for the purpose of leading persons to an experience with and devotion to Christ, the Lordship of Christ in one's personal life, and conservatism on social issues.

The association elects a president and a coordinating committee. Made up of seven persons chosen from the member congregations, the committee maintains a clergy roster and fosters cooperation between churches in ministry to youth, evangelism, parish education, and other matters. Association members also sponsor a theological seminary and a Bible school in Minneapolis, Minnesota, through a schools corporation consisting of fifty persons drawn from member churches.

CHURCH OF THE LUTHERAN BRETHREN OF AMERICA

Founded: 1900
Membership: 13,920 in 115 congregations (1999)

This is an independent Lutheran (see LUTHERAN CHURCHES) body made up of autonomous congregations scattered across the U.S. and Canada. The synod was organized in 1900 for the purpose of serving its member congregations in the larger ministries of Christian education and in home and world missions.

The church maintains a firm commitment to the supreme authority of the scriptures. It accepts the basic Lutheran teachings and emphasizes the need for a personal faith in the Lord Jesus Christ that demonstrates itself in daily life. Membership in the local congregation is based on an individual's personal profession of faith. Worship services are characterized by a nonliturgical style, the use of both traditional and contemporary music, lay participation, and biblical teaching and preaching that is evangelistic and personal in application.

The congregations support a seminary, a Bible school, and a four-year secondary academy. These institutions, as well as the headquarters, are located in Fergus Falls, Minnesota. Home mission congregations are being planted in many areas of the U.S. and Canada. Extensive missions projects are carried on in Chad, Cameroon, Japan, and Taiwan.

CHURCH OF THE LUTHERAN CONFESSION

Founded: 1960
Membership: 8,631 in 72 congregations (1999)

This confessional church was organized by clergy and laypeople who had withdrawn from several synods of the Synodical Conference of North America over the issue of uniting with other synods. The Church of the Lutheran Confession holds firmly to the doctrine of verbal inspiration and inerrancy of the Bible, and it maintains that there can be no church union (even with other Lutherans) unless there is full agreement in doctrine. It holds without reservation to all the historic confessions of the Lutheran faith (see LUTHERAN CHURCHES).

209

Membership is concentrated in South Dakota, Minnesota, and Wisconsin. It also engages in mission work in India and Nigeria. A high school, a college, and a seminary in Eau Claire, Wisconsin, are supported by the church.

EVANGELICAL LUTHERAN CHURCH IN AMERICA

Founded: 1988
Membership: 5,149,668 in 10,851 congregations (1999)

On January 1, 1988, the Evangelical Lutheran Church in America (ELCA) was formed by a union of the Lutheran Church in America (LCA), the American Lutheran Church (ALC), and the Association of Evangelical Lutheran Churches (AELC), making this body not only the largest Lutheran denomination, but also one of the largest religious bodies in the U.S. Two of the uniting denominations themselves were the result of mergers. The ALC was formed in 1960 of Midwestern synods, three of which were Scandinavian. This merger marked a movement away from ethnic identity for Lutherans. The LCA was formed in 1962 in New York and Philadelphia from four synods, including a Finnish synod. The LCA descended from the old General Synod and represented a reunification with the Southern Lutherans. The AELC, on the other hand, broke away from the Missouri Synod in 1976 in a doctrinal dispute. Therefore, this new body represents the historical continuity of Lutherans from colonial days to the present as well as the unity of Lutherans across ethnic lines.

Efforts to form the ELCA began in 1982 when the three uniting churches elected a 70-member commission to draft the constitution and other documents for their new church. In August 1986, the conventions of the individual bodies approved the constitution, and the following May, the ELCA Constituting Convention elected Herbert Chilstrom as bishop. The ELCA's headquarters is located in Chicago, and its congregations are grouped into 65 synods throughout the U.S. and the Caribbean. Nine regions coordinate the work between synods, and between synods and churchwide organizations.

The biennial Churchwide Assembly, which includes about 600 lay voting members equally divided by gender and about 400 clergy voting members, is this church's highest legislative authority. A 37-member Church Council, elected by the assembly, serves as the board of directors and interim legislative authority between assemblies.

The bishop is the church's chief pastor and executive officer. The term of office is four years, eligible for re-election by the Churchwide Assembly. Also elected to four-year terms are the treasurer, secretary, and executive directors.

The organization of the ELCA provides for divisions for Congregational Life, Higher Education, Global Mission, Ministry, Outreach, and Church in Society Ministries. Its publishing house, with primary offices in Minneapolis, produces and distributes printed and other media resources for the church. Among the publications is the magazine of the church, *The Lutheran*. The Department for Ecumenical Affairs coordinates ecumenical, inter-Lutheran, and interfaith activities and administers relationships with the Lutheran World Federation, the National Council of the Churches of Christ in the U.S.A., and the World Council of Churches. In 1997 the ELCA approved full communion partnerships with the Presbyterian Church (U.S.A.), the United Church of Christ, and the Reformed Church in America; similar status was approved for The Moravian Church in America and The Episcopal Church, U.S.A., in 1999.

EVANGELICAL LUTHERAN SYNOD

Founded: 1918
Membership: 22,264 in 139 congregations (1999)

This synod traces its roots to Norwegian immigration in the middle of the nineteenth century. A Norwegian synod was formed in 1853, and the present body was organized in 1918 by a minority group that declined to join the other Norwegian groups when they united in the Norwegian Lutheran Church (later, the Evangelical Lutheran Church) in 1917.

The jurisdiction of the synod is entirely advisory; all synod resolutions are ultimately accepted or rejected by the local congregations. The officers and boards of the synod, however, direct work of common interest insofar as they do not interfere with congregational rights or prerogatives.

For some years the synod used the facilities of the colleges and seminaries of the Missouri and Wisconsin synods, within the framework of the Synodical Conference. In 1963 the Evangelical Lutheran Synod withdrew from the conference because of doctrinal differences with the Missouri Synod, but it is in fellowship with the

Wisconsin Synod. It has maintained Bethany Lutheran College at Mankato, Minnesota, since 1927 and Bethany Lutheran Theological Seminary, also at Mankato, since 1946.

LUTHERAN CHURCH—MISSOURI SYNOD

Founded: 1847
Membership: 2,582,440 in 6,220 congregations (1999)

This second largest Lutheran denomination in the U.S. was founded in Missouri by German immigrants in 1847. Many of these immigrants had rejected the planned merger of the Lutheran and Reformed churches in Prussia, and from the beginning, this synod has been devoted to the maintenance of confessional Lutheranism, coupled with a strong sense of mission outreach. It stresses the authority of the classic Lutheran confessional statements and the inerrancy of Scripture.

The synod has long been considered a leader in the field of communications. It operates the world's oldest religious radio station, KFUO in St. Louis, Missouri; provides the fifty-year-old "Lutheran Hour," heard in more than 100 countries; and produces "This Is the Life," after thirty years the longest-running syndicated dramatic series on television. It also operates Concordia Publishing House, one of the largest religious publishers in the U.S. In addition, the church has given great attention to ministry to deaf and blind persons, producing literature in Braille and supporting nearly sixty congregations for the hearing impaired.

Because of differences in doctrine and practice, the Missouri Synod was not a part of the 1988 merger that united three other Lutheran denominations. However, it continues to cooperate with those churches in a variety of ministries, particularly in areas of social work, such as world hunger relief and the resettlement of refugees.

The church's headquarters are in the International Center, in suburban St. Louis. Directors for the church body are set by a triennial convention of pastors and laypeople, whose members represent the congregations of the synod. Christian education for members of all ages has always been stressed. The synod operates twelve colleges and seminaries in North America, with an enrollment of more than 8,000. Its elementary and secondary system of more than 1,500 schools is the largest of any Protestant denomination in the U.S. Mission work is conducted in thirty foreign countries.

WISCONSIN EVANGELICAL LUTHERAN SYNOD

Founded: 1850
Membership: 411,295 in 1,239 congregations (1999)

Organized in Milwaukee as the German Evangelical Lutheran Synod of Wisconsin, this church merged with the Minnesota and Michigan synods in 1917 to become the Evangelical Lutheran Joint Synod of Wisconsin and Other States. In 1959 the present name was adopted. This synod subscribes to confessional Lutheranism and is committed without reservation to the inspiration and infallibility of Holy Scripture. It is opposed to fellowship with other church bodies unless there is full agreement in doctrine and practice.

Divided into twelve districts, it maintains its national headquarters in Milwaukee. Mission churches are supported in Zambia, Malawi, Brazil, Mexico, Puerto Rico, Colombia, Japan, Taiwan, Hong Kong, Indonesia, India, Cameroon, Nigeria, Russia, Bulgaria, and among Native Americans in Arizona. For the education of its pastors and Christian day-school teachers, the synod maintains two colleges, three academies, and a theological seminary. Associations of congregations operate seven homes for the aged and a social-service agency.

MENNONITE CHURCHES

Dating from the 1520s in Central Europe, these Protestants take their name from Menno Simons (ca. 1496–1561), an early Dutch leader of the "Radical Reformation." "Radical" in yearning to get to "the roots" of the biblical manner of living, they rejected the "magisterial Reformation" of Martin Luther (1483–1546) and John Calvin (1509–64). Called Anabaptists by others, they were treated as outsiders, heretics, and even outlaws by Catholics and Protestants alike. Their concerns were not with proper theology, the sacraments, or liturgy. Rather, they believed themselves called to exemplify godly living based on the Sermon on the Mount (Matt. 5:1–7:29). Until

213

recently, most (and still some) of those quietly dedicated Christians frowned on involvement in secular activity, refusing to take oaths, bear arms, vote, or hold public office. They are a called-out (from the state, from conventional society) fellowship of believers. Always emphasizing the local congregation, some groups insist on living in "intentional communities." In many ways akin to the Brethren family (see BRETHREN and PIETIST CHURCHES), Mennonites pursue their own course in giving primacy to lifestyle rather than to cultivated piety.

The first Anabaptist congregation of historical record was organized at Zurich, Switzerland, in 1525 by those who disagreed with Ulrich Zwingli (1484–1531) in his readiness to forge a union of church and state. They also denied the scriptural validity of infant baptism and hence were labeled Anabaptist, or Rebaptizers.

Anabaptist congregations were organized in Holland by Obbe Philips (ca. 1500–68) as early as 1534. Philips baptized Menno Simons in 1536, and Simons, a converted Roman Catholic priest, organized so many Anabaptist congregations that his name became identified with the movement. Simons's writings, which emphasize pacifism, continued to influence the Mennonites. Their pacifism and rejection of the state religion brought severe persecution, and the number of martyrs might have been much greater had it not been for the haven offered by William Penn (1644–1718) in the American colonies.

Thirteen families settled in Germantown near Philadelphia in 1683, and eventually a Mennonite congregation was established there. Mennonite immigrants from Germany and Switzerland spread over Pennsylvania, Ohio, Virginia, Indiana, Illinois, and into the far western U.S. and Canada; these were later joined by others from Russia, Prussia, and Poland. Thanks to their historic insistence on nonresistance, their colonial settlements were comparatively peaceful and prosperous.

Mennonite beliefs are based on a confession of faith signed at Dordrecht, Holland, in 1632. In eighteen articles, the following doctrines were laid down: faith in God as Creator; humanity's fall and restoration at the coming of Christ; Christ as the Son of God, who redeemed humankind on the cross; obedience to Christ's law in the gospel; the necessity of repentance and conversion for salvation; baptism as a public testimony of faith; the Lord's Supper as an expression of common union and fellowship; matrimony only among the "spiritually kindred"; obedience to and respect for civil government, except in the use of armed force; exclusion from the church and social ostracism of those who sin willfully; and future reward for the faithful and punishment for the wicked.

The Lord's Supper is served twice a year in almost all Mennonite congregations; in most, baptism is by pouring. Most also observe the foot-washing ordinance in connection with the Lord's Supper, after which they salute one another with the "kiss of peace." The sexes are separated in the last two ceremonies. All Mennonites baptize only on confession of faith, refuse to take oaths before magistrates, oppose secret societies, and strictly follow the teachings of the New Testament. They have a strong intra-church program of mutual aid and provide worldwide relief through the Mennonite Central Committee.

The local congregation is more or less autonomous and authoritative, although in some instances appeals are taken to district or state conferences. The officers of the church are bishops (often called elders), ministers, and deacons (almoners). Many ministers are self-supporting, working in secular employment when not occupied with the work of the church. Other officers are appointed for Sunday school, young people's work, and other duties.

The Amish movement within the ranks of the Mennonites takes its name from Jacob Amman (ca. 1656–c. 1730), a Swiss Mennonite bishop of the late seventeenth century who insisted on strict adherence to the confession of faith, especially in the matter of shunning excommunicated members. This literalism brought about a separation in Switzerland in 1693.

Early Amish immigrants to the U.S. concentrated in Pennsylvania and spread into Ohio, Indiana, Illinois, Nebraska, and other western states and into Canada. Many Amish, distinguished by their severely plain clothing, are found in the Conservative Amish Mennonite Church and Old Order Amish Mennonite Church. They are still the literalists of the movement, clinging tenaciously to the Pennsylvania Dutch language and seventeenth-century culture of their Swiss-German forebears. They oppose the use of automobiles, telephones, and higher education and are recognized as extremely efficient farmers.

BEACHY AMISH MENNONITE CHURCHES

Founded: 1927
Membership: 7,853 in 114 churches (1997)

These churches are made up mostly of Amish Mennonites (see MENNONITE CHURCHES) who separated from the more conservative Old Order Amish (see OLD ORDER AMISH CHURCHES) over a period of years, beginning in 1927 in Somerset County, Pennsylvania. They were led by Bishop Moses M. Beachy, and they are now found principally in Pennsylvania and Ohio. They believe in the Trinity and that the Bible is the infallible Word by which all people will be judged, the righteous going to heaven and the wicked to eternal suffering.

To some degree, they resemble the Old Order Amish in garb and general attitude, but their discipline is milder. These Mennonites worship in church buildings, have Sunday schools, and are active in supporting missionary work. Nearly all of the churches sponsor Christian day schools. They sponsor a monthly publication, *Calvary Messenger,* and an annual twelve-week Calvary Bible School. The Mission Interests Committee sponsors homes for the aged and handicapped as well as missions in the U.S. and Europe.

BRUDERHOF COMMUNITIES

Founded: 1920
Membership: 2,500 worldwide (2000)

One of the newest manifestations of the Anabaptist communal witness is the Bruderhof movement that began in Germany following the economic and social devastation of the First World War. Founded by Eberhard Arnold (1883–1935), a theologian and writer, it gained attention in North America during the 1960s, and has now grown to nine communities in the U.S., England, and Australia, where about 2,500 men, women, and children live in common in accordance with the witness of the early Christians as described in the book of Acts (chaps. 2 and 4). They live together in full community, share their property, work and worship together, and in all things seek unity. Many more people are associated with the movement without being members.

Theologically the Bruderhof affirm the Apostles' Creed but place their emphasis on the expectation of God's kingdom coming to this earth. They hold that followers of Jesus are empowered by the Spirit to live now in accordance with God's rule and reign as expressed in the Sermon on the Mount (Matt. 5:1–7:29). The mission of the Bruderhof is to witness to the good news that in Christ it is possible to live a new life and to share this life together with others in brotherhood, community, and justice.

Because of Jesus' teachings, the Bruderhof affirm the sanctity of every life; thus they oppose every form of violence and killing, including abortion, capital punishment, war, and physician-assisted suicide. They also believe in the sanctity of marriage (between one man and one woman) and the sanctity of sex (sexual intimacy within marriage only). They do not proselytize but instead seek to work together with others, whatever their belief and wherever possible, in the spirit of Christian unity and common concern.

CHURCH OF GOD IN CHRIST, MENNONITE

Founded: 1859
Membership: 12,144 in 102 churches (1999)

This church grew out of the preaching and labors of John Holeman (1832–1900), a member of the Mennonite (see MENNONITE CHURCHES) church in Ohio, who became convinced that the church was in error in many of its teachings and practices, having moved from the doctrines and practices of its forebears. He preached ardently on the necessity of the new birth, Holy Ghost baptism, more adequate training of children in the fundamentals of the faith, disciplining of unfaithful members, avoidance of apostates, and condemnation of worldly minded churches. He separated from the Mennonite Church and in 1859 began to hold meetings with a small group of followers. They then formally organized into the Church of God in Christ, Mennonite.

The church holds that the same confession of faith must be believed and practiced by all churches, "from the time of the apostles to the end of the world," and that the Bible, as the inspired, infallible Word of God, must govern all doctrine and teaching. It accepts the Eighteen Articles of Faith drawn up at Dordrecht, Holland, in 1632. Women are required to cover their heads and men to wear

217

beards. Noninvolvement in the military and in secular government is enforced.

The highest decision-making authority is the General Conference, a convention of ministers, deacons, and delegates that convenes every five years or as the need arises. The church teaches nonconformity to the world in dress, bodily adornment, sports, and amusements.

Most congregations in the church maintain a Christian school for the education of their children. Missions are operated in the U.S., Canada, Mexico, Guatemala, Haiti, the Philippines, India, Nigeria, and other countries. Kansas is the state of heaviest concentration.

CONSERVATIVE MENNONITE CONFERENCE

Founded: 1910
Membership: 10,334 in 102 churches (1999)

The Conservative Mennonite Conference (CMC) is an autonomous affiliation of congregations within the Mennonite (see MENNONITE CHURCHES) church that was formed in 1910 in a meeting of concerned Amish Mennonite church leaders at Pigeon, Michigan. Five ministers were in attendance, representing Amish Mennonite churches that were reluctant to adopt the Old Order Amish Mennonite (see OLD ORDER AMISH CHURCHES) conservatism toward cultural expressions. However, they were also more conservative than the prevailing Amish Mennonite and Mennonite approach of that time. The organization was known as Conservative Amish Mennonite Conference from 1912 until the present name was adopted in 1954.

The CMC subscribes to the Mennonite Confession of Faith (1963) and to the Conservative Mennonite Statement of Theology (1991). These documents affirm the full humanity and full divinity of Jesus Christ, the full inspiration and autographical inerrancy of the scriptures, believers' baptism, and nonviolence. Members are expected to refrain from gambling, alcohol, tobacco, immodest attire, swearing oaths, and premarital and extra-marital sexual activity.

The highest decision making body in the Conservative Mennonite Conference is the semiannual Minister's Business Meeting, which elects an executive board and a general secretary to oversee the day to day operations of the conference. The missions arm of the CMC is Rosedale Mennonite Missions. Internationally affiliated church bodies are found in Costa Rica, Nicaragua, Ecuador, Haiti, Germany, and Kenya. Rosedale Bible Institute in Irwin, Ohio offers college-level courses in various Christian studies. The conference sponsors Bethel Mennonite Camp for youth in eastern Kentucky. The official publication of CMC is the *Brotherhood Beacon.*

EVANGELICAL MENNONITE CHURCH

Founded: 1865
Membership: 4,929 in 33 churches (2000)

Formerly the Defenseless Mennonite Church (see MENNONITE CHURCHES), this body was founded as a result of a spiritual awakening among the Amish in Indiana under the leadership of Henry Egly, who stressed the need for repentance and regeneration before baptism. Egly's practice of rebaptizing Amish who experienced conversion led to conflict within the Amish community, leading to the formation of the evangelical church. It continues to emphasize regeneration, separation and nonconformity to the world, and nonresistance.

The Evangelical Mennonite Church's program today is largely one of missions and church-extension evangelism. A children's home in Flanagan, Illinois, and a camp near Kalamazoo, Michigan, are maintained. The present name was adopted in 1949; however, by 2000 the denomination was studying the possibility of dropping the word *Mennonite* from its name.

FELLOWSHIP OF EVANGELICAL
BIBLE CHURCHES

Founded: 1889
Membership: 1,917 in 16 churches (1990)

Formerly known as the Evangelical Mennonite Brethren (see MENNONITE CHURCHES), this group emanates from the Russian immigration of Mennonites into the U.S. and Canada during 1873 and 1874. The Conference was founded in 1889 in order to emphasize the evangelical doctrines of repentance, conversion, baptism on confession of faith, and living lives committed to Jesus Christ. It also adheres to belief in the inerrant, inspired Word of God and to the dispensational interpretation of history and biblical prophecy that looks for the imminent return of Christ.

The majority of the fellowship's churches lie outside the U.S., in Canada, Argentina, and Paraguay. Despite its size, it carries on an active world mission program.

GENERAL CONFERENCE OF MENNONITE BRETHREN CHURCHES

Founded: 1860
Membership: 82,130 in 368 churches (1996)

Dutch and German in background, this church was organized in the Ukraine by a small group of Mennonites (see MENNONITE CHURCHES) seeking greater attention to prayer and Bible study than they found in their native Mennonite church. Its founders were heavily influenced by German Pietism (see BRETHREN AND PIETIST CHURCHES), but they retained the congregational polity common to Mennonite churches. Small bodies reached Kansas in 1874, then spread to the Pacific Coast and Canada.

A general conference meets biennially as the chief administrative body, gathering delegates from its two areas (Canada and the U.S.). Each area has a number of districts. The area conferences supervise work in home missions, education, and publications. General offices are maintained in Fresno, California.

The Krimmer Mennonite Brethren merged with this church in 1960, and General Conference Mennonites continue to work closely with other Mennonites in mission. Foreign missions are found in Africa, Asia, Europe, South America, and Mexico; a radio ministry broadcasts worldwide in English, German, and Russian; and a French-language Bible Institute was established in Quebec in 1976.

MENNONITE CHURCH

Founded: 1525 (organized in the U.S. in 1725)
Membership: 92,002 in 935 churches (1999)

This major Mennonite (see MENNONITE CHURCHES) body was brought to Germantown, Pennsylvania, in 1683 by Dutch and German immigrants. The Dordrecht Confession was adopted at a conference of Pennsylvania Mennonite ministers in 1725 as a Mennonite statement of faith. In 1921, Christian Fundamentals was adopted. A confession adopted in 1963 sought, without attempting to make the body into a creedal church, to set forth the major doctrines of Scripture as understood in the Anabaptist-Mennonite tradition. The confession stresses faith in Christ, the saved status of children, the importance of proclaiming God's Word and "making disciples," baptism of believers, absolute love, nonresistance rather than retaliation as one's personal response to injustice and maltreatment, and the church as a nonhierarchical community. Because of their insistence on freedom from the traditional Mennonite regulations on attire, this group has been regarded as "liberal in conduct" by some other Mennonites.

The General Assembly meets every two years. It brings together representatives from all area conferences and from many congregations throughout North America. Discussion is open to all; however, only elected delegates (women and men, ordained and nonordained) may vote.

Churchwide program boards are in charge of mission, congregational ministries, education, publishing, and mutual aid work; all are under the supervision of the church's general board. Home missions stress evangelism, and missions are found in Asia, Africa, Europe, and Central and South America. The church sponsors hospitals, retirement homes, and child-welfare services. Membership is strongest in Pennsylvania and the Midwest states.

In 2001 this church will merge with the General Conference Mennonite Church (founded in 1860). The membership of the new body should be about 125,000 people in 1,020 churches. The united church will have a "one denomination-two country structure," with the new Mennonite Church divided into Mennonite Church U.S.A. and Mennonite Church Canada.

In 1995, General Conference Mennonites and members of the Mennonite Church adopted a new Confession of Faith in a Mennonite Perspective. The confession is the most recent in a series of historical Anabaptist faith statements, beginning with the Schleitheim Articles, written in 1527. The new confession of faith includes twenty-four articles that interpret Mennonite beliefs about God, Jesus Christ, the Holy Spirit, Scripture, creation, sin, salvation, the church, Christian life and mission, peace and justice, and the reign of God.

Associated Mennonite Biblical Seminary in Elkhart, Indiana, trains General Conference and Mennonite Church pastors, missionaries, pastoral counselors, peace workers, and lay leaders.

MISSIONARY CHURCH

Founded: 1969
Membership: 46,015 in 334 churches (1999)

The Missionary Church is made up of two groups that merged in March 1969: the Missionary Church Association founded at Berne, Indiana, in 1889 and the United Missionary Church, formed in 1883 in Englewood, Ohio as the Mennonite Brethren in Christ. Both former denominations had a Mennonite (see MENNONITE CHURCHES) heritage and came into existence through the holiness revivals of the late 1800s.

The Missionary Church is conservative and evangelical in theology and practice. Local churches are free to manage their own affairs, but recognize and adhere to the authority of a general conference made up of clergy, missionaries, and laity, held biennially. Working under the general conference is a general board that oversees a variety of agencies and missions activities. The president, vice president, and secretary are elected for terms of four years.

The U.S. Missionary Church works jointly with the Missionary Church of Canada in overseas ministry in the joint venture named World Partners. Church planting, Bible translation, correspondence courses, Bible schools, a theological college, extension seminaries, clinics, youth camps, and other programs are carried out by 139 missionaries who work in cooperation with the national churches. Countries served include Brazil, the Dominican Republic, Ecuador, France, Haiti, Jamaica, Nigeria, Sierra Leone, Spain, and others. There are also indigenous churches in India, Mexico, and Venezuela. Further outreach is achieved through other evangelical mission boards in twenty-three countries worldwide.

The church is affiliated with one educational institution in the U.S.: Bethel College in Mishawaka, Indiana.

OLD ORDER AMISH CHURCHES

Founded: 1720s
Membership: est. 80,800 in 898 districts (1993)

The Old Order (*Ordnung*) Amish hold to the old traditions of the Amish movement more strictly than do the so-called Church Amish. For example, their "plain dress" requires the use of hooks and eyes instead of buttons or zippers, and members do not own automobiles.

It is impossible to give precise membership statistics since the Old Order is not a denomination in the usual sense of the word. There are no church buildings because believers worship in private homes. Moreover, there are no conferences. Members do not believe in missions or benevolent institutions or centralized schools; some, however, do contribute to the missions and charities of the Mennonite Church (see MENNONITE CHURCHES). There are nearly 900 Old Order Amish districts, each averaging 100 to 150 members, with approximately half that number baptized.

OLD ORDER (WISLER) MENNONITE CHURCH

Founded: 1872
Membership: statistics not available

This church was named for Jacob Wisler, the first Mennonite see (MENNONITE CHURCHES) bishop in Indiana, who led a separation from that church in 1872 to protest the use of English in the services and the introduction of Sunday schools. Similar to Old Order (*Ordnung*) Amish, these Mennonites maintain the old style of clothing, make only limited use of modern technology, and keep separate from the world. Joined in 1886, 1893, and 1901 by groups with similar ideas from Canada, Pennsylvania, and Virginia, the church is still maintained on the basis of those protests.

Each section of the church has its own district conference, and there are conferences twice each year in each community. All churches take part in relief work, especially for the needy at home and in foreign lands, and some contribute to the work of the Mennonite Church.

METHODIST CHURCHES

For decades, the Methodist Church was the largest religious organization in the United States, and it still has the greatest geographical scope of any church. Beginning as a Pietist (see BRETHREN and PIETIST CHURCHES) movement within the Church of England in the 1730s, Methodism expanded greatly during the eighteenth century under the leadership of the Wesley brothers, John (1703–91) and Charles (1707–88), who preached and wrote hymns on the need for a personal experience of salvation and change of life. Although Methodism remains history-minded and respectful of liturgy, it typically has been concerned with ministry to the poor and disadvantaged, expressing its faith in compassion for the human condition. In a variety of ways, the witness of the Spirit among Methodists has been an impelling force for worship, love of neighbor, personal piety, and evangelization.

History. The origins of the Methodist Church can be traced to a small group of serious-minded students and fellows at Oxford University who were dubbed "Methodists" (also "Bible Bigots" and the "Holy Club") because of their strict regimen of prayer, fasting, Bible reading, and charitable works inspired by William Law's (1686–1761) *A Serious Call to a Devout and Holy Life* and *A Treatise on Christian Perfection.* Among the members of the group were the Wesleys and the future evangelist George Whitefield (1714–70).

John Wesley had been ordained in the Church of England (see EPISCOPAL/ANGLICAN CHURCHES) in 1728 and had served a parish with his father for two years before the older man's death, when John returned to Oxford as a Fellow of Lincoln College. Charles was ordained in 1735. The two left Oxford and traveled to the Colonies, arriving in Georgia in 1735. Charles came as secretary to General James Oglethorpe (1696–1785), and John was sent by the Society for the Propagation of the Gospel to be a missionary to the Native Americans. It was an unsuccessful and unhappy two years for John, but while aboard ship on the way to the Colonies, he met a group of Moravians (see MORAVIAN CHURCH) and was deeply impressed by their piety and humble Christian way of life. After his return to London, he went to the meeting of a Moravian religious society in Aldersgate Street. There he heard the preacher read Luther's "Preface to the Epistle to the Romans," and he felt his heart "strangely warmed" as the meaning of the Reformer's doctrine of "justification by faith" sank into his soul. That was the evangelistic spark that energized his life and started the flame of Wesleyan revival in England.

The Wesleys and Whitefield soon began preaching the need for a personal experience of conversion and holiness of life. When the staid Church of England closed its pulpits to them, they took to the open air and sought audiences among the large and ignored working class of the new industrial revolution. Charles wrote hymns of revival for the streets, barns, private homes, and mining pits of Cornwall. John preached repentance, regeneration, justification, holiness, and sanctification to coal miners and textile laborers. Converts came thick and fast; it became necessary to organize into "societies." One was attached to a Moravian congregation in Fetter Lane, London, in 1739 and later moved to its own quarters in an abandoned government building known as the Foundry, where in 1740 it became the first self-sustaining Methodist society in London.

Between 1739 and 1744 the organizational elements of Methodism were instituted: a circuit system and itinerant ministry, class meetings and class leaders, lay preachers, and annual conferences. There was phenomenal growth in membership; more than 26,000 Methodists were worshiping in England, Ireland, Scotland, and Wales in 1767.

Methodism was primarily a lay movement, and Wesley did his best to keep it within the Church of England. An evangelical party grew within that church that would include luminaries such as hymn writer Isaac Watts (1674–1748) and philanthropist and abolitionist William Wilberforce (1759–1833), but it became evident that a separate Methodist organization was needed to deal with the large numbers recruited from among the unchurched. As early as 1739 John Wesley drew up a set of general rules that are still held by modern Methodists as an ideal delineation of biblical rules of conduct. *A Deed of Declaration* in 1784 gave legal status to the yearly Methodist conference.

Methodists in the United States. Meanwhile, the movement had reached Ireland and the American colonies, and Wesley began to send out leaders. The first in the Colonies were Joseph Pilmoor

(1739–1835) and Richard Boardman (1738–82). By 1769, New York Methodists had built Wesley Chapel, now known as John Street Methodist Church. Captain Thomas Webb (ca. 1726–96) established societies in Philadelphia; Robert Strawbridge (d. 1781) started a revival in Maryland and built a log-cabin church at Sam's Creek. Devereux Jarratt (1733–1801), a transplanted Anglican minister, led a revival in Virginia that won thousands.

The true center of Methodism in those days lay in the South; of 3,148 Methodists in the Colonies in 1775, about 2,000 lived south of Mason and Dixon's line. Wesley, aware of the rapid spread of the movement, sent emissaries to take charge, among them Francis Asbury (1745–1816) and Thomas Rankin (1738–1810), the latter as "superintendent of the entire work of Methodism in America." Rankin presided over the first conference in the Colonies, called at Philadelphia in 1773.

At the time of the Revolution, Methodism seemed doomed to disappear in North America. Wesley's pro-British attitude aroused resentment, and Asbury, working almost singlehandedly, found it difficult to keep some of the churches alive. Surprisingly, of all the religious groups in the Colonies, Methodists alone actually seemed to prosper during the Revolution. By the end of the war, membership had grown to 14,000, and there were nearly 80 preachers. It was now an American church, free of both England and the Church of England. Wesley accepted the inevitable; he ordained ministers for the Colonies and appointed Asbury and Thomas Coke (1747–1814) as superintendents.

Coke brought with him from England certain instructions from Wesley, a service book and a hymnal, and authority to proceed with the organization. The Christmas Conference, held at Baltimore in December 1784, organized the Methodist Episcopal Church and elected Coke and Asbury as superintendents (later called bishops). *The Sunday Service* (an abridgment of *The Book of Common Prayer*) and Articles of Religion were adopted as written by John Wesley with the addition of an article that the Methodists should vow allegiance to the United States government.

Under Asbury's energetic direction, Methodism was adapted to the American rural setting. Circuit riders, preachers on horseback who traveled the expanding frontier, went to mountain cabins, prairie churches, schoolhouses, and camp meetings, preaching the need for conversion and regeneration. The Methodist Book Concern was established in 1789, putting into the saddlebags of the circuit riders religious literature that followed the march of the American empire south and west. The revivalistic flavor of the camp meeting, born among the Presbyterians, was adopted by the Methodists and exploited to the limit. By the middle of the nineteenth century there were some 1.3 million Methodists in the U.S.

All was not peaceful among the Methodists. Objecting to what they considered abuses of the episcopal system, several bodies broke away: the Republican Methodists, later the Christian Church, withdrew in Virginia; Methodist Protestants seceded in 1830. Between 1813 and 1917, large groups of African Americans formed independent churches: the African Methodist Episcopal Church; the Union Church of Africans, now the Union American Methodist Episcopal Church; and the African Methodist Episcopal Zion Church. In 1844 came the most devastating split of all, the bisecting of the Methodist Episcopal Church into the Methodist Episcopal Church, the Northern body, and the Methodist Episcopal Church, South, organized in 1845.

The cause of this major split was, of course, slavery. Bishop J. O. Andrew (1794–1871), a Georgian, owned slaves through inheritance, and his wife also was a slaveholder. It was not possible for them to free their slaves under the laws of Georgia, but the General Conference of 1844, held in New York City, requested that the bishop desist from the exercise of his office while he remained a slaveholder. Incensed, the Southern delegates rebelled; a provisional plan of separation was formulated, and the Southerners went home to organize their own church.

Basic to the separation was the constitutional question of the power of the General Conference, which, the Southerners maintained, assumed supreme power in virtually deposing a bishop who had violated no law of the church and against whom no charges had been brought. It was a split that was not healed until 1939, when the Methodist Episcopal Church; the Methodist Episcopal Church, South; and the Methodist Protestant Church were reunited at Kansas City, Missouri, to form The Methodist Church.

The uniting conference of that year adopted a new constitution in three sections: an abridgment of the Articles of Religion drawn up by John Wesley; the General Rules, covering the conduct of church members and the duties of church officials; and the Articles of Organization and Government, outlining the organization and conduct of conferences and local churches. This constitution cannot be changed by any General Conference unless and until every annual conference has acted upon the proposed changes.

Another Methodist body with a distinct history was The Evangelical United Brethren Church, which had arisen from a series of mergers of two groups: United Brethren in Christ and the Evangelical Church. The Evangelical Church, originally Evangelical Association, began as a result of the labors of Jacob Albright (1759–1808) among the German people of Pennsylvania. Preaching first as a Lutheran and then as a Methodist exhorter, Albright was made a bishop at the first annual conference of the Evangelical Association in 1807. He used the Methodist *Discipline*, preached Methodist doctrine, and was so effective that for quite some time his followers were known as "the Albrights." A split in 1891 resulted in a separate denomination, the United Evangelical Church. The two groups were reunited in 1922 under the name "Evangelical Church."

Another group, Church of the United Brethren in Christ, developed in a parallel manner through the preaching of the Pietists (see BRETHREN and PIETIST CHURCHES) Philip William Otterbein (1726–1813) and Martin Boehm (1725–1812) among the Germans in Pennsylvania, Maryland, and Virginia. They were elected bishops at a conference in September 1800. That conference created the Church of the United Brethren in Christ, which also was strongly Methodist in polity, doctrine, and practice. Each group had a *Discipline* modeled on that of the Methodists. The Church of the United Brethren in Christ and the Evangelical Church were merged into the Evangelical United Brethren Church (E.U.B.) at Johnstown, Pennsylvania, in 1946.

In April of 1968, The Methodist Church merged with the Evangelical United Brethren (E.U.B.) to form The United Methodist Church. In this union no significant changes were made in either doctrine or polity.

Representatives from the African Methodist Episcopal Church, the African Methodist Episcopal Zion Church, the Christian Methodist Episcopal Church, and The United Methodist Church have met since the mid-1980s as the Commission on Pan-Methodist Cooperation. A newer body, the Commission on Union, was formed in 1996, again with representatives from the four churches. Members of the two bodies have recommended that the commissions be merged; the recommendation must be approved by the general conferences of each of the four churches before it can be adopted.

Beliefs and Practices. In matters of faith, there has been very little occasion for confusion or difference; doctrinal quarrels have been noticeably absent. Historically, Methodists have not built theological fences to keep anyone out; they have stressed the foundational beliefs of Protestantism and have offered theological common ground. Not all of the churches repeat the Apostles' Creed in their worship, though the discipline of the church provides for its use in formal worship. The theology is Arminian, stressing the free will of the individual and the death of Jesus Christ as atonement for all human beings, as interpreted by Wesley in his sermons, his *Notes on the New Testament,* and his *Articles of Religion.*

The church preaches and teaches the doctrines of the Trinity; the natural sinfulness of humankind, its fall and the need of conversion and repentance; freedom of the will; justification by faith; sanctification and holiness; future rewards and punishments; the sufficiency of the scriptures for salvation; and the enabling grace of God. Two sacraments, baptism and Communion, are observed; baptism is administered to both infants and adults, usually by sprinkling. Membership is based on confession of faith or by letter of transfer from another church; admission of children to membership is usually limited to those thirteen years of age or older, but in the South the age may be a few years younger.

There is wide freedom in the interpretation and practice of all doctrines, with some congregations more liberal and others more conservative. Methodists played major roles in many significant American religious movements, especially the Temperance Movement, the Social Gospel, the Holiness Movement, and the Ecumenical Movement. Some of these movements produced new denominations.

Worship and liturgy are based on the English prayer book, with widespread modifications. The language of the prayer book is much in evidence in the sacraments of Methodist churches. In many forms of worship, however, each congregation is free to use or change the accepted pattern as it sees fit.

Polity. The local churches of Methodism are called charges; clergy are appointed by the bishop at the Annual Conference, and each church elects its own administrative board, which initiates planning and sets goals and policies on the local level. It is composed of staff members, chairs of various committees, those representing various program interests, and members at large. Charge, Annual, and

General Conferences prevail in most Methodist bodies. While the government is popularly called episcopal, it is largely governmental, through this series of conferences. The Charge Conference meets at the local church or on the circuit, with the district superintendent presiding. It fixes the salary of the pastor, elects the church officers, and sends delegates to the Annual Conference. It may delegate responsibility for many of these duties to the administrative board.

Some areas have a district conference between the Charge and the Annual Conference, but it is not a universal arrangement. Annual Conferences cover defined geographical areas; they ordain and admit ministers, vote on constitutional questions, supervise pensions and relief, and exchange pastors with other Annual Conferences through acts of the bishop; and, every fourth year, elect lay and ministerial delegates to the General Conference. The General Conference is the lawmaking body of the church, meeting quadrennially; the bishops preside, and the work of the conference is done largely in committees, whose reports then may be adopted by the General Conference.

AFRICAN METHODIST EPISCOPAL CHURCH

Founded: 1814
Membership: est. 2,500,000 in 6,200 congregations (1999)

The African Methodist Episcopal Church (AMEC) is one of the oldest and largest Methodist (see METHODIST CHURCHES) bodies in the world. It was founded by Richard Allen (1760–1831), a former slave from Delaware who had bought his freedom. Allen had been converted while still a slave, and he began preaching to freed African Americans in Philadelphia up to five times a day. He regularly attended St. George's Methodist Church, where African Americans were generally welcomed, but were segregated from whites. In 1787 Absalom Jones (1746–1818), who later became the first African American Episcopal priest, was kneeling in prayer when white trustees physically removed him to the back of the church. When the congregational leadership supported this discrimination, Allen and Jones led the black members out of the congregation. In 1793, Allen established the Bethel Church for Negro Methodists in Philadelphia.

Although Francis Asbury dedicated the chapel in Philadelphia and ordained Richard Allen as its minister, Bethel Church was the center of controversy within the Methodist system. The whites in the denomination tried to keep Allen and his congregation from controlling their own property, but in 1816 the Pennsylvania Supreme Court ruled in favor of Allen. It was during the course of this struggle that the Bethel Congregation and five other predominantly black Methodist churches left the Methodist Church and formed the AMEC in 1814. Allen was consecrated by Asbury as the first bishop in 1816.

Other African American churches throughout the urban North followed suit. Bishop Allen held strongly to the connectional system of the Methodists and tried to bring the new Zion Church (see AFRICAN METHODIST EPISCOPAL ZION CHURCH) under his umbrella after 1816, but the members of Zion responded by forming their own denomination. In the years preceding the Civil War, the AMEC was largely confined to the Northern states; following the war its membership increased rapidly in the South. Today it is found all across the nation.

There are 19 bishops (including the first woman bishop, elected in 2000), 12 general officers, and 18 connectional officers in thirteen districts; a General Conference is held quadrennially. Foreign missions are supported in South Africa; West Africa; India; London, England; the Caribbean; and South America. The church supports six colleges and two theological schools. Journalism has been a central part of the church's work from its early years; the AME Book Concern dates to 1816, and the weekly *Christian Reader* has been published since 1848.

AFRICAN METHODIST EPISCOPAL ZION CHURCH

Founded: 1821
Membership: 1,276,662 in 3,125 congregations (1999)

This church dates from 1796, when it was organized by a group of people protesting racial discrimination in the John Street Methodist Church in New York City. Their first church, named Zion, was built in 1800, and that word was later made part of the denominational name. Richard Allen tried to bring the new Zion church under the authority of the African Methodist Episcopal Church (see AFRICAN METHODIST EPISCOPAL CHURCH), but Zion maintained its independence. The first annual conference was held in that church in 1821, with nineteen preachers from six black Methodist churches in New Haven, Connecticut; Philadelphia, Pennsylvania; and Newark, New Jersey. James Varick (ca. 1750–1827), who had led the John Street dissension, was elected the first bishop. The present name was approved in 1848. The church spread quickly over the northern states, and by 1880 there were fifteen annual conferences in the South.

Livingstone College, in Salisbury, North Carolina, the largest educational institution of the church, was established in 1879. Departments of missions, education, and publications were created in 1892. Later administrative boards were established to direct work in church extension, evangelism, finance, ministerial relief, and so on. Home missions are supported in Louisiana, Mississippi, and several western states, principally Oklahoma. Missionaries are found also in Liberia, Ghana, Nigeria, South America, and the West Indies. The church maintains five secondary schools and two colleges.

CHRISTIAN METHODIST EPISCOPAL CHURCH

Founded: 1870
Membership: 784,114 in 3,069 congregations (1999)

This body was established in 1870, in an amicable agreement between white and black members of the Methodist Episcopal Church, South (see METHODIST CHURCHES). At the time of Emancipation there were at least 225,000 slave members of the Southern church, but following the Civil War, all but 80,000 joined one of the two independent black bodies, the African Methodist Episcopal Church or the African Methodist Episcopal Zion Church. When the general conference of the Methodist Episcopal Church, South, met at New Orleans in 1866, a commission from the black membership asked to separate into a church of its own. The request was granted, and the Colored Methodist Episcopal Church was organized. That name was held until the meeting of its general conference at Memphis in May 1954, when it was changed to the present name.

The doctrine of the church is Methodist, but this denomination adds a quarterly conference to the district, annual, and quadrennial conferences usual in Methodism. There are ten episcopal districts, each supervised by a presiding bishop, who together form the College of Bishops. Ten departments oversee the national work, each chaired by a bishop assigned by the College of Bishops. The general secretaries of the various departments are elected every four years by the General Conference, and the president of the Women's Missionary Council is elected every four years by the quadrennial assembly of the Missionary Council. The church issues two periodicals and supports five colleges, a seminary, a hospital, and several low-rent and senior-citizen housing complexes. In the latter decades of the twentieth century, the church encouraged economic growth for African Americans as part of its ministry.

CONGREGATIONAL METHODIST CHURCH

Founded: 1852
Membership: 14,738 in 187 churches (1995)

This church was established in Georgia in protest against certain features of the episcopacy and itinerancy of the Methodist Episcopal Church, South (see METHODIST CHURCHES). In the late 1880s more than half of this body in turn withdrew to join the Congregational Church (see CONGREGATIONAL CHURCHES).

Local pastors are called by the local churches; annual conferences grant licenses, ordain ministers, and review local reports. Annual and general conferences are recognized as church courts, empowered to rule on violations of church law and to coordinate, plan, and promote general church activities. There is a missionary program among the Navajo in New Mexico and Mexico. Wesley College and the denominational headquarters are in Florence, Mississippi.

EVANGELICAL CHURCH OF NORTH AMERICA

Founded: 1968
Membership: 12,369 in 132 congregations (1998)

When the Methodist Church merged with the Evangelical United Brethren to form The United Methodist Church in 1968 (see UNITED METHODIST CHURCH), a number of churches in the Brethren body withdrew to form The Evangelical Church of North America. The new church was organized at Portland, Oregon, and eventually

233

came to include congregations across the country, although the strength still lies in the Northwest. In 1982, union occurred with the Holiness Methodist Church and the Northwest Canada Conference.

The doctrinal position of the Evangelical Church is Wesleyan-Arminian. In organization, conference superintendents oversee each district and annual conference; the general administration is carried on by annual conference sessions, the conference Council of Administration, and program agencies, such as evangelism, missions, Christian education, and stewardship. A general superintendent is the overseer of the work of the denomination.

EVANGELICAL CONGREGATIONAL CHURCH

Founded: 1894 and 1928, with roots to 1800
Membership: 22,349 in 143 congregations (1999)

This denomination traces its origin to the work of Jacob Albright (1759–1808), a Methodist (see METHODIST CHURCHES) evangelist among the German people of Pennsylvania in the early 1800s. Albright helped to organize the Evangelical Association that later became the Evangelical Church, which eventually merged with the United Brethren Church to form the Evangelical United Brethren Church. In a bitter dispute over episcopal authority, seven Annual Conferences and some 60,000 members of the Evangelical Church withdrew from that body in 1891 to organize the United Evangelical Church.

The two churches were reunited in 1922, but again a minority objected and remained aloof from the merger. The East Pennsylvania Conference and several churches in the Central, Pittsburgh, Ohio, Illinois, and West Virginia conferences continued their separate existence under the old name, which was changed to the Evangelical Congregational Church in 1928. This church, like its parent Evangelical Church, is "Methodist in polity, Arminian in doctrine." Emphasis is on the inspiration and integrity of the Bible and "fellowship of all followers of Christ."

Each congregation owns its property, determines its membership, manages its affairs, and chooses its ecclesiastical affiliation. Within set geographical areas there are Annual Conferences that supervise the local congregations through regional elders/conference superintendent. The supervisory/stationing committee, composed of the bishop and the stationing elders/conference superintendent, annually assigns pastors to the churches. The several Annual Conferences send representatives to a General Conference every four years.

The Division of Missions, with two adult auxiliaries, supervises the missionary programs. There are missionaries abroad and in the U.S., with 163 nationals at work in various lands. Summer camping is held at three campsites, strategically located in the conferences, with four ten-day camp meeting sessions. Church headquarters, the Evangelical School of Theology, and the Evangelical Congregational Church Retirement Village are located at Myerstown, Pennsylvania.

EVANGELICAL METHODIST CHURCH

Founded: 1946
Membership: 8,615 in 123 congregations (1997)

The Evangelical Methodist Church is "fundamental in doctrine, evangelistic in program, and congregational in government." It represents a double protest against what was considered an autocratic and undemocratic government, on the one hand, and a tendency toward modernism, on the other hand, in the Methodist Church (see METHODIST CHURCHES).

The church is Arminian in theology and Wesleyan in doctrine. Members seek to apply the spirit and revivalistic fervor of original Wesleyanism to the needs of society today. Fundamentalist in theology, they oppose the "substituting of social, educational, or other varieties of cultural salvation for the gospel message."

Local churches own and control their own property and select their own pastors. There are six districts, each with a district superintendent, and a general superintendent. The General Conference meets quadrennially; international headquarters are in Indianapolis, Indiana. The church maintains missionary work in Bolivia and in Mexico.

FREE METHODIST CHURCH OF NORTH AMERICA

Founded: 1860
Membership: 70,556 in 971 congregations (1999)

The Free Methodist Church is one of the more conservative among the larger bodies of American Methodism in both doctrine

235

and standards of Christian practice. Its founders were the Reverend B. T. Roberts (1823–93) and his associates, who objected to "new school" Methodism, which they believed compromised the Wesleyan standards of the church. They called for a return to stricter doctrine and lifestyle in the Methodist Church (see METHODIST CHURCHES). This included the abolition of slavery, abolishing the practice of pew rentals, opposition to secret societies, and more freedom in worship. They were "read out" of their churches and organized the Free Methodist Church in Pekin, New York.

Doctrinally, the Free Methodists stress the virgin birth, the deity of Jesus, and his vicarious atonement and resurrection. No one may be received into membership without undergoing confession and forgiveness of sin, and the experience of entire sanctification is sought in all members.

The church is connectional, with a board of four bishops who supervise the four basic geographic areas of the church, a general conference that meets every four years, annual conferences, and districts, in a basic Methodist pattern. Headquarters are in Indianapolis, Indiana. The publishing arm of the church is Light and Life Communications.

The Free Methodist Church has become a world fellowship, consisting of ten general conferences (Burundi, Canada, Congo, Egypt, Dominican Republic, Japan, Mozambique, Rwanda, South Africa, and U.S.) with a common constitution. Free Methodist churches are found in fifty-nine countries; membership outside the U.S. is over 500,000.

The church operates six four-year colleges and a seminary and maintains a seminary foundation in cooperation with Asbury Theological Seminary and Western Evangelical Seminary. Social services include a hospital, a home for unwed mothers, five retirement and nursing facilities for the elderly, and many day-care centers for children.

PILLAR OF FIRE

Founded: 1901
Membership: statistics not available

The Pillar of Fire originated in the evangelistic efforts of its founder, Alma White (1892–1946), who often preached from the pulpit of her husband, the Reverend Kent White, a circuit-riding Methodist minister in Colorado. At a time when the Methodist Episcopal Church (see METHODIST CHURCHES) was reluctant to have female ministers in its pulpits, Alma White's fervent exhortations on regeneration and holiness, or sanctification, as a second definite work of grace brought her into conflict with church leaders. Eventually, White withdrew to establish the Pentecostal Union in 1901. The name was changed to "Pillar of Fire" in 1917, drawing on imagery from Exodus 13:21.

The Pillar of Fire states that the organization's purpose is "the building up of Christian character among all people." Their theology is essentially Wesleyan, with emphasis on repentance, justification, second-blessing holiness, pre-millennialism, future judgment, and the inspiration and authority of the scriptures. Sacraments include baptism and the Lord's Supper.

Pillar of Fire churches are found in California, Colorado, Illinois, New Jersey, Ohio, and Pennsylvania. From headquarters in Zarephath, New Jersey, a bishop and general secretary oversee the activities of the organization. The church has specialized in radio ministries and Christian academies throughout its history. A pioneer Christian radio station, KPOF, which went on the air in 1928, is recognized by the National Religious Broadcasters as "the oldest radio station of the oldest Christian network" in the United States. Pillar of Fire sponsors Christian schools in California, Colorado, Illinois, and New Jersey, and supports Belleview College in Westminster, Colorado. Mission work is carried on in England, India, and Malawi.

PRIMITIVE METHODIST CHURCH, U.S.A.

> Founded: 1840
> Membership: 6,031 in 77 congregations (1999)

This church came into being as a result of camp-meetings in England inspired by the American evangelist Lorenzo Dow (1777–1834). At an all-day meeting held at Mow Cop, Staffordshire, on May 31, 1807, two local preachers, Hugh Bourne and William Clowes, were dismissed from the Wesleyan Church. A group of people, converted as a result of the open-air meetings, joined with Bourne and Clowes in 1810. Growth was such that by February 1812 the group took the name Society of the Primitive Methodists (see

METHODIST CHURCHES), a name that refers to the practice of early Methodist evangelists who preached in the open air. Four missionaries were sent to the U.S. in 1829 to work with Primitive Methodists who had settled mainly in the East and the Midwest. Their ministries prospered, and the American Primitive Methodist Church was established in 1840.

The denomination has an Annual Conference that is both administrative and legislative, the churches being divided into six districts. The president is elected every four years, and there is one salaried official, an executive director. The relationships and arrangements of clergy are reviewed annually, and vacancies are filled with student ministers or ordained deacons and elders. The general offices are located in Wilkes-Barre, Pennsylvania.

Doctrinally, the Primitive Methodists embrace a Wesleyan form of fundamentalism that emphasizes the Bible as the inspired Word of God, the deity of Christ, the fall of Adam and Eve, the necessity of repentance and regeneration for all believers, the return of Christ, and eternal rewards and punishments for all people. This denomination has close ties to the Evangelical Congregational Church, the United Brethren in Christ Church, and the Southern Methodist Church.

SOUTHERN METHODIST CHURCH

Founded: 1939
Membership: 7,686 in 117 congregations (1999)

The Southern Methodist Church grew out of the Methodist Episcopal Church, South (see METHODIST CHURCHES). Its members opposed the merger of that church with the northern Methodist Episcopal Church in 1939, on grounds of the "alarming infidelity and apostasy found therein." They regard the Southern Methodist Church not as a separatist body but as a church "brought into existence to perpetuate the faith of John Wesley."

There are no bishops, but there are the usual Methodist Annual and General Conferences; a president is elected every four years from the elders of the clergy. Laypeople and clergy have equal voice and voting privileges in the conferences.

Local churches own and control their own property and buildings and call their own pastors, who must be approved by their Annual

Conferences. There is one college and a publishing house, Foundry Press, both located at Orangeburg, South Carolina.

UNITED METHODIST CHURCH

Founded: 1968, with roots to 1784
Membership: 8,377,662 in 35,609 congregations (1999)

Two mergers of major importance produced The United Methodist Church. The first merger was actually a rejoining of three separated Methodist (see METHODIST CHURCHES) groups in 1939 when the Methodist Episcopal Church, the Methodist Episcopal Church, South, and the Methodist Protestant Church were reunited under a new name, The Methodist Church. In 1968, this body merged with the Evangelical United Brethren (E.U.B.) to form The United Methodist Church.

Both the Methodist and the E.U.B. churches, across the years, had been deeply conscious of their common historical and spiritual heritage. Their doctrines were similar. Both were episcopal in government and traced their origins to John Wesley. They had similar books of discipline. Their preachers often exchanged pulpits and congregations, worked together, and shared the same buildings. The only major difference was that of language: German among the Brethren, English among the Methodists; but in time this barrier began to mean less and less. Conversations concerning a merger began as early as 1803; but the long considered merger was not consummated until the two churches became The United Methodist Church at Dallas, Texas, on April 23, 1968.

There was some dissent at Dallas; fifty-one congregations and nearly eighty ministers of the Evangelical United Brethren withdrew from the Pacific Northwest Conference to establish the Evangelical Church of North America (see EVANGELICAL CHURCH OF NORTH AMERICA); eighteen E.U.B. congregations in Montana left to establish the Evangelical Church of North America in Montana. However, roughly 750,000 Brethren accepted the union, and their strength gave the new United Methodist Church a membership of nearly 11 million at its inception.

In this union no significant changes were made in either doctrine or polity. The Confession of Faith of the Evangelical United Brethren Church, adopted in 1962, was placed beside the Methodist Articles

239

of Religion. Similar systems of bishops and conferences were in use in both denominations, and the format is still maintained.

Above the sixty-four Annual Conferences are five jurisdictional conferences, established for geographical convenience in administrative matters. These meet quadrennially, at times determined by the Council of Bishops, to elect new bishops and to name the members of the larger boards and commissions. Outside the continental U.S., central conferences correspond to jurisdictional conferences; they meet quadrennially and, when authorized to do so, may elect their own bishops. All bishops are elected for life (except in some overseas conferences, where the term is four years), and a Council of Bishops meets at least once a year "for the general oversight and promotion of the temporal and spiritual affairs of the entire church."

The General Conference consists of 1,000 delegates, half laity and half clergy, elected on a proportional basis by the Annual Conferences. The Judicial Council determines the constitutionality of any act of the General Conference that may be appealed, and it hears and determines any appeal from a bishop's decision on a question of law, in any district or annual, central, or jurisdictional conference.

The agencies of the church nationally are the General Council on Finance and Administration, the General Council on Ministries, the General Board of Church and Society, the General Board of Discipleship, the General Board of Global Ministries, the General Board of Higher Education and Ministry, the General Board of Pension and Health Benefits, the General Commission on Archives and History, the General Commission on Christian Unity and Inter-religious Concerns, the General Commission on United Methodist Men, the General Commission on Religion and Race, the General Commission on the Status and Role of Women, the General Commission on Communication, and The United Methodist Publishing House.

In social ministries and education, the church operates or supports 225 retirement homes and long-term care facilities, 70 hospital and health-care facilities, 50 child-care facilities, 30 ministries for persons with disabilities, 8 two-year colleges, 82 four-year colleges, 10 universities, and 13 theological schools. United Methodists give more than $3.65 billion annually for clergy support and benevolences, local church building and debt retirement, and operating expenses. The church also gives considerable financial support to the National Council of the Churches of Christ in the U.S.A.

The World Methodist Council was organized in 1881. Headquartered at Lake Junaluska, North Carolina, the council is designed to draw the whole Wesleyan movement closer together in fellowship and devotion to the Wesleyan heritage.

The 1972 General Conference broadened the basis of doctrine in the church in the first restatement since the eighteenth century. The classic documents of the merging Methodist and Evangelical United Brethren churches were maintained, but the doctrinal door was left open to theological change and revision. A revised statement was adopted in 1988: "In theological reflection, the resources of tradition, experience, and reason are integral to our study of Scripture without displacing Scripture's primacy for faith and practice."

Unusual among churches, The United Methodist Church has adopted a Social Creed that stresses human rights and ecological concerns. The church has considered the question of homosexuality at several General Conferences. At the 2000 conference, a substantial majority of lay and clergy delegates affirmed by vote that the practice of homosexuality is incompatible with Christian teaching and that no self-avowed practicing homosexual can be ordained as clergy or be given a pastoral appointment.

NATIVE AMERICAN RELIGION

Contrary to popular belief, the largest single religion among the native peoples of North America is Christianity in one form or another. Early missions were primarily Roman Catholic (see CATHOLIC CHURCHES), particularly in the Southwest. There the Pueblo and Yaqui peoples adapted Christian beliefs and practices to tribal traditions, creating an innovative religious syncretism. The various Protestant denominations were generally more hostile to tribal ritual. Most Native American Christian congregations today are evangelical in orientation, teaching that members must have a personal conversion experience. Cook Christian Training School in Phoenix is an important institution for contemporary Native American missions.

Tribal religions are still practiced throughout the U.S. wherever native peoples have communities. Since tribal religion is based on oral tradition, it is difficult to determine how much it has changed since contact with Europeans, but oral tradition has been one glue that has held tribes together in the face of white hostility. It is impossible to give a concise statement of the details of the various tribal religions. Suffice it to say that there is more variety than uniformity among traditional native religions in terms of both practice and belief.

In the latter years of the twentieth century there was a revival of interest in traditional beliefs and practices among the tribes, and schools have been established to preserve the languages in which the old stories are passed down. Native American spirituality has also become a topic of great interest in the dominant culture, primarily through the so-called new age movement. The book *Black Elk Speaks* has been a major guide for whites and natives alike who are seeking to connect with a nature-based mysticism in which "Mother Earth" and all her inhabitants live in ecological and spiritual harmony. Shamanism, sweat lodges, vision quests, and other features of some tribal religions have become part of the American religious economy.

There have also been attempts to form new types of native religion that unite people across tribes without endorsing Christianity. Beginning around the turn of the last century, a group of Native Americans formed the Native American Church with principal concentration of membership in the Southwest. Its beliefs and practices are syncretistic, blending elements of Christianity with various traditional tribal practices. It was chartered in 1918 and reports about 300,000 members.

Popularly, but inaccurately, called the "peyote religion" because its ceremonies frequently make use of the button or crown of the hallucinogenic peyote, a plant in the cactus family, the Native American Church is a uniquely American religion dedicated to the Peyote spirit. Worshipers hold all-night ceremonies filled with chanting to the rhythms of a water drum, during which peyote is consumed. The reason for its use is not individual ecstasy but to serve as a communal ritual, to foster bonded relationships. Males perform the leadership functions; the central figure is the shaman, who is thought to be endowed with psychic abilities.

Despite its reputation as a "drug" church, the Native American Church is quite conservative and has been effective in dealing with drug and alcohol abuse among Native Americans.

ORTHODOX AND ORIENTAL ORTHODOX CHURCHES

With more than 200 million members around the world, the Orthodox churches represent one of the three major branches of Christianity (the others being Roman Catholic and Protestant). Unlike the Roman Catholic Church (see ROMAN CATHOLIC CHURCH), the Orthodox churches (also known as the Eastern or Eastern Orthodox churches) do not have a single hierarchical institution. Instead there are dozens of national bodies, each of which worships in its native language with its own independent (autocephalous) hierarchy. Each Orthodox church thus reflects its own national heritage and ethnic customs in its liturgy. Unlike the Protestant churches, which also demonstrate a wide variety of institutions and forms, most of the Orthodox churches are in communion with one another and hold to the same basic theology based on the ancient creeds of Christianity.

A few of the main Eastern bodies, however, reject the statements of the Council of Chalcedon (451 C.E.), in particular the phrase relating to Jesus Christ being one person in two natures, divine and human. These are known as non-Chalcedonian or Oriental Orthodox Churches. Included among these bodies are the Armenian Church, the Coptic Church, the Ethiopian Church, the Eritrean Church, the Syrian Church of Antioch, and the Syrian Indian Church of South India. A few Orthodox bodies are also in communion with the Roman Catholic Church and are known as Uniate churches (see EASTERN RITE CATHOLIC/UNIATE CHURCHES).

Orthodox church services are elaborate, ritualistic, and beautiful. Virtually every architectural feature of the sanctuary, every movement of the priest's body, and every word spoken by the worshipers has symbolic value. The liturgy is an ancient drama that celebrates Christ's incarnation, crucifixion, and resurrection. Lighting, clerical vestments and altar adornments, icons, music, and consecrated bread and wine bring the kingdom of God into the present. The word *orthodox* means "true glory" (as well as "straight teaching"), and "giving glory to God is the purpose of life" is the keynote of this tradition. Praising God, giving God thanks, and receiving God's presence in the sanctified gifts capture the heart of worship. Through worship, and in God-informed relationships and responsibilities,

243

these Christians mean to move toward sanctification. The Christian goal is *theosis,* "perfection" or "deification," living in genuine unity with God in the here and now and for eternity.

History. Western history books will often state that the Orthodox churches of the East separated from the Catholic Church (see CATHOLIC CHURCHES) of the West, but that is not an accurate presentation. The Eastern Orthodox tradition claims direct descent from Christ and the apostles. For centuries, Christianity was primarily Eastern in orientation, with most of the episcopal sees of the early church being in Greece, Turkey, Egypt, and Syria. The ecumenical councils that continue to define the beliefs of most of the world's Christians were held in the East and were attended primarily by Eastern bishops and theologians. Of the five patriarchal Sees—Rome, Alexandria, Antioch, Constantinople, and Jerusalem—only the Roman one was in the West. For centuries councils and patriarchs guided the church. The bishops of the two capitals of the Roman Empire after 330, Constantinople and Rome, had the greatest authority. In 1054, the bishops of Constantinople and Rome mutually excommunicated each other along with their followers, creating a formal breach in Christianity that has only recently begun to heal. It is still the practice in the Orthodox churches that no one patriarch is responsible to any other patriarch. All are within the jurisdiction of an ecumenical council of all the churches, in communion with the patriarch of Constantinople, who holds the title Ecumenical Patriarch.

Long before the official schism between East and West, the two churches had already developed certain basic differences that made for confusion. The East was primarily Greek in speech and attitude, while the West was Latin and Roman. The transference of the capital from West to East meant a shifting of the center of political, social, and intellectual influences. The church in the East was integrally related to the Byzantine Empire, and the great cathedral of Hagia Sophia ("Holy Wisdom") in Constantinople was the center of both the church and the empire. A number of the schisms in the East were both political and theological in nature, the most important of which involved the understanding of the person of Christ. In Syria, some churches embraced the views of Nestorius (b. after 351; d. after 451), who held that there were two separate persons in the incarnate Christ, one divine and one human. In Egypt and Armenia other churches accepted the teaching of Cyril of Alexandria (d. 444), as

244

expressed in the phrase "one Incarnate nature of the Word." Most of the Eastern churches, though, remained in communion with the patriarch of Constantinople.

As the Roman Empire decayed in the West and barbarians began pouring into Italy and Gaul, the bishop of Rome became a symbol of unity and stability for Westerners. When the pope crowned Charlemagne as Holy Roman Emperor in 800, it marked a clear break with the Roman Empire in the East (commonly called the Byzantine Empire). Conflict deepened between the pope at Rome and the patriarch at Constantinople. One major point of controversy was the addition of the words "and the son" (*filioque*) to the Nicene Creed in referring to the procession of the Holy Spirit.

As the Byzantine Empire expanded to the west and north, Orthodox missionaries, such as the celebrated brothers Cyril (826–69) and Methodius (ca. 815–85), converted the Slavic peoples of Bulgaria, Serbia, and Russia to Christianity. The Divine Liturgy and holy books were translated into Slavic tongues, and monasteries and schools were established throughout Eastern Europe. As these peoples gained political independence, national Orthodox churches were gradually established, the first being the Bulgarian Orthodox Church.

The Orthodox churches were profoundly affected by the dramatic rise of Islam in the seventh century. Three of the ancient patriarchal sees (Antioch, Alexandria, and Jerusalem) quickly came under Muslim control and were effectively separated from Constantinople. Christianity in Muslim countries continued to exist as a minority faith living under severe restrictions.

The strongest blow to Orthodoxy came when the Turks captured Constantinople in 1454 and put an end to the Byzantine Empire. Hagia Sophia was converted into a mosque, and the Ecumenical Patriarch was forced to give allegiance to the Muslim rulers. For centuries the Orthodox churches in the Balkans would struggle for existence under Turkish rule. During this time, the Russian Orthodox Church would rise in power and prestige until Moscow was declared to be "the third Rome." As the Ottoman Empire declined, other Slavic churches asserted their independence from Greek and Russian rule while still remaining in communion with the Ecumenical Patriarch.

The Russian Revolution of 1917 and the spread of Communism to Eastern Europe following the Second World War led the Eastern Orthodox churches in Poland, Finland, Estonia, and Latvia to assert their independence. The Orthodox Church managed to survive Communist rule despite persecution. After World War II, Estonia and Latvia were reintegrated into the Russian Orthodox Church.

Nearly all European and Asiatic bodies of this ancient church have established dioceses in the United States; some are governed by one of the five patriarchates, while others have declared themselves independent and self-governing (autocephalous). In the U.S. today, Albanian, Bulgarian, Greek, Romanian, Russian, Serbian, Ukrainian, Carpatho-Russian, and Syrian churches are under the supervision of bishops of their respective nationalities and usually are related to their respective mother churches in tradition and spirit, if not in administration. The patriarch of Moscow and of Alexandria each has jurisdiction over a few parishes.

Beliefs and Practices. The Nicene Creed in its original form is central to the Orthodox faith in all its branches. It is recited whenever the Divine Liturgy is celebrated and is the heart of Orthodox theology and mysticism. Since for the Eastern churches a creed is "an adoring confession of the church engaged in worship," its faith is expressed more fully in its liturgy than in a doctrinal statement.

It is the long tradition of the church, not the pronouncements of individual theologians or canon law, that defines what is orthodox. This tradition includes the decisions of the seven Ecumenical Councils as well as the tradition of the Divine Liturgy itself. Many of the doctrines and practices of the Roman Catholic and Protestant churches are rejected as inappropriate innovations. For instance, the dogma of the pope as the sole "vicar of Christ on earth" is rejected, together with that of papal infallibility. Members of Orthodox churches honor the Virgin Mary as *theotokos* ("the bearer of God") but do not subscribe to the dogmas of the immaculate conception and the assumption. They show reverence to the cross, the saints, and nine orders of angels but reject the teaching of the treasury of merits of the saints and the doctrine of indulgences.

Icons (consecrated pictures) of revered persons and events are central to Orthodox devotion, and Protestant iconoclasm or opposition to icons is condemned. Orthodox Christians hold that since God became incarnate in Christ, God's human nature may be depicted in a sacred image. Refusal to venerate an icon is seen as denying the concrete reality of the Incarnation; however, the Orthodox reject three-dimensional carvings.

The mysteries, or what are called sacraments in the Western

church, are central in Orthodox life. The mysteries are physical items or actions that communicate spiritual reality. The seven that are definitive in the Roman Catholic Church—baptism, confirmation, the Eucharist, penance, extreme unction, holy orders, and matrimony—are present and important in the Orthodox tradition as well, but there is little disposition to restrict that number formally. Other rites have a sacramental character. In fact, for the Orthodox, worship itself is a mystery or sacrament. For some Orthodox theologians and mystics, even creation is a sacrament.

The Holy Eucharist, or Communion, is the "mystery of mysteries." It is the chief service on all Sundays and holy days and is treated with great reverence. All Orthodox churches teach that the bread and wine are the body and blood of Christ, but this is not described as transubstantiation. Mysteries cannot be defined by human intellect. Purgatory is denied, but prayers are offered for the dead. It is believed that the dead can and do pray for those on earth. Both faith and works are considered necessary for salvation.

Polity. The government of all Orthodox churches is episcopal and hierarchical to a degree. There is usually a synod of bishops over which an elected archbishop, metropolitan, or patriarch presides. In the U.S., each jurisdiction is incorporated, with a church assembly of bishops, clergy, and laity.

There are three orders in the ministry: deacons (who assist in parish work and in administering the sacraments), priests, and bishops. Deacons and priests may be either secular or monastic. Candidates for the deaconate and priesthood may marry before ordination but are forbidden to marry thereafter. Bishops are chosen from members of the monastic communities and, therefore, are under lifelong vows of poverty, chastity, and obedience.

The history of the Orthodox in North America is primarily the story of immigration and ethnic identity. The church was a way for immigrants to keep a connection with their homeland, their language, and their customs. Membership statistics are confusing and often unreliable, however, inasmuch as membership is based on baptismal records rather than communicant status. There are at least 3.5 million Orthodox in the U.S.

After a century or so of "creeping disunity" within U.S. Orthodoxy, during the period of heavy immigration and the formation of various Orthodox communities of faith, there have been movements toward closer cooperation. One such movement was the organization in 1960

247

of the Standing Conference of Canonical Orthodox Bishops in the Americas, which is composed of nine jurisdictions that represent the majority of the Orthodox in North America. Another was the formation of two pan-Orthodox seminaries.

There are a number of so-called Orthodox churches in the U.S. that are not recognized as canonically "Orthodox." These irregular Eastern churches might be called autogenic, or self-starting, but they cannot properly be called Orthodox, since Orthodox churches must be in canonical relationship with the Patriarch of Constantinople and with one another.

AFRICAN ORTHODOX CHURCH

Founded: 1921
Membership: est. 5,000 (1999)

This body is not in communion with Orthodox churches (see ORTHODOX and ORIENTAL ORTHODOX CHURCHES) generally, but it claims to be in apostolic succession through the West Syrian Church of Antioch. It was established in 1921 by George Alexander McGuire (1866–1934), who was an immigrant to the United States from Antigua. McGuire had served as a priest in the Protestant Episcopal Church until 1918. He left that body because of racial discrimination and decided that equality and spiritual freedom would be attained only in a denomination of blacks with a black administration. This quest for equality led him to Marcus Garvey's (1887–1940) Universal Negro Improvement Association. Once McGuire founded the African Orthodox Church, Garvey used his periodical, entitled *The Negro World,* to disseminate news about the denomination throughout Africa. The periodical also carried the story of McGuire's consecration by a white bishop named Joseph Rene Vilatte (1854–1929). In 1924, the church was established in South Africa, where it became a potent force among the black population.

The church puts strong emphasis on the apostolic succession and historic sacraments and rituals; it celebrates the original seven sacraments of the Roman Catholic Church (see ROMAN CATHOLIC CHURCH): baptism, confirmation, the Eucharist, penance, extreme unction, holy orders, and matrimony. Its worship is a blend of Western and Eastern liturgy, creeds, and symbols, though the liturgy is usually

Western with a mingling of Anglican (see EPISCOPAL/ANGLICAN CHURCHES), Greek, and Roman patterns. The common creeds, Athanasian, Nicene, and Apostles', are used.

The denomination maintains the position that no priest may perform a marriage ceremony for the guilty party in a divorce, and innocent parties are remarried only with special permission from a bishop. The government is, of course, episcopal; bishops are in charge of dioceses, or jurisdictions; and groups of dioceses form a province, each led by an archbishop and a primate. The primate, in turn, presides over the provincial synod. At the head stands a primate archbishop metropolitan, general overseer of all the work of the church, which now extends over the U.S. into Canada, Latin America, and South Africa.

ALBANIAN ORTHODOX ARCHDIOCESE IN AMERICA

Founded: 1919
Membership: est. 40,000 (1999)

The Albanian Orthodox Archdiocese in America has been part of the Orthodox Church of America (see ORTHODOX CHURCH OF AMERICA) since 1971, but its bishops and clergy continue to minister to the special needs of the Albanian community in the U.S. The history of the church in Albania is complex, filled with a series of persecutions and changes in the religious and political struggles of the Balkans. Christianized by both Latin and Greek missionaries, Albania, as part of Illyricum, had both Latin- and Greek-rite Christians and was at various times under the authority of the patriarch of Constantinople (see ORTHODOX and ORIENTAL ORTHODOX CHURCHES) and the pope. When the Turks conquered Albania in 1478–79, half of its people became Muslim. The Christian minority remained divided between Latin-rite Christians in the North and Greek-rite Christians in the South.

When Albania became an independent nation in the twentieth century, its people demanded a liturgy in their language rather than in Greek. They turned to the Russian Orthodox Church for assistance, and in 1908 the Russian Orthodox Church in America set up an Albanian diocese under an Albanian archimandrite-administrator, Father Theophan S. Noli (1880–1965), who translated the liturgy

249

into Albanian. With the outbreak of the Russian revolution, the ties with the Russian Church were severed, and Noli was consecrated the bishop in 1923 at the Korche Cathedral in Albania as the Archbishop and Metropolitan of Durres. In doing so, he became the first bishop of a completely independent Albanian Archdiocese, a "mother church" that, strangely enough, spread its influence back into Albania. Noli returned home to establish a metropolitan throne with its See in Boston. Because of the official closing of all religious institutions in Albania in 1967, communication between the American church and the Albanian church was not possible until the collapse of communism.

Another body, the Albanian Orthodox Diocese of America, was established in 1950 under the authority of the Ecumenical Patriarchate of Constantinople. It has two parishes with about 2,000 members.

AMERICAN CARPATHO-RUSSIAN ORTHODOX GREEK CATHOLIC CHURCH

Founded: 1938
Membership: 13,120 in 80 parishes (1999)

The Carpatho-Russian people derive their name from the Carpathian mountain region of eastern Europe, where they have resided for centuries. For many years the mother church endured strife between Orthodoxy and Roman Catholicism. Under political pressure in the seventeenth century, it became a Uniate (see EASTERN RITE CATHOLIC/UNIATE CHURCHES) church, with Eastern rites and customs, but recognized the supremacy of the Roman Catholic pope.

The struggle to separate from Rome and become completely Eastern was transferred to North America when large numbers of members emigrated to the U.S., especially to the coal-mining and industrial areas of the northeast. In 1891, Alexis Toth, a Carpatho-Russian Uniate priest, led his Minneapolis parish back to the Orthodox Church (see ORTHODOX and ORIENTAL ORTHODOX CHURCHES). Along with several other pastors and parishes they were absorbed into the Russian Orthodox Church in the U.S. (see ORTHODOX CHURCH IN AMERICA).

In 1938, a new American Carpatho-Russian Orthodox Greek

Catholic diocese was established and canonized by Benjamin I, the ecumenical patriarch of Constantinople. Orestes P. Chornock (1883–1977) became its first bishop. Both the diocesan headquarters (Christ the Saviour Cathedral) and Christ the Saviour Seminary are located in Johnstown, Pennsylvania. The diocese maintains a youth camp, a retreat, and a conference center in Mercer, Pennsylvania, and a monastery in Tuxedo Park, New York.

ANTIOCHIAN ORTHODOX CHRISTIAN ARCHDIOCESE OF NORTH AMERICA

Founded: 1975, with roots to 1895
Membership: est. 65,000 in 227 parishes (1999)

Antioch, in Syria, was one of the first cities to be evangelized by the apostles and in the early church was one of the most important patriarchal Sees. The faithful managed to maintain the existence of the church through centuries of Muslim rule, even adopting Arabic as a liturgical language, but as the Ottomon Empire collapsed in the late nineteenth century, thousands of Antiochene Christians emigrated to North America. Their spiritual needs were first met through the Syro-Arabian Mission of the Russian Orthodox Church (see ORTHODOX CHURCH IN AMERICA). In 1895, a Syrian Orthodox Benevolent Society was organized by Antiochian immigrants in New York City, with Dr. Ibrahim Arbeely, a prominent Damascene physician, serving as its first president.

Arbeely convinced Raphael Hawaweeny, a young Damascene clergyman serving as Professor of the Arabic Language at the Orthodox Theological Academy in Kazan, Russia, to come to New York to organize and pastor the first Arabic-speaking parish on the continent. Hawaweeny was consecrated as a bishop in New York in 1904, making him the first Orthodox bishop of any nationality to be consecrated in North America. He crisscrossed the United States and Canada, gathering the scattered immigrants into parish communities. He founded *al-Kalimat* (*The Word*) magazine in 1905, and published many liturgical books in Arabic for use in his parishes, in the Middle East, and in immigrant communities around the world.

The mission suffered because of the early death of Hawaweeny in 1915, the disruptions of the First World War, and the Russian Revolution. The Syro-Arabian Mission fell into divisiveness until

1975, when jurisdictional and administrative unity was restored with the merger of the Antiochian Orthodox Christian Archdiocese of New York and the Antiochian Archdiocese of Toledo. The resulting Archdiocese is divided into four chancellories located in New Jersey, Ohio, Kansas, and California. The General Assembly, the largest legislative body of the Archdiocese, consists of all the pastors and representatives of every parish and mission. It meets in convention every other summer. There are nearly four hundred priests and deacons who minister at the local level. Candidates for ordination complete an undergraduate program and then receive their theological education at either St. Vladimir's Orthodox Theological Seminary in New York or St. John of Damascus Orthodox Theological Academy near Tripoli, Lebanon. Their program is augmented by specialized courses offered annually by the Antiochian House of Studies, held for two weeks at the Heritage and Learning Center in Ligonier, Pennsylvania. Twenty-four established departments and commissions deal with specific needs of the Archdiocese, such as communications, translations, clergy education, and parish development.

A pioneer in the use of the English language in the Orthodox churches (see ORTHODOX and ORIENTAL ORTHODOX CHURCHES), since the 1930s the church has translated and published liturgical and devotional works into English. The Antiochian Village, a 280-acre property located in southwestern Pennsylvania, serves as a retreat center and popular summer camp that attracts children and young adults from throughout North America. The St. John of Damascus Sacred Art Academy is also headquartered at the Village.

ARMENIAN CHURCH

Founded: 301 C.E. (came to the U.S. in 1887)
Membership: est. 774,000 in approx. 108 parishes (1999)

Armenia is generally recognized as the first nation to become Christian when Christianity became the state religion in 301. Tradition holds that the apostles Thaddeus and Bartholomew first brought the message of Christ to Armenia. Saint Gregory the Illuminator became the first head of the national church in 314 and was given the title Patriarch Catholicos of All Armenians. A translation of the scriptures by St. Sahag and St. Mesrob and their students in the early part of the fifth century is accepted as the authoritative Armenian version of the Bible. The translators created an Armenian alphabet in order to give the Armenians the scriptures in their own language.

The Armenian Church administers seven sacraments: baptism, confirmation or chrismation, Eucharist, penance, matrimony, ordination, and extreme unction or order of the sick. Baptism, ordinarily of infants, is administered by immersion. Chrismation (anointing with oil) and Communion follow immediately after baptism. The Eucharist is offered on Sundays and on special feast days of the church. At the conclusion of the Eucharist, fragments of thin unleavened bread, simply blessed, are distributed to those not receiving Communion.

The hierarchical organization of the Armenian Church consists of the Catholicos, the supreme head of the church, who resides in the ancient city of Etchmiadzin, Armenia, and the Catholicate of Cilicia, located in Antelias, Lebanon. The two patriarchates are Jerusalem and Constantinople. There are three major orders of clergy, according to the tradition of all ancient churches: deacon, priest, and bishop. Parish priests are ordinarily chosen from among married men, but bishops are chosen from among the celibate clergy. Widowed priests may be promoted to the episcopate. Clergy are trained in seminaries attached to Etchmiadzin, Jerusalem, and Antelias. One of the most important aspects of the Armenian Church administration is its conciliar system. The administrative, doctrinal, liturgical, and canonical norms are set and approved by a council through a participatory decision-making process. The Council of Bishops (or the Synod) is the highest religious authority in the church.

The Armenian Church has sustained its people throughout a history marked by tragedy. It suffered in the conflict between the Byzantine Empire and Persia and sustained persecutions by the Turks, culminating in the genocide of 1915. Thousands of Armenians escaped to North America before World War I, but the bulk of emigration occurred after the war. The first Armenian Church in the U.S. was established in Worchester, Massachusetts, in 1891. The Armenian Diocese of America was organized in 1898, headed by a primate appointed by the Mother See of Holy Etchmiadzin in Armenia, under whose jurisdiction the diocese functioned.

In 1933 a dispute over matters related to the church in Soviet

Armenia led to a split in the church in the United States. One group of churches, the Armenian Apostolic Church of America, chose to remain independent until 1957, when these churches placed themselves under the jurisdiction of the Holy See of Cilicia in Antelias. The other group, the Armenian Church of America, remained within the jurisdiction of the Mother See of Etchmiadzin. Dogma and liturgy were not affected by the division. Deacons, priests, bishops, and archbishops are ordained and elevated by the hierarchical authorities of the respective jurisdictions. The Armenian Church of America has seventy-two churches; the separated Apostolic Church has thirty-six.

The Armenian Church is in communion with the Oriental Orthodox Churches (see ORTHODOX and ORIENTAL ORTHODOX CHURCHES), sometimes referred to as the Lesser Eastern Orthodox Churches. Also known as Monophysites ("one nature of Christ"), these are churches that did not ascribe to the doctrinal statements adopted at the Council of Chalcedon in 451 C.E. It should be noted that the Armenian Church accepts the decisions of the first three ecumenical councils. It affirms the Christological formula of St. Cyril of Alexandria (d. 444): "One is the nature of the divine Word incarnate. The union of Godhead and the manhood are without confusion, without change, and indivisibly." In 1990, the theologians and official representatives of both Eastern and Oriental Orthodox churches agreed in a formal statement that their theological understanding, especially their Christology, is "orthodox." The statement called for unity and communion among the Eastern and Oriental Orthodox churches.

BULGARIAN EASTERN ORTHODOX CHURCH

Founded: 1938
Membership: 70,000 in 23 parishes (1990)

Christianity was introduced to the Bulgar peoples in the ninth century during the reign of Tsar Boris. For centuries, the church struggled for independence from Constantinople, an independence won for brief periods. There was a schism between the Bulgarians and the Ecumenical Patriarch until the end of World War II. Before the outbreak of the Macedonian revolution in 1903, very few Bulgarians emigrated to the U.S. In 1940, there were still only about 60,000 residents. They brought with them memories of the church's long struggle for independence from Constantinople. The first Bulgarian Orthodox Church in the U.S. was built in Madison, Illinois, in 1907. In 1922 the Bulgarian Orthodox Mission of the Holy Synod of Bulgaria began attempts to organize the Bulgars. It established a bishopric in 1938.

Attached directly to the Holy Synod of Bulgaria, the membership of this church is made up of descendants of immigrants from Bulgaria, Macedonia, Thrace, Dobruja, and other parts of the Balkan peninsula. Services are in the Bulgarian and English languages, and doctrine is in accord with that of other Eastern Orthodox churches (see ORTHODOX and ORIENTAL ORTHODOX CHURCHES).

GREEK ORTHODOX ARCHDIOCESE OF NORTH AMERICA

Founded: 1922
Membership: 1,954,500 in 555 parishes (1998)

The Greek Orthodox Church is one of the largest Orthodox (see ORTHODOX and ORIENTAL ORTHODOX CHURCHES) bodies in the U.S., due to the massive immigration of Greeks to the U.S. between 1890 and 1929. Greece was one of the earliest and most vital centers of Christianity, but the capture of Constantinople by the Turks and the subjugation of the patriarch to Muslim rule was a severe blow to the Greek Orthodox Church. In the nineteenth century, the church in Greece established a Holy Synod independent from (but in communion with) the Ecumenical Patriarch. Orthodox priests were sent to the U.S. either by the Holy Synod of Greece or by the Ecumenical Patriarchate of Constantinople. In 1864, the first Greek Orthodox Church in the United States was founded in New Orleans, Louisiana. By 1910 there were approximately thirty-five congregations in various parts of the country. A period of confusion existed from 1908 to 1922, during which time the jurisdiction of American churches shifted from the Ecumenical Patriarchate of Constantinople to the Holy Synod of Greece and back again. This was finally resolved with the Founding Tome of 1922, which established the Greek Orthodox Archdiocese of North and South America.

Archbishop Athenagoras Spyrou of Corfu was appointed to head the Greek Church in America in 1931, and under his leadership the church increased to 286 parishes. In 1948, Athenagoras was elected Patriarch of Constantinople and was succeeded by Archbishop Michael Constantinides of Corinth, who was enthroned in the New York Cathedral of the Holy Trinity. Since 1996, Archbishop Spyridon, appointed by Constantinople's Ecumenical Patriarch, has led the Greek Orthodox Archdiocese of North America. He oversees work in nine dioceses, each headed by a bishop. Worship, doctrine, and polity follow historical Orthodox patterns, with the service of worship being the center of congregational life.

The church supports eighteen parochial schools; nine summer camps; a school for orphans and children from broken homes; Hellenic College and Holy Cross Greek Orthodox School of Theology, both in Brookline, Massachusetts; three homes for teenage boys; and a home for the aged.

HOLY EASTERN ORTHODOX AND APOSTOLIC CHURCH IN NORTH AMERICA, INC.

Founded: 1927
Membership: est. 4,300 in 19 parishes (1998)

This church traces its heritage back to the Russian Orthodox Church. Also known as the American Orthodox Catholic Church, it has a claim to being the first Orthodox church (see ORTHODOX and ORIENTAL ORTHODOX CHURCHES) established in North America specifically to serve English-speaking worshipers, but this claim is not recognized by other Orthodox bodies. The church was chartered by the Synod of Bishops in North America of the Russian Patriarchal Church (Moscow and all Russia). Archbishop Aftimios Ofiesh of the Syrian Mission was selected to head the new church.

Over the years, the church has adopted more of the Western rite, but remains theologically in the Eastern tradition. It is found in twelve states and has one religious order, the Society of St. Basil.

MALANKARA ORTHODOX SYRIAN CHURCH and MAR THOMA ORTHODOX SYRIAN CHURCH
(Indian Orthodox)

Founded: in the U.S. 1978; 1988
Membership: est. 42,000 in 125 parishes (1997)

These are the two major bodies of independent Indian Christian churches in the U.S. Both bodies claim descent from Thomas the apostle, whom legend says went to India as an evangelist after the resurrection of Christ. The church in India is ancient and historically had close ties to the Nestorian church in Persia, which was made up of refugees from Syria. (The Indian church actually used Syriac in worship.) The Persian/Syrian church was called "Nestorian" because of its adherence to the doctrine attributed to the fourth/fifth century theologian Nestorius that Christ was two distinct persons, one human and one divine. In 1599, under the influence of Portuguese missionaries, most Malankara Christians (living in southwest India) rejected Nestorianism. Many united with Rome as a Uniate church (see EASTERN RITE CATHOLIC/UNIATE CHURCHES). Others, however, turned to the Syrian Orthodox Church (see ORTHODOX and ORIENTAL ORTHODOX CHURCHES) for guidance. In the nineteenth century, Christianity in India experienced further fracture during the period of British rule.

The Malankara church was named for a town where Thomas is believed to have arrived in India in 52 C.E. It uses the liturgy, calendar, language, and traditions of the Syrian Orthodox Church. The American Diocese was established in 1978 to serve Indian immigrants to the U.S. and their children. It includes about 12,000 members in 60 parishes.

The Mar Thoma Church was established to preserve the native Indian church from forced Latinization by the Portuguese colonizers of the Malankara region. It is in communion with the Syrian Orthodox Church of Antioch and uses the Orthodox liturgy and calendar. The church is independent, however, and is also in communion with the Anglican Church. The American diocese was organized in 1988 to serve members in the immigrant community. It has about 25,000 members in 65 parishes.

ORTHODOX CHURCH IN AMERICA
(Russian Orthodox)

Founded: 1970, with roots to 1794
Membership: est. 1,000,000 in 710 parishes (1999)

The Orthodox (see ORTHODOX and ORIENTAL ORTHODOX CHURCHES) faith came to the U.S. by way of Alaska, which was part of Russia until 1867. Russia itself joined the Orthodox fold with the baptism of Grand Prince Vladimir of Kiev in 988 C.E. The church was ruled at first by metropolitans appointed or approved by the Patriarch of Constantinople, but eventually an independent patriarchate was established in Moscow, which came to be regarded by Slavs as "the Third Rome."

Eight Russian Orthodox monks entered Alaska in 1794, established headquarters at Kodiak, and built the first Eastern Orthodox Church in North America. Orthodox monks and bishops created an alphabet and printed a grammar in the Aleutian language, translated portions of the Bible, and built a cathedral at Sitka.

Early in the nineteenth century, a chapel was built at a Russian trading post near present-day San Francisco. The Episcopal See was transferred to that city in 1872, but moved to New York City in 1905 as waves of immigration brought thousands of Slavs to the eastern states. For many years, the Russian hierarchy in the U.S. cared for immigrants from other Orthodox countries, such as Serbia, Syria, and Bulgaria. Many Eastern-rite Catholics (see EASTERN RITE CATHOLIC/UNIATE CHURCHES) from the old Austro-Hungarian Empire also transferred to the jurisdiction of the Russian Orthodox Church rather than accept the administration of Irish and Italian Catholic bishops.

Bishop Tikhon, who later became Patriarch of the Russian Church, founded the first Russian Orthodox Theological Seminary in Minneapolis, Minnesota, in 1905. Bishop Tikhon also transferred the Episcopal See and its Ecclesiastical Consistory from San Francisco to New York City, where the Russian Orthodox headquarters for this hemisphere are still located. Under Tikhon, St. Nicholas Cathedral in New York was built in 1901. In 1919 the Russian Church in America held its first Sobor, or general council, at Pittsburgh.

The history of the church in the United States has been tied to political events in Russia. In 1917 the Bolsheviks took over the gov-

258

ernment of Russia and instituted restrictive religious policies. The patriarch and the Holy Synod resisted, but the government found some priests and bishops ready to support the new regime. These officials held an assembly that deposed the patriarch, endorsed communism, and declared itself the governing body of the Russian church.

Calling itself the Renovated, or Living, Church, this group changed the ancient disciplinary rules and instituted liturgical reforms. With the support of Soviet authorities, who hoped thus to divide and weaken the church, that body held control for several years but was never recognized by the great majority of clergy or people. The government considered opposition to the Living Church a civil offense and, on this basis, banished thousands of bishops, clergy, monks, and laypersons to labor camps.

The Living Church faction in Russia, supported by the communist government, sent an emissary to secure control of Russian Orthodox Church property in the U.S.; through action in the civil courts, it gained possession of the cathedral in New York City. In 1924, an assembly of the Diocese of North America, in an attempt to prevent further seizures, declared that, on a temporary basis, it was administratively, legislatively, and jurisdictionally independent of the church in Russia. But this independence was not recognized by the Patriarchate of Moscow or by the Russian Orthodox Church Outside Russia, headquartered at that time in the former Yugoslavia.

In 1927 the Soviet government prevailed upon Metropolitan Sergius, the *locum tenens* (that is, temporary substitute) of the then vacant patriarchal See, to submit the policy of the church totally to the Soviet regime. Stalin engineered the meeting of a small group of bishops to elect Metropolitan Sergius as Patriarch of Moscow and All Russia. Sergius called upon his people to support the government in the defense of their country during World War II, and this marked a turning point in the Soviet policy toward the church. The Living Church was discarded, and the patriarch's authority was recognized by the state. Many surviving clergy and bishops who had been banished were permitted to return, and gradually the patriarchal administration became again the sole authority in the Orthodox Church of Russia.

A body of Russian émigrés, though, formed the Russian Orthodox Church Outside Russia in 1920 under the authority of the Ecumenical Patriarch. They hold that the Moscow Patriarchate has forfeited its right to be considered a true Orthodox church because it adopted a position of submission to the atheistic Soviet regime, not only in regard to politics and external matters but also with respect to its internal policies and affairs. In 1950 this church came to the U.S. It has about 175 parishes dedicated to the traditions of the pre-Soviet Russian church.

Despite the conflicts in the church in Russia, the main body of believers in the U.S. maintained their institutional life and worked to bring other Slavic peoples together into a vibrant Orthodox Church. On May 18, 1970, a delegation of hierarchs, clergy, and laity of the Russian Orthodox Metropolia in America, headed by Bishop Theodosius (presently Primate of the Orthodox Church of America), went to Moscow to receive the Thomos of Authocephaly—that is, the document of independence, from the head of the Russian Orthodox Church. Since that time, the Orthodox Church in America has been independent.

From administrative offices in New York City, the primate of the Orthodox Church in America oversees the work of eleven dioceses, which are in turn headed by bishops. The primate and bishops make up the Holy Synod of Bishops, which is the highest decision making body in the church. Church ministry units include education and community life ministries, mission and stewardship ministries, pastoral life ministries, witness and communication ministries, and church order ministries. The church administers three theological seminaries: St. Tikhon's in Pennsylvania, St. Vladimir's in New York, and St. Herman's in Alaska.

ROMANIAN ORTHODOX EPISCOPATE OF AMERICA

Founded: 1929
Membership: est. 25,000 in 55 parishes (2000)

Christianity came to Romania in the fourth century. Originally Western and Latin in orientation, the church there gradually came under the authority of Constantinople and adopted Greek liturgical practices and customs (see ORTHODOX and ORIENTAL ORTHODOX CHURCHES). In 1859, the church declared itself independent of Constantinople as a national church, a move that was officially acknowledged twenty-five years later.

The church in the U.S. was organized at a congress convened in Detroit, Michigan, by clergy and lay representatives of Romanian Orthodox parishes in the U.S. and Canada. It remained under the canonical jurisdiction of the Romanian Orthodox Patriarchate in Bucharest until political conditions forced its separation; it is now a diocese under the autocephalous Orthodox Church in America (see ORTHODOX CHURCH IN AMERICA).

The worship and theology of the church accord with Orthodox practice and thought. As for polity, the church is governed by a church congress and an episcopate council, both of which are made up of representatives from parishes and from auxilliary organizations. An archbishop presides over the two bodies; he is also a member of the Holy Synod of the Orthodox Church in America, and the diocese is recognized as an administratively self-governing body. The church maintains offices in Jackson, Michigan, and publishes the monthly magazine *Solia/The Herald* in Romanian and English.

SERBIAN EASTERN ORTHODOX CHURCH

Founded: 1921
Membership: 65,000 in 140 parishes (1998)

Saints (and brothers) Cyril (826–69) and Methodius (815–85) were instrumental in establishing Christianity among the Serbian people. From the seventh century until the thirteenth, the church in Serbia was under the jurisdiction of the Patriarchate of Constantinople (see ORTHODOX and ORIENTAL ORTHODOX CHURCHES). It became the independent National Serbian Church in 1219 during the Western occupation of Constantinople. The church made notable contributions to art and architecture during the glory days of the medieval Serbian empire, and it played an important part in the Serbian struggle for independence through the long period of Turkish invasion and domination. In 1879 the church again achieved independence from Constantinople following the freedom of the nation from Turkish control.

Through the close of World War I, the ecclesiastical and political situation in the Balkans was turbulent and complicated. Attempts were made to unite several Orthodox groups into one church, with these efforts becoming successful in 1920 when the union of five autonomous bodies was proclaimed. Metropolitan Dimitriji of

261

Belgrade was appointed patriarch, uniting in himself the historic titles of Archbishop of Ipek, Metropolitan of Belgrade and Karlovci, and Patriarch of Serbs.

Serbian immigrants to the U.S., coming more for political than economic reasons, began to arrive in large numbers around 1890. They worshiped at first in Russian churches, accepting the ministrations of Russian priests and the supervision of Russian bishops. The Serbian Patriarchate of Yugoslavia approved the organization of the Diocese of the United States and Canada in 1921, and in 1926, with thirty-five Serbian churches making up the American Diocese, Archimandrite Mardary Uskokovich was consecrated by Patriarch Dimitriji of Serbia as the first bishop of the Serbian Orthodox Church of America.

As of 2000, the Serbian Eastern Orthodox Church has two dioceses in North America: the New Gracanica Metropolinate Diocese of America and Canada, based in Libertyville, Illinois; and the Diocese of Western America, based in Alhambra, California. The cathedral of the Serbian Church, built and opened in 1945, is located in New York City.

The extended conflict in the Balkans during the 1990s brought great distress to Serbs living in North America. The Serbian Eastern Orthodox Church played an important role in conveying information to Serbs in the U.S. and Canada and in offering them spiritual and psychological support. It also sought to present a comprehensive picture of Serbian life and culture to the American public.

SYRIAN ORTHODOX CHURCH OF ANTIOCH
(Archdiocese of the U.S.A. and Canada)

Founded: 1957
Membership: 32,500 in 22 parishes (1999)

The Syrian Orthodox Church dates back to the apostolic age, and tradition holds that Peter established the first patriarchate in Antioch. Christianity in Syria was divided during the Nestorian controversy. The followers of Nestorius, who taught that there were two separate persons in the incarnate Christ, one divine and one human, were persecuted and found refuge in Persia. The main body of Christians in Syria adopted a monophysite (one nature) position that they understood to be the teaching of the first three ecumenical councils. When

262

the Council of Chalcedon adopted a formula that seemed to endorse Nestorius's ideas, the Syrian Orthodox refused to comply with the Patriarch of Constantinople. The church was persecuted under the Byzantine Empire, but found toleration under Muslim rule in the Middle Ages. It continues to have its patriarchal See in Damascus with twenty-three archdioceses in other countries.

The Syrian Orthodox use the ancient liturgy of St. Mark in worship. The Syriac Scripture is one of the oldest translations of the Bible and continues to be vital for Syrian Christianity.

Syrians were few in number in the U.S. until the turn of the twentieth century. Syrian Orthodox silk weavers from Diyarbakir, Turkey, settled in New Jersey, a major area of the silk industry. Families from Harput, Turkey, were drawn to Massachusetts. The first priest, the Very Rev. Hanna Koorie, arrived in 1907; their first patriarchal vicar, Archbishop Mar Athanasius Y. Samuel, was appointed in 1949. On November 15, 1957, Patriarch Ignatius Yacoub III set his seal upon the document officially establishing the Archdiocese of the Syrian Orthodox Church in the United States and Canada. The next year, a cathedral in the name of St. Mark was consecrated in Hackensack, New Jersey. It was relocated in 1994 to a new complex in Teaneck, New Jersey.

From the 1960s through the 1980s, new Syrian Orthodox parishes were established in California, Michigan, Illinois, Massachusetts, Oregon, and New York. Following the death of Archbishop Samuel in 1995, the Holy Synod of the Syrian Orthodox Church of Antioch divided the North American Archdiocese into three separate Patriarchal Vicariates: the Syrian Orthodox Archdiocese for the Eastern United States under His Eminence Mor Cyril Aphrem Karim, the Syrian Orthodox Archdiocese of Los Angeles and Environs under His Eminence Mor Clemis Eugene Kaplan, and the Syrian Orthodox Archdiocese of Canada under His Eminence Mor Timotheos Aphrem Aboodi.

UKRAINIAN ORTHODOX CHURCH OF THE U.S.A.

Founded: 1924
Membership: est. 20,000 in 105 parishes (2000)

Tradition has it that Andrew the apostle preached the gospel in the early years of his apostolic ministry in what is presently Kyyiv

263

(Kiev), the capital of the Ukraine. Around the year 862, the first Orthodox Christian community was founded on the outskirts of Kyyiv, during the reign of two princes, Askold and Dyr. Instrumental in making Orthodox Christianity (see ORTHODOX and ORIENTAL ORTHODOX CHURCHES) known in Rus-Ukraine was the Kyyivian Princess Olha, baptized in 975, grandmother of St. Volodymyr (Vladimir) the Great. After considerable reflection and investigation, Volodymyr (baptismal name Basil) proclaimed Orthodox Christianity the official faith of his kingdom of Rus-Ukraine in 988.

For over six hundred years, the Kyyivan Metropolia enjoyed autonomy within the jurisdiction of the Ecumenical See of Constantinople (see ORTHODOX and ORIENTAL ORTHODOX CHURCHES). This autonomy ended in 1686 with the forced subjugation of Ukraine's mother church to the Patriarchate of Moscow. As a consequence of the 1917 revolution, the Ukrainian Orthodox Church sundered jurisdictional ties with Moscow and declared autocephaly in 1921. The autocephalous Ukrainian Orthodox Church was reestablished twice in the twentieth century, first in 1941 and again in 1989 as a result of glasnost and perestroika. The June 5, 1990, Sobor (council) of the Ukrainian Autocephalous Orthodox Church in newly independent Ukraine established its own patriarchate and elected as its first patriarch Metropolitan Mstyslav, at that time Primate of the Ukrainian Orthodox Church of the U.S.A. Mstyslav held the title of Patriarch of Kyyiv and All Ukraine until his death in 1993. Following his death, two patriarchs were elected, Dmytrij to head the Ukrainian Autocephalous Orthodox Church jurisdiction, and Volodymyr to head the Ukrainian Orthodox Church-Kyyivan Patriarchate.

The Ukrainian Orthodox Church of the U.S.A., presently headed by His Eminence Metropolitan Constantine, was established in 1924, when its first bishop, Metropolitan Ioan (John) Teodorovych arrived from the Ukraine. He served as leader of the church until his death in 1971. He was followed as Metropolitan by Mstyslav, who served from 1971 until his death in 1993, at age 95, when he was succeeded by Constantine. Metropolitan Constantine led the church through its merger with the former Ukrainian Orthodox Church of America in 1996.

The church has congregations in twenty-five states; heaviest concentration is in the New York-New Jersey-Pennsylvania area. Three eparchies (episcopal areas), divided geographically, are headed by archbishops. The church maintains St. Andrew Center, a Ukrainian cultural center, in South Bound Brook, New Jersey. The center is home to St. Andrew Memorial Church, a monument to Ukrainian Cossak Baroque architecture, and to St. Sophia Seminary.

PENTECOSTAL CHURCHES

Pentecostalism is a modern American Christian movement that emerged out of the Holiness movement (see HOLINESS CHURCHES) around the turn of the twentieth century. Two key figures in the genesis of Pentecostalism were Charles Fox Parham (1873–1929), the founder of Bethel Bible College in Topeka, Kansas, and William J. Seymour (1870–1922), an African American Holiness evangelist from Louisiana. Through his study of Paul's letters, Parham became convinced that the gifts of the Holy Spirit that were evident in apostolic times are available to Christians in modern times as well. Of particular interest was speaking in tongues, the first incidence of which occurred at Bethel Bible College in 1901. Five years later, Seymour, who had studied at Bethel with Parham, led a revival on Azusa Street in Los Angeles that lasted for several months. Participants experienced a "baptism in the Holy Ghost." Some were healed of illnesses, while others spoke in tongues. Thousands from across the U.S. traveled to Azusa Street and carried the message back to their home states.

The movement eventually became known as "Pentecostal" because of its similarity to the first Pentecost, fifty days after Christ's resurrection, when the Spirit came upon the early Christians and enabled them to speak in unfamiliar languages. There are a great variety of Pentecostal churches, most of which are theologically and socially conservative. In general, Pentecostals are in the evangelical tradition and teach that the Holy Spirit continues to act as it did at the first Pentecost. Teaching that contemporary Christians can receive the same spiritual gifts that the apostles did, many Pentecostal churches use the word *apostolic* in their names.

Seeking and receiving the gift of tongues is regarded as a sign of the baptism of the Holy Spirit, and in many Pentecostal churches this is a requirement for full discipleship. Other spiritual gifts, such as healing, love, joy, prophecy, and answers to prayer, also make up Pentecostals' experience of God. Pentecostals are generally less bound to traditional forms of worship than are other churches, and many have adapted contemporary music for evangelistic purposes. Pentecostal churches that minimize traditional liturgical practice refer to rites such as baptism as "ordinances" rather than as "sacraments." The term "Neo-Pentecostalism" is often used to describe churches that embrace charismatic practices, such as speaking in tongues, but not the Holiness tradition of the older Pentecostal bodies. Even traditional, liturgical churches, such as the Episcopal Church (see EPISCOPAL/ANGLICAN CHURCHES), now have charismatic or Pentecostal parishes.

In general, Pentecostal denominations are Protestant and evangelical, but many have been influenced by the fundamentalist movement (see FUNDAMENTALIST/BIBLE CHURCHES). They commonly hold to beliefs in original sin, salvation through the atoning blood of Christ, the virgin birth and deity of Jesus, the divine inspiration and literal infallibility of the scriptures, pre-millennialism (the return of Jesus Christ prior to his thousand-year reign on earth), and future rewards and punishments. Two sacraments are found in most groups: baptism, usually by immersion, and the Lord's Supper. Some of the smaller bodies also observe foot washing. Pentecostals are generally trinitarian; but they place great emphasis on the direct action of the Holy Spirit, which is manifested in a "baptism in the Spirit" accompanied by spiritual gifts.

Originally strongest among the rural peoples of the South and the Midwest, early Pentecostalism also found a home among the urban poor in the 1930s. Now the movement has spread to all fifty states and represents a cross-section of American society.

ASSEMBLIES OF GOD, GENERAL COUNCIL OF

Founded: 1914
Membership: 2,574,531 in 12,055 churches (1999)

The General Council of the Assemblies of God is actually a group of churches and assemblies that joined together at Hot Springs, Arkansas, in 1914. The founders were former pastors of evangelical persuasion who wished to unite in the interest of doctrinal unity, more effective preaching, and an enlarged missionary crusade.

266

Theologically, the Assemblies of God is Arminian (after Jacobus Arminius, 1560–1609), stressing Christ's atoning death for all persons, the freedom of human will, and the need for conversion. There is also a strong belief in the infallibility and inspiration of the Bible, the fall and redemption of the human race, baptism in the Holy Spirit, a life of holiness and separation from the world, divine healing, the second advent of Jesus and his millennial reign, eternal punishment for the wicked, and eternal bliss for believers. Two ordinances, baptism and the Lord's Supper, are practiced. Assemblies of God members are especially insistent that baptism in the Holy Spirit be evidenced by speaking in tongues. They hold that all the gifts of the Spirit should be evident in a church modelled after that of the New Testament.

The government of the assemblies is an unusual mixture of presbyterian and congregational systems. Local churches are independent in polity and in the conduct of local affairs. District officers have a pastoral ministry to all the churches and are responsible for the promotion of home missions. Work is divided into fifty-six districts in the U.S. and Puerto Rico, including ten foreign-language districts, each with a district presbytery that examines and recommends credentialing of ministers. The General Council consists of all ordained ministers and lay representatives from local churches. This biennial General Council elects general officers, sets doctrinal standards, and provides for church expansion and development. The General Superintendent and other general church officers serve at the national headquarters in Springfield, Missouri.

The denomination's publishing arm, the Gospel Publishing House, produces curriculum and other resources and several periodicals, including the weekly *The Pentecostal Evangel,* which has a circulation of approximately 280,000. In the U.S. there are nine Bible colleges; an Arts and Sciences college; six institutes; and a nontraditional college and a seminary in Springfield. Missionary work is conducted under the guidance of a central missionary committee; there are over 1,500 foreign missionaries at work. The church sponsors 417 Bible schools abroad.

ASSEMBLIES OF THE LORD JESUS CHRIST

Founded: 1952
Membership: 413 churches (2001)

Three Pentecostal groups, known as the Assemblies of the Church of Jesus Christ, Jesus Only Apostolic Church of God, and the Church of the Lord Jesus Christ, formulated a merger in 1952, adopting the name "Assemblies of the Lord Jesus Christ." The Assemblies promotes many basic Pentecostal doctrines (see PENTECOSTAL CHURCHES), including the infallibility and direct divine inspiration of Scripture, the fall of humankind, salvation by grace, a premillennial tribulation, water baptism and baptism by the Holy Spirit, Holy communion, the service of foot washing, divine healing, and holiness in life. However, the church is not trinitarian, believing rather that the "one True God manifested Himself in the Old Testament in divers ways, in the Son while he walked among men, as the Holy Ghost after the ascension." Members are forbidden to attend dances or theatrical events, even in public schools; thus private Bible schools are preferred. Another distinctive teaching of the church is that Christians are to obey the government in all matters except for the bearing of arms. Members are thus conscientious objectors.

The Assemblies of the Lord Jesus Christ has churches in thirty-five states, with particular strength in the Midwest and the South. It maintains offices in Memphis, Tennessee. Administration includes a general superintendent and three assistant superintendents. The church maintains Parkersburg Bible College in West Virginia and the Memphis School of Ministries in Tennessee; it supports missions in eight countries outside the U.S.; and it carries out prison ministry, ministry to Native Americans, and church building programs throughout the U.S.

BIBLE WAY CHURCH OF OUR LORD JESUS CHRIST, WORLD WIDE, INC.

Founded: 1957
Membership: est. 300,000 in 350 churches worldwide (1995)

The Bible Way Church is an organization of Pentecostal churches. At a ministerial conference of African American Pentecostal pastors in September 1957, Apostle Smallwood Edmond Williams led some seventy churches out of the Church of Our Lord Jesus Christ of the Apostolic Faith (see CHURCH OF OUR LORD JESUS CHRIST) to form the Bible Way Church, World Wide. The vision of the founder was to promote evangelistic goals. The church's basic beliefs include Christ's resurrection and pre-millennial Second Coming, the resurrection and translation of the saints, the priesthood of all believers, and the final judgment of humankind. Baptism is by immersion, and baptism of the Holy Spirit is necessary for second birth. Foot washing is also practiced.

Phenomenal growth has been reported by the church, but precise numbers are dificult to obtain. The Bible Way Church has twenty-seven dioceses, six of which lie outside the U.S. A board of bishops directs the church, and individual bishops preside over the various dioceses. A general conference is held annually in July, and the church sponsors various convocations. A publishing house at Washington, D.C., circulates periodicals, religious pamphlets, and recordings.

CHRISTIAN CATHOLIC CHURCH

Founded: 1896
Membership: 2,728 in 7 churches (1996)

The Christian Catholic Church (catholic in the sense of "universal") was formally organized by John Alexander Dowie (1847–1907), a Congregational preacher who embraced divine healing. He also founded Zion City, Illinois, in 1901 as a theocratic center for his church. Dowie had extensive plans for educational and cultural projects. He criticized the injustices of capitalism and the excesses of labor leaders, alcoholic beverages, tobacco, medicine and the medical profession, secret lodges, and the press. He was also a tireless advocate of racial equality and integration. Several years after the church was located at Zion, Dowie claimed to be Elijah the Restorer. He maintained leadership of the group until 1906, when he was deposed and followed successively by Wilbur Glen Voliva, Michael J. Mintern, Carl W. Lee, and, currently, Roger W. Ottersen.

Theologically, the Christian Catholic Church is rooted in evangelical orthodoxy. The scriptures are accepted as the rule of faith and

269

practice. Other doctrines call for the necessity of repentance from sin and personal trust in Christ for salvation, baptism by triune immersion, the Second Coming of Christ, and tithing as a practical method of Christian stewardship.

Some of Dowie's followers joined the Assemblies of God (see ASSEMBLIES OF GOD) in 1914. Since then, the Christian Catholic Church has placed less emphasis on healing. It has increasingly identified itself as evangelical in doctrine and practice.

CHRISTIAN CHURCH OF NORTH AMERICA, GENERAL COUNCIL

Founded: 1948
Membership: 7,200 in 96 churches (1999)

Originally known as the Italian Christian Church, this body originated in a gathering of Italian Pentecostal ministers held in 1927 at Niagara Falls, New York. The leader was Luigi Francescon (1866–1964) who had left the Roman Catholic Church in 1892, joining the First Italian Presbyterian Church in Chicago. He embraced believer's baptism in 1903 and established the first Italian American Pentecostal congregation in 1907 in Chicago. When the church was incorporated in 1948 at Pittsburgh, it took the name "Missionary Society of the Christian Church of North America." The present name was adopted in 1963 when the body was reorganized as a denomination.

The Christian Church of North America, General Council holds to basic Pentecostal (see PENTECOSTAL CHURCHES) beliefs, emphasizing the infallibility of Scripture, the trinitarian (Father, Son, and Holy Spirit) understanding of God, and salvation through faith in Jesus Christ. Although affirming the experiences of salvation and spirit baptism, the body does not teach the doctrine of entire sanctification. Two ordinances are recognized: baptism and the Lord's Supper. Members are exhorted to pursue a life of personal holiness, setting an example for others. A conservative position is held in regard to marriage and divorce.

The governmental form is congregational in nature, but district and national agencies are led by overseers. General departments direct missions programs in over forty countries, establish credentials for ministers, develop resources for Christian education programs in the churches, and support various lay organizations for men, women, youth, and children. Headquarters are in Transfer, Pennsylvania. *Vista Magazine* is the official organ of the church.

CHURCH OF GOD (Cleveland, Tennessee)

Founded: 1886; 1907
Membership: 870,039 in 6,328 churches (1999)

The Church of God (Cleveland, Tennessee) claims the distinction of the being the oldest Pentecostal body. It traces its founding to 1886 in Monroe County, Tennessee, when the Christian Union was organized by Richard Spurling (1810–91), a Baptist (see BAPTIST CHURCHES) and his son, R. G. Spurling (1857–1935). The Spurlings had been led to the Bible to stem the tide of the church's "spiritual indifference, formality, and accommodation to modern culture." In 1892 a second church was formed in Cherokee County, North Carolina, under the leadership of William F. Bryant (1863–1949); four years later, this group experienced speaking in tongues for the first time. R. G. Spurling met with the North Carolina group and others, and two more congregations were added over the next few years. The small organization was renamed the Holiness Church in 1902.

In 1903, Ambrose J. Tomlinson (1865–1943) of the American Bible Society joined the Holiness Church. In January of 1907 the name was changed once more, to Church of God, and headquarters were moved to Cleveland, Tennessee. Tomlinson was elected general overseer in 1909, and the church began publishing *The Church of God Evangel* the following year. The Church of God embraced Pentecostal (see PENTECOSTAL CHURCHES) practices and grew rapidly across the South and Midwest.

A crisis occurred in 1923 that raised concerns over the personal role of Tomlinson (see CHURCH OF GOD OF PROPHECY) and, more important, the nature of the church's government and the leader's authority. The majority, those with whom the Church of God (Cleveland, Tennessee) is continuous, rejected Tomlinson's leadership and selected F. J. Lee as overseer.

The church's major doctrines blend many Protestant themes with those that are specifically Pentecostal: justification by faith, sanctification, baptism of the Holy Spirit, speaking in tongues, the need to

271

be born again, fruitfulness in Christian living, and a strong interest in the pre-millennial Second Coming of Christ (Christ to return before reigning on earth for a thousand years). The Church of God professes reliance on the Bible "as a whole rightly divided rather than upon any written creed." It practices divine healing; condemns the use of alcohol and tobacco; opposes membership in secret societies; and accepts baptism, the Lord's Supper, and foot washing as ordinances.

The Church of God elects its officers at a biennial General Assembly. The administration of the church includes a general over-seer, three assistant overseers, a secretary general, and an eighteen member International Executive Council, which is responsible for the day-to-day operations of the church. Administrative divisions include education, world evangelism, church ministries, care ministries, and support services. Pathway Press is the publishing arm of the church, producing resources for Christian education and books for ministers and lay people. The Church of God operates Lee University and the Church of God School of Theology in Cleveland, Tennessee; a school of ministry; and a preparatory school. Its foreign missions enterprise is extensive, serving in Africa, Asia, Europe, Central America, and South America.

CHURCH OF GOD IN CHRIST

Founded: 1897
Membership: est. 5,500,000 in 15,300 churches (1991)

Ministers Charles H. Mason (1866–1961) and Charles P. Jones, expelled by Baptist groups (see BAPTIST CHURCHES) in Arkansas for what was considered an overemphasis on holiness (see HOLI-NESS CHURCHES), together founded the Church of Christ (Holiness) U.S.A. in 1895. This church stressed the doctrine of entire sanctification. Mason also organized a congregation in Lexington, Mississippi, in 1897, to which he gave the name Church of God in Christ. In 1907 Mason went to Azusa Street in Los Angeles, California, to observe the Pentecostal revival taking place there (see PENTECOSTAL CHURCHES); while in attendance, he had his first experience of speaking in tongues. Subsequently, Mason raised the issue of Pentecostal experience in a gathering of leaders of the Church of Christ (Holiness) U.S.A. Charles P. Jones and others did not share Mason's enthusiasm for the Pentecostal movement and withdrew fellowship from him. Mason then called for a meeting in Memphis, Tennessee, of ministers who endorsed Pentecostal doctrine. With this group, he organized a general assembly of the Church of God in Christ, of which he was named general overseer and chief apostle. Mason remained head of the church until his death in 1961.

Church of God in Christ doctrine is trinitarian, stressing repentance, regeneration, justification, sanctification, speaking in tongues, and the gift of healing as evidence of the baptism of the Spirit. The sanctifying power of the Holy Spirit is considered a prerequisite to living a holy life, separate from the sin of the present world. Ordinances include baptism by immersion, the Lord's Supper, and foot washing.

Generally acknowledged to be the largest African American Pentecostal body in the U.S., the Church of God in Christ organization is held to have its authority in Scripture. There are presiding, assistant presiding, and state bishops; a general board and a national trustee board; district superintendents; pastors; evangelists; deacons; and departmental presidents. Officers are chosen at a general assembly that meets every four years. General departments include Sunday school, youth, evangelism, and missions. The denomination's headquarters are in Memphis, Tennessee, as is the department of publications and a Sunday school publishing house to supply the denomination with literature. Missionaries are found in South Africa, Thailand, Jamaica, Haiti, Liberia, and on the west coast of Africa. The Charles H. Mason Theological Seminary is one unit in the Interdenominational Theological Center in Atlanta, Georgia.

CHURCH OF GOD OF PROPHECY

Founded: 1923
Membership: 75,112 in 1,862 churches (1999)

Church of God of Prophecy is one of the churches that grew out of the work of A. J. Tomlinson (1865–1943; see CHURCH OF GOD [CLEVELAND, TENNESSEE]). At his death, his son M. A. Tomlinson was named General overseer, a position he held until 1990. He emphasized church unity and fellowship unlimited by social, racial, and political differences. The present general overseer, Billy D. Murray, Sr., has made promoting Christian unity and worldwide evangelism his priorities.

273

From its beginnings, the church has based its beliefs on "the whole Bible, rightly divided" and has accepted the Bible as God's Holy Word, inspired, inerrant, and infallible. The church affirms that there is one God, eternally existing in three persons. It believes in the deity, virgin birth, sinlessness, miracles, atoning death, bodily resurrection, ascension to the Father, and physical second coming of Christ. The church professes that salvation results from grace alone through faith in Christ, that regeneration by the Holy Spirit is essential for the salvation of sinners, and that sanctification by the blood of Christ makes personal holiness possible. The church stresses the ultimate unity of believers, based on John 17, and the sanctity of marriage and family.

Other official teachings include baptism by the Spirit with the speaking of tongues as evidence; divine healing; the pre-millennial Second Coming of Christ; baptism by immersion; abstinence from tobacco, alcohol, and narcotics; and holiness in lifestyle. In addition to the Lord's Supper, the church practices foot washing.

The church is racially integrated on all levels, and women play a prominent role in church affairs, including serving in pastoral roles. The General Oversight Group consists of at least two bishops who, along with the General Overseer, are responsible for setting the vision for the entire church body. The Area Presbyters are bishops who are strategically placed around the world to assist in doctrinal matters and in leadership development. Doctrinal and business concerns of the church are addressed at the biennal General Assembly. Administrative divisions of the church include global outreach, leadership development and discipleship, specialized ministries, communications and publishing, and administrative services.

CHURCH OF OUR LORD JESUS CHRIST OF THE APOSTOLIC FAITH, INC.

Founded: 1919
Membership: est. 30,000 in 450 churches (1998)

This church was organized in 1919 at Columbus, Ohio, by Robert C. Lawson as "a continuation of the great revival begun at Jerusalem on the day of Pentecost in 33 C.E. . . . ." Lawson moved to New York City later that year, where he founded Refuge Temple, which he pastored until his death in 1961. He also led the wider organization as chief apostle until his death. He was succeeded as pastor of the church (now Greater Refuge Temple) by William L. Bonner, who later also became chief apostle of the Church of Our Lord Jesus Christ of the Apostolic Faith, Inc.

Church doctrine is held to be "that of the apostles and the prophets," with Christ as the cornerstone. The basic emphases are Christ's resurrection and pre-millennial Second Coming, the resurrection and translation of the saints, the priesthood of all believers, and the final judgment of humankind. The church is non-trinitarian, maintaining belief "in the oneness of God, who was the Father in creation, the Son in redemption, and today, He is the Holy Ghost in The Church." Baptism is by immersion, and baptism of the Holy Spirit is necessary for second birth. Foot washing is practiced, but not as an ordinance.

The Church of Our Lord Jesus Christ of the Apostolic Faith, Inc. has congregations in 32 states, the British West Indies, Africa, the Philippines, Haiti, the Dominican Republic, and London, England. It operates a Bible college in New York City, where general offices are maintained, and carries out various ministries of caring in the communities in which it serves. A national convocation meets every year. National officers include a chief apostle, a presiding apostle, a board of apostles, a board of bishops, and a board of presbyters.

CHURCH OF THE LIVING GOD, CHRISTIAN WORKERS FOR FELLOWSHIP

Founded: 1889
Membership: approx. 100 temples (2000)

This body claims to be the first black church in the U.S. that was not begun by white missionaries. The Church of the Living God, Christian Workers for Fellowship came out of an organization formed in 1889 at Wrightsville, Arkansas, by William Christian (1856–1928), a former slave. At a time when many white Christians treated blacks as less than human, Christian began a group that maintained that many of the prominent people of the Bible, including Jesus and David, were black. Christian held the office of "Chief" in the new church, and was succeeded in the office by his wife and, eventually, by their son.

Christian held to trinitarian doctrine and accepted Pentecostal (see

PENTECOSTAL CHURCHES) practices, such as speaking in tongues, without requiring the practices of members; he did, however, hold that inspired speaking must be in recognizable languages. The Church of the Living God, Christian Workers for Fellowship observes three ordinances: water baptism, washing of feet, and the Lord's Supper celebrated with water and unleavened bread.

Christian also was fascinated by Freemasonry, and he developed a church structure that resembled a fraternal organization. He insisted that his "organism" be known as "operative Masonry" and characterized the three ordinances as the "first three corporal degrees." A chief bishop is the presiding officer of the organization. Members tithe their incomes to support their churches, which they call temples.

CHURCH OF THE LIVING GOD, THE PILLAR AND GROUND OF THE TRUTH, INC.

Founded: 1903
Membership: est. 2,000 in 100 churches (1988)

Mary Lena Lewis-Tate (1871–1930), later known as Mary Magdalena Lewis-Tate, was the "First Chief Overseer and Mother in True Holiness" of the Church of the Living God, the Pillar and the Ground of Truth, Inc. Lewis-Tate felt moved by the Holy Ghost to go out into the world and preach the gospel, first at Steele Springs, Tennessee. She chose as her co-laborers her two sons, Walter Curtis Lewis and Felix Early Lewis. Two of her first converts were her sisters in Paducah, Kentucky, who also became ministers and bishops in the church. By 1908, Lewis-Tate had a number of local congregations in many places, and she organized the first general assembly of the church that year at Greenville, Alabama. At her death in 1930, her son Felix became Chief Overseer of the church; and in 1968, upon Lewis's death, Helen M. Lewis became Chief Overseer. The church has experienced two major schisms, one during the founder's lifetime and one after.

Doctrinally, the church promotes basic Holiness (see HOLINESS CHURCHES) and Pentecostal (see PENTECOSTAL CHURCHES) beliefs, including belief in the Holy Trinity, water baptism by immersion, Spirit baptism with evidence of speaking in unknown/foreign tongues, the Lord's Supper (with water rather than wine), sanctification, praying, and fasting. The King James Version of the Bible is given precedence in worship and study.

The Church of the Living God, the Pillar and Ground of Truth, Inc., maintains offices in Nashville, Tennessee, which is also the home of the church's publishing arm, New and Living Way Publishing Company. A general assembly meets annually.

CONGREGATIONAL HOLINESS CHURCH

Founded: 1921
Membership: est. 10,000 in 187 churches (2000)

The Congregational Holiness Church was organized in January of 1921 by ministers formerly connected with the Pentecostal Holiness Church (see INTERNATIONAL PENTECOSTAL HOLINESS CHURCH). The divisive issue was the nature of divine healing; those who founded the new church held that although all blessings including divine healing come through the merits of Christ's atonement, God has given the gift of medicine for human well-being. The church identifies with the Holiness wing (see HOLINESS CHURCHES) of the Pentecostal movement (see PENTECOSTAL CHURCHES). It stresses holiness of life in opposition to what is sees as the prevailing worldliness of contemporary culture.

Doctrinally, the Congregational Holiness Church affirms the inspiration of Holy Scripture; the trinitarian understanding of the Godhead; the virgin birth of Jesus Christ; the death and resurrection of Christ for the salvation of human beings; the gift of eternal salvation through Christ for those who repent of sin and believe in Christ; the eternal punishment of those who reject Christ; sanctification as a second work of divine grace in the life of believers; and the imminent, personal return of Christ prior to his reign on earth. The church emphasizes the baptism of the Holy Ghost, with speaking in tongues as the Spirit gives utterance being the initiatory evidence of that experience. Ordinances include baptism by immersion, the Lord's Supper, and foot washing.

Church government is congregational. In the early days of the denomination, there were no elected leaders. A General Conference was held every two years. This arrangement continued until 1935, when there was an organizational change. The local churches are grouped into eight geographical districts, all in the southeast region

277

of the U.S. Each district has a presbytery of five members. The districts have the power to license and ordain ministers. The District Judicial Presbytery serves as the committee that examines candidates for the ministry and makes recommendations to the District Conference. The District Presbytery members, the General Executive Board (which includes the General Superintendent), and General Department heads comprise the General Committee, which governs the church between the General Biennial Conferences. The General Conference is the highest ruling body of the church. Offices are maintained in Griffin, Georgia.

Congregational Holiness Church pastors are elected by a majority vote of the congregation to which they are called; both women and men are ordained. While the church does not have a seminary of its own, it endorses several conservative evangelical schools as training centers for those going into the ministry. The church has missions in India, Cuba, Brazil, Venezuela, Costa Rica, Nicaragua, Honduras, Guatemala, El Salvador, Belize, Panama, and Mexico.

ELIM FELLOWSHIP

Founded: 1947
Membership: est. 21,000 in 190 churches (1997)

This body is an outgrowth of the missionary-oriented Elim Ministerial Fellowship, formed in 1933, and the work of graduates of the Elim Bible Institute in Lima, New York, founded in 1924 by Ivan and Minnie Spencer. The group was incorporated in 1947 as the Elim Missionary Assemblies; the present name was adopted in 1972.

Members of the Elim Fellowship hold to basic Pentecostal (see PENTECOSTAL CHURCHES) tenets of belief, beginning with affirmation of the Bible as the inspired and infallible Word of God. The fellowship espouses the trinitarian understanding of the Godhead, the atoning death and resurrection of Jesus Christ, salvation, sanctification, water baptism, the celebration of Communion among believers, the baptism of the Holy Spirit as evidenced in charismatic gifts and ministries, divine healing, and resurrection of the saved and unsaved for eternal reward or punishment.

The organizational pattern of Elim Fellowship is congregational, with individual churches autonomous in decision making. An annual assembly meets in Lima, where the General Chairman maintains

278

offices. Over 150 missionaries affiliated with the fellowship are at work in Africa, Asia, Europe, and South America.

FULL GOSPEL FELLOWSHIP OF CHURCHES AND MINISTERS, INTERNATIONAL

Founded: 1962
Membership: 275,200 in 896 churches (1998)

This fellowship was founded in Dallas, Texas, at a meeting called by Gordon Lindsay to support, encourage, and promote apostolic, that is, Pentecostal ministry (see PENTECOSTAL CHURCHES). As Lindsay and others envisioned it, the organization would give expression to the essential unity of those who believe in Christ and in the active work of the Holy Spirit. It was not to be a denomination as such but a fellowship of ministries. The organization also made it easier for independent churches to have tax-exempt status with the Internal Revenue Service.

Although individual churches or groups of churches affiliated with the Full Gospel Fellowship have doctrinal and ecclesial autonomy, certain core beliefs form the basis for fellowship. Among the suggested tenets of faith are belief in the Bible as the inspired Word of God, in the trinitarian understanding of the Godhead, in the atoning death and resurrection of Jesus Christ, in the need for personal salvation and sanctification, in the return and reign of Jesus Christ, and in heaven and hell. The fellowship strongly advocates baptism by the Holy Spirit, as evidenced by the gift of speaking in tongues.

Regional conventions and an annual international convention are held; and various cooperative ministries, including curriculum development, are facilitated by the organization. The fellowship maintains offices in Irving, Texas.

INDEPENDENT ASSEMBLIES OF GOD, INTERNATIONAL

Founded: 1922
Membership: statistics not available

This group is to be distinguished from the Assemblies of God (see ASSEMBLIES OF GOD), but it shares a common heritage in the early Pentecostal movement (see PENTECOSTAL CHURCHES). It traces its origins to the Azusa Street revival in Los Angeles in 1906 that soon spread across the country and across ethnic lines. In 1918, Scandinavian Pentecostals, who were particularly concerned to preserve the principles of Congregationalism (see CONGREGATIONAL CHURCHES), formed the Scandinavian Assemblies of God in the United States, Canada, and Foreign Lands. This group operated essentially as a fellowship of like-minded churches until 1935, when they merged with the Independent Pentecostal Churches to form the Independent Assemblies of God, International.

Doctrinally, the church's statement of faith includes the common tenets of Pentecostalism, such as belief in the Bible as the inspired and infallible Word of God, in the Trinity, in the reality of Satan, and in the need for baptism by the Holy Spirit as evidenced through speaking in tongues. Ordinances include baptism by immersion and the Lord's Supper.

The churches in this assembly are autonomous but work together on common ministries. The leadership of the Assemblies of God International includes a general overseer, an assistant general overseer, and an international missions director. The Independent Assemblies of God, International maintains offices in Santa Ana, California. The church supports missionaries and national pastors in Africa, Central America, South America, Mexico, India, and the Philippines.

INTERNATIONAL CHURCH OF THE FOURSQUARE GOSPEL

Founded: 1927
Membership: 233,412 in 1,836 congregations (1999)

Founded during the evangelistic work of Aimee Semple McPherson (1890–1944), this church is a tribute to the organizing genius and striking methods of its founder. Born in Ontario in 1890, McPherson was converted under the preaching of her first husband, Robert Semple, an evangelist. Semple died while they were serving as missionaries in China, and Aimee Semple returned to the U.S. in 1911, where she conducted evangelistic crusades throughout North America.

In 1918, after her remarriage, Aimee Semple McPherson and her children, Roberta and Rolf, settled in Los Angeles. With the help of her followers, she built and dedicated Angelus Temple on January 1, 1923. She also founded the Echo Park Evangelistic Association, the Lighthouse of International Foursquare Evangelism (L.I.F.E.) Bible College, and the International Church of the Foursquare Gospel.

With her speaking ability and faith in prayer for the sick, McPherson attracted thousands to her meetings. Her critics felt that the meetings were too spectacular, but others appreciated her type of presentation. There was great interest in the sick and the poor; "more than a million and a half" are said to have been fed by Angelus Temple during the depression years. McPherson was president of the church during her lifetime and, together with a board of directors, oversaw the denomination's expansion. Upon her death in 1944, her son, Rolf Kennedy McPherson, became president. Upon his retirement in 1988, John R. Holland assumed the office, followed by Paul C. Risser in 1998.

The "four-fold gospel" refers to four central Pentecostal (see PENTECOSTAL CHURCHES) teachings that pre-date McPherson but that she popularized nationally. They are (1) salvation, (2) baptism by the Spirit, (3) divine physical healing, and (4) the Second Coming of Jesus Christ. The broader teaching of the church is set forth in a 21-paragraph Declaration of Faith written by McPherson. Strongly fundamentalist (see FUNDAMENTALIST/BIBLE CHURCHES), it stresses the return of Christ prior to his reign on earth, personal holiness (see HOLINESS CHURCHES), and the trinitarian conception of God. The Bible is affirmed as "true, immutable, steadfast, unchangeable, as its author, the Lord Jehovah." Baptism with the Holy Spirit, with the initial evidence of speaking in tongues, is subsequent to conversion, and the power to heal is given in answer to believing prayer. The ordinances of baptism and the Lord's Supper are observed in the church.

The official business of the church is conducted by a board of directors, a missionary cabinet, and an executive council made up of corporate officers. The highest seat of authority is the annual Foursquare Convention, which alone has the power to make or amend the bylaws of the church and which elects the president of the church to a four-year term. District supervisors are appointed for ten districts in the United States and are ratified by pastors of the respective districts every four years. Pastors are appointed by the board of directors of the denomination and are assisted by a local church council. Congregations are subordinated units of the denomination and contribute monthly to home and foreign missionary work. The official publication of the church is the *Foursquare World ADVANCE* magazine, published bimonthly.

While membership is highest on the West Coast, there are Foursquare churches in all fifty states. Overseas, the Foursquare Gospel is preached in 107 countries, with over three million members and adherents in over 26,000 churches and meeting places. In addition to L.I.F.E. Bible College in Los Angeles and L.I.F.E. Bible College East in Christiansburg, Virginia, the church supports numerous Bible colleges and institutes around the world. There is also an extensive youth camping program. The church sponsors radio station KFSG-FM in Los Angeles.

INTERNATIONAL PENTECOSTAL CHURCH OF CHRIST

Founded: 1976
Membership: 5,572 in 69 churches (1999)

The International Pentecostal Church of Christ, with headquarters in London, Ohio, grew as a result of a 1976 consolidation of the International Pentecostal Assemblies and the Pentecostal Church of Christ (see PENTECOSTAL CHURCHES). The International Pentecostal Assemblies was organized in 1921 and was based in Atlanta, Georgia. It grew out of the founding of *The Bridegroom's Messenger* in 1907, which continues to be the official organ of the present denomination. The Pentecostal Church of Christ was organized in 1917 by John Stroup, a former Methodist elder (see METHODIST CHURCHES), in Flatwoods, Kentucky; this group subsequently was headquartered at Ashland, Kentucky, and then London, Ohio, where the general offices of the church are located today.

The International Pentecostal Church of Christ subscribes to the basic doctrines of the Holiness (see HOLINESS CHURCHES) and Pentecostal movements, with a stress on the body of saints' being perfected in the image of Christ. The church affirms the Bible as the revealed Word of God and the New Testament as the sole rule for discipline and government; and it proclaims a Trinity of God the Father, Jesus Christ the Son, and the Holy Spirit. Baptism by the Holy Ghost as evidenced in speaking with tongues as the spirit gives utterance and divine healing as provided by the atoning death of Christ are central elements in the body's statement of faith. Ordinances include baptism by immersion, Holy Communion, foot washing, and child dedication.

Beulah Heights Bible College of Atlanta, Georgia, is owned and operated by the International Pentecostal Church of Christ. Other denominational ministries include Christian education, global missions, home missions and evangelism, women's ministries, and youth ministries. The denomination also maintains a home for the elderly in West Virginia and a conference center in Ohio. Active missions work is conducted in Brazil, French Guiana, India, Kenya, Mexico, the Philippines, and Uruguay.

INTERNATIONAL PENTECOSTAL HOLINESS CHURCH

Founded: 1911
Membership: 185,431 in 1,771 churches (1999)

The International Pentecostal Holiness Church traces its origins to an organization founded in 1898 at Anderson, South Carolina, by a number of Holiness associations (see HOLINESS CHURCHES); at that time the group was called the Fire-Baptized Holiness Church. In the same year, in Goldsboro, North Carolina, another group was organized as the Pentecostal Holiness Church. In 1907, G. B. Cashwell (1826–1916), a participant in the Azusa Street revival, led a Pentecostal revival in North Carolina and brought these two groups into Pentecostalism (see PENTECOSTAL CHURCHES). The two bodies united in 1911 as the Pentecostal Holiness Church; and a third body, the Tabernacle Pentecost Church, joined them in 1915. The present name was adopted in 1975.

The theological standards of Methodism (see METHODIST CHURCHES) prevail in the International Pentecostal Holiness Church, with certain modifications. The denomination accepts the pre-millennial teaching of the Second Coming, holding that Christ's return will precede his thousand year reign on earth, and believes that provision was made in the atonement for healing of the human body. Divine healing is practiced, but not to the exclusion of medicine. Three distinctive experiences are taught: two works of grace—justification by faith and sanctification—and Spirit baptism, attested to by speaking in other tongues. Services are often characterized by "joyous demonstrations." Two ordinances are observed: water baptism and Holy Communion.

The church's general executive board of ten members is elected by a quadrennial conference for a four-year term; members are limited to two consecutive terms in any one office. There is a general superintendent, three assistant general superintendents, a secretary-treasurer, and five board members who represent geographical areas and the church at large. The assistant superintendents serve as directors of the world missions, evangelism, and Christian education departments of the general church. Twenty-eight conferences or regional judicatories cover the U.S., but principal strength lies in the Carolinas, Virginia, Oklahoma, Florida, Texas, and California. General offices are in Bethany, Oklahoma.

The International Pentecostal Holiness Church sponsors Emmanuel College in Georgia and Southwestern College of Christian Ministries in Oklahoma, both four-year accredited colleges. The church operates a children's home at Falcon, North Carolina; a children's convalescent center at Bethany, Oklahoma; and a home for the aged. Foreign mission work takes place in ninety countries.

OPEN BIBLE STANDARD CHURCHES, INC.

Founded: 1935
Membership: est. 46,000 in 371 churches (2000)

This association of churches was originally composed of two revival movements rooted in the Azusa Street meetings of 1906 (see PENTECOSTAL CHURCHES): Bible Standard, Inc., founded in Eugene, Oregon, by Fred Hornshuh in 1919 and Open Bible Evangelistic Association, founded in Des Moines, Iowa, by John R. Richey in 1932. The Pacific Coast group, with activities centered in Oregon, spread through Washington, California, and into the Rocky Mountain areas of the West; the Iowa group expanded into Illinois, Missouri, Ohio, Florida, and Pennsylvania. Similar in doctrine and government, the two groups joined on July 26, 1935, taking the combined name Open Bible Standard Churches, Inc., with headquarters in Des Moines. There are now churches in thirty-one states, concentrated in the central and far west regions of the U.S.

The teachings of the Open Bible Standard Churches are "fundamental in doctrine, evangelical in spirit, missionary in vision, and Pentecostal in testimony." They include emphasis on the infallibility of the Word of God, the blood atonement of Christ, divine healing, baptism of the Holy Spirit, personal holiness, the return of Jesus Christ prior to his reign on earth, and baptism by immersion.

Open Bible Standard Churches are grouped into five geographical regions, subdivided into 25 districts; district superintendents guide the work under the supervision of regional superintendents. Individual churches are congregationally governed, locally owned, and affiliated by charter with the national organization. Sixteen areas of ministry function under the leadership of six executive directors, aided by the counsel of committees under the supervision of the national board of directors. The highest governing body is the general convention, which meets biennially. The convention is composed of all licensed and ordained ministers, with a lay delegate for each 100 church members.

The association ministers in 32 countries outside the U.S. and sponsors 12 Bible institutes serving over 440 students. Mission emphasis is on the training of nationals for ministry. The missions department publishes a monthly *World Vision* and a semiannual *Outreach* magazine. A separate board of publications is responsible for the preparation of books and Bible studies, publishes a monthly periodical, *Message of the Open Bible,* and provides lesson material for Sunday schools in cooperation with a Christian education department. Open Bible Standard Churches sponsor Eugene Bible College in Oregon and many Institute of Theology by Extension (INSTE) groups throughout the U.S.

PENTECOSTAL ASSEMBLIES OF THE WORLD, INC.

Founded: 1907
Membership: est. 1,500,000 in 1,750 churches (1998)

Tracing its origin to the Azusa Street revival in 1906, this body is the oldest "oneness" Pentecostal body (see PENTECOSTAL CHURCHES), meaning that its baptism is in the name of Jesus only. The goal of the Pentecostal Assemblies of the World, Inc., is to spread the message that Jesus Christ is Lord to all people. From its beginning, the group, including its leadership, has been interracial; however, the church is predominantly African American today. Two of it most influential leaders were G. T. Haywood, who directed the church during a period of consolidation from 1924 until his death in 1931, and Samuel Grimes, a former missionary, who led the church through a period of expansion from 1937 until his death in 1967.

Basic Pentecostal and Holiness (see HOLINESS CHURCHES) doctrine and practice are followed, except for rejection of the trinitarian understanding of God. The church stresses holiness of life, holding that believers must be wholly sanctified to fully participate in salvation. Strict codes governing dress and leisure pursuits are maintained. Water baptism and the Lord's Supper are practiced, with wine used in the latter. Only the King James Version of the Bible is accepted as the true Word of God.

The Pentecostal Assemblies of the World hosts two major conferences annually, to which its constituents come from around the globe to worship God and to fellowship with one another. The church is headed by a presiding bishop who guides its members spiritually. There is also an executive board, including an assistant presiding bishop, a general secretary, a general treasurer, and lay directors. The organization's administrator and staff handle its business affairs from general offices in Indianapolis, Indiana. This body is heavily concentrated in urban areas, such as Chicago, Detroit, and Indianapolis, but there are ministers serving in all fifty states.

The Aenon Bible College, located in Indianapolis, Indiana, serves to train Pentecostal Assemblies ministers and lay members. The college has affiliate institutes all over the U.S. and two foreign affiliates in Liberia: the Samuel Grimes Bible Institute and the Haywood Mission.

PENTECOSTAL CHURCH OF GOD

Founded: 1919
Membership: 105,200 in 1,237 churches (1999)

This body was organized in Chicago under the name "Pentecostal Assemblies of the U.S.A." in order to better organize early Pentecostalism (see PENTECOSTAL CHURCHES) in the Midwest for evangelism and to preserve congregations from unethical preachers pretending to be Spirit-filled. When the church was reorganized in 1922, the name was changed to "Pentecostal Church of God." For a number of years "of America" was a part of the name, but this was dropped in 1979.

The Pentecostal Church of God is evangelical and Pentecostal in faith and practice. The doctrines of salvation, divine healing, baptism in the Holy Spirit (with the evidence of speaking in tongues), and the Second Coming of Christ are strongly emphasized. Ordinances include water baptism, the Lord's Supper, and foot washing.

A General Convention of the church meets biennially. Executives of the denomination include a general superintendent, a general secretary, a director of world missions, a director of home missions/evangelism, and a director of (American) Indian missions. Headquarters are located in Joplin, Missouri. The church has six regional divisions, each presided over by an assistant general superintendent. Most of the divisions have annual conventions.

The Pentecostal Church of God conducts mission work in 49 countries in Europe, Asia, Africa, and the Americas; 37 missionaries serve in the field. Over 4,950 churches have been established outside the U.S., and over 2,500 national ministers have been commissioned. The group sponsors 22 Bible schools, 57 training centers, and 51 day schools across the globe. Messenger College, Messenger Publishing House, and Messenger Towers, all in Joplin, are supported by the church. *The Pentecostal Herald* is the official publication.

PENTECOSTAL FREE WILL BAPTIST CHURCH, INC.

Founded: 1959
Membership: est. 28,000 in 150 churches (1998)

The Pentecostal Free Will Baptist Church came into existence through the merging of four Free-Will Baptist conferences in North Carolina in 1959. These various groups traced their origins as Free Will Baptists (see BAPTIST CHURCHES) to the work of Paul Palmer (d. 1750) in the Carolinas during the first half of the eighteenth century. The Pentecostal aspect of the church's doctrine was developed in response to the preaching of G. W. Cashwell (1826–1916), who had participated in the Azusa Street revival of 1906 in Los Angeles, California (see PENTECOSTAL CHURCHES). Cashwell launched a series of meetings in North Carolina on New Year's Eve, 1906; in response, many Free Will

Baptist individuals and churches adopted Pentecostal doctrine and practice.

The church's doctrine is a mixture of Baptist and Pentecostal beliefs. Central affirmations include the inerrancy of the Bible, regeneration through faith in the shed blood of Christ, sanctification as a second definite work of grace (subsequent to regeneration), Pentecostal baptism of the Holy Spirit as evidenced through speaking in tongues, divine healing, and the pre-millennial Second Coming of Christ. Ordinances include baptism by immersion, the Lord's Super, and foot washing.

A general meeting of the Pentecostal Free Will Baptist Church is held biennially in August; lay and ministerial representatives attend. Church officials include a general superintendent, a general secretary, and a general treasurer. Offices are maintained in Dunn, North Carolina, where Heritage Bible College was established in 1971. Most of the group's churches are in eastern North Carolina; but mission work is carried on in nine foreign countries, and Bible institutes are operated in Mexico, the Philippines, and Venezuela.

UNITED HOLY CHURCH OF AMERICA, INC.

Founded: 1918; 1886
Membership: statistics not available

This is a Pentecostal/Holiness body that was first organized in 1886 in Method, North Carolina as a regional body (see PENTE-COSTAL CHURCHES; HOLINESS CHURCHES). Known originally as the Holy Church of North Carolina, it was reorganized in 1918 as the United Holy Church of America, Inc. Its purpose is to establish and maintain holy convocations, assemblies, conventions, conferences, public worship, and missionary and educational efforts.

Articles of faith contain statements of belief in the Trinity, the record of the revelation of God in the Bible, redemption through Christ, justification with instantaneous sanctification, baptism of the Holy Spirit, divine healing, and the ultimate reign of Christ over the earth. Baptism by immersion, the Lord's Supper, and foot washing are observed as ordinances. The United Holy Church believes in speaking in tongues and views Spirit baptism as normative, although it shares the position held by many Pentecostal groups that speaking in tongues is not required for full membership, full discipleship, or even spirit baptism.

288

The church maintains headquarters in Greensboro, North Carolina. The chief officer is the General President. Other officials include two general vice presidents, a general recording secretary, a general financial secretary, and a general treasurer. A board of bishops supervises the work of the church. The United Holy Church's primary publication is *The Holiness Union.*

UNITED PENTECOSTAL CHURCH INTERNATIONAL

Founded: 1945
Membership: est. 600,000 in 3,876 churches (2000)

The United Pentecostal Church International (UPCI) was founded in 1945 by the union of the Pentecostal Assemblies of Jesus Christ and the Pentecostal Church, Inc. Each of those bodies was itself the result of mergers of other Pentecostal bodies in the 1930s. All the constituent members were "oneness" ("Jesus only") Pentecostals who withdrew from the Assemblies of God in 1916.

The doctrinal views of the UPCI reflect most of the beliefs of the Holiness-Pentecostal movement (see HOLINESS CHURCHES; PENTECOSTAL CHURCHES), with the exception of the "second work of grace," the historic doctrine of the Trinity, and the traditional trinitarian formula in water baptism. Holiness of life is understood to be an aspect of God's salvation of an individual, not the result of a subsequent experience. The oneness view held by the UPCI asserts that God "revealed Himself in the Old Testament as Jehovah and in the New Testament revealed Himself in His Son, Jesus Christ." Jesus Christ is thus the one true God manifested in flesh and the Holy Ghost is the Spirit of God/the resurrected Christ. Baptism is carried out in Jesus' name only. The church embraces the Pentecostal view that speaking in tongues is the initial sign of receiving the Holy Spirit. For the UPCI, the Bible is the inerrant and infallible Word of God, and the church rejects all extra-biblical revelations and writings, such as church creeds and articles of faith.

UPCI polity is essentially congregational, with autonomous local churches. The General Conference of the church meets annually to elect officials. A general superintendent, two assistants, and a secretary-treasurer are members of a general board that also includes district superintendents, executive presbyters, and division heads.

Denominational offices are located at Hazelwood, Missouri, as is World Aflame Press, the church's publishing house. The press publishes books, Sunday school materials, and a wide variety of religious literature. *The Pentecostal Herald* is the official organ of the UPCI, and there are various divisional publications. The church also sponsors "Harvest Time," an international radio broadcast.

UPCI's foreign missions program sponsors work in 136 countries outside the U.S. Over 15,800 national ministers serve some 21,000 churches with a membership of just under 2,000,000. Within the U.S., the church supports seven Bible colleges and will open a graduate school of theology in St. Louis, Missouri in 2001. Other UPCI ministries include children's homes in Tupelo, Mississippi and Hammond, Louisiana; a chaplaincy program for persons in prison; and a chaplaincy program for the armed services.

VINEYARD CHURCHES INTERNATIONAL

Founded: 1983
Membership: approx. 500 churches (2000)

The Vineyard movement began in California in the 1970s and has grown rapidly since that time. In the early 1980s the church embraced charismatic tenets and was centered around the work of musician John Wimber among students at Fuller Theological Seminary. Christian rock music was used effectively in evangelical outreach through recordings and radio broadcasts. The church embraces evangelical and charismatic/Pentecostal (see PENTE-COSTAL CHURCHES) theology regarding the infallibility of Scripture, the fall of the human race, the need for an experience of salvation, and the spiritual gifts of healing and speaking in tongues. The Vineyard also emphasizes informal worship and provides fellowship for disaffected youth.

With the death of founder John Wimber in 1997, the movement has been struggling with issues of organization and future direction. The U.S. division, known both as the Association of Vineyard Churches and as VineyardUSA, moved its offices from California to Stafford, Texas at the end of 2000.

PRESBYTERIAN CHURCHES

Originating between 1534 and 1560 during the Protestant Reformation in France and Switzerland, the Presbyterian denomination is so named because it is a church governed by presbyters (from the Greek word *presbuteros,* meaning "elder") who represent the local congregation. The central theologian of the Presbyterians (as well as the Reformed churches; see REFORMED CHURCHES) was the Protestant Reformer John Calvin (1509–64). Calvin left his native France for Switzerland during the tumultuous years of the early Reformation. He helped to reorganize the religious, social, and political life of Geneva, making the Swiss city the capital of the Reformed movement throughout Europe.

Basic to Calvin's thought is God's sovereignty over the world and people's lives, including people's response to God's authority and will, known through Word and Spirit. His system has been summarized in five main points: human impotence, unconditional predestination, limited atonement, irresistible grace, and final perseverance. God, according to Calvin, is the sovereign and eternal ruler of the world; humans are completely dominated by and dependent upon God. More cerebral and verbal than emotional and aesthetic, Reformed theology places particular value on understanding, learning, and propriety.

Because of their covenantal understanding of the relation between God and people, Presbyterian and Reformed churches stress active human responsibility. Calvinism contributed to the building of an intelligent ministry, the liberation of the oppressed and persecuted, and the establishment of democratic forms of government in both church and state. In Calvin's thought lay the germ that in time destroyed the divine right of kings; it gave a new dignity to the people and brought representative government to parliaments and church officials. Calvin struck the final blow at feudalism and offered a spiritual and moral tone for dawning capitalism.

Strictly speaking, however, Calvin did not found Presbyterianism; he merely laid the foundations upon which it was constructed in Switzerland, Holland, France, England, Scotland, and Ireland. The work of John Knox (ca. 1513–72) in Scotland was particularly important for the Presbyterians in North America, since

291

Presbyterianism was brought to the U.S by Scot and Scots-Irish immigrants during the Colonial period.

A delegation of Scots sat in the Westminster Assembly of Divines (1643–48) with 121 English ministers, ten peers, and twenty members of the House of Commons to resolve the struggle over the compulsory use of the Anglican *Book of Common Prayer*. That assembly was a milestone in Presbyterian history because it produced a Larger and a Shorter Catechism; a directory for the public worship of God; a form of government; and the Westminster Confession of Faith, which became the doctrinal standard of Scottish, British, and American Presbyterianism.

Dominant in the Westminster Assembly, Presbyterians soon also dominated the British government during the English Civil War and the Interregnum. Oliver Cromwell completed the ousting of King Charles I in 1649 and established the Commonwealth. When the Commonwealth fell apart after Cromwell's death in 1658 and the monarchy was restored, British Presbyterians fled to North America with the Puritans. An attempt to establish episcopacy in Scotland after 1662 sent many Presbyterians out of Scotland into Ireland, where economic difficulties and religious inequalities then drove them on to the U.S. From 1710 until the middle of the 18th century, between 3,000 and 6,000 Scottish immigrants arrived annually, settling at first in New England and the middle colonies.

Presbyterians in the United States. The first American presbytery or association of local churches was founded in Philadelphia in 1706. In a General Synod in 1729 Presbyterians adopted the Westminster Confession of Faith, together with the Larger and the Shorter Catechism, "good forms of sound words, and systems of Christian doctrine." The same synod denied civil magistrates any power over the church and banned the persecution of anyone for religious faith.

Presbyterians quickly began to procure trained ministers. In the 1720s, William Tennent, Sr. (1673–1746), organized a "log college" in a cabin at Neshaminy, Pennsylvania, with three of his four sons as his first pupils. This family school grew into the most important Presbyterian institution of higher learning in the colonies. From it came the College of New Jersey (later Princeton University) and a stream of revivalistic Presbyterian preachers who played leading roles in the Great Awakening of the early eighteenth century.

Prominent among them were William Tennent, Jr. (1705–77), and his brother Gilbert (1703–64). They met and followed British revivalist George Whitefield (1714–70) in preaching an emotional "new birth" revivalism, which conflicted with the old creedal Calvinism. The camp-meeting revival, born as a Presbyterian institution, grew out of that Great Awakening enthusiasm. However, Presbyterian objection to emotional revivalism went deep, and in 1740 it split the church. Preachers on the "old side" opposed revivalism, while those of the "new side" endorsed it, claiming that less attention should be paid to college training of ministers and more to recruiting regenerated common men.

The two sides quarreled until they reunited in 1757. The next year, in the first united synod, there were 94 ministers in the colonial Presbyterian Church, with 200 congregations and 10,000 members. One of the ablest of the new-side preachers was John Witherspoon (1723–94), president of Princeton, a member of the Continental Congress and the only member of the clergy to sign the Declaration of Independence. Witherspoon may have been instrumental in the general synod's decision to call upon Presbyterian churches to "uphold and promote" the resolutions of the Continental Congress. The Scots-Irish accepted the Revolution with relish; their persecution in England and Northern Ireland had made them solid anti-British dissenters. Their old cry, "No bishop and no king," was heard back in England—Horace Walpole (1717–97) supposedly remarked that "Cousin America" had run off with a Presbyterian parson.

Presbyterians moved swiftly to strengthen their church after the colonial victory at Yorktown; the synod met in Philadelphia in 1788 while the new nation's Constitution was being drafted in the same city. From 1790 until 1837, membership in the Presbyterian Church in the U.S.A. (as it was called at that time) increased from 18,000 to 220,557, due to the revivalism sweeping the country and to a plan of union with the Congregationalists (see CONGREGATIONAL CHURCHES). Under that plan, Presbyterian and Congregational preachers and laypeople moving into the new western territory worked and built together. Ministers of the two groups preached in one another's pulpits, and members held the right of representation in both the congregational association and the presbytery. The plan worked well on the whole, absorbing the fruits of the national revivals and giving real impetus to missionary work at home and abroad.

In 1810 some Presbyterian ministers in Tennessee withdrew from

the church over the issue of predestination and ordination requirements. Over time, their group grew in number, eventually holding a
general assembly in 1829. This body, known as Cumberland
Presbyterians, has continued as a separate denomination, despite the
decision of the majority of its members to affiliate with another
Presbyterian group in the early years of the 20th century.

Then came disagreements between "Old School" and "New
School" Presbyterians over matters of discipline and the expenditure
of missionary money. The General Assembly of 1837 expelled four
New School synods, which promptly met in their own convention to
form a new General Assembly. The Presbyterian Church in the
U.S.A. (PCUSA) remained split between New School advocates,
who wanted to continue to work with Congregationalists, and those
of the Old School, who were suspicious of Congregational theology.

The Southern Church. In 1846, the Old School assembly
regarded slavery as no bar to Christian communion, but in that same
year, the New School condemned the practice strongly. By 1857,
several Southern New School synods had withdrawn to form the
United Synod of the Presbyterian Church. The greater schism came
in 1861, following the outbreak of the Civil War, when forty-seven
Southern presbyteries of the Old School formed the Presbyterian
Church in the Confederate States of America. In 1867, following the
war, the United Synod and the Confederate churches merged to form
the Presbyterian Church in the United States (PCUS).

The PCUS, initially Old School in doctrine, continued to develop
its own style of faith and practice. Presbyterianism was well established in the South since Colonial days. In fact, Presbyterian leaders
helped bring law and order to many parts of the South before colonial
officials could assume such duties, and the ministers taught school
before the establishment of public school systems. Presbyterians were
prominent during both the French and Indian War and the American
Revolution, and with Baptists they laid the political, spiritual, moral,
and intellectual foundations for the famous Jeffersonian Act for
Establishing Religious Freedom, the Virginia statement that preceded
similar ones in the Constitution and elsewhere.

The PCUS church government developed parallel to that of the
northern churches. Offices were gradually centralized in Atlanta
under the General Assembly Mission Board; mission work was
always undertaken on a worldwide scale, a special source of pride to
southern Presbyterians. In 1982, just prior to reunion with the north-

ern churches to form the Presbyterian Church (U.S.A.), PCUS members numbered 814,931 in 2,704 churches, with 61 presbyteries (17 already functioning as "united" with United Presbyterian Church in the U.S.A. [UPCUSA] presbyteries) and seven synods. There were 6,077 ordained ministers on the rolls. Church-supported seminaries were in Austin, Texas; Columbia, Georgia; Louisville, Kentucky; and Union, in Richmond, Virginia, as well as the Presbyterian School of Christian Education (Virginia), a unique institution. Several secondary schools and mission schools, as well as colleges, children's homes, and homes for the elderly also were supported.

The National (Northern) Church. The Old School and New School bodies of the Presbyterian Church in the U.S.A. (PCUSA) had held separate assemblies since 1837, but were united in 1870 on the basis of the Westminster Confession. Most of the Cumberland Presbyterian churches joined them in 1907; the Welsh Calvinist Methodists joined in 1920. In the decades from 1920 until 1950, an emphasis on theology was evident in a liberal/conservative struggle. There was also an emphasis on unity, manifest in the proposed merger with the Protestant Episcopal Church (see EPISCOPAL/ ANGLICAN CHURCHES), which did not take place, and the accomplished merger with the United Presbyterian Church of North America (UPCNA) in 1958.

The UPCNA had been formed exactly a century earlier by a merger of the Associate Presbyterian Church with the Associate Reformed Presbyterian Church. Their doctrines, traditions, and institutions were preserved in the new church's presbyterian style of government by local sessions, presbyteries, synods, and general assembly. A 1925 confessional statement of forty-four articles contained the substance of the Westminster Confession, but restricted divorce to marital infidelity, denied infant damnation, extended the sacraments to all who professed faith in Christ and led Christian lives, and withdrew the old protest against secret societies. It also abandoned the exclusive use of psalms in worship, maintained belief in the verbal inspiration of Scripture, affirmed the sufficiency and fullness of the provisions of God for the needs of the church, emphasized the renewing and sanctifying power of the Holy Spirit, and held that salvation is free to all sinners.

There were no insurmountable differences when the UPCNA and the PCUSA merged in 1958 to become the United Presbyterian Church in the U.S.A. (UPCUSA); however, there remained disagreements between conservatives and liberals. On the whole, all found agreement in the Westminster Confession, their accepted doctrinal statement. The UPCUSA eventually reorganized its offices into three agencies based in New York City. In 1982, on the eve of reunion with the southern churches, the UPCUSA had 2,351,119 members nationwide and 15,178 ordained ministers. Its 8,975 churches were grouped in 151 presbyteries and 15 synods; 17 of the presbyteries were joint "union" bodies with similar units in PCUS.

Polity. Presbyterian churches typically exhibit a basic organizational structure. Each congregation has a local session made up of elders, with the pastor as moderator. The session governs the local church, receiving and disciplining members as well as acting for the church's welfare. Presbyteries, made up of congregations in a local district, examine, ordain, and install ministers; review reports from sessions; and hear any complaints. The synods, occupying larger boundaries, review the presbytery records, organize new presbyteries, and help to administer denominational matters.

The highest judicial body is a general assembly, which meets yearly and is made up of lay and clergy delegates elected by their presbyteries on a proportional plan of representation. The general assembly settles all matters of policy and doctrine referred to it by the lower governing bodies, establishes new synods, appoints agencies and commissions, and reviews all appeals. There are two key officers of the general assembly: a chief (principal, stated) clerk, who is essentially the chief executive officer of the church; and a moderator, who presides over the assembly and often speaks for the church during the year.

ASSOCIATE REFORMED PRESBYTERIAN CHURCH

Founded: 1782
Membership: 40,600 in 238 congregations (1997)

The Associate Reformed Presbyterian Church traces its origin to controversies in the national Presbyterian Church in Scotland in the eighteenth century, when a group of presbyters seceded from the national church in protest over a number of issues of polity and worship. The controversy over the "Seceders" and "Covenanters" was carried to Northern Ireland with the Scottish migration there. The Scots-Irish immigrants to North America established congregations along the lines followed in the British Isles, but in 1782 two of the seceding branches united to form the Associate Reformed Synod in Philadelphia (see PRESBYTERIAN CHURCHES).

Eight years later, the Associate Reformed Presbytery of the Carolinas and Georgia was formed in Abbeville County, South Carolina, followed in 1803 by the division of the entire church into four Synods and one General Synod. In 1822 the Synod of the South was granted separate status, and by the end of the nineteenth century was the sole remaining body of the Associate Reformed Presbyterian Church, as several mergers over the years had absorbed the rest of the denomination into the old United Presbyterian Church. There are now nine presbyteries in North America, primarily in the Southeast.

The doctrinal standards of the Apostles' Creed and the Westminster Confession are followed. For some years the only music in this church was the singing of psalms; this was modified in 1946 to permit the use of hymns.

The General Synod of the church meets annually to elect officers and conduct business. The chief officers are the Moderator (one-year term), who presides over the General Synod and is the spokesperson for the church during the year, and the Principal Clerk (four-year term), who establishes and maintains the official records for the General Synod. These and other officers serve as the Executive Board of the General Synod.

Associate Reformed Presbyterian Church foreign mission fields are located in Germany, Mexico, Pakistan, Turkey, Asia, and the Middle East. *The Associate Reformed Presbyterian* is published monthly at Greenville, South Carolina; Erskine College and Erskine Theological Seminary are in Due West, South Carolina. The church supports an assembly ground, Bonclarken, at Flat Rock, North Carolina, and three retirement centers.

CUMBERLAND PRESBYTERIAN CHURCH

Founded: 1810
Membership: 86,049 in 775 congregations (1999)

An outgrowth of the great revival known as the Second Great Awakening that swept across the new nation around 1800, the Cumberland Presbyterian Church dates its origin from February 4, 1810, in Dickson County, Tennessee, where three Presbyterian ministers, Finis Ewing (1773–1841), Samuel King (1775–1842), and Samuel McAdow (1760–1844), constituted a new presbytery (see PRESBYTERIAN CHURCHES). They objected to the doctrine of predestination in the Westminster Confession of Faith and insisted that Presbyterian standards for ordination of the clergy be more flexible in view of the extraordinary circumstances that then existed on the American frontier. The General Assembly of the church was organized in 1829.

Attempted union with the Presbyterian Church (U.S.A.) in 1906 was only partially successful. A considerable segment of the Cumberland Presbyterian membership, to whom the terms of merger were unsatisfactory, perpetuated the church as a separate denomination.

A confession of faith was formulated in 1814, drawing on the Westminster Confession, but affirming key points made by the founders of the Cumberland Presbyterian Church in 1810: (1) There are no eternal reprobates; (2) Christ died for all humankind, not for the elect alone; (3) there is no infant damnation; and (4) the Spirit of God operates in the world coextensively with Christ's atonement, so "as to leave all men inexcusable." This confession was revised in 1883 and again in 1984, in each instance to better articulate for its time the historic truths of the Christian faith. The 1984 document expresses a clear recognition of God's action in the salvation of human beings, noting that repentance is a necessary condition of salvation but not a sufficient one, as God's grace is the fundamental element.

Congregations are located for the most part in southern and border states, with some congregations in Indiana, Illinois, Michigan, Iowa, New Mexico, Arizona, and California. The church sponsors missionaries in Colombia, Japan, Hong Kong, and Liberia in West Africa. It supports Bethel College in McKenzie, Tennessee; Memphis Theological Seminary; and a children's home in Denton, Texas. Denominational headquarters and a resource center are located in Memphis, Tennessee.

CUMBERLAND PRESBYTERIAN CHURCH IN AMERICA

Founded: 1874
Membership: 15,142 in 152 congregations (1996)

This church developed after the Civil War, when African American pastors and lay members of the Cumberland Presbyterian Church (see CUMBERLAND PRESBYTERIAN CHURCH) sought to establish their own organization. It has been estimated that some 20,000 African Americans were associated with the parent church at the time. Led by Moses T. Weir, a former slave, black ministers formed the Synod of Colored Cumberland Presbyterians in 1869. Other presbyteries and synods were formed in various regions (see PRESBYTERIAN CHURCHES), and in 1874 the first General Assembly of the Colored Cumberland Presbyterian Church was held. The parent church offered some financial support in the early years of the denomination and has continued to work with the African American body on various issues, including theological formulations. The Colored Cumberland Presbyterian Church eventually became known as the Second Cumberland Presbyterian Church and, late in the twentieth century, as the Cumberland Presbyterian Church in America.

The church's doctrinal position is similar to that of the Cumberland Presbyterian Church. Members of the two bodies worked together on the 1984 Confession of Faith. This document gives contemporary expression to the historic Presbyterian witness, with particular emphasis on God's saving grace.

The Cumberland Presbyterian Church in America now has four synods, primarily in the Midwest and the South. The church's ministers are trained at the Cumberland Presbyterian Church College in McKenzie, Tennessee, and at its seminary in Memphis. Serious conversation continues concerning unification with the Cumberland Presbyterian Church.

EVANGELICAL PRESBYTERIAN CHURCH

Founded: 1981
Membership: 63,447 in 197 congregations (1999)

The Evangelical Presbyterian Church (EPC) grew out of a series of meetings among pastors and church elders held in St. Louis Missouri in 1980–81. Representing various mainline Presbyterian groups (see PRESBYTERIAN CHURCHES), these leaders wished to form a church informed by Scripture and the historic confessions of the Christian faith and committed to evangelism. From those meetings, a General Assembly was convened in Detroit, Michigan, in 1981, at which the EPC was born.

The EPC is a conservative denomination composed of eight geographical presbyteries in the U.S., with churches in twenty-nine states. It is presbyterian in polity (governance by elders), with the courts of the church being the Session (local), the Presbytery (regional), and the General Assembly (national).

"Reformed in doctrine, presbyterian in polity, and evangelical in spirit," the EPC places high priority on church planting along with world missions. About fifty world outreach missionaries serve the church's mission at home and abroad. High priority is also placed on developing its women's ministries and youth ministries.

The Westminster Confession and its catechisms are the church's doctrinal standards. Unlike other conservative Presbyterian bodies, it includes chapter 34, "Of the Holy Spirit," and chapter 35, "Of the Love of God and Missions" in the Confession. The historic motto "In essentials, unity; in nonessentials, liberty; in all things, charity" expresses the irenic spirit of the EPC.

To the broader world, the General Assembly bears witness on particular issues through position papers. To date, position papers on the Holy Spirit, abortion, AIDS/HIV, divorce and remarriage, the value of and respect for human life, the ordination of women as elders, homosexuality, and problems of suffering and dying have been adopted.

KOREAN-AMERICAN PRESBYTERIAN CHURCH

Founded: 1976
Membership: statistics not available

The Korean-American Presbyterian Church (KAPC) was established to serve Korean immigrants in North America. The Presbyterian Church (see PRESBYTERIAN CHURCHES) is the largest Christian body in Korea, a country in which many Christian denominations are represented. The KAPC is theologically conservative; in addition to the Westminster Confession and the Larger and Shorter Catechisms, pastors ascribe to a creed that emphasizes biblical inerrancy, the absoluteness of God, the sin of Adam and Eve, and the necessity of faith. Works and obedience to the law of God result from saving faith. The church is headquartered in Phoenix, Arizona.

ORTHODOX PRESBYTERIAN CHURCH

Founded: 1936
Membership: 25,302 in 204 congregations (1999)

This church originated in protest against what were believed to be modernistic practices by the Presbyterian Church in the U.S.A. (see PRESBYTERIAN CHURCHES). The dissenters, led by Princeton professor J. Gresham Machen (1881–1937), were suspended from the Presbyterian Church in the U.S.A. and organized the Presbyterian Church of America. However, an injunction was brought against the use of that name by the parent body, and in 1938 the name was changed to Orthodox Presbyterian Church.

Orthodox Presbyterians lay strong emphasis on the infallibility and inerrancy of the Bible. They believe that the writers of the books of the Bible were "so guided by [God] that their original manuscripts were without error in fact or doctrine." Fundamental doctrines include original sin; the virgin birth, deity, and substitutionary atonement of Christ; his resurrection and ascension; his role as judge at the end of the world and the consummation of the kingdom; the sovereignty of God; and salvation through the sacrifice and power of Christ for those "the Father purposes to save." Salvation is "not because of good works [but] in order to do good works." The Westminster Confession and the Larger and the Shorter Catechisms

301

are accepted as subordinate doctrinal standards or creedal statements.

The church constitution contains the creedal statement, the form of government, the book of discipline, and the directory for the worship of God. Local churches are governed by sessions, which include teaching elders (ministers) and ruling elders (laymen); women are not allowed to hold office, based on interpretation of New Testament practice. The local church focuses on worship, education, evangelism, ministries of mercy, and godly discipline. The denomination has sixteen regional churches, each composed of several local congregations and governed by a presbytery made up of all the teaching elders and ruling elders from those congregations. The presbytery cares for the well-being of the several churches in the region and helps resolve conflicts. A general assembly oversees the work of the Orthodox Presbyterian Church as a whole. This assembly includes teaching and ruling elders from each presbytery; it appoints committees that conduct work in home and foreign missions, Christian education, and general benevolence.

The Orthodox Presbyterian Church has published *Trinity Hymnal,* probably the only hymnal designed as a worship supplement to the Westminster Confession of Faith. Membership is spread throughout the country, with concentration in eastern Pennsylvania, New Jersey, and southern California.

PRESBYTERIAN CHURCH IN AMERICA

Founded: 1973
Membership: 299,055 in 1,206 congregations (1999)

This denomination was formed in 1973 when delegates from 260 conservative congregations that had withdrawn from the Presbyterian Church, U.S. (PCUS) in protest over liberalism convened a general assembly (see PRESBYTERIAN CHURCHES). These congregations opposed the PCUS's ecumenical involvements in the National Council of the Churches of Christ, the World Council of Churches, and the Consultation on Church Union; they also opposed the impending merger with the more liberal United Presbyterian Church in the U.S.A. The Presbyterian Church in America (PCA) also maintained the traditional position on the ordination of women. At first known as the National Presbyterian Church, the present name was adopted in 1974.

The Westminster Confession of Faith is the Presbyterian Church in America's primary doctrinal standard. The church teaches that the Holy Spirit guided the writers of the scriptures so that the writings are free of error of fact, doctrine, and judgment. Other doctrines emphasized are human depravity, salvation by grace, Christ's death for the elect, and perseverance of the saints.

The PCA maintains the historic polity of Presbyterian governance: rule by presbyters (or elders) and the graded courts, the session governing the local church; the presbytery for regional matters; and the general assembly at the national level. It makes a distinction between the two classes of elders: teaching elders (ministers) and ruling elders (laymen).

In 1982, the Reformed Presbyterian Church, Evangelical Synod (RPCES), joined the PCA, bringing with it Covenant College on Lookout Mountain, Georgia, and Covenant Theological Seminary in St. Louis, Missouri. The PCA headquarters is in Atlanta, where work by three program committees is coordinated: Mission to the World, Mission to North America, and Christian Education and Publications.

PRESBYTERIAN CHURCH (U.S.A.)

Founded: 1983
Membership: 3,561,184 in 11,216 congregations (1999)

Following formal separation that began during the Civil War and lasted for 122 years, the two largest American Presbyterian churches (PCUS [southern] and UPCUSA [national]) were reunited on June 10, 1983 (see PRESBYTERIAN CHURCHES). The setting was a historic Communion service celebrated by some 15,000 persons in the Georgia World Congress Center in Atlanta and by many more on a nationwide television link. The Rev. J. Randolph Taylor, pastor of Myers Park Presbyterian Church in Charlotte, North Carolina, was elected the new group's first moderator. Over the next fifteen years, great effort was expended to work out the administrative details of combining the two denominations and their numerous presbyteries and ministry groups.

Under the Presbyterian Church (U.S.A.) system of government,

303

each congregation has a local session made up of elders, with the pastor as moderator. The session governs the local church, receiving and disciplining members as well as acting for the church's welfare. Presbyteries, made up of congregations in a local district, examine, ordain, and install ministers; review reports from sessions; and hear any complaints. The synods, occupying larger boundaries, review the presbytery records, organize new presbyteries, and help to administer denominational matters.

The highest judicial body is the General Assembly, which meets yearly and is made up of lay and clergy delegates elected by their presbyteries on a proportional plan of representation. The General Assembly settles all matters of policy and doctrine referred to it by the lower governing bodies, establishes new synods, appoints agencies and commissions, and reviews all appeals. Its decisions are final, except that it cannot, of itself, amend the church's constitution. There are two officers of the General Assembly: a stated clerk (the chief executive officer of the church) is elected for a four-year term and may be reelected; a moderator is chosen each year to preside over the meetings and often speaks for the church during the year.

The Westminster Confession (1647) had been the basic doctrinal statement of American Presbyterians since Colonial times; however, when the UPCUSA was formed in 1958 it was noted that the Westminster Confession was more than 300 years old and reflected the concerns of an earlier time. Many Presbyterians had come to believe that a new statement was needed to proclaim the gospel in twentieth-century language. So in 1967, after eight years of work, a special committee presented a draft of the first new major doctrinal statement since 1647 to the General Assembly, and it was ratified.

The brief (4,200 words) Confession of 1967 avoided what many saw as the confusing terminology of the Westminster Confession, instead stressing the concepts of love, sin, eternal life, and especially the work of reconciliation in God, Christ, and the church. Christ-centered, it generally repeats the Westminster tenets in modern speech. Some opposition persisted, on the ground that the new document watered down the Westminster Confession, but most United Presbyterians accepted the document as reflecting true Presbyterianism and as offering a wide theological basis on which all Presbyterians could stand together.

With the acceptance of the new creed, the UPCUSA now had a *Book of Confessions* with nine creeds: the Nicene Creed of 325 C.E., the Apostles' Creed of the second century, the Scots Confession of 1560, the Heidelberg Confession of 1563, the Westminster Confession of 1647, the Larger Catechism of 1647, the Shorter Catechism of 1647, the 1934 Theological Declaration of Barmen, and the Confession of 1967. These were grouped together in the *Book of Confessions* to trace the development of the great Christian affirmations, especially in the Reformed tradition; to make clear the common beliefs of most of the world's Christians; and to offer common ground for unity. This *Book of Confessions* was adopted by the Presbyterian Church (U.S.A.) with the reunification of 1983.

While Presbyterians are found throughout the U.S., about 40 percent live in the area of the former PCUS—the South. Membership is greatest in large cities, with concentrations in Ohio, Pennsylvania, New York, Virginia, North Carolina, Florida, Texas, Illinois, and New Jersey. In 1988 the national headquarters of the new denomination was dedicated in Louisville, Kentucky, representing the marriage of the old national church's offices from New York and the southern church's from Atlanta. The church has operated two publishing companies, now united in Louisville as Westminster John Knox Press. The official periodical is the monthly *Presbyterian Survey,* published in Louisville. There are sixty-eight Presbyterian-related colleges, eleven seminaries, and six secondary schools in the U.S.

REFORMED PRESBYTERIAN CHURCH OF NORTH AMERICA

Founded: 1809
Membership: 6,105 in 86 congregations (1997)

This church traces its roots to the Covenanter Presbyterians of Scotland in the eighteenth century who resisted the king's attempts to impose religious beliefs and practices on them. Most of the early membership merged with the Associate Presbytery in 1782, but a small group reorganized in 1798 under the name Reformed Presbytery. A synod was constituted at Philadelphia in 1809, only to split into Old Light and New Light groups in 1833. This dispute concerned citizenship and the right of members to vote or participate in public affairs. The New Lights formed the general synod of the Reformed Presbyterian Church and imposed no restrictions on participation. The Old Lights perservered in resisting involvement in

305

public affairs, and the Reformed Presbyterian Church of North America is their heritage. However, restriction was finally removed in 1964, and members are free to participate in civil government and to vote on issues and for political candidates committed to Christian principles of civil government.

The church places special emphasis on the inerrancy of Scripture, the sovereignty of God, and the Lordship of Christ over every area of human life. Church government is thoroughly Presbyterian (see PRESBYTERIAN CHURCHES), except that there is no general assembly. Members use only the Psalms in their worship services; no instrumental music is permitted. Members cannot join secret societies.

Home missionaries work in seven states under a Board of Home Missions and Church Extension; foreign missionaries are stationed in Japan, Cyprus, and Taiwan. Geneva College is located at Beaver Falls, Pennsylvania, and the Reformed Presbyterian Theological Seminary is at Pittsburgh. A home for elderly persons is also located in Pittsburgh. Crown and Covenant Publications provides print and music resources for the church.

REFORMED CHURCHES

The Reformed family of Protestant churches, like the Presbyterians (see PRESBYTERIAN CHURCHES), originated in the Swiss Reformation, whose greatest theologian was John Calvin (1509–64). Commonly called Calvinist, the Reformed churches were closely connected to the Presbyterians in Scotland, the Puritans (see CONGREGATIONAL CHURCHES) in England and New England, and the Huguenots in France. The Reformed churches organized nationally, particularly in the Netherlands (Holland), Germany, Hungary, Bohemia, and Poland. During the formative period of the Reformed churches, they were outlawed throughout Europe until the Peace of Westphalia in 1648. Their theology and church structure were thus formed in the midst of persecution and a struggle for religious and political independence.

Reformed church government is generally a modified presbyterian form. The doctrine is based on the Belgic Confession (1561), the

306

Heidelberg Catechism (1563), and the Canons of the Synod of Dort (1618). The Reformed churches stress the theological dimension of church life, placing emphasis on the sermon and sound doctrine. More rationalist than Pietist (see BRETHREN and PIETIST CHURCHES), Reformed conservatism takes the form of strict theological orthodoxy.

As they moved overseas to the American colonies, three major ethnic groups of adherents to the Reformed tradition formed different churches with minor theological variations. Germans, primarily from the Palatinate, founded the Reformed Church in the United States, later known as the Evangelical and Reformed Church, which later became one of the main bodies in the United Church of Christ (see UNITED CHURCH OF CHRIST). Dutch settlers founded the Reformed Church in America and the Christian Reformed Church. And Hungarians founded the Free Magyar Reformed Church in America.

German Reformed in the United States. Although most of the Reformed churches today can be traced to Dutch immigration to the Midwest, Reformed churches in the U.S. originated in the flood tide of German immigrants to Pennsylvania in the eighteenth century. More than half the Germans there in 1730 were Reformed, but the congregations were widely separated along the frontier and, lacking ministers, often employed school teachers to lead the services.

Johann Philip Boehm (1683–1749) had come to southeastern Pennsylvania from Germany in 1720 as a schoolmaster. Boehm was asked to lead worship services shortly after his arrival and, by 1725, to assume the pastoral office among Reformed settlers in the Perkiomen Valley. Boehm was deeply influenced by Michael Schlatter (1718–90), who had been sent to the U.S. by the (Dutch Reformed) Synod of South and North Holland. In 1747, they organized a coetus (synod) in Philadelphia, directly responsible to, and in part financially supported by, the synod in Holland. The American synod declared its independence in 1793, taking the name German Reformed Church; in that year it reported 178 congregations and 15,000 communicants. The word *German* was dropped from the name in 1869, and thereafter the denomination was called the Reformed Church in the United States.

Difficulties arose in the early years of the nineteenth century. Older Germans preferred the use of the German language; second-generation members demanded English. Some churches withdrew to form a separate synod, but returned in 1837 when compromises were made. District synods of both German-speaking and English-speaking congregations were created, and two Hungarian classes from the Old Hungarian Reformed Church were added in 1924.

The Evangelical and Reformed Church was the product of a union established at Cleveland, Ohio, on June 26, 1934, by two bodies with basic agreements in doctrine, polity, and culture: the Evangelical Synod of North America and the Reformed Church in the United States. Few difficulties were encountered in reconciling the doctrines of the two bodies when the union was finally accomplished. Both churches were German in ethnicity and Calvinistic in doctrine. The Reformed Church had been based historically on the Heidelberg Catechism (1563); the Evangelical Synod, on the Heidelberg Catechism, the Augsburg Confession (1530), and Martin Luther's (1483–1546) Catechism. These three standards of faith were woven into one in the new constitution of the Evangelical and Reformed Church, which in 1957 became part of the United Church of Christ.

Dutch Reformed in the United States. As early as 1614, what is now known as the Reformed Church in America had an unorganized membership along the upper reaches of the Hudson River in the area of Fort Orange (Albany), New York. There were no regularly established congregations or churches, but members were numerous enough to require the services of Reformed lay ministers, two of whom came from Holland in 1623 as "comforters of the sick." By 1628 the Dutch in New Amsterdam had a pastor of their own, Jonas Michaelius (b. 1577), and an organized collegiate church, the oldest church in the middle colonies and the oldest church in the U.S. with an uninterrupted ministry.

When the English took possession of New Amsterdam in 1664, Dutch churches were thriving in Albany, Kingston, Brooklyn, and Manhattan in New York and at Bergen, New Jersey. When immigration from Holland ceased, perhaps 8,000 Dutch church people were holding services in their own language, served primarily by pastors sent from Holland. It was difficult and expensive to send native-born ministerial candidates to Holland for education and ordination, so a college and seminary were established at New Brunswick, New Jersey. This institution later became New Brunswick Theological Seminary and Rutgers University.

A large majority of the clergy and laypeople of the Reformed Church supported the American Revolution. Two generals, Philip

Schuyler (1733–1804) and Nicholas Herkimer (1728–77), were members of the Reformed Church. As the Dutch became more and more Americanized, the English language gradually became accepted in churches, but not without a struggle.

A second emigration from the Netherlands began in the middle of the nineteenth century, bringing entire congregations with their pastors. One group, led by Albertus van Raalte (1811–76), established a community called Holland in western Michigan. Van Raalte and his group became part of the Reformed Church in America in 1850. Another colony, led by Hendrick Scholtem (1805–68), settled in Pella, Iowa in 1846, and, except for a small dissenting group, merged with the Reformed Church in America in 1856.

Doctrine and Polity. The explicit statements and principles of the Belgic Confession (1561), the Heidelberg Catechism (1563), and the Canons of the Synod of Dort (1618) are still the doctrinal standards of most Reformed churches in America. The mild and gentle spirit of the Belgic Confession, with its emphasis on salvation through Christ, is a central theme; the primacy of God's power in human life is at the heart of the preaching, as it is at the heart of the Canons of Dort; and the Heidelberg Catechism, based on the threefold division of the epistle to the Romans, is employed in many Christian doctrine classes. The divine authority of Scripture is important. Worship is semi-liturgical, with an optional liturgy; only the forms for baptism and the Lord's Supper, the two recognized sacraments, are obligatory.

The government of Reformed churches is essentially presbyterian. The governing body in the local church is the consistory or council, made up of elders, deacons, and ministers, who together undertake the administrative duties common to congregational life. A number of churches in a limited area are grouped into a classis, which has immediate supervision of the churches and clergy within its bounds. The classis is composed of elder delegates from each congregation and the ministers in the area. Classes are grouped into regional synods that supervise the planning and programming of the churches within the area. The highest legislative and judicial body of the church is the General Synod, which meets once a year. It is composed of clergy and elder delegates from each classis; the size of the delegation depends on the size of the classis.

309

CHRISTIAN REFORMED CHURCH
IN NORTH AMERICA

Founded: 1857
Membership: 198,400 in 732 congregations (1998)

This Dutch Reformed group originated in Michigan in 1847 and was affiliated with the Reformed Church in America from 1850 until 1857, when it found itself in disagreement with the parent church on matters of doctrine and discipline (see REFORMED CHURCHES). A conference held at Holland, Michigan, effected the separation of the True Holland Reformed Church, which, after a series of name changes, became the present Christian Reformed Church in North America. Emigration from Holland brought several other groups into the new organization, rapidly increasing its membership.

The Christian Reformed Church (CRC) today is largely English speaking, although the Dutch, Spanish, French, Navajo, Zuni, Korean, Chinese, and Vietnamese languages are used in some of the churches. Conservative theologically, the CRC holds to the three historic Reformed statements as the basis of union: the Belgic Confession (1561), the Canons of Dort (1618), and the Heidelberg Catechism (1563). Organization bears the usual Reformed characteristics, including the local session or council, 47 classes (35 in the U.S., 12 in Canada) that meet every four months (in some cases every six months), but with no intermediate or regional synods between the classes; and a general synod made up of two clergy and two elders from each classis that meets annually. The general synod makes decisions regarding theological, liturgical, and ethical matters. It also oversees the ministries shared by CRC churches generally. To this end, the synod has created eight boards and agencies to govern each ministry, including general church administration, radio ministry, Calvin Theological Seminary, Calvin College, home missions, world relief, publications, and world missions.

Christian Reformed Home Missions provides guidance and financial assistance to some 200 new and established churches that maintain ministries among Navajos, Zunis, African Americans, Asian Americans, Hispanic Americans, and on many university campuses. Almost 300 foreign missionaries are stationed in Latin America, the Caribbean, Africa, Eastern Europe, and Asia. The Christian

Reformed World Relief Committee carries on a relief program serving in 27 countries.

The "Back to God Hour" radio program, broadcast from a chain of stations in the U.S. and abroad, reaches Europe, Africa, and Asia as well as South America; a television ministry also broadcasts in the U.S. and Canada. The church sponsors Calvin College and Calvin Theological Seminary in Grand Rapids, Michigan. A publishing house in Grand Rapids provides literature for the church and its agencies, as well as educational material for many other churches.

HUNGARIAN REFORMED CHURCH IN AMERICA

Founded: 1924
Membership: est. 6,000 in 27 congregations (1998)

Work in the U.S. among Hungarian Reformed people began in 1891. With the breakup of the Austro-Hungarian Empire and the impoverishment of the Reformed Church in Hungary, the church in Hungary transferred jurisdiction of its U.S. churches to the Reformed Church in the United States in an agreement reached at Tiffin, Ohio, in 1921 (see REFORMED CHURCH IN THE UNITED STATES). Three of the original congregations refused to accept the agreement. In 1924 in Duquesne, Pennsylvania, they united with four other congregations to form the Free Magyar Reformed Church in America, a fully independent, autonomous church. The church's name was changed in 1958 to Hungarian Reformed Church in America.

The church's polity is a combination of synod-presbyterian elements gradually developed in Hungary from the mid-sixteenth century. At present it is made up of three classes—New York, Eastern, and Western—which form a synod headed by an elected bishop and a chief lay curator. Doctrinal standards are those of the Heidelberg Catechism (1583) and the Second Helvetic Confession (1566). The synod meets every two years, and a constitutional General Synod is held every four years.

311

NETHERLANDS REFORMED CONGREGATIONS IN NORTH AMERICA

Founded: 1907
Membership: 9,047 in 24 congregations (1999)

The Netherlands Reformed Congregations in North America broke away from the Christian Reformed Church (see CHRISTIAN REFORMED CHURCH) over doctrinal differences. This body stresses the classic doctrines of the Reformed tradition as expressed in the Belgic Confession of Faith (1561), the Heidelberg Catechism (1563), and the Canons of Dort (1618). It supports several home and foreign missions and eleven schools with over 2,000 students. A seminary was established in Grand Rapids, Michigan in 1996.

PROTESTANT REFORMED CHURCHES IN AMERICA

Founded: 1926
Membership: 6,730 in 27 congregations (1999)

In 1924, three consistories and the pastors of the Classes Grand Rapids East and Grand Rapids West of the Christian Reformed Church in North America (see CHRISTIAN REFORMED CHURCH) were deposed from that denomination as the result of a disagreement over the doctrine of common grace. This doctrine states that grace is extended in some measure to those who are not part of God's elect. Those who objected to the doctrine and were forced out of the church formally organized as the Protestant Reformed Churches in America in 1926; foremost among the founders was Herman Hoeksema (1886–1965). He and the other leaders of the new church taught that particular grace, that is, grace for the elect alone, is an essential aspect of Reformed faith.

The Protestant Reformed Church holds to the three basic Reformed confessions (the Heidelberg Catechism of 1563, the Belgic Confession of 1561, and the Canons of Dort of 1618) as the basis of their belief in the infallible Word of God. In government they are Presbyterian (see PRESBYTERIAN CHURCHES). There are two classes, organized geographically; a general synod meets annually in June. Membership is found mainly in the upper Midwest.

312

The church maintains a theological seminary at Grand Rapids, Michigan. The Reformed Free Publishing Association publishes a bimonthly periodical, *The Standard Bearer.* A monthly publication, *Beacon Lights,* is issued by the young people's federation. Several home mission fields and work in the United Kingdom is supported; mission efforts in Singapore established independent churches there.

REFORMED CHURCH IN AMERICA

Founded: 1792
Membership: 293,147 in 901 congregations (1999)

A sharp controversy over the authority of the Classis of Amsterdam resulted in complete independence for the Dutch Reformed churches in the U.S. (see REFORMED CHURCHES). A general body and five particular bodies were created, a constitution was drawn up in 1792, and a general synod was organized in 1794. In 1819 the body was incorporated as the Reformed Protestant Dutch Church, and in 1867 it became the Reformed Church in America.

The church holds to the traditional Reformed doctrinal statements, especially the Belgic Confession (1561), the Heidelberg Catechism (1563), and the Canons of Dort (1618); but it interprets them more flexibly than do other Reformed groups. The church also affirms the Apostles' Creed, the Athanasian Creed, and the Nicene Creed. A contemporary statement of faith, Our Song of Hope, was approved in 1978.

Local Reformed Church in America congregations are governed by consistories, composed of ministers, elders, and deacons. The next higher assembly is the classis, made up of representative ministers and elders from local churches in a particular region. A number of classes together form a regional synod. The church has over 900 congregations, 46 classes, and 8 regional synods. The highest assembly, the General Synod, meets annually to consider matters that affect the entire denomination. The various program and service functions of the denomination are supervised by a sixty-three member General Synod Council, composed of a representative from each classis, thirteen at-large members, and a representative from each of four racial-ethnic councils. The council is subdivided into six committees: Congregational Services; Evangelism and Church Development Services; Finance Services; Ministry and Personnel Services; Mission Services; and Policy, Planning, and

313

Administration Services. Denominational staff are located at the Interchurch Center in New York City and at several regional centers throughout the U.S. and Canada. In 1998, the church entered into full communion with Evangelical Lutheran Church in America (see EVANGELICAL LUTHERAN CHURCH IN AMERICA), the Presbyterian Church (U.S.A.) (see PRESBYTERIAN CHURCH [U.S.A.]), and the United Church of Christ (see UNITED CHURCH OF CHRIST).

The Reformed Church in America has a strong mission history and is at work in more than twenty-five countries. North American mission work began in 1786, although work among Native Americans had started much earlier. Needy churches in New York, Pennsylvania, and Kentucky were assisted by the classis of Albany until 1806, when the General Synod assumed administration of all missionary agencies, in cooperation with the American Board of Commissioners for Foreign Mission. In 1832 the Board of Foreign Missions was created; it continued to work through the American Board until 1857, when it began to operate independently. Through ethnic/racial councils in North America, the denomination relates to African Americans, Pacific and Asian Americans, Hispanic Americans, and Native Americans.

Insisting on seven years of college and seminary training for its clergy, the church in 1828 established the Education Society of the Reformed Church in America, later called the Board of Education of the General Synod. The denomination has two theological seminaries (New Brunswick, in New Jersey, and Western, in Holland, Michigan) and three colleges (Central, in Pella, Iowa; Hope, in Holland, Michigan; and Northwestern, in Orange City, Iowa). The church's greatest numerical strength is in Michigan, New York, New Jersey, Iowa, and California.

REFORMED CHURCH IN THE UNITED STATES

Founded: 1942
Membership: 4,257 in 40 congregations (1998)

This body originated with Swiss and German immigrants who arrived in the U.S. in the 1700s. It operated under the auspices of the Dutch Reformed Synod of South and North Holland, but separated from that synod in 1793. Since 1869 it has been known as the

Reformed Church in the United States. In 1934, most of its churches merged with the Evangelical Church to become the Evangelical and Reformed Church (see UNITED CHURCH OF CHRIST).

The Eureka Classis in South Dakota refused to become a part of the united church in 1934, primarily over the issue of the authority of Scripture. The classis maintained that the Bible "is the very Word of God" and opposed what it saw as liberal interpretation of Scripture. It remained a separate and independent body for over fifty years. Over the decades, several ministers and congregations joined with the classis, and in 1986 it dissolved to re-form as the Synod of the Reformed Church in the United States. The church follows the Reformed pattern of governance (see REFORMED CHURCHES): local churches are governed by consistories of ministers, elders, and deacons; four classes of local congregations are organized geographically and are made up of representatives from local churches; and the synod of the church, with representatives from each classis, elects denominational officers, including a president, a vice-president, a stated clerk, and a treasurer. Twelve committees of the synod oversee the ongoing ministries of the church.

In addition to the authority of Scripture, the Reformed Church in the United States accepts the Belgic Confession (1561), the Heidelberg Catechism (1563), and the Canons of Dort (1618) as standards of doctrine. The denomination emphasizes that Christ is the head of the church and that all human activity is to be done for the glory of God.

The church maintains fraternal relations with several other conservative Reformed bodies around the world and endorses three seminaries in the Reformed tradition: Mid-America Reformed Seminary in Dyer, Indiana; New Geneva Theological Seminary in Colorado Springs, Colorado; and Westminster Theological Seminary in Philadelphia, Pennsylvania. The official publication is *The Reformed Herald*.

SALVATION ARMY
(and related organizations)

The Salvation Army and its related organizations grew out of the Methodist Church's (see METHODIST CHURCHES) concern for outreach to the impoverished peoples of the growing metropolises in England. In order to bring the gospel to these neglected souls, a new type of religious organization was created. It is neither a traditional denomination nor a traditional service organization, but a creative union of both.

William Booth (1829–1912), an ordained minister in the Methodist New Connexion in England, left that church in 1861 to become a freelance evangelist. In 1865 he dedicated his life to the poverty-stricken unchurched masses in the slum areas of London's East End. He first planned to supplement the work of the churches, but this proved impractical because many converts did not want to go where they were sent, and often when they did go, they were not accepted. Moreover, Booth soon found that he needed the converts to help handle the great crowds that came to his meetings.

He began his work under the name "Christian Mission," and in 1878 the name was changed to the Salvation Army. Booth first organized his movement along lines of Methodist polity, with annual conferences at which reports were made and programs planned, but when the name was changed, the whole organization became dominated by the new title. Articles of War (a declaration of faith) were drawn up, and soon the mission stations became corps, members became soldiers, evangelists became officers, and converts were called seekers. Booth was designated as general, and his organization was gradually set up on a military pattern, which provided a direct line of authority and a practical system of training personnel for effective action. He reasoned that it was "just as valid to build an army of crusaders to save souls as it has been to send armies to recover a sepulchre."

The work spread quickly over England, Scotland, and Wales and was officially established in the United States in 1880 by a pioneer group under the direction of George Scott Railton (1849–1913). Once committed to a policy of expansion, Booth lost no time in sending pioneering parties in different directions. They reached Australia and France in 1881; Switzerland, Sweden, India, and Canada in 1882; New Zealand and South Africa in 1883; and Germany in 1886. Today the Salvation Army works in over 100 lands with approximately 25,000 officers; preaches the gospel in some 140 languages at over 14,000 evangelical centers; and operates more than 5,000 social institutions, hospitals, schools, and agencies.

316

AMERICAN RESCUE WORKERS

Founded: 1913
Membership: est. 2,500 in 15 churches (1999)

Incorporated in 1884 as the Salvation Army (see SALVATION ARMY) and in 1896 as the American Salvation Army, with its name amended when the organizational charter was drawn up in 1913, American Rescue Workers, a religious and charitable movement, is a branch of the Christian Church. Its membership includes officers (clergy), lay members (called soldiers or adherents), participants in varied activity groups, and volunteers who serve as advisers. It offers emergency aid (lodging, clothing, food), halfway houses and rehabilitation centers for alcoholics and drug addicts, homeless shelters, workshops and social-service programs for the socially and physically handicapped, and evangelism.

The fact that American Rescue Workers attempts to perform so many community-service programs does not alter its status as a full-fledged denomination. The rites of baptism and Communion are administered by ministers in charge of local churches (corps), and church and Sunday school services are held in community churches. A minister is ordained after serving three years as an officer and must have graduated from a seminary and/or the study courses of the organization and been approved by it.

The articles of religion include belief in the Trinity, the inspiration of the scriptures, the fall of humankind, redemption through Christ, and other basic orthodox doctrines. The motivation of the organization is love of God and a practical concern for the needs of humanity. Its purposes are to preach the gospel, disseminate Christian truths, supply basic human necessities, and undertake the spiritual and moral regeneration and physical rehabilitation of all persons in need, regardless of race, color, creed, sex, or age.

Government is by a board of managers elected by the members of the Grand Field Council. Structure follows a quasi-military pattern, with territorial and divisional commanders in charge. National headquarters are in Williamsport, Pennsylvania. A periodical, *The Rescue Herald,* is published in Hagerstown, Maryland.

SALVATION ARMY

Founded: 1880
Membership: 472,871 in 1,355 corps (1999)

The Salvation Army conducts its religious and social programs in all fifty states, preaching the gospel in order to effect the spiritual, moral, and physical reclamation of those who come under its influence. Through 9,037 centers of operation, including 3,793 service units, that are administered by more than 5,400 officers, assisted by some 43,300 employees and 1,700,000 volunteers, the Army reaches out to communities throughout the U.S. While the Salvation Army has a dual function of church and social agency, its first purpose is salvation "by the power of the Holy Spirit combined with the influence of human ingenuity and love." Its social services are a means of meeting the needs of the "whole person," putting the socially disinherited—the needy both physically and spiritually—into a condition to be uplifted.

Administratively, the Army is under the command of a general. The primary unit of the Army is the corps, of which there may be several in a city. Each corps is commanded by an officer, ranging in rank from lieutenant to major, who is responsible to divisional headquarters. A number of corps make up each of the forty divisions in the U.S., with the work of each division under the direct supervision of a divisional commander. Divisions are grouped into four territories—Eastern, Central, Southern, and Western—with headquarters in West Nyack, New York; Des Plaines, Illinois; Atlanta, Georgia; and Rancho Palos Verdes, California, respectively. Territorial commanders are in charge of each territory, and the four territorial headquarters are composed of departments to facilitate all phases of Army work.

The national headquarters in Alexandria, Virginia, is the coordinating office for the entire country. The national commander is the chief administrative officer, official spokesperson, and president of all Salvation Army corporations in the U.S. Property and revenues are in the custody of a board of trustees, or directors, and citizen advisory boards assist in interpreting the work of the Army to the general public.

Within the structure of the Army, converts who desire to become soldiers (members) are required to sign the Articles of War (a statement of belief), after which, as members, they give volunteer service. The function of officers, who are commissioned to full-time Salvation Army service, is similar to that of clergy of other churches.

Basic training for each officer is a two-year, in-residence course at one of the Army's four schools in Suffern, New York; Chicago; Atlanta; and Rancho Palos Verdes. The chief source of officer candidates is the Salvation Army corps. A soldier who has served actively for at least six months may make application and, if accepted, may enter the School for Officers' Training, where the curriculum, in addition to formal study, includes field experience as well as orientation in all possible areas of Salvation Army service. The officer graduates from the school as a lieutenant and, following additional study, is eligible to attain the rank of captain, major, lieutenant colonel, colonel, or commissioner.

The motivating force of the Salvation Army is the religious faith of its officers and soldiers, and the fundamental doctrines of the organization are stated in the eleven cardinal affirmations of its Foundation Deed of 1878. These statements include the Army's recognition of the Bible as the only rule of Christian faith and practice; God as the Creator and Father of all humankind; the Trinity of Father, Son, and Holy Ghost; Jesus Christ as Son of God and Son of man; sin as the great destroyer of soul and society; salvation as God's remedy for human sin and the ultimate and eternal hope made available through Christ; sanctification as the individual's present and maturing experience of a life set apart for the holy purposes of the kingdom of God; and an eternal destiny that may triumph over sin and death.

The work of the Army in the U.S. includes 162 rehabilitation centers, aiding over 174,000 annually. Over 176,000 people are served each year in 53 medical facilities; 51 camps provide camping facilities for more than 177,000 children, mothers, and senior citizens. The Army maintains more than 300 boys' and girls' clubs, with more than 113,000 members; some 28,000,000 meals are served annually; and basic social services are offered to almost 18,000,000. About 150,000 persons make life-changing spiritual decisions under the Army's ministry each year. There are also hotels and lodges for men and women, missing person bureaus, day-care centers, alcoholic care facilities, correctional service bureaus for prisoners and their families, programs for homeless persons, and other allied services. These services are given without

319

respect to race, color, creed, or condition; the whole work is financed largely through voluntary subscriptions, federal funds, and annual appeals.

VOLUNTEERS OF AMERICA, INC.

Founded: 1896
Membership: statistics not available

Volunteers of America (VOA) is a Christian church and human-service organization founded in 1896 by Ballington (1857–1940) and Maud (1865–1948) Booth, son and daughter-in-law of William Booth, founder of the Salvation Army (see SALVATION ARMY). The mission of VOA is to reach and uplift all people, bringing them to the immediate knowledge and active service of God.

VOA is present in communities across the U.S., providing over 160 different human-service programs and opportunities for individual and community involvement. From rural areas to inner-city neighborhoods, VOA engages more than 11,000 full-time employees and over 30,000 volunteers in operating programs that deal with today's most pressing social needs. It responds to individual community needs to help abused and neglected children, youth at risk, the frail elderly, the disabled, homeless individuals and families, and many others. Each year, it helps more than 1.5 million people in need.

Volunteers of America adheres to a defined set of beliefs, or Cardinal Doctrines, that conform to biblical teaching and traditional Christian thought and practice. Individuals who are commissioned as VOA ministers (having met all requirements for religious study and spiritual formation) become fully accredited clergy and may perform sacramental and evangelical functions.

Volunteers of America is governed by both a religious body, the Grand Field Council, and a corporate body, the National Board of Directors. The Council is made up of all VOA clergy and represents the membership of the organization. The Council is responsible for framing the articles of incorporation, constitution, bylaws, and regulations and for electing its president. The National Board of Directors consists of thirty-one volunteer members and is responsible for the direction and effective functioning of the organization. The National Ecclesiastical Board is a smaller body of VOA clergy charged with ministerial affairs.

320

The chief officer of Volunteers of America, Inc., elected for a five-year term, is president of the corporation as well as head of the church. The national office, in Alexandria, Virginia, provides technical and administrative support to local VOA programs and directs other strategic initiatives to address the organization's mission.

SCHWENKFELDER CHURCH

Founded: 1782, with roots to 1519
Membership: est. 2,800 in 6 congregations (2000)

This church represents a unique branch of the Protestant Reformation, but it has now almost disappeared. The church is named for Caspar Schwenckfeld von Ossig (1489–1561), a Silesian nobleman who experienced a spiritual awakening in 1518. Disappointed in his hope to help reform the Roman Catholic Church from within, he played a leading role in the Reformation, advocating wider reading of the Bible by laypeople, urging the need for the power, guidance, and leading of the Holy Spirit and preaching that the sacramental consumption of the Lord's Supper is a mystical partaking of Christ as food for the soul—but that the food is really bread. This interpretation of the Lord's Supper, together with his insistence on complete separation of church and state, led Schwenkfelder into disagreement with Lutheranism (see LUTHERAN CHURCHES). Espousing a "Reformation of the Middle Way," Schwenkfelder and his followers emphasized the supremacy of the Spirit over literalistic interpretations of scriptural faith and practice. By the end of the sixteenth century, the movement numbered several thousand, gathered basically by Schwenkfelder's writings and sermons, for he organized no church; but the group was persecuted by other religious bodies and remained small and rather dispersed.

Schwenkfelders, as members are called, arrived in Philadelphia in six migrations between 1731 and 1737. Unable to find land for common purchase, the immigrants spread out and settled in the region between Philadelphia and Allentown, Pennsylvania. The Society of Schwenkfelders was formed in 1782, and the Schwenkfelder Church was incorporated in 1909. Although descendants of the original set-

321

tlers live in all regions of the U.S., the remaining Schwenkfelder churches are found within a fifty-mile radius of Philadelphia.

All theology, the members hold, should be constructed from the Bible, but Scripture is considered dead without the indwelling Word. They believe that Christ's divinity was progressive, his human nature becoming more and more divine without "losing its identity." Faith, regeneration, and subsequent spiritual growth change human nature, but justification by faith must not obscure the positive regeneration imparted by Christ; thus the theology is Christocentric.

SPIRITUALIST AND THEOSOPHICAL BODIES

The Spiritualist movement dates to the nineteenth century and is a forerunner of the modern new age movement. Central to the beliefs and practices of spiritualism is the ability to communicate with the spirits of those who have departed this earthly life. This may be done through such things as mediums, séances, and mystical rites. In recent years there has been greater interest in psychic experiments and extrasensory perception. Many spiritualists hold to a belief in reincarnation and seek to reconnect with past-life experiences.

The soul is often called the astral body; at death the material body dissolves, and the soul, as the body of the spirit, progresses through a series of spheres to a higher and higher existence. In two lower spheres, persons of bad character or sinful record are purified and made ready for higher existences. Most of the departed are to be found in a third sphere, the summer land; beyond this are the philosopher's sphere, the advanced contemplative and intellectual sphere, the love sphere, and the Christ sphere. All reach the higher spheres eventually; Spiritualists do not believe in heaven or hell or that any are ever lost. Christ is often recognized as a medium; the annunciation was a message from the spirit world, the transfiguration was an opportunity for materialization of the spirits of Moses and Elias, and the resurrection was evidence that all people live on in the spirit world.

The following principles are provided by the National Spiritualist Association of Churches but apply broadly to most spiritualist organizations:

322

1. We believe in Infinite Intelligence.
2. We believe that the phenomena of Nature, both physical and spiritual, are the expression of Infinite Intelligence.
3. We affirm that a correct understanding of such expression, and living in accordance therewith, constitute true religion.
4. We affirm that the existence and personal identity of the individual continue after the change called death.
5. We affirm that communication with the so-called dead is a fact scientifically proven by the phenomena of Spiritualism.
6. We believe that the highest morality is contained in the Golden Rule: "Whatsoever ye would that others should do unto you, do ye also unto them."
7. We affirm the moral responsibility of the individual, and that we make our own happiness or unhappiness as we obey or disobey Nature's physical and spiritual laws.
8. We affirm that the doorway to reformation is never closed against any human soul here or hereafter.
9. We affirm that the precepts of Prophecy and Healing are divine attributes proven through Mediumship.

Services or séances are held in private homes, rented halls, or churches. Most Spiritualist churches have regular services with prayer, music, selections from writings by various spiritualists, a sermon or lecture, and spirit messages from the departed. Churches and ministers are supported by free will offerings; mediums and ministers also gain support from classes and séances in which fees are charged. Attendance at church services is invariably small, averaging twenty to twenty-five.

Administration and government differ slightly in the various groups, but most have district or state associations and an annual general convention. All have mediums, and most have ministers in charge of the congregations. Requirements for licensing and ordination also differ, but a determined effort is being made to raise the standards of education and character in the larger groups. Spiritualism and its cognates have a greater impact on American culture and religion than is evident from the enduring institutional forms.

Closely related to American Spiritualism is Theosophy, or divine wisdom. Theosophists view this divine wisdom as the universal perennial philosophy that underlies all religions. Thus it draws from both Eastern and Western philosophy and religious teachings.

The chief founder of the modern theosophical movement was Helena Petrovna Blavatsky (1831–91), who was born in Russia in 1831 and traveled over the world in search of "knowledge of the laws which govern the universe." She arrived in the U.S. in 1872 and, with Henry Steel Olcott (1831–1907) and William Q. Judge (1851–96), founded the Theosophical Society of New York in 1875. Her aim was "to form a nucleus of the Universal Brotherhood of Humanity, without distinction of race, creed, sex, caste, or color; to encourage the study of comparative religion, philosophy, and science; and to investigate the unexplained laws of nature and the powers latent in man."

Blavatsky drew on the teachings of the great thinkers of various religions, sciences, and philosophies, both ancient and current at that time. Proceeding from the premise that God is immanent in the hidden forces of nature and that people can attain perfection through their own powers, she described God as the Absolute Principle of pantheistic Hinduism, the Tao of Taoism, and the Godhead of Christianity. Each person is a part of God, and within each is a divine potential; therefore, all are related.

Blavatsky held that all religions stem from a hierarchy that includes Jesus, Buddha, and other master thinkers who have experienced a series of rebirths, or reincarnations, ultimately to attain divinity. Reincarnation is a central theme in Theosophy. It is the method through which persons rid themselves of all impurities and unfold their inner potentials through varied experiences. Closely connected with the concept of reincarnation is that of karma, the law of cause and effect; each rebirth, then, is seen as the result of actions, thoughts, and desires brought from the past.

Olcott and Blavatsky left New York in late 1878 and established the headquarters of the society at Adyer, near Madras in southern India, in 1882. When Blavatsky died in 1891, Annie Besant (1847–1933) took over leadership of the movement, with Olcott as president, until his death in 1907. During that period, conflicts developed between Besant and the leaders of other theosophical groups in Europe and the U.S. In 1895, William Q. Judge, one of the three founders and president of the American society, established an independent Theosophical Society in America. Those loyal to Besant worked in the society whose headquarters was in India. Other splits developed in the years that followed, and the fragmentation is still evident; but the basic teachings of Blavatsky still hold in all groups.

No accurate report of membership seems possible among these groups, but it is estimated that there are some 40,000 Theosophists worldwide, perhaps 5,000 in the U.S. The Theosophical Society was the first group to bring out the philosophy behind occultism. Its influence, thanks to the current interest in Eastern philosophy and religion, is felt in many other occult groups unconnected with any Theosophical Society.

NATIONAL SPIRITUAL ALLIANCE OF THE U.S.A.

Founded: 1913
Membership: statistics not available

This body was founded by G. Tabor Thompson and was incorporated at Lake Pleasant, Massachusetts; its headquarters are at Keene, New Hampshire. Holding general Spiritualist doctrines, the alliance stresses paranormal and impersonal manifestations and intercommunication with the spirit world. Salvation is held to be through the development of personal character: "One reaps as he sows, yet . . . all things are working together for good and evolution obtains perpetually in all persons."

Local groups of the alliance elect their own officers and choose their own ministers. A three-day convention is held annually, at which delegates from all the churches elect national officers—president, secretary, and treasurer. An official board of directors steers the work of ministers and certified mediums; college training is not required, but a minister must have passed a course of study arranged by the alliance. Mediums may baptize, but only ministers may officiate at ceremonies of ordination and marriage. Work of the alliance involves benevolent, literary, educational, musical, and scientific activities.

NATIONAL SPIRITUALIST ASSOCIATION OF CHURCHES

Founded: 1893
Membership: est. 3,000 in 136 churches (1999)

The National Spiritualist Association of Churches was organized in Chicago around the time of the World's Parliament of Religions, which had heightened American interest in Eastern religions and esoteric philosophies. Basic to the association is the conviction that spiritualism is a science, religion, and philosophy based on the reality of communication with the world beyond. Influential far beyond its immediate membership, this association furnishes literature for the whole American Spiritualist movement.

In 1994, the Association established the College of Spiritual Science in Lily Dale, New York, that offers a course of study for members, licentiates, healers, mediums, National Spiritualist Teachers, and ordained ministers, leading to an Associate of Arts in Religious Studies. The Morris Pratt Institute, established in Milwaukee in 1901, presents a correspondence course in modern spiritualism, offers a two-week residential course in pastoral skills and special seminars on spiritualism, and maintains an extensive research library. The NSAC also has a "Spiritualist Benevolent Society" that issues stipends to dedicated members in financial need. An annual legislative convention is held, and officers are elected triennially.

SWEDENBORGIAN CHURCH
(The General Convention of the New Jerusalem in the U.S.A.)

Founded: 1817
Membership: 2,104 in 44 churches (2000)

One of the primary figures in both Spiritualism and Theosophy was Emmanuel Swedenborg (1688–1772). He was born in Stockholm, Sweden, and was an Enlightenment-era scientist distinguished in the fields of mathematics, geology, cosmology, and anatomy before he turned seriously to theology. Although certain he was divinely commissioned to teach the doctrines of the "New Church," Swedenborg never preached or founded a church. His followers, however, felt that the need for a separate denomination was implicit in the new revelation given in Swedenborg's monumental work *Arcana Celestia,* in which, they believed, he unlocked the hidden meaning of Scripture and recorded his conversations with great figures long dead.

The Swedenborgian church centers its worship on the risen and glorified present reality of Christ and looks for the establishment of the kingdom of God in the form of a universal church on earth. In this new church all people will strive for peace, freedom, and justice. Swedenborgian bodies have often used the name "Churches of the

New Jerusalem" to indicate the inbreaking of the eschatological reality described in the New Testament.

The New Church as an organization arose in London in 1783 when Robert Hindmarsh (1759–1835), a printer, gathered a few friends to discuss the writings of Swedenborg. They formed a general conference of their societies in 1815. The first Swedenborgian Society in the U.S. was organized at Baltimore, Maryland, in 1792, and in 1817 the General Convention of the New Jerusalem in the U.S.A. was established. It was incorporated in 1861.

The Faith and Aims of the church state that the "Lord Jesus Christ has come again, not in a physical reappearance, but in spirit and in truth; not in a single event only, but in a progressive manifestation of his presence among men." Adherents claim that tokens of Christ's coming appear in the burst of scientific development, the rise of the spirit of inquiry, the progress toward political and intellectual freedom, and the deepening sense of national and international responsibility that has characterized the modern era.

The doctrines of the General Convention of the New Jerusalem are founded on the Bible, which is understood to have both a literal, historical meaning and a deeper, spiritual meaning. The church teaches that there is one God, known by many names, and that the Christian Trinity denotes aspects of this God. Human beings are believed to be essentially spirits clothed in material bodies, which are laid aside at death; the human spirit lives on in a spirit world, in a manner determined by its attitudes and behavior on earth. Therefore, Swedenborgians hold that adherents are to live out their religious beliefs in all aspects of life.

Societies are grouped into a General Convention that meets annually. Each society is self-regulating, with ministers and general pastors (in charge of state associations). Services are liturgical, based on the *Book of Worship* issued by the General Convention. A theological school is in Newton, Massachusetts, and the Swedenborg Foundation is in West Chester, Pennsylvania; J. Appleseed & Co. in San Francisco distributes books and pamphlets based on Swedenborg's writings.

Another Swedenborgian body, The General Church of the New Jerusalem, broke away from the older group in 1890. It shares many of the doctrines of the larger body, but acknowledges the writings of Swedenborg as divinely inspired. Headquarters is at Bryn Athyn, Pennsylvania, where a cathedral has been built.

TRIUMPH THE CHURCH AND KINGDOM OF GOD IN CHRIST, INTERNATIONAL

Founded: 1902
Membership: statistics not available

This Christian body grew out of the Holiness (see HOLINESS CHURCHES) movement but developed some unique qualities, particularly a stress on ongoing revelation. It was founded by Elias Dempsey Smith, a Methodist pastor in Mississippi who was proclaimed an apostle by his followers. Through revelation, Smith taught that entire sanctification is an instantaneous work of grace and that baptism by the Holy Spirit is obtainable by faith.

Bishops lead the church and administer its business; the chief executive is chief bishop. There is a quadrennial International Religious Congress. Triumph has a strong presence in Africa, particularly in Liberia.

UNIFICATION CHURCH

Founded: 1954
Membership: statistics not available

One of the most controversial churches born in modern times is the Unification Church of the Rev. Sun Myung Moon. This church originated in Korea and burst upon the American scene in the 1970s. Its teaching is a blend of Eastern traditional philosophy and evangelical Christianity. Members hold that Satan distorted the original harmony of creation, but through the sacrifice of Jesus and revelations given to the Rev. Moon that harmony is being restored. Central to Moon's teaching is that God is a balance of masculine and feminine traits (basically the yin and yang of Taoism) and that humans can restore this harmony of polarities through spiritual marriage. Humans can also connect with the spiritual world and experience spiritual growth through proper actions, attitudes, and devotions that blend Eastern and Western elements.

328

Sun Myung Moon was born in 1920 in Korea and studied at a Confucian school. Around 1930, his parents became fervent Presbyterians, and the young Moon became a Sunday school teacher. At Easter 1935, as he was praying in the Korean mountains, Moon had a vision of Jesus, who asked him to continue the work Jesus had begun on earth nearly 2,000 years before. Sun Myung Moon studied the Bible and many other religious teachings in order to unravel the mysteries of life and human history. Embracing asceticism, he came to an understanding of God's own suffering and longing to be reunited with God's children.

By 1945, Moon had organized the teachings that came to be known as the Divine Principle, and he began his public ministry. On May 1, 1954, in Seoul, Moon founded the Holy Spirit Association for the Unification of World Christianity, popularly called the Unification Church. Despite opposition from other churches and the government, including imprisonment of Moon and other leaders, the church quickly spread throughout South Korea. In 1959, the first missionaries arrived in the U.S.

Marriage is central to the teachings of the church, and the wedding of Moon to Hak Ja Han in 1960 was seen by his followers as the marriage of the Lamb foretold in the book of Revelation, marking the beginning of the restoration of humankind back into God's lineage. Sun Myung Moon and Hak Ja Han established the position of True Parents and are considered the first couple to have the complete blessing of God and to be able to bring forth children with no original sin. The church teaches that all people, whether previously married or single, can receive the blessing of God upon their marriages through the Moons' standing as the True Parents. The number of couples who have received this blessing in large wedding ceremonies was 360,000 by 1995.

In 1971, Moon expanded his ministry by coming to the United States. He conducted a "Day of Hope" speaking tour throughout the U.S. in the early 1970s with the purpose of reviving traditional Judeo-Christian values. He was invited to the White House, where he met with President Richard Nixon. On two occasions, Moon addressed members of the U.S. Congress from both the House and the Senate. In 1975, Reverend Moon sent missionaries to 120 countries, making the Unification Church a worldwide faith. Controversy followed Moon and his followers, however, and in the 1980s he was convicted of tax evasion and imprisoned in the U.S. for thirteen months.

In 1992 Reverend Moon declared that he and his wife are the Messiah and True Parents of all humanity. For adherents, this marks the beginning of the Completed Testament Age. Since then, Mrs. Moon has taken a more active role in the worldwide work of the church.

UNITARIAN UNIVERSALIST ASSOCIATION

Founded: 1961
Membership: 216,931 in 1,040 churches (1999)

In May 1961, the Unitarian and Universalist churches in the U.S. and Canada were consolidated as the Unitarian Universalist Association of Congregations in North America, one of the most influential liberal churches. The two bodies had separate and interesting origins and history.

Unitarian. The basic tenet of Unitarianism is that there is only one God; thus, Jesus was not divine in essence. Unitarians often claim that their thought reaches back into the early Christian centuries, before the concept of the Trinity was developed. Unitarianism as we know it today, however, began with the Protestant Reformation, among anti-trinitarians. The movement spread from independent thinkers, such as Michael Servetus (ca. 1511–53) and Faustus Socinus (1539–1604), and Anabaptists (see MENNONITE CHURCHES) in Switzerland, Hungary, Transylvania, Holland, Poland, and Italy. In England it found champions in such leaders as the scientist and mathematician Isaac Newton (1642–1727), the philosopher John Locke (1632–1704), and the poet John Milton (1608–74), but no attempt was made to organize the movement until late in the eighteenth century.

American Unitarianism developed in New England Congregational churches that were known as Liberal Christian. The split within Congregationalism (see CONGREGATIONAL CHURCHES) came into the open in 1805 when Henry Ware (1764–1845), a Unitarian, was appointed professor of theology at Harvard University, the bastion of Congregationalist education. The split widened in 1819 when William Ellery Channing (1780–1842) of Boston preached his famous Baltimore sermon outlining the Unitarian view. Channing defined the true church in these words: "By his Church our Savior does not mean a party bearing the name of a human leader, distinguished by a form or an opinion, and on the ground of this distinction, denying the name and character of Christians to all but themselves. . . . These are the church—men made better, made holy, virtuous by his religion—men who, hoping in his promises, keep his commands."

Eventually Unitarian Congregationalists organized the American Unitarian Association in 1925. It was devoted to certain moral, religious, educational, and charitable purposes, which may be as enlightening to the non-Unitarian as an analysis of its religious or doctrinal statements. They were:

1. Diffuse the knowledge and promote the interests of religion that Jesus taught as love to God and love to man;
2. Strengthen the churches and fellowships that unite in the association for more and better work for the kingdom of God;
3. Organize new churches and fellowships for the extension of Unitarianism in our own countries and in other lands; and
4. Encourage sympathy and cooperation among religious liberals at home and abroad.

The organization was liberally congregational. Independent local churches were grouped in local, county, district, state, and regional conferences and were united in an international association for purposes of fellowship, counsel, and promotion of mutual interests. At the time of the merger in 1961, there were four Unitarian seminaries, two preparatory schools, 386 churches, and approximately 115,000 members.

Universalist. Universalism refers to the belief that all persons are saved regardless of religious belief or non-belief. Universalists find evidence of their thinking and philosophy in many cultural streams, and the teaching has much in common with several religions throughout the world. Universalists claim roots in the early Christian gnostics Clement of Alexandria (ca. 150–ca. 215) and Theodore of Mopsuestia (ca. 350–428), certain Anabaptists (see MENNONITE CHURCHES), and the seventeenth- and eighteenth-century German mystics, such as Jacob Boehme (1575–1624).

In 1759, James Relly (1722–78) of England wrote *Union,* in which he opposed the Calvinistic doctrine of election of the few. Relly's

331

conviction of universal salvation deeply influenced John Murray (1741–1815), a Wesleyan evangelist who came to New Jersey in 1770 and found groups of universalist-minded people scattered along the Atlantic coast. He became minister to one such group in Gloucester, Massachusetts, and later served briefly as a Revolutionary War chaplain in the armies of Washington and Greene. His Independent Christian Church of Gloucester became the first organized Universalist church in the U.S. in 1779.

A group of Universalists met at Philadelphia in 1790 to draft their first declaration of faith and plan of government. They promoted pacifism, abolition of slavery, testimony by affirmation rather than by oath, and free public education. This Philadelphia declaration was adopted by a group of New England Universalists in 1793.

At about the same time, Hosea Ballou (1771–1852), a school teacher and itinerant preacher in Vermont, was ordained in the Universalist ministry. He broke radically with Murray's thought, in 1805 publishing the *Treatise on Atonement,* which gave Universalists their first consistent philosophy. Ballou rejected the theories of total depravity, endless punishment in hell, the Trinity, and miracles. Humankind, said Ballou, was potentially good and capable of perfectibility; God, being a God of infinite love, recognized humanity's heavenly nature and loved the human race as God's own offspring. The meaning of the atonement was not found in bloody sacrifice to appease divine wrath, but in the heroic sacrifice of Jesus, who was not God but a Son of the universal God who revealed the love of God and wanted to win all persons to that love.

Universalists in the nineteenth century were active very early in reform movements for prison inmates and working women. They opposed slavery from their earliest days, stood for separation of church and state, and have maintained a continuing interest in the fields of science, labor, management, civil rights, and human concern. Universalists founded several non-sectarian colleges and universities, including Tufts, St. Lawrence, Lombard (now linked to the University of Chicago), Goddard, and the California Institute of Technology. At the time of the merger, there were 68,949 members in 334 churches.

Unitarian Universalist Association. In this association, neither body seems to have lost any of its original ideology, theology, or purpose. Flexibility, freedom of conscience, and local autonomy are prime values. No minister, member, or congregation "shall be required to subscribe to any particular interpretation of religion, or to any particular religious belief or creed." The aims of the association were set forth in 1985 in a revised statement:

> The Principles and Purposes of the member congregations of the Unitarian Universalist Association covenant to affirm and promote:
> (a) The inherent worth and dignity of every person;
> (b) Justice, equity, and compassion in human relationships;
> (c) Acceptance of one another and encouragement to spiritual growth in our congregations;
> (d) A free and responsible search for truth and meaning;
> (e) The right of conscience and the use of the democratic process within our congregations and in society at large;
> (f) The goal of world community with peace, liberty, and justice for all;
> (g) Respect for the interdependent web of all existence of which we are a part.

In recent years the Association has been heavily involved in numerous causes and concerns: the issue of racial and cultural diversity in what have been historically white congregations; the rise of feminist consciousness; scholarship in church history and process theology; inner-city ministries; and the rights of gay, lesbian, and bisexual persons.

A General Assembly, with clergy and lay representatives, is the overall policy-making body, meeting annually. The elected officers of the Association (moderator, president, two vice-moderators, secretary, and treasurer) all elected for four-year terms, together with twenty-four other elected members, constitute a Board of Trustees, which appoints the executive and administrative officers and generally carries out policies and directives. Members of this board have the usual powers of corporate directors as provided by law; they meet four times a year, between regular meetings of the general assembly.

Among the most notable and successful achievements of the Association are its publishing house, Beacon Press, which produces fifty new titles each year and is one of the most distinguished independent publishing houses in the U.S.; a periodical, *The World,* circulated six times a year to more than 110,000 member families; the Unitarian Universalist Service Committee, which provides leadership and materials in the field of social change; and a highly respected religious education curriculum.

Continental headquarters are in Boston; twenty-three district offices have been established. Principal numerical strength lies in the Northeast, the Midwest, and the Pacific West Coast. Foreign work is now conducted through the International Association for Religious Freedom, with headquarters at Oxford, England; the International Association has correspondents in sixty-five countries.

UNITY SCHOOL OF CHRISTIANITY AND ASSOCIATION OF UNITY CHURCHES

Founded: 1886
Membership: est. 31,000 in 664 churches (1995)

Unity is not a church or a denomination, but a nonsectarian religious educational institution devoted to demonstrating that following the teaching of Jesus Christ is a practical, seven-day-a-week way of life. Unity teaches that "the true church is a state of consciousness in man." The Association of Unity Churches helps provide resources for congregations dedicated to Unity teachings.

Unity has been described as "a religious philosophy with an 'open end,' seeking to find God's truth in all of life, wherever it may be." Unity has no strict creed or dogma; it finds good in all religions and teaches that people should keep their minds open to receive that goodness. Unity teaches that reality is ultimately spiritual and that realization of spiritual truth will illuminate, heal, and prosper humanity. Cultivation of health-conducive emotions such as love, confidence, and joy is encouraged. Overcoming health-inhibiting emotions such as anger, hatred, and despair is also encouraged. Unity has no rules concerning health but concentrates on spiritual goals, knowing that healthful living habits will follow. Some Unity students are vegetarians in the interest of health.

Unity began in 1886 when Charles Fillmore (1854–1948), bankrupt and crippled, and his wife, Myrtle (1845–1931), seriously ill with tuberculosis, discovered a way of life based on affirmative prayer. They studied Christian Science (see CHURCH OF CHRIST, SCIENTIST), the Bible, Transcendentalism, New Thought, Quakerism (see FRIENDS), Theosophy (see SPIRITUALIST and

334

THEOSOPHICAL BODIES), Rosicrucianism, Spiritism, and Hinduism; out of their studies came an ideology built on ancient truth and concepts, but moving in a new direction. This approach is offered today in the Unity School of Christianity as a curative in many areas beyond physical healing.

The Fillmores held that "whatever man wants he can have by voicing his desire in the right way into the Universal Mind." Unity teaches that God is "Principle, Law, Being, Mind, Spirit, All Good, omnipotent, omniscient, unchangeable, Creator, Father, Cause and Source of all that is." Human beings are children of God, with potential for Christ consciousness. It is through Christ, or the Christ consciousness, that the human gains eternal life and salvation. Salvation means the attainment of true spiritual consciousness, becoming like Christ. This transformation takes place not in any hereafter, but "here in this earth" through a process of unfolding and regeneration. A person suffers no final death, but changes into increasingly better states until finally becoming like Christ. Members of Unity believe that all people will have this experience.

Prayer and meditation are suggested for every human want and illness. The Unity way of prayer and meditation involves relaxation and affirmation of spiritual truth to develop the consciousness of the individual and silent receptivity to the "Divine Mind" for whatever the seeker needs. The Bible is used constantly and is highly valued, but is not considered the sole or final authority in faith and practice; people must be in direct, personal communion with God, not dependent upon such secondary sources as the scriptures.

The Association of Unity Churches, an independent but related organization of ministers and licensed teachers, evolved out of the work of the founding generations. The Association ordains ministers, provides educational and administrative support, and is self-supporting.

Unity School trains ministers in a two-year program. It also educates teachers and offers retreat programs. Unity School's central work is done through what is called Silent Unity. A large staff in Unity Village, near Kansas City, Missouri, is available to pray with people day and night; workers answer an average of one million calls and nearly two million letters annually. This service of prayer and affirmation offers help on every conceivable problem; each case or call is assigned to a member of the staff who suggests the proper affirmations. The whole staff joins in group prayer and meditation several times a day. All calls and requests are answered; there is no charge for this service, but love offerings are accepted. Most calls come from members of various Christian churches; correspondents are never asked to leave the churches to which they belong.

Unity School publishes some 75 million copies of booklets, brochures, and magazines annually. These materials are used by many who never contact headquarters or become members of a Unity church.

UNIVERSAL FELLOWSHIP OF METROPOLITAN COMMUNITY CHURCHES

Founded: 1970
Membership: est. 44,000 in 300 churches (1998)

This Protestant body is unique among Christian bodies in that it was founded specifically to reach out to and affirm homosexual persons. The church holds the belief that theology is the basis to present the good news of God's love to a segment of society often excluded from, and sometimes ridiculed for, participation in church life. This awareness prompted Troy D. Perry to create a denomination in which such marginalized people could find genuine acceptance in a context of Christian worship and service. Perry, himself a homosexual, had been discharged from the church he served as pastor and ostracized from his denomination. He called a congregation into being in Los Angeles, and soon churches were organized in other cities. In the summer of 1970, the first general conference was held.

Heterosexuals may and do belong to the church, but a large percentage of the membership is homosexual. The denomination describes its ministry as a shared one—lay and clergy, women and men, privileged and underprivileged, lesbian, gay, and heterosexual. Forty-three percent of its clergy are women.

The church professes traditional Christian theology on such doctrines as Scripture, the Trinity, and the sacraments. The Bible, "interpreted by the Holy Spirit in conscience and faith," is the guide for faith and discipline. Since its members come from all types of Christian churches, the worship style, liturgy, and practice of congregations is eclectic and varied. Some congregations are more or less

336

Pentecostal (see PENTECOSTAL CHURCHES), while others are very liturgical. Baptism and Holy Communion are the sacraments.

The membership of this denomination is active in a variety of ministries, reflecting its primary orientation to such traditions as the social gospel and liberation theology. In particular, it has sought to address the needs of the hungry, the homeless, and the powerless. It supports a freeze on nuclear weapons and is committed to eradicating sexism in its theology and in society at large. The civil rights of all people are a major concern. It also addresses the AIDS epidemic as a major social issue, partly because incidences of the disease are so prevalent among its own membership.

The church faces the controversial nature of its existence by stating that its members accept homosexuality as "a gift from God," just as heterosexuality is "a gift from God." Nonetheless, it holds that "our sexuality is not and should not be the focal point of our lives. The MCC emphasizes that everything in our life, including our sexuality, must center on our relationship with God, through faith in Jesus Christ."

The government of the church is vested in a General Council, consisting of Elders and District Coordinators, clergy, and lay delegates. The body applied for membership in the National Council of the Churches of Christ in the U.S.A. in 1983 and was declined, but it hopes eventually to become a part of that ecumenical organization, with which it remains in dialogue. It does participate as an official observer in World Council of Churches events.

WORLDWIDE CHURCH OF GOD

Founded: 1933
Membership: est. 70,000 worldwide (2000)

The Worldwide Church of God (formerly the Radio Church of God) began its work in 1933 under the leadership of Herbert W. Armstrong (1892–1986). The mission statement of the church was to proclaim the gospel of Jesus Christ around the world and to help members grow spiritually. The church grew rapidly from 1964 to 1974, but controversy erupted in the 1970s. Garner Ted Armstrong, the founder's son, took part of the membership with him when he founded the rival Church of God International. The original church weathered a bitter legal battle, and its situation became more unstable in the 1980s. After Herbert Armstrong's death in 1986, Joseph W. Tkach became Pastor General. Tkach and, after his death in 1995, his son Joseph W. Tkach, Jr., led the church through an experience nothing short of religious conversion in the late 1980s and 1990s.

The elder Armstrong saw himself as the apostle-messenger of the Last Days and so assumed absolute authority in the organization. His church was to be the Philadelphian church described in Revelation. Congregations generally worshipped in rented facilities or private homes rather than building separate structures. At the time of his death, he left a church with some 120,000 members, a budget of $2,000,000, and a publication, *Plain Truth*, with a circulation of eight million copies a month. His organization was a worldwide ministry, with churches in 100 countries and territories, carried out from a headquarters in Pasadena, California.

The Worldwide Church of God held to some traditional Christian teachings, but it maintained several unique theological ideas. Herbert Armstrong taught that there is one God, who is the Father. Jesus was accepted as divine, constituting with the Father a divine family. Armstrong did not, however, believe the Holy Spirit was a distinct person. Concerning human nature, the inspiration of the scriptures, Christ's bodily resurrection, and baptism, the church held traditional positions, and it took a strong stand against bearing arms and the taking of human life. It rejected the concept of everlasting conscious torment in hell for the unsaved.

Accepting a number of Jewish (see JUDAISM) observances as scripturally mandated, the church observed the Lord's Supper, or Passover of Jesus Christ, annually as a memorial of the death of Jesus. The sabbath (Friday sunset to Saturday sunset) was honored as a day of worship. Seven annual holy days were kept, and certain "unclean" meats were avoided. Holidays, such as Halloween, Easter, and Christmas, were condemned as pagan. The three ordinances of baptism, the Lord's Supper, and foot washing were practiced. Such was Armstrong's theological conviction that he did not acknowledge as Christian those who failed to observe the liturgical calendar and practices he maintained.

However, under the leadership of the Tkaches, the Worldwide Church of God made a dramatic theological turn, essentially moving

338

to an evangelical position. While continuing to honor Armstrong's sincerity, the church has repudiated his more unusual doctrinal and practical ideas. Key changes include affirmation of traditional Christian understanding of the Trinity (1993) and renunciation of Old Testament covenant laws (1994). The church issued formal apologies for error to the wider Christian community, and in 1997 it was accepted as a member of the National Association of Evangelicals. The wholesale conversion of the entire movement, from "an unorthodox church on the fringes of Christianity, into an evangelical church that believes and teaches orthodox doctrines," is one of the singular events in American religious history.

Many adherents were disillusioned by the changes following Armstrong's death, and thousands left the church. Hundreds of staff were laid off, finances and programs were depleted, radio and television ministries were cut back, and the church's educational institution, Ambassador University, was closed. However, the church moves into the twenty-first century with an expressed confidence that God will persist in forming and shaping it for the divine purpose. The church continues to publish *The Plain Truth* and to engage in various forms of electronic ministry. Over 900 churches remain affiliated around the world, and the Ambassador Center at Azusa Pacific University (Wesleyan theological heritage; see METHODIST CHURCHES) helps provide church members with Christian education in a liberal arts setting.

.

Appendix 1
Members of the National Association of Evangelicals
(and date they joined)

Advent Christian General Conference (1986)
Assemblies of God (1943)
Baptist General Conference (1966)
The Brethren Church (1968)
Brethren in Christ Church (1949)
Christian Catholic Church (Evangelical Protestant) (1975)
The Christian and Missionary Alliance (1966)
Christian Church of North America (1953)
Christian Reformed Church in North America (1943-51; 1988)
Christian Union (1954)
Church of God (1944)
Church of God, Mountain Assembly, Inc. (1981)
Church of the Nazarene (1984)
Church of the United Brethren in Christ (1953)
Churches of Christ in Christian Union (1945)
Congregational Holiness Church (1990-92, 1994)
Conservative Baptist Association of America (1990)
Conservative Congregational Christian Conference (1951)
Conservative Lutheran Association (1984)
Elim Fellowship (1947)
Evangelical Church of North America (1969)
Evangelical Congregational Church (1962)
Evangelical Free Church of America (1943)
Evangelical Friends International of North America (1971)
Evangelical Mennonite Church (1944)
Evangelical Methodist Church (1952)
Evangelical Presbyterian Church (1982)
Evangelistic Missionary Fellowship (1982)
Fellowship of Evangelical Bible Churches (1948)
Fire Baptized Holiness Church of God of the Americas (1978)
Free Methodist Church of North America (1944)
General Association of General Baptists (1988)
International Church of the Foursquare Gospel (1952)
International Pentecostal Church of Christ (1946)
International Pentecostal Holiness Church (1943)
Mennonite Brethren Churches, USA (1946)
Midwest Congregational Christian Fellowship (1964)
Missionary Church, Inc. (1944)
Open Bible Standard Churches (1943)

Pentecostal Church of God (1954)
Pentecostal Free Will Baptist Church, Inc. (1988)
Presbyterian Church in America (1986)
Primitive Methodist Church USA (1946)
Reformed Episcopal Church (1990)
Reformed Presbyterian Church of North America (1946)
Regional Synod of Mid-America (Reformed Church in America) (1989)
The Salvation Army (1990)
The Wesleyan Church (1948)
Worldwide Church of God (1997)

Appendix 2
Member Communions of the National Council of the Churches of Christ in the U.S.A.

African Methodist Episcopal Church
African Methodist Episcopal Zion Church
The Alliance of Baptist Churches in the USA
American Baptist Churches in the USA
The Antiochian Orthodox Christian Archdiocese of North America
Diocese of the Armenian Church of America
Christian Church (Disciples of Christ)
Christian Methodist Episcopal Church
Church of the Brethren
The Coptic Orthodox Church in North America
The Episcopal Church
Evangelical Lutheran Church in America
Friends United Meeting
Greek Orthodox Archdiocese of North and South America
Hungarian Reformed Church in America
International Council of Community Churches
Korean Presbyterian Church in America
Malankara Orthodox Syrian Church
Mar Thoma Church
Moravian Church in America Northern Province and Southern Province
National Baptist Convention of America
National Baptist Convention, U.S.A., Inc.
National Missionary Baptist Convention of America
Orthodox Church in America
Patriarchal Parishes of the Russian Orthodox Church in the USA
Philadelphia Yearly Meeting of the Religious Society of Friends
Polish National Catholic Church of America
Presbyterian Church (U.S.A.)
Progressive National Baptist Convention, Inc.
Reformed Church in America
Serbian Orthodox Church in the U.S.A. and Canada
The Swedenborgian Church
Syrian Orthodox Church of Antioch
Ukrainian Orthodox Church of America
United Church of Christ
The United Methodist Church

Appendix 3: Relationships of Church Bodies to One Another

The Early Church

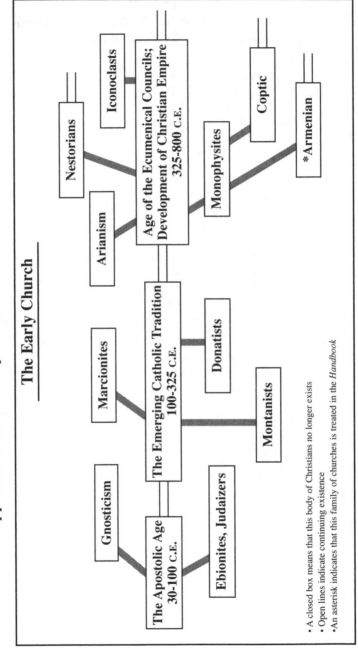

- A closed box means that this body of Christians no longer exists
- Open lines indicate continuing existence
- An asterisk indicates that this family of churches is treated in the *Handbook*

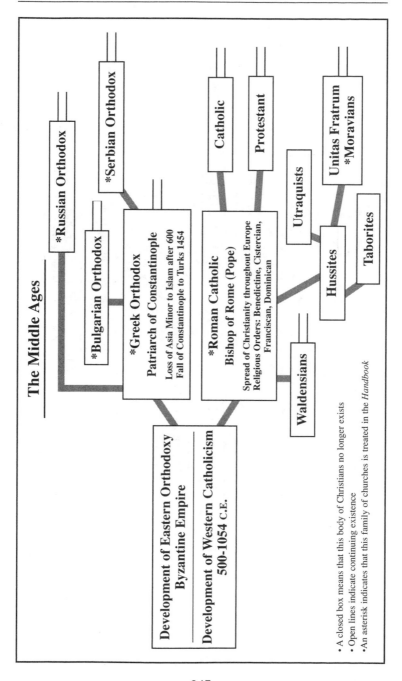

The Middle Ages

**Russian Orthodox

**Serbian Orthodox

**Bulgarian Orthodox

**Greek Orthodox
Patriarch of Constantinople
Loss of Asia Minor to Islam after 600
Fall of Constantinople to Turks 1454

Catholic

Protestant

Utraquists

Unitas Fratrum
**Moravians

Hussites

Taborites

**Roman Catholic
Bishop of Rome (Pope)
Spread of Christianity throughout Europe
Religious Orders: Benedictine, Cistercian,
Franciscan, Dominican

Waldensians

Development of Eastern Orthodoxy
Byzantine Empire

Development of Western Catholicism
500-1054 C.E.

• A closed box means that this body of Christians no longer exists
• Open lines indicate continuing existence
•An asterisk indicates that this family of churches is treated in the *Handbook*

345

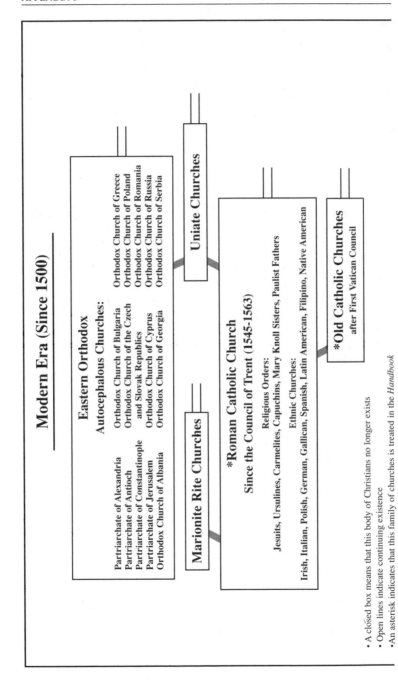

Modern Era (Since 1500)

Eastern Orthodox

Autocephalous Churches:

Partriarchate of Alexandria
Partriarchate of Antioch
Partriarchate of Constantinople
Partriarchate of Jerusalem
Orthodox Church of Albania

Orthodox Church of Bulgaria
Orthodox Church of the Czech
and Slovak Republics
Orthodox Church of Cyprus
Orthodox Church of Georgia

Orthodox Church of Greece
Orthodox Church of Poland
Orthodox Church of Romania
Orthodox Church of Russia
Orthodox Church of Serbia

Uniate Churches

Marionite Rite Churches

*Roman Catholic Church
Since the Council of Trent (1545-1563)

Religious Orders:
Jesuits, Ursulines, Carmelites, Capuchins, Mary Knoll Sisters, Paulist Fathers

Ethnic Churches:
Irish, Italian, Polish, German, Gallican, Spanish, Latin American, Filipino, Native American

*Old Catholic Churches
after First Vatican Council

• A closed box means that this body of Christians no longer exists
• Open lines indicate continuing existence
•An asterisk indicates that this family of churches is treated in the *Handbook*

346

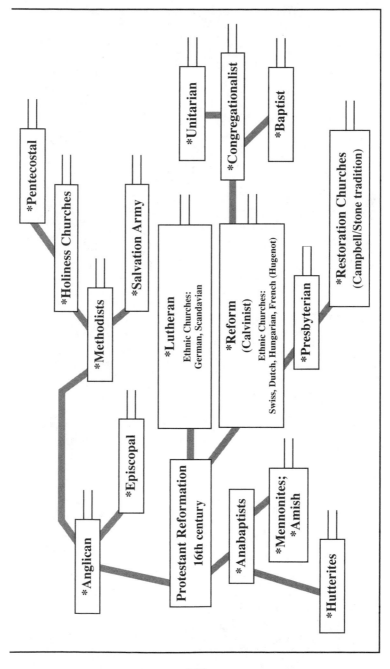

Appendix 4: Directory of Denominational Headquarters and Web Sites

Denomination	Address	Web Site
Advent Christian Church	14601 Albemarle Road, P.O. Box 23152, Charlotte, NC 28227	www.adventchristian.org
African Methodist Episcopal Church	1134 11th Street NW, Washington, D.C. 20001	www.amecnet.org
African Methodist Episcopal Zion Church	P.O. Box 32843, Charlotte, NC 28323	www.amezion.org
African Orthodox Church	137 Alston Street NW, Cambridge, MA 02139	
Albanian Orthodox Archdiocese in America	523 East Broadway, South Boston, MA 02127	www.oca.org/oca/al
American Association of Lutheran Churches	801 West 106th St., #203, Minneapolis, MN 55420	www.taalc.org
American Baptist Association	4605 N. State Line Avenue, Texarkana, TX 75503	www.abaptist.org
American Baptist Churches in the U.S.A.	P.O. Box 851, Valley Forge, PA 19482-0851	www.abc-usa.org
American Carpatho-Russian Greek Catholic Church	312 Garfield Street, Johnston, PA 15906	www.goarch.org
American Catholic Church	P.O. Box 725, Hampton Bays, NY 11946	www.geocities.com/westhollywood/4136
American Evangelical Christian Churches	P.O. Box 47312, Indianapolis, IN 46277	www.aecministries.com
American Jewish Committee	165 East 56th Street, New York, NY 10022	www.ajc.org
American Rescue Workers	643 Elmira Street, Williamsport, PA 17701	www.arwus.com
Anglican Catholic Church	107 West Broadway, Gettysburg, PA 17325	www.anglicancatholic.org
Anglican Rite Synod in the Americas	875 Berkshire Valley Road, Wharton, NJ 07885	www.anglicanrite.org
Antiochian Orthodox Christian Archdiocese of North America	550 West 50th Street, New York, NY 10019	www.antiochian.org
Apostolic Christian Church (Nazarene)	1135 Sholey Road, Richmond, VA 23231	
Apostolic Christian Church of America	3420 North Sheridan Road, Peoria, IL 61604	www.apostolicchristian.org
Apostolic Episcopal Church — Order of Corporate Reunion	P. O. Box 2401, Apple Valley, CA 92307	www.celticsynod.org/aec.htm
Apostolic Faith Mission of Portland, OR	6615 SE Duke Street, Portland, OR 97206	www.apostolicfaith.org
Apostolic Lutheran Church of America	332 Mt. Washington Way, Clayton, CA 94517-1546	www.apostolic-lutheran.org
Apostolic Orthodox Catholic Church	P.O. Box 1834, Glendora, CA 91740-1834	www.pe.net/~idyll/para1.htm (unofficial)
Apostolic Overcoming Holy Church of God, Inc.	1120 North 24th Street, Birmingham, AL 35234	www.prairienet.org/staoh
Armenian Apostolic Church of America	138 E. 39th Street, New York, NY 10016-4885	www.armprelacy.org

Denomination	Address	Web Site
Assemblies of God International	1445 Boonville Avenue, Springfield, MO 65802	www.ag.org
Assemblies of God International Fellowship	P.O. Box 22410, San Diego, CA 92192-2410	www.agifellowship.org
Assemblies of the Lord Jesus Christ	875 N. White Station Road, Memphis, TN 38122	www.aljc.org
Associate Reformed Presbyterian Church	3132 Grace Hill Road, Columbia, SC 29204	www.arpsynod.org
Association of Free Lutheran Congregations	3110 E. Medicine Lake Boulevard, Minneapolis, MN 55441	www.aflc.org
Baha'i	866 UN Plaza, Suite 1202, New York, NY 10017	www.bahai.org
Baptist Bible Fellowship International	P.O. Box 191, Springfield, MO 65801	www.bbfi.org
Baptist General Conference	2002 South Arlington Heights Road, Arlington Heights, IL 60005	www.bgc.bethel.edu
Baptist Missionary Association of America	P.O. Box 193920, Little Rock, AR 72219-3920	www.bmaa-missions.com
Beachy Amish Mennonite Churches	3015 Partridge Road, P.O. Box 73, Partridge, KS 67566	www.mhsc.ca (unofficial)
Berean Fundamental Church	P.O. Box 6103, Lincoln, NE 68506	
Bible Fellowship Church	3000 Fellowship Dr., Whitehall, PA 18052	www.bfc.org
Bible Way Church of Our Lord Jesus Christ World Wide, Inc.	4949 Two-Notch Road, Columbia, SC 29204	www.biblewaychurch.org
Brethren Church (Ashland)	524 College Avenue, Ashland, OH 44805	www.brethrenchurch.org
Brethren in Christ Church	P.O. Box A, Grantham, PA 17207-0901	www.bic-church.org/index.htm
Bulgarian Eastern Orthodox Church	550-A West 50th Street, New York, NY 10019	
Charismatic Episcopal Church	46797 Trailwood Place, Potomac Falls, VA 20165	www.diochi.org
Christadelphians	1000 Mohawk Drive, Elgin, IL 60120-3148	www.christadelphia.org
Christian and Missionary Alliance	P.O. Box 35000, Colorado Springs, CO 80935-3500	www.cmalliance.org
Christian Brethren	327 Prairie Avenue, Wheaton, IL 60187-3408	
Christian Catholic Church	Dowie Memorial Drive, Zion, IL 60099	
Christian Church (Disciples of Christ)	130 East Washington Street, P.O. Box 1986, Indianapolis, IN 46206	www.disciples.org
Christian Church of North America, General Council	1294 Rutledge Road, Transfer, PA 16154-9005	www.ccna.org
Christian Churches and Churches of Christ	4210 Bridgetown Road, P.O. Box 11326, Cincinnati, OH 45211	www.cwv.net/christ'n (unofficial)
Christian Congregation, Inc.	804 West Hemlock Street, LaFollette, TN 37766	
Christian Methodist Episcopal Church	4466 Elvis Presley Blvd., Memphis, TN 38116	www.c-m-e.org
Christian Reformed Church in North America	2850 Kalamazoo Avenue SE, Grand Rapids, MI 49560	www.crcna.org
Church of Christ (Holiness) U.S.A.	329 East Monument Street, P.O. Box 3622, Jackson, MS 39207	www.cochusa.com/main.htm

Denomination	Address	Web Site
Church of Christ (Temple Lot)	200 S. River Boulevard, P.O. Box 472, Independence, MO 64501-0472	www.church-of-christ.com
Church of Christ, Scientist	175 Huntington Avenue, Boston, MA 02115	www.tfccs.com
Church of God and Saints of Christ	3825 Central Avenue, Cleveland, OH 44115	www.churchofgod1896.org
Church of God (Anderson, IN)	P.O. Box 2420, Anderson, IN 46018-2420	www.chog.org
Church of God (Cleveland, TN)	2490 Keith St., P.O. Box 2430, Cleveland, TN 37320-2430	www.chofgod.org
Church of God (General Conference)	P.O. Box 100,000, Morrow, GA 30260	www.abc-coggc.org
Church of God (Holiness)	7407 Metcalf, P.O. Box 4711, Overland Park, KS 66204	www.kccbs.edu/cogh
Church of God (Seventh Day)	330 West 152nd Avenue, P.O. Box 33677, Denver, CO 80233	www.cog7.org
Church of God by Faith, Inc.	1315 South Lane Avenue, Suite 6, Jacksonville, FL 32206	www.cogbf.org
Church of God in Christ	272 South Main Street, Memphis, TN 38101	
Church of God in Christ, International	170 Adelphi Street, Brooklyn, NY 11205	www.bibleviews.com
Church of God in Christ, Mennonite	P.O. Box 230, Moundridge, KS 67107	
Church of God of Prophecy	3720 North Keith Street, P.O. Box 2910, Cleveland, TN 37320-2910	www.cogop.org
Church of Jesus Christ	P.O. Box 1414, Cleveland, TN 37311	
Church of Jesus Christ (Bickertonites)	2007 Cutter Drive, McKees Rocks, PA 15136	
Church of Jesus Christ of Latter-day Saints	15 East South Temple Street, Salt Lake City, UT 84150	www.lds.org
Church of Our Lord Jesus Christ of the Apostolic Faith	444 W. Penn Street, Philadelphia, PA 19144	www.apostolic-faith.org
Church of the Brethren	1451 Dundee Avenue, Elgin, IL 60120	www.brethren.org
Church of the Living God (Christian Workers for Fellowship)	430 Forest Avenue, Cincinnati, OH 45229	
Church of the Living God, the Pillar and Ground of Truth, Inc.	4520 Ashland City Hwy., Nashville, TN 37208	www.clgpgt.org
Church of the Lutheran Brethren of America	P.O. Box 655, Fergus Falls, MN 56538	www.clba.org
Church of the Lutheran Confession	501 Grover Road, Eau Claire, WI 54701	www.clclutheran.org
Church of the Nazarene	6401 The Paseo, Kansas City, MO 64131	www.nazarene.org
Church of the United Brethren in Christ	302 Lake Street, Huntington, IN 46750	www.ub.org
Churches of Christ	P.O. Box 726, Kosciusko, MS 39090	www.church-of-christ.org
Churches of Christ in Christian Union	1426 Lancaster Pike, Box 30, Circleville, OH 43113	www.bright.net/~ccuhq

350

Denomination	Address	Website
Churches of God, General Conference	700 Melrose Ave., P.O. Box 926, Findlay, OH 45839	www.cggc.org
Congregational Christian Churches	P.O. Box 1620, Oak Creek, WI 53154	www.naccc.org
Congregational Holiness Church	3888 Fayetteville Hwy., Griffin, GA 30223	www.ch.church.com
Congregational Methodist Church	P.O. Box 9, Florence, MS 39073	
Conservative Baptist Association of America	1501 West Mineral Ave., Suite B, Littleton, CO 80120-5612	www.cbamerica.org
Conservative Congregational Christian Conference	7582 Currell Boulevard, Suite 108, St. Paul, MN 55125	www.cccusa.org
Conservative Mennonite Conference	9910 Rosedale-Milford Center Road, Irwin, OH 43029	www.cmcrosedale.org
Cooperative Baptist Fellowship	P.O. Box 450329, Atlanta, GA 31145-0329	www.cbfonline.org
Coptic Orthodox Church	P.O. Box 384, Cedar Grove, NJ 07009	www.nacopticchurch.org
Cumberland Presbyterian Church	1978 Union Avenue, Memphis, TN 38104	www.cumberland.org
Cumberland Presbyterian Church in America	226 Church Street, Huntsville, AL 35801	www.cumberland.org/cpca
Divine Science	2025 35th Street NW, Washington, D.C. 20007	www.divinescience.org
Elim Fellowship	1703 Dalton Road, Lima, NY 14485	www.elim.edu
Episcopal Church	815 Second Avenue, New York, NY 10017	www.ecusa.org
Episcopal Missionary Church	600 Oak Hollow Lane, Fort Worth, TX 76112	www.emchome.org
Evangelical Church	7733 West River Road, Minneapolis, MN 55444	
Evangelical Congregational Church	100 West Park Avenue, Myerstown, PA 17067	www.eccenter.com
Evangelical Covenant Church	5101 North Francisco Avenue, Chicago, IL 60625	www.covchurch.org
Evangelical Free Church of America	901 East 78th Street, Minneapolis, MN 55420-1300	www.efca.org
Evangelical Friends International	1975 Raisin Center Hwy., Adrian, MI 49221	www.evangelical-friends.org
Evangelical Lutheran Church in America	8765 West Higgins Road, Chicago, IL 60631	www.elca.org
Evangelical Lutheran Synod	6 Browns Court, Mankato, MN 56001	www.evluthsyn.org
Evangelical Mennonite Church	1420 Kerrway Court, Fort Wayne, IN 46805	www.brookside.org
Evangelical Methodist Church	P.O. Box 17070, Indianapolis, IN 46217	www.emchurch.org
Evangelical Presbyterian Church	29140 Buckingham Avenue, Suite 5, Livonia, MI 48154	www.epc.org
Fellowship of Evangelical Bible Churches	5800 South 14th Street, Omaha, NE 68107	
Fellowship of Grace Brethren Churches	P.O. Box 386, Winona Lake, IN 46590	www.fgbc.org
Free Methodist Church of North America	P.O. Box 535002, Indianapolis, IN 46253	www.fmcna.org
Free Will Baptists, National Association	P.O. Box 5002, Antioch, TN 37011-5002	www.nafwb.org

Denomination	Address	Web Site
Friends General Conference	1216 Arch St, #2B, Philadelphia, PA 19107	www.fgcquaker.org
Friends United Meeting	101 Quaker Hill Drive, Richmond, IN 47374-1980	www.fum.org
Full Gospel Assemblies International	P.O. Box 1230, Coatesville, PA 19320	
Full Gospel Fellowship of Churches and Ministries, International	4325 W. Ledbetter Drive, Dallas, TX 75233	www.fgfcmi.org
General Association of General Baptist Churches	100 Stinson Drive, Poplar Bluff, MO 63901	www.angelfire.com
General Association of Regular Baptist Churches	1300 North Meacham Road, Schaumburg, IL 60173	www.garbc.org
General Church of the New Jerusalem	P.O. Box 711, Bryn Athyn, PA 19009	www.newchurch.org
Grace Gospel Fellowship	2125 Martindale SW, P.O. Box 9432, Grand Rapids, MI 49509	www.ggfusa.org
Greek Orthodox Archdiocese of America	8-10 East 79th Street, New York, NY 10021	www.goarch.org
Holy Eastern Orthodox Catholic and Apostolic Church	HC74, Box 419-2, Mountain View, AR 72560	www.theocacna.org
House of God, Which is the Church of the Living God, the Pillar and Ground of the Truth	866 Georgetown Street, Lexington, KY 40508	www.houseofgod.org
Hungarian Reformed Church in America	13 Grove Street, Poughkeepsie, NY 12601	www.calvinsynod.org
Hutterian Brethren	Crystal Spring Colony, Box 10, Ste Agathe, MB R0G 1Y0 Canada	www.hutterianbrethren.com (unofficial)
Independent Fundamental Churches of America (IFCA International, Inc.)	3250 Fairlanes, P.O. Box 810, Grandville, MI 49468	www.ifca.org
International Church of the Foursquare Gospel	1910 W. Sunset Blvd., Suite 210, P.O. Box 26902, Los Angeles, CA 90026-0176	www.foursquare.org
International Council of Community Churches	21116 Washington Parkway, Frankfort, IL 60423-3112	www.akcache.com/community/iccc.html
International Pentecostal Church of Christ	2245 State Route 42 SW, P.O. Box 439, London, OH 43140	http: members.aol.com/hqipcc/
International Pentecostal Holiness Church	P.O. Box 12609, Oklahoma City, OK 73157	www.iphc.org
Islamic Center of Washington	2551 Massachusetts Avenue NW, Washington, D.C. 20008	
Islamic Society of North America	P.O. Box 38, Plainfield, IN 46168	www.isna.net
Jehovah's Witnesses	25 Columbia Heights, Brooklyn, NY 11201-2483	www.watchtower.org
Jewish Reconstructionist Federation	78 Montgomery Avenue, Suite 9, Elkins Park, PA 19027	www.jrf.org
Korean Presbyterian Church in America	P.O. Box 457, Morganville, NJ 07951	
Korean-American Presbyterian Church	2853 W. 7th Street, Los Angeles, CA 90005	www.kapc.org

Denomination	Address	Web Site
Liberal Catholic Church International	1206 Ayers Ave., Ojai, CA 93023	www.thelcc.org
Lubavitch World Headquarters	7700 Eastern Parkway, Brooklyn, NY 11213	www.chabad-centers.com
Lutheran Church—Missouri Synod	1333 South Kirkwood Road, St. Louis, MO 63122-7295	www.lcms.org
Malankara Orthodox Syrian Church	80-34 Commonwealth Boulevard, Bellerose, NY 11426	www.malankara.org/american.html
Mar Thoma Orthodox Syrian Church of India	2320 S. Merrick Avenue, Merrick, NY 11566	www.marthomachurch.org
Mennonite Brethren Churches, General Conference	4824 Butler Avenue, Fresno, CA 93727-5097	www.mbconf.org
Mennonite Church USA	421 South Second Street, Suite 600, Elkhart, IN 46516	www.mennonites.org
Missionary Church	3811 Vanguard Drive, P.O. Box 9127, Fort Wayne, IN 46899-9127	www.mcusa.org
Moravian Church (Unitas Fratrum)	1021 Center Street, P.O. Box 1245, Bethlehem, PA 18016-1245	www.moravian.org
Muslim American Society (W. Deen Muhammed)	P.O. Box 1944, Calumet City, IL 60409	
National Baptist Convention of America	777 S. R.L. Thornton Freeway, Suite 205, Dallas, TX 75203	http://members.aol.com/nbyc1/nbca.html
National Baptist Convention U.S.A., Inc.	1700 Baptist World Center Dr., Nashville, TN 37207	
National Missionary Baptist Convention of America	P.O. Box 512096, Los Angeles, CA 90051-0096	www.natl-missionarybaptist.com
National Primitive Baptist Convention U.S.A.	6433 Hidden Forrest Drive, Charlotte, NC 28213	www.natlprimbaptconv.org
National Spiritual Alliance of the U.S.A.	67 Mine Road, Winchester, NH 03470	
National Spiritualist Association of Churches	P.O. Box 217, Lily Dale, NY 14752	www.nsac.org
Netherlands Reformed Congregations	1261 Beckwith N.E., Grand Rapids, MI 49505	http://home.earthlink.net/~vogelaar /nrc/church.htm (unofficial)
New Apostolic Church of North America	3753 North Troy Street, Chicago, IL 60618	www.nak.org
North American Baptist Conference	1 South 210 Summit Avenue, Oakbrook Terrace, IL 60181	www.nabconference.org
Old Catholic Church of America	409 N. Lexington Parkway, DeForest, WI 53532	www.oldcatholic.org
Old German Baptist Brethren	6952 N. Montgomery County Line Rd, Englewood, OH 45322-9748	www.cob-net.org/docs/groups.htm (unofficial)
Old Roman Catholic Church of North America	1207 Potomac Place, Louisville, KY 40214	www.orccna.org
Open Bible Standard Churches	2020 Bell Avenue, Des Moines, IA 50315	www.openbible.org
Orthodox Church in America	P.O. Box 675, Sysosset, NY 11791-0675	www.oca.org
Orthodox Presbyterian Church	607 North Easton Road, Bldg. E, Box P, Willow Grove, PA 19090-0920	www.opc.org
Orthodox Union in America	333 Seventh Ave, New York, NY 10001	www.ou.org
Pentecostal Assemblies of the World, Inc	3939 Meadows Drive, Indianapolis, IN 46205	http://members.tripod.com/paw_inc/ index.html

353

Denomination	Address	Web Site
Pentecostal Church of God	4901 Pennsylvania, P.O. Box 850, Joplin, MO 64802	www.pcg.org
Pentecostal Free Will Baptist Church, Inc		www.pfwb.org
Pillar of Fire	P.O. Box 9159, Zarephath, NJ 08890	www.gospelcom.net/pof
Polish National Catholic Church of America	1006 Pittston Avenue, Scranton, PA 18505	www.pncc.org
Presbyterian Church (U.S.A.)	100 Witherspoon Street, Louisville, KY 40202	www.pcusa.org
Presbyterian Church in America	1852 Century Place, Atlanta, GA 30345-4305	www.pcanet.org
Primitive Baptists		www.pb.org (unofficial)
Primitive Methodist Church in the U.S.A.	1045 Laurel Run Road, Wilkes-Barre, PA 18702	www.primitivemethodistchurch.org
Progressive National Baptist Convention, Inc.	601 50th Street, NE, Washington, DC 20019	www.pnbc.org
Protestant Reformed Churches in America	4949 Ivanrest Avenue, Grandville, MI 49418	www.prca.org (unofficial)
Reformed Church in America	Office of the General Secretary, 475 Riverside Dr., 18th Floor, New York, NY 10115	www.rca.org
Reformed Church in the United States	6121 Pine Vista Way, Elk Grove, CA 95758	www.rcus.org
Reformed Episcopal Church	826 Second Ave, Blue Bell, PA 19422-1257	www.recus.org
Reformed Methodist Union Episcopal Church	1136 Brody Ave., Charleston, SC 29407	
Reformed Presbyterian Church of North America	7408 Penn Avenue, Pittsburgh, PA 15208	www.reformedpresbyterian.org
Religious Society of Friends (Conservative)		www.quaker.org
Reorganized Church of Jesus Christ of Latter-day Saints	P.O. Box 1059, 1001 Walnut Street, Independence, MO 64501	www.rlds.org
Roman Catholic Church Council	3211 Fourth Street, Washington, DC 20017	www.vatican.va
Romanian Orthodox Episcopate of America	2535 Grey Tower Road, Jackson, MI 49201-9120	www.roea.org
Russian Orthodox Church outside of Russia	75 East 93rd Street, New York, NY 10128	www.rocor.org
The Salvation Army	615 Slaters Lane, Alexandria, VA 22313	www.sarmy.org
Schwenkfelder Church	105 Seminary St., Pennsburg, PA 18073	www.schwenkfelder.org
Separate Baptists in Christ	10102 N Hickory Lane, Columbus, IN 47203	www.separatebaptist.org
Serbian Eastern Orthodox Church in the U.S.A. and Canada	Office of External Affairs, 2311 M St, NW (Suite 402), Washington, DC 20037	http://oca.serbian-church.net
Seventh Day Baptist General Conference	P.O. Box 167, Janesville, WI 53547-16788	www.seventhdaybaptist.org
Seventh-day Adventist Church	12501 Old Columbia Pike, Silver Spring, MD 20904-6600	http://northamerica.adventist.org
Southern Baptist Convention	901 Commerce Street, Suite 750, Nashville, TN 37203	www.sbc.net

Denomination	Address	Web Site
Southern Episcopal Church	234 Willow Lane, Nashville, TN 37211-4945	www.angelfire.com/biz/Southern
Southern Methodist Church	P.O. Box 39, Orangeburg, SC 29116-0039	www.southernmethodistchurch.org
Swedenborgian Church	11 Highland Avenue, Newtonville, MA 02460	www.swedenborg.org
Syrian (Syriac) Orthodox Church of Antioch (Archdiocese of the Eastern United States)	260 Elm Avenue, Teaneck, NJ 07661	www.syrianorthodoxchurch.org
Theosophical Society in America	P.O. Box 270, Wheaton, IL 60189	www.theosophical.org
Triumph the Church and Kingdom of God in Christ Inc. (International)	213 Farrington Ave SE, Atlanta, GA 30315	
Ukrainian Orthodox Church of the USA	135 Davidson Avenue, Somerset, NJ 08873	www.uocofusa.org
Unification Church	4 West 43rd St., New York, NY 10036	www.unification.org
Union of American Hebrew Congregations	838 Fifth Avenue, New York, NY 10021	www.uahc.org
Unitarian Universalist Association of Congregations	25 Beacon Street, Boston, MA 02108	www.uua.org
United Church of Christ	700 Prospect Avenue, Cleveland, OH 02108	www.ucc.org
United Holy Church of America, Inc.	312 Umstead Street, Durham, NC 27702	http://members.aol.com/newpent/nphca (unofficial)
United Methodist Church	P.O. Box 320, 810 Twelfth Ave. S., Nashville, TN 37202-0320	www.umc.org
United Pentecostal Church International	8855 Dunn Road, Hazelwood, MO 63042	www.upci.org
United Synagogues of Conservative Judaism	155 Fifth Ave, New York, NY 10010	www.uscj.org
Unity Churches, Association of	P.O. Box 610, Lee's Summit, MO 64063	www.unity.org
Unity of the Brethren		www.unityofthebrethren.org
Universal Fellowship of Metropolitan Community Churches	8704 Santa Monica Boulevard, 2nd Floor, West Hollywood, CA 90069	www.ufmcc.com
Vineyard Churches USA	5340 E. LaPalma Ave., Anaheim, CA 92807	www.vineyardusa.org
Volunteers of America	1660 Duke Street, Alexandria, VA 22314-3421	www.voa.org
Wesleyan Church	P.O. Box 50434, Indianapolis, IN 46250	www.wesleyan.org
Wisconsin Evangelical Lutheran Synod	2929 N Mayfair Road, Milwaukee, WI 53222	www.wels.net
Worldwide Church of God	300 West Green Street, Pasadena, CA 91123	www.wcg.org

355

SUGGESTED READINGS

General Works on Western Religions

Armstrong, Karen. *Islam: A Short History*. New York: Modern Library, 2000.

Atwood, Craig D. *Always Reforming: A History of Christianity Since 1300*. Macon, GA: Mercer University Press, 2001.

Esposito, John L. *Islam: The Straight Path*. New York: Oxford University Press, 1988.

————, ed. *The Oxford Encyclopedia of the Modern Islamic World*. 4 vols. New York: Oxford University Press, 1995.

Neusner, Jacob. *An Introduction to Judaism: A Textbook and Reader*. Louisville: Westminster/John Knox Press, 1991.

————. *The Way of Torah: An Introduction to Judaism*. 4th ed. Belmont, CA: Wadsworth, 1988.

Occhiogrosso, Peter. *The Joy of Sects: A Spirited Guide to the World's Religious Traditions*. New York: Image Books, 1996.

Oxtoby, Willard G., ed. *World Religions: Western Traditions*. New York: Oxford University Press, 1996.

Pelikan, Jaroslav. *The Christian Tradition: A History of the Development of Doctrine*. 5 vols. Chicago: University of Chicago Press, 1971–1989.

Steinberg, Milton. *Basic Judaism*. New York: Harcourt Brace, 1986.

Walker, Williston, et al. *A History of the Christian Church*. 4th ed. New York: Scribner, 1985.

Wuthnow, Robert. *Growing Up Religious: Christians and Jews and Their Journeys of Faith*. Boston: Beacon Press, 1999.

General Works on Religion in the United States

Ahlstrom, Sydney E. *A Religious History of the American People.* 2 vols. New Haven: Yale University Press, 1972.

Bloom, Harold. *The American Religion: The Emergence of the Post-Christian Nation.* New York: Simon and Schuster, 1992.

Bowden, Henry W., ed. *Dictionary of American Religious Biography.* 2nd. ed. Westport, CT: Greenwood Press, 1993.

Butler, Jon, and Harry S. Stout, eds. Religion in American Life Series. New York: Oxford University Press, 1999–.

Butler, Jon. *Awash in a Sea of Faith: Christianizing the American People.* Cambridge, MA: Harvard University Press, 1990.

Gaustad, Edwin Scott. *A Religious History of America.* Rev. ed. San Francisco: Harper & Row, 1990.

Gaustad, Edwin Scott and Philip L. Barlow. *New Historical Atlas of Religion in America.* New York: Oxford University Press, 2000.

Hatch, Nathan O. *The Democratization of American Christianity.* New Haven: Yale University Press, 1989.

Hill, Samuel S, ed. *Encyclopedia of Religion in the South.* Macon, GA: Mercer University Press, 1984.

———. *The South and the North in American Religion.* Athens: University of Georgia Press, 1980.

Lindner, Eileen W., ed. *Yearbook of American and Canadian Churches 2000: Religious Pluralism in the New Millennium.* 68th ed. Nashville: Abingdon Press, 2000.

Lippy, Charles H., and Peter W. Williams, eds. *Encyclopedia of American Religious Experience: Studies of Traditions and Movements.* 3 vols. New York: Scribner, 1988.

Marty, Martin E. *Modern American Religion.* 2 vols. Chicago: University of Chicago Press, 1986.

Melton, J. Gordon. *Encyclopedia of American Religions.* 6th ed. 3 vols. Detroit: Gale Research, 1999.

Moore, R. Laurence. *Religious Outsiders and the Making of Americans.* New York: Oxford University Press, 1986.

———. *Selling God: American Religion in the Marketplace of Culture.* New York: Oxford University Press, 1994.

Neusner, Jacob, ed. *World Religions in America: An Introduction.* Louisville: Westminster/John Knox Press, 1994.

Noll, Mark A. *A History of Christianity in the United States and Canada.* Grand Rapids: Eerdmans, 1992.

358

Wuthnow, Robert. *The Restructuring of American Religion: Society and Faith Since World War II*. Princeton, NJ: Princeton University Press, 1988.

Works on Specific Themes in American Religion

Balmer, Randall. *Mine Eyes Have Seen the Glory: A Journey into the Evangelical Subculture of America*. New York: Oxford University Press, 1989.

Frazier, E. Franklin. *The Negro Church in America*. New York: Schocken Books, 1974.

James, Janet W., ed. *Women in American Religion*. Philadelphia: University of Pennsylvania Press, 1980.

Lincoln, C. Eric, and Lawrence H. Mamiya. *The Black Church in the African-American Experience*. Durham, NC: Duke University Press, 1990.

Lincoln, C. Eric. *The Black Church Since Frazier*. New York: Shocken Books, 1973.

Marty, Martin E. *Protestantism in the United States: Righteous Empire*. 2nd ed. New York: Scribner; London: Collier Macmillan, 1986.

Raboteau, Albert J. *Slave Religion: The "Invisible Institution" in the Antebellum South*. New York: Oxford University Press, 1978.

Ruether, Rosemary Radford, and Rosemary Skinner Keller, eds. *Women and Religion in America*. 3 vols. San Francisco: Harper & Row, 1981.

Sernett, Milton C., ed. *Afro-American Religious History: A Documentary Witness*. Durham, NC: Duke University Press, 1985.

Works on Specific Movements and Churches

Ammerman, Nancy T. *Baptist Battles: Social Change and Religious Conflict in the Southern Baptist Convention*. New Brunswick, NJ: Rutgers University Press, 1990.

Beckford, James A. *The Trumpet of Prophecy: A Sociological Study of Jehovah's Witnesses*. Oxford: Basil Blackwell, 1975.

Blumhofer, Edith L. *Restoring the Faith: The Assemblies of God, Pentecostalism, and American Culture*. Urbana: University of Illinois Press, 1993.

359

Bokenkotter, Thomas S. *Concise History of the Catholic Church.* Rev. ed. New York: Image Books, 1990.

Brackney, William H. *The Baptists.* New York: Greenwood Press, 1988.

Bratt, James D. *Dutch Calvinism in Modern America.* Grand Rapids: Eerdmans, 1984.

Bucke, Emory S., ed. *History of American Methodism.* Nashville: Abingdon Press, 1964.

Buehrens, John A., et al. *A Chosen Faith: An Introduction to Unitarian Universalism.* Boston: Beacon Press, 1998.

Burgess, Stanley M., and Gary B. McGee, eds. *Dictionary of Pentecostal and Charismatic Movements.* Grand Rapids: Regency Reference Library, 1988.

Crews, Mickey. *The Church of God: A Social History.* Knoxville: University of Tennessee Press, 1990.

Dayton, Donald W., and Robert K. Johnston, eds. *The Variety of American Evangelicalism.* Downer's Grove, IL: InterVarsity Press, 1991.

De Witt, John. *The Christian Science Way of Life.* Boston: Christian Science Publishing Society, 1971.

Doan, Ruth A. *The Miller Heresy, Millennialism, and American Culture.* Philadelphia: Temple University Press, 1987.

Durnbaugh, Donald F., ed. *The Brethren Encyclopedia.* 3 vols. Philadelphia: Brethren Press, 1983–84.

Eddy, Mary Baker. *Science and Health with Key to the Scriptures.* Reprint. Boston: Christian Science Board of Directors, 1994.

Eisen, Arnold M. *The Chosen People in America: A Study in Jewish Religious Ideology.* Bloomington: Indiana University Press, 1983.

Fitts, Leroy. *A History of Black Baptists.* Nashville: Broadman Press, 1985.

Garrison, W. E., and A. T. DeGroot. *The Disciples of Christ: A History.* St. Louis: Bethany Press, 1958.

Greeley, Andrew. *The American Catholic: A Social Portrait.* New York: Basic Books, 1977.

Hall, Francis. *Friends in the Americas.* Philadelphia: Friends World Committee, 1976.

Hamilton, J. T., and K. G. Hamilton, *History of the Moravian Church: The Renewed Unitas Fratrum, 1722–1957.* Bethlehem, PA: Interprovincial Board of Christian Education, Moravian Church in America, 1967.

Hamm, Thomas D. *The Transformation of American Quakerism: Orthodox Friends: 1800–1907*. Bloomington: University of Indiana Press, 1988.

Hansen, Klaus J. *Mormonism and the American Experience*. Chicago: University of Chicago Press, 1981.

Hardon, John A. *Modern Catholic Dictionary*. Garden City, NY: Doubleday, 1980.

Hart, D. G., and Mark A. Noll, eds. *Dictionary of the Presbyterian and Reformed Tradition in America*. Downers Grove, IL: InterVarsity Press, 1999.

Horton, Douglas. *The United Church of Christ. Its Origins, Organization, and Role in the World Today*. New York: Thomas Nelson, 1962.

Hostetler, Beulah Stauffer. *American Mennonites and Protestant Movements: A Community Paradigm*. Scottdale, PA: Herald Press, 1987.

Hughes, Richard T. *Reviving the Ancient Faith: The Story of Churches of Christ in America*. Grand Rapids: Eerdmans, 1996.

Idel, Moshe. *Hasidism: Between Ecstasy and Magic*. Albany: State University of New York Press, 1995.

Johnson, Kevin Orlin. *Why Do Catholics Do That? A Guide to the Teachings and Practices of the Catholic Church*. New York: Ballantine, 1995.

Langford, Thomas A., ed. *Doctrine and Theology in The United Methodist Church*. Nashville: Kingswood Books, 1991.

Leonard, Bill J., ed. *Dictionary of Baptists in America*. Downers Grove, IL: InterVarsity Press, 1994.

Marsden, George M. *Fundamentalism and American Culture: The Shaping of Twentieth-century Evangelicalism, 1870–1925*. New York: Oxford University Press, 1980.

Meyendorff, John. *The Orthodox Church: Its Past and Its Role in the World Today*. 4th ed. Crestwood, NY: St. Vladimir's Seminary Press, 1996.

Nelson, E. Clifford, ed. *Lutherans in North America*. Philadelphia: Fortress Press, 1975.

Neufeld, Don. F., ed. *Seventh-Day Adventist Encyclopedia*. Rev. ed. Washington, DC: Review and Herald Publishing, 1961.

Paris, Arthur Ernest. *Black Pentecostalism: Southern Religion in an Urban World*. Amherst: University of Massachusetts Press, 1982.

361

Penton, James. *Apocalypse Delayed: The Story of Jehovah's Witnesses.* Toronto: University of Toronto Press, 1985.

Prichard, Robert W. *A History of the Episcopal Church.* Harrisburg, PA: Morehouse, 1991.

Pruter, Karl. *A History of the Old Catholic Church.* Scottsdale, AZ: St. Willibrord's Press, 1973.

Richardson, Harry V. *Dark Salvation: The Story of Methodism as It Developed Among Blacks in America.* Garden City, NY: Anchor Press, 1976.

Rosenthal, Gilbert S. *The Many Faces of Judaism: Orthodox, Conservative, Reconstructionist, and Reform.* Edited by S. Rossel. New York: Behrman House, 1978.

Schlink, Edmund. *Theology of the Lutheran Confessions.* Trans. Paul F. Keohneke and Herbert J. A. Bouman. Philadelphia: Muhlenberg Press, 1961.

Shipps, Jan. *Mormonism: The Story of a New Religious Tradition.* Urbana: University of Illinois Press, 1985.

Sklare, Marshall. *Conservative Judaism: An American Religious Movement.* New ed. New York: Schocken Books, 1972.

Smith, Jane I. *Islam in America.* Columbia Contemporary American Religion Series. New York: Columbia University Press, 1999.

Smith, Joseph. *The Book of Mormon.* Reprint. Salt Lake City: Church of Jesus Christ of Latter-day Saints, 1986

Smith, Timothy L. *Called unto Holiness: The Story of the Nazarenes: The Formative Years.* Kansas City, MO: Nazarene Publishing House, 1962.

Smylie, James H. *A Brief History of the Presbyterians.* Louisville: Geneva Press, 1996.

Synan, Vinson. *The Holiness-Pentecostal Movement in the United States.* Grand Rapids: Eerdmans, 1971.

VandenBerge, Peter M., ed. *Historical Directory of the Reformed Church in America: 1628–1978.* Grand Rapids: Eerdmans, 1978.

Ware, Kallistos T. *The Orthodox Way.* Crestwood, NY: St. Vladimir's Seminary Press, 1995.

Williams, George H. *American Universalism: A Bicentennial Historical Essay.* Boston: Universalist Historical Society, 1971.

INDEX

Humanae Vitae, 85
Hungarian Reformed Church in America. *See* Reformed churches
Hunt, Robert, 130
Hus, John, 78
Hutchinson, Anne, 121
Hutter, Jacob, 170
Hutterian Brethren, 170

Ignatius of Antioch, 83
Independent Assemblies of God, International. *See* Pentecostal churches
Independent Fundamental Churches of America. *See* Fundamentalist/Bible
    churches
Independent Pentecostal Churches, 280
Institute of Theology by Extension, 285
Interdenominational Theological Center, 273
International Association for Religious Freedom, 334
International Bible Students, 179
International Church of the Foursquare Gospel. *See* Pentecostal churches
International Communion of the Charismatic Episcopal Church. *See*
    Episcopal/Anglican churches
International Council of Christian Churches, 155
International Council of Community Churches. *See* Community Churches,
    International Council of
International New Thought Alliance, 129
International Pentecostal Assemblies, 282
International Pentecostal Church of Christ. *See* Pentecostal churches
Irving, Edward, 137
Isabella (Queen), 184
Islam, 37, 171-78, 183, 245
    Nation of Islam, 173, 175-77
    Shi'ism, 173, 174, 177
    Sufism, 177-78
    Sunnism, 174, 178
Islamic Society of North America, 178
Italian Christian Church, 270

J. Appleseed & Co., 327
Jabbar, Kareem Abdul, 175
Jackson, Joseph H., 57
Jacob, 182
James, apostle, 196
James, Fannie Brooks, 128
Jarratt, Devereux, 226
Jay, John, 131
Jefferson, Thomas, 19, 131
Jeffersonian Act for Establishing Religious Freedom, 294
Jehovah's Witnesses, 21, 178-81

Muslim American Society, 177
Muslims. *See* Islam
Napoleon III, 39
Nation of Islam. *See* Islam
National Association of Evangelicals, The, 23, 339
National Association of Free Will Baptists. *See* Baptist churches
National Baptist Convention of America, Inc. *See* Baptist churches
National Baptist Convention, U.S.A., Inc. *See* Baptist churches
National Catholic Register, The, 98
National Catholic Reporter, The, 98
National Conference of Synagogue Youth, 192
National Conference on Catholic Charities, 99
National Council of the Churches of Christ in the U.S.A., The, 49, 146, 155, 211, 240, 302, 337
National Council of the Congregational Christian Churches. *See* Congregational churches
National Missionary Baptist Convention of America. *See* Baptist churches
National Organization of the New Apostolic Church of North America. *See* Episcopal/Anglican churches
National Primitive Baptist Convention, U.S.A. *See* Baptist churches
National Religious Broadcasters, 237
National Serbian Church, 261
National Spiritual Alliance of the U.S.A. *See* Spiritualist and Theosophical bodies
National Spiritualist Association of Churches. *See* Spiritualist and Theosophical bodies
Native American church, 241-42
Navajoland Episcopal Church. *See* Episcopal/Anglican churches
Nazarene Publishing House, 168
Negro World, The, 248
Nero, Emperor, 93
Nestorius, 244, 257, 263, 264
Netherlands Reformed Congregations in North America. *See* Reformed churches
New and Living Way Publishing Company, 277
New Brunswick Theological Seminary, 308
New Geneva Theological Seminary, 315
New Hampshire Confession of Faith, 43, 53, 65
Newsletter (Church of God and Saints of Christ), 118
Newton, Isaac, 330
Niagara Christian College, 71
Nicene Creed, 81, 89, 95, 133, 137, 206, 246, 249, 304, 313
Nixon, Richard, 329
Noble Drew Ali, 175, 176
Noli, Father Theophan S., 249
North American Baptist Conference. *See* Baptist churches
North American Baptist Seminary, 59